The 9th Ed

M000209048

THE GENTLEMAN'S GUIDE TO

Passages

South

by Bruce Van Sant

Sailing directions for easier windward passage making
in the islands from Florida to Venezuela,
and a handbook for Caribbean cruising.

Distributed by:

CRUISING GUIDE PUBLICATIONS

P.O. Box 1017
Dunedin, FL 34697-1017
Phone: (727) 733-5322 • Fax: (727) 734-8179
www.cruisingguides.com
info@cruisingguides.com

IMPORTANT NOTICE:

The chartlets in this guide intend to assist the reader in following the sailing tactics described, not to give meaningful measurements for navigation. The prudent mariner will avail himself of official charts and publications, some of which this guide recommends, as well as any navigational methods and tools required to ensure the safety of the vessel and the accuracy of its navigation. There exist no warranties, either expressed or implied, as to the usability of the information contained herein for any purpose whatever.

PUBLISHED BY:
Bruce Van Sant & Cruising Guide Publications, Inc.
P.O. Box 1017, Dunedin, FL 34697-1017
Phone: (727) 733-5322
www.cruisingguides.com

by Bruce Van Sant

NINTH EDITION

ISBN 0-944428-79-7

Library of Congress 90-102996

Printed in the U.S.A.
Written in E-prime

PREFACE

THE THORNLESS PATH, and by that I mean cruising with *comfort, safety and pleasure*, gets disdain from gung-ho yachties who punch the rhumbline from island A to island B — as they imagine the iron men of old had, but didn't. This book actually began in 1978 while I, still a gung-ho yachtie, lay ahull in a North Sea full storm — Force 10 in a forest of oil rigs — and for the second time! Somewhere between quitting the job and casting off I had lost sight of those first principles of cruising: safety, comfort and pleasure. I promised myself then that I would take all future passages thornlessly or *not at all*.

I've kept that promise. Since 1979 I've racked up well over 70,000 miles playing the island lees to South America, most of it single handed on the route through the islands which they call the Thorny Path. Every passage, every harbor hop, has for me become an unalloyed pleasure, while I watch others senselessly bang into it, sometimes losing it all.

THE THORNY PATH had little or no traffic until the age of steam. Owners who valued their sailing ships didn't find the windward routes commercially viable. Even the slaves-for-sugar-for-rum trade swept *downwind* from Africa to Boston. Now, with the fiberglass revolution, come the gung-ho yachties braving the thorny path.

Vague notions of iron men on wooden ships have shamed us into navigating on the "you have to take whatever comes" principle. But for four and a half centuries practically no merchants agreed to take what came by sailing this route. Yet yuppies, retiring baby boomers, brokers and lawyers regularly think they've got the stuff the old iron men did not. And Mom and Pop, who know for sure they haven't got it, come too.

After hearing their brave and knowledgeable talk at the bar I find that few actually take my safe and comfortable sailing route across the Mona Passage. Halfway across they crank up the revs and bash straight east like I used to zip by graveyards as a kid. In their fear of the dark and deep some take two days and a night to cross, instead of vice versa. Predictably, their path turns *thorny*, while the **night lee**, a calming of wind and sea caused by cooling land on each side of the passage, would have given them a **Thornless Path**.

ISLAND EFFECTS from islands big and small, even reefs and banks, alter the trade winds and currents which pass through, over and around the islands. These effects alter the conditions forecast by the National Weather Service (NWS) in a *predictable* manner. Playing these island effects in concert, you can make safe, comfortable and pleasant progress against normally impenetrable trade winds and seas. To do that, you need to study those effects and apply your knowledge while underway with Teutonic rigor.

I had racked up more single handed island hopping through the Antilles than anyone I knew. Winters I shuttled between my home in Puerto Plata and charters in the Bahamas. Summers I refit in Venezuela. When friends in Georgetown sent cruisers to me for advice on going south, their naïvete apalled me. Gentle retired folks planned to buck 25 knot tradewinds with their 23hp auxiliaries and their 32 foot cutters. I did what I could to help insure their safety and comfort.

A MANUAL OF INSTRUCTION for windward tricks would fill the need, if it also included demostrations of how to use them on key passages and in specific harbors. I remembered my early passages south as rather arduous. I shared some with them. I had lots of rum for my charter guests, and we had fun with the chart talks. Later, when the Peso began to dive, and the charters ran thin, the Georgetown chart talk parties became BYOB.

Soon questions got redundant. I began to answer them with typed notes from com-

i

puter printer tear sheets. I had quite a database of *disjointed* passage and harbor notes on my computer where I kept my log. These notes along with copies of my log's harbor sketches, got passed around for the costs of copying. They raised more questions which made me write more notes. Cockpit sessions expanded to beach seminars with a syllabus laboriously copied at the church's Xerox machine. In Puerto Plata, where it cost little to copy, I found cruisers copying and selling my notes for profit, including some of their own bad skinny. I figured I'd make an official version to safeguard the readers -- *and* my name.

With encouragement from Milt Baker at Bluewater Books and Charts, I printed a *manual*. The U.S. prohibited copying charts back then, so I drew some by hand. The result sold out in three months, and of course it raised more questions, and I wrote more notes. Each edition funded an improved printing with answers to more questions. Thus, without really meaning to, I *snowballed* my way toward eventually answering all the relevant questions and including all the relevant harbors and hurricane holes in a fat book.

PASSAGES SOUTH TODAY, if followed, can your island hopping thornless. Its windward strategies, backed by many years of continuous observation and testing, beat any instant expertise based on just a few voyages. Tune out the two-trip Globetrotter who says, "Aw, that's malarkey! Why, I did that last year and ...." He'll get his on the third trip.

I surveyed every recommended anchorage several times prior to printing each edition. I sounded them with my long-keeled, 6½ foot draft ketch, *Jalan Jalan*. Her shy 37 shaft horsepower easily took her seven times the 1200 windward miles to South America, gave me around 50 tranquil cruises between the Bahamas and the Virgins, and at least a hundred sails on the coasts of Hispaniola before I entered trawlerdom.

ME, my experience and background? An American working internationally as a systems engineer, I lived aboard and cruised in the Baltic, the North Sea, English Channel and the Mediterranean, with stints in Asia and Central America. En route back to Indonesia, I broke off and sensibly settled into continually cruising from Florida to South America .

Forty-five years of sailing ended grudgingly, however. The signs piled up: skin cancers, a stroke leaving me with bouts of vertigo and missteps at night while single-handing a big ketch around the Caribbean. Clearly, to stay on the water, and to continue running the island chain, I had to get out of the cockpit, under cover and into something I couldn't easily fall out of. I transferred to an unmasted motorsailer, upon which I continued my peripatetic cruising. Before *Jalan Jalan* blessed me for 15 years, I cruised on *Rasa Saya*, *Sayang* and *Tingal*. Now I have *Tidak Apa*, also a Malayu idiom for *never mind — it doesn't make any difference.* The trawler versus sail, I mean. And it really hasn't.

THE RISK CURVE gets pushed by an undermanned small boat jamming to windward with sexagenarians at the helm. *Passages South* documents my research and recurrent experience cruising to windward through the islands — under both sail and power. It always works for me.

If followed, it will work for you too.

Bruce, *KEMBALI KE TANAH*
Luperón, Dominican Republic

Contents

HOW TO USE THIS GUIDE

I write a *windward* guide, not a *yachtsman's guide*. I show you how to safely and comfortably take any boat against the wind in places where you hardly ever get the winds you want. In these areas you usually don't want so-called *favorable* winds because they often directly precede deteriorating weather.

I write to the crew of a small boat jamming 1200 miles to *windward* between Florida and South America. For them I've pruned the hedges and peeled back the quibbles to give them a book of plain-spoken, straightforward skinny unsoftened by *perhapses* and *maybes*. If, as a result of my candor, you think me huffy, dogmatic or opinionated, you shall miss many systematic solutions that *work* to bring you safe and comfortable passaging.

All bold face phrases appear in the INDEX. Most bold type not geographical names appear in the GLOSSARY at the back of the book. I will define these terms the first time I use them, but if in doubt, or to refresh yourself, look them up in the GLOSSARY.

I use **true degrees** (e.g. 45°T, where 0° points to the physical North Pole along your longitude) to assist with chart work. I use **magnetic degrees** (e.g. 15°M, where 0° starts at the magnetic north pole in Canada) to provide compass bearings for deck work.

Wherever you read the unmodified word *wind*, I always refer to the **gradient wind**, or the wind arising from atmospheric pressure gradients; neither harbor wind nor coastal wind, but the wind about a hundred feet (33 meters) above the surface of the open sea as forecast by the National Weather Service (**NWS**) in its **Offshore Report**s. The plethora of weather reports available to the electronic navigator notwithstanding, I refer exclusively to the NWS forecasters' definitive determination of sea conditions (wind and wave) found only in their Offshore Reports. The Offshore Reports summarize NWS analyses in a manner specifically useful to mariners at sea. Occasionally I use **Wx** to mean *weather*.

The techniques I have for navigating through the islands against the wind explicitly conform to only the Offshore Report. I have over 6,000 times copied these reports underway on the actual passages I describe. Therefore my navigation rules calibrate against those reports, *no others*. Nonetheless, for reasons you can learn in the chapter *Playing the Island Lees*, your deck level observations shall rarely match the exact conditions of that forecast. I will give you rules with which you can translate the difference between the Offshore Report and your deck observations to a navigation plan. *If you apply them to any other report, you break the rules, and you risk your safety and comfort.*

RULES, RULES, RULES

It took many trips south before I dared give the least advice to anyone. But my compendium of notes and sketches steadily gave evidence that they saved cruisers from repeating my own, and others', misadventures. Even after decades gunkholing the path described in this book, I still quail at giving unhedged counsel, but I've bitten the bullet and written down unequivocal sailing directions, *rules* I follow for safe and comfortable progress against the wind. Then I illustrate their application on each passage. Finally, I tell you what happens to you if you don't follow the rules using real life stories.

I've given special shore-side attention to Puerto Rico and the Dominican Republic because no other yachtie guides exist, and you must spend significant time in those countries, and because, basing from both for many years, I know them well.

I don't want you to follow a rigid path through the islands. This book's advice for *thornless* cruising against the wind tells you *HOW* and *WHEN* to go, not necessarily *WHERE*.

1

WHY A *GENTLEMAN*'S GUIDE?

When yachting began in England in the mid 1800's the young ladies and gentlemen of the privileged classes would take the train down to the south coast where paid crews had delivered their yachts, usually made-over workboats. They lounged on the white canvas-covered decks in their white duck trousers and their white linen dresses. They rolled home under a billow of running white sail. Deck stewards served gin and tonic to the gents and cooled Advocaat to the ladies. "*A gentleman never sails to windward*," they said. This book, *especially for Ladies*, gives the lie to that oldest of yachting's traditional sayings.

The Gentleman's Guide to Passages South connects the major cruising grounds with 18 windward passages between Florida and Venezuela. I divide each passage into an average of 4 safe and easy sails for a total of over 190 anchorages enroute, most of which I've used dozens of times, and in many different conditions, with my 6½ foot draft ketch.

Dawdle to your heart's content in any major cruising area. But to change from Bahamas to the DR, or DR to PR, PR to VI, you must return to these tried and true passages.

WHY *THORNLESS*?

The windward way south through the islands gets referred to as the **Thorny Path** to the Caribbean for good reason. As a mostly single-handed senior, living aboard a sailboat in the Caribbean, I always sought to take the thorns out of my travels by taking the most comfortable and safe passages. I have researched a *thornless* way south since sailing into these waters from Europe in 1979. I wanted an alternative to beating my brains out in the ocean, bypassing all the island cruising grounds that I wanted to enjoy. Why not *baysail* and *daysail* to Venezuela? I discovered I could!

In the tropics, each season brings its own surprises in the weather: no year just like another, no *day* just like another. My thornless strategies count on and rely on this constant variation in wind and wave. With a 6½ foot draft, long-keeled ketch, and now my small trawler, I have hoofed up and down my **Thornless Path** and found it *thornless* in any season, given careful study of the weather and patience in applying my methods.

WHO NEEDS THIS GUIDE?

The live-aboard, long-term cruiser who can take the time necessary to have a safe and leisurely cruise south; cruisers like Mom and Pop on their dream retirement cruise, the neophyte cruisers who just bought their first boat, singlehanders who must reduce risk, and sailors like me who don't want to get their boats (or themselves) broken, who seek comfort before challenge, who like me, easily — and sensibly — get scared of the sea.

If not among the above, you probably don't want this guide. It purposes to deliver these cruisers to their various paradises with themselves, their boats and their relationships still intact and healthy. While illustrating each passage with *real* examples of *first hand* experience, I will also try to debunk some of the bar story bugbears with which the tellers want to intimidate you, and which could keep you from enjoying the cruise of a lifetime.

DO YOU NEED OTHER GUIDES?

You bet! So-called "yachtsman's guides" will tell you where to go, what to do, who to see and why. This book does that for Hispaniola and Puerto Rico. For the other cruising grounds, see my recommendations in *Boat Stuff: Navigation Aids*. But for *WHEN* and *HOW* to go use this book everywhere for its sections treating *Island Weather, Island Strategies, Playing the Island Lees, Copying the Weather.* Use also my *South from the Virgins*.

HOW TO USE THE CHARTLETS

You need the lastest edition. Depths change in the harbors of the Greater Antilles due to massive rains and flooding from, for example, Hurricane George. Also, due to rapid Caribbean development, my transits for harbor entrances often change. You should have a planning chart in front of you. I use Waterproof Charts #16: Florida to Puerto Rico.

Follow the directions given for entrances. Your intuition or experience elsewhere may not count. Example: *Set your anchors to the* **Trades** means just that. The unrelenting easterly **Trade Winds** below 22° latitude shall shock you with their persistence. I see the majority of skippers that enter Luperón with this book in their hands set their anchors to the *west* where the creek's flow and the night's breeze points the anchored boats overnight. Later in the day, when 25 knots of trades make up from the *east*, their anchors pivot and the random loops of night-chain snag their anchor shanks and they drag.

When details for plotting and making passages between anchorages can be found in the standard cruising guide for an area, I don't repeat them here. Chartlets get included, however, when you need data relevant to **Thornless** strategies for those harbors.

All sailing directions relate to the **prevailing conditions** at the location: e.g., trade winds in the Caribbean, light easterlies in the Bahamas. They use the weather features and **land effects** which predictably modify prevailing contrary winds. If you use the chartlets in this guide without an understanding of the sailing directions in the text, and the frame of reference of local prevailing conditions, you shall undoubtedly screw up

All chartlet depths show feet Mean Low Water unless otherwise specified.

GPS WAYPOINTS AND COMPASS BEARINGS

Most GPS coordinates in this guide show to the nearest tenth of a mile. This satisfies either WGS-84 (NAD83) and WGS-72 datum. I have confirmed these waypoints by using them myself on-site several times a year. I have intentionally made all the bearings as simple and mnemonic as possible, given the marks they refer to. I've made every attempt to make GPS waypoints with safe searoom, and which coincide with the chartlet compass bearings — no easy task!

My chartlets, hand drawn before one could legally copy official charts, have GPS waypoints proven by many thousands of boats. If you plot them on official charts with *inaccurate* Lat/Longs, you shall put yourself into grave danger.

Notation

I use the format **DDMM** (Degrees, Minutes), eliminating the folderol and fritter of ° and ' signs, and **N** and **W** designations for Latitude and Longitude. For example, I write **2845** instead of **28° 45' N**. Since this book covers the area 15° to 26°N latitude and 60° to 80°W longitude, it shouldn't confuse anyone with this simpler notation. If you do get it twisted up, you will no doubt recover your error since Faial, in the Azores, lies at 28°45'W longitude, and you probably don't want that right now.

To summarize, Georgetown, in the Bahamas has the coordinates

| 2330 |
| 7545 |

while Kalaallit Nunaat, in the eastern *skærgaard* of Greenland has | 7545 | .
| 2330 |

3

GPS Cautions

Don't lose your nav skills. If you haven't any, get them quick. Despite your use of the GPS, while planning or executing a crossing, make **estimated positions** (EPs), *not* **DRs (dead reckoning)**. EPs include current, leeway, tide, variation and compass deviation.

With the full availability of GPS, cruisers have taken to giving each other precise coordinates of reef entrances and channel markers. Use these at your peril! I have adjusted all my arrival waypoints to give you: (1) a safe offing with which to proceed *visually*, and (2) a safe approach from sea at any reasonable arrival angle.

Take this example of a dangerous yet common practice. A helpful yachtie, the leader type with a radio voice the envy of every Pan Am Flight 001 captain, dinghied out to the red ball inside the entrance at **Luperón**, and holding the ball, did several GPS clickety-clicks. Proud as Columbus, he told the cruiser nets of his adventure with the "Luperón seabuoy" and advised them to replace my arrival waypoint in this book with his "more accurate" numbers. Three yachts on a southeast course went onto the reef in the next two weeks. Look at the chartlet for Luperón to see why. You'll find that guy still around.

And how about the 53 foot Australian yacht lost coming into **Salinas**, Puerto Rico, through **Boca de Infierno**, on a clear night, calm sea, at four knots headed due west, for a waypoint someone had given them for the exact center of the cut? He had a really accurate waypoint. Take a look at the chart for Boca de Infierno. What happened to them?

Or take the group of gooners yakking incessantly on the VHF while crossing the Caicos Banks: "Watch for this!" "Oops for that!" "Which waypoint are you using?" "Try the Wavy Line one!" "Pavlidis' looks better!" "I've gone back to Van Sant's!" They coupled the start waypoint for the Starfish Channel from Wavy Line Graphics' excellent chart to the ending waypoint from *Passages South*, then changed the destination waypoint back and forth, forth and back, every time they saw a cloud's shadow on the bank, just to check and double check. But they never checked back-bearings to start points which cohered with their changed destination points. They busily sailed their gizmos, *but not their boats*.

Heads down in two charts and two guides, eyes agoggle at electronic charts fed by GPSs with correction offsets they had put in for another chart and forgot to erase, charts displaying their little cursor boat just where they wanted it — all following the leader anyway — someone finally went bang! They checked all their LCD readouts and they all indignantly agreed they had the right of things and the guides and charts had the wrong.

One boat moved my tried and true arrival waypoint to the inaccurate lat/longs of an official chart and proceeded to steer around the fanciful crosses on the chart's "unsurveyed" area, crosses basically meaning "Here be Dragons". That boat sank.

1. Load up on guides and embellished charts that have *proven lat/long data. Do not* put correction and offset information into your computer, your GPS or your autopilot. You shall surely leave one of them behind like a computer virus when you make the transition between charts, between chart media or between the chart and the helm.

2. Proceed *visually* in all channels, cuts and harbors of the Caribbean or the Bahamas.

3. While coasting, make fixes regularly by compass bearings, and confirm with both GPS and chart to ensure your continuous recognition of land features *and chart error.*

4. Treat all Bahamian and Caribbean beacons and lights as unreliable.

5. Throw the damned chart plotter away rather than use it within 2 nm of land not belonging to the United States of America. *Most charts* have Lat/Longs uncorrected for GPS!

THE BASIC PATH

Thornless cruising means less *where* to cruise than *how*. Yet the principle of threading island lees to windward results in a basic path which links the major cruising areas: The Bahamas, Hispaniola, Puerto Rico, The Virgins, Leewards, Windwards and South America.

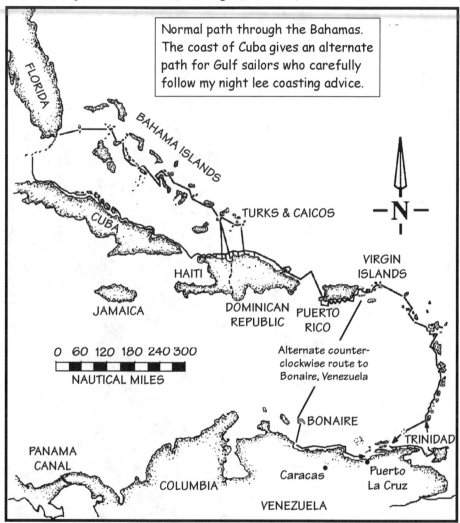

Normal path through the Bahamas. The coast of Cuba gives an alternate path for Gulf sailors who carefully follow my night lee coasting advice.

FLORIDA

BAHAMA ISLANDS

CUBA

TURKS & CAICOS

—N—

HAITI

VIRGIN ISLANDS

JAMAICA

DOMINICAN REPUBLIC   PUERTO RICO

0 60 120 180 240 300
NAUTICAL MILES

Alternate counter-clockwise route to Bonaire, Venezuela

BONAIRE

TRINIDAD

PANAMA CANAL

Caracas

Puerto La Cruz

COLUMBIA

VENEZUELA

KEY STOPS AT WHICH TO WAIT FOR WEATHER

I have divided the route between Florida and South America into short and easy passages, between way stations where you can wait for a good weather window before proceeding. I then divide each passage into short and easy sails that I know well. Every small step means to put you in a snug harbor in time to fish up dinner and relax with a **Sundowner**. I have learned the hard way to skip as few steps of the path as I can.

Some typical stations on the **Thornless Path** from Florida to the Virgin Islands follow. Short sailing legs separate these key anchorages in order to put boat and crew into snug and safe havens where they can wait for their next good weather opportunity.

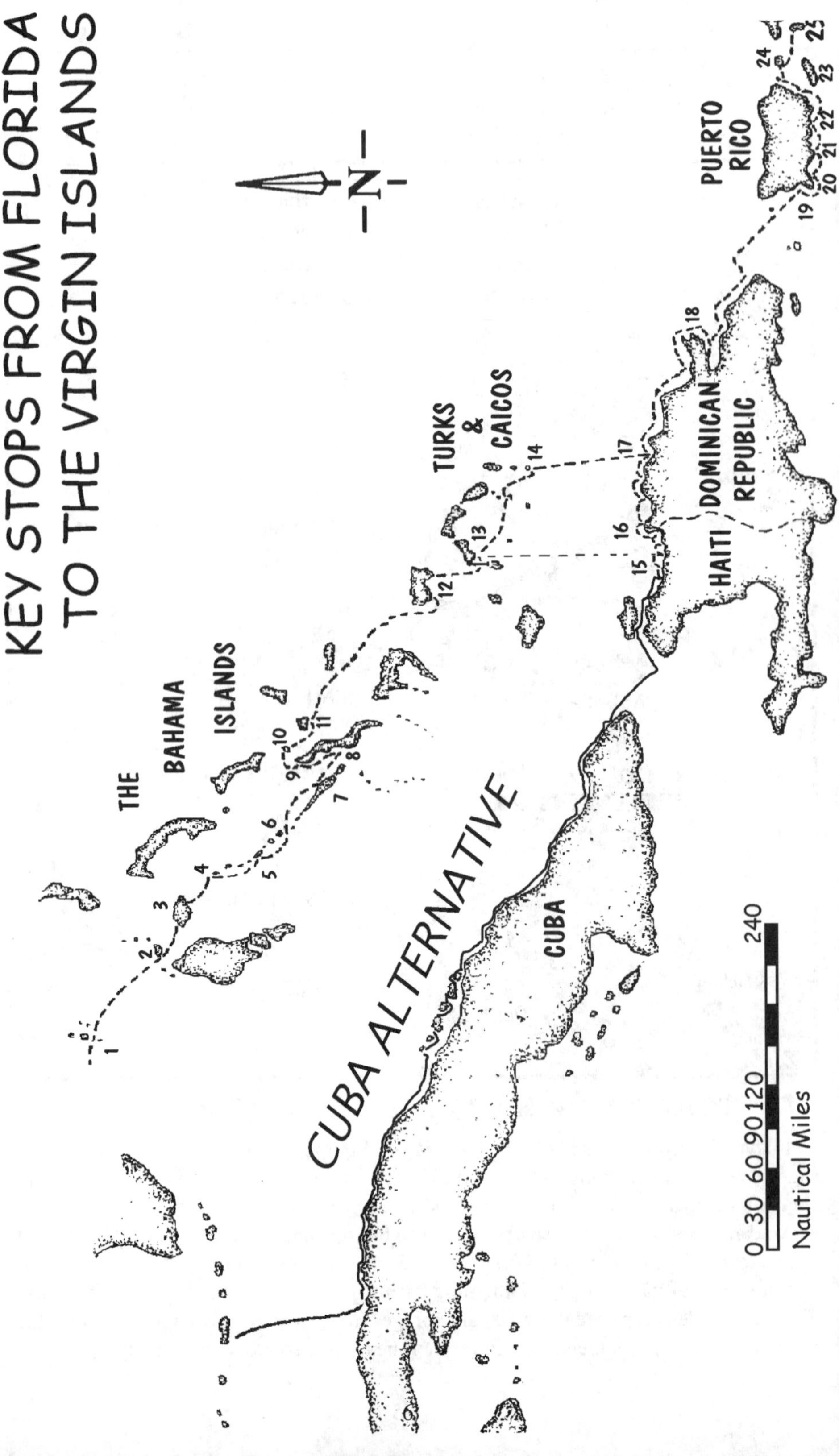

PASSAGES SOUTH   Bruce Van Sant

KEY STOPS FROM FLORIDA
TO THE VIRGIN ISLANDS

THE
BAHAMA
ISLANDS

TURKS
&
CAICOS

PUERTO
RICO

DOMINICAN
REPUBLIC

HAITI

CUBA

CUBA ALTERNATIVE

0 30 60 90 120   240
Nautical Miles

Some short term anchorages which show up in the sailing dirctions don't show on the list below, and you might choose to bypass some do show. For instance, **Georgetown** to **Conception Island** can make a fun seven hour sail in a good southeaster, missing **Long Island** entirely. But you shouldn't miss Long Island, and seven hours of beating amounts to twice too much when you don't have to. Other stations (e.g., **San Salvador**), lie slightly off the path but may become useful in the right conditions. (See *Flexible Route Planning*). I include **Haiti** and the western half of the north coast of the **Dominican Republic** as an alternate path for the cruiser who wants to tour **Hispaniola** properly. For older cruisers and singlehanders I recommend **West Caicos** to **Manzanillo** (13-16) as an easier route with smaller, less windward steps. You can tour Haiti by land while the boat stays at Manzanillo or **Luperón**, if you don't want to sail to Haiti's ports of entry at **Cap Haïtien** or **Fort Liberté**.

1.	Gun Cay		11.	Rum Cay	F	19.	Boquerón	
2.	Chub Cay		12.	Mayaguana	A	20.	Guánica	
3.	Nassau	FA	13.	Sapodilla Bay	FA	21.	Ponce	FA
4.	Allen's Cay		14.	Big Sand Cay		22.	Salinas	HFA
5.	Sampson Cay	F	15.	La Badie		23.	Puerto del Rey	HFA
6.	Cave Cay		15.	Cap Haïtien	A	24.	Culebra	A
7.	Georgetown	FA	15.	Fort Liberté		25.	St. Thomas	FA
8.	Salt Pond	FA	16.	Manzanillo	A			
9.	Calabash Bay	A	17.	Luperón	HFA		(*from tanker boat)	
10.	Conception Island		18.	Samaná	FA			

Note H: Stops at which you can safely leave the boat in hurricane season.

Note F: Fuel can get pumped from barrels almost everywhere, but these stops have dockside fuel accommodating a draft of up to seven feet.

Note A: Access to airline connections for the embarking and receiving of guests.

GOING WEST, DOWNWIND

After crossing the Atlantic many Europeans tell me they can't do the Bahamas with their keel depth. Don't make that mistake. Get all **Explorer Chartbooks** and relevant **Wavy Line Graphics** charts, the only Lat/Long corrected charts around and carrying detail from decades of first-hand on-site experience. Look closely at the charts, and you'll find the Bahamas has deep enough water everywhere you want it. Trust these charts, and you'll have a dream cruise.

Get all your charts for the Bahamas in St.Thomas or Puerto Rico. Follow my notes (admittedly brief) to the letter for boats westbound from PR and northbound from Luperón. For too many reasons to explain here, don't miss a beat of it. Put all your time available in Luperón to experience that island, and do the straight line route I show through the Bahamas, *not* the **Old Bahama Channel** unless you sail to Cuba or Key West. The Old Bahama Channel reminds me of Mediterranean sailing with its pyramidial seas, and anyway it makes a longer passage than the rhumbline straight through the Bahamas. If you must hurry, you can bypass Turks and Caicos. But plan lots of time in the Dominican Republic and the Bahamas **Far Out islands**, the best cruising goals on the route -- especially if you've got YCB (Yachtie Center Burnout) from the eastern Caribbean.

THE CUBA ALTERNATIVE

My techniques using an island's **night lee** to advance against the trades provides a boon to Gulf sailors if applied successfully to Cuba's north coast. I must emphasize that I only twice sailed this coast to evaluate its land effects, versus well over 100 times that I've done the same off Hispaniola. If you understand and have experience with the techniques involved, go for it. But prepare yourself for longer waits for weather or shorter legs.

From Florida to Hispaniola I've rarely used less than 15 stops in playing the lees through the Bahamas against prevailing conditions. Cuba from Varadero eastward may need up to 20 stops, averaging 23 miles apart. Worst case means 20 pre-dawn runs of 5-7 hours each, or at least a month of passage making May through November. It might take up to two months during the period December through April with the fronts active in that season.

Both Cuba guide authors counsel against easting on the northeast coast of Cuba. The coast slants a bit southerly into the trades, which takes the wind onshore. Cuba barely lies on the edge of the trade belt, so you get less reliable winds. Narrow and less than half as high as Hispaniola, Cuba does not give you great **land effects**. Fronts nearly always pass through most of Cuba, albeit weakened, while they rarely make it to Hispaniola. Dying and stalled fronts play a key role in my methods. All told, you don't leave Cuban harbors in **gradient wind** forecasts much over 10 knots, and then only between moving fronts.

Many alternative anchorages exist beyond those shown in the table below. However, the waypoints shown fit the criteria of (1) offering nearby refuge to wait for weather, and (2) providing the most easterly staging point prior to a series of unprotected anchorages. After two cruises in Cuba I added "No Guardia Post" as a definitely positive criterion.

20 Planned Anchorages (out of 56 Available)	Facilities	Latitude	Longitude	Miles
Varadero	1,2,3,4	23 07	81 19	
Cayo Libertad		23 11	81 07	12
Pasa de la Manuy	1	23 06	80 58	10
Cayo Cádiz		23 11	80 29	27
Cayo Esquivel del Sur		23 04	80 05	23
Pasa Boca Chica	1	22 56	79 48	18
Pasa Marcos		22 47	79 38	13
Cayo Francés	1	22 38	79 13	25
Cayo Guillermo (west)	4	22 37	78 43	28
Cayo Paredón		22 28	78 10	32
Cayo Confites	4	22 11	77 40	33
Pasa Carabelas (reef)		21 48	77 25	27
Nuevitas (entrance)	1,4	21 35	77 07	21
Manatí (entrance)	1,4	21 23	76 49	21
Puerto Padre (entrance)	1,4	21 16	76 32	17
Gíbara	4	21 06	76 08	25
Bahía Vita	1,2,3,4	21 06	75 53	9
Bahía Nipe	1,4	20 48	75 33	29
Cayo Moa Grande	1,4	20 41	74 54	37
Baracoa	1,3,4	20 21	74 30	30

1=Protection from a front   2=Marina   3=Provisioning   4=Guardia Post

CREW STUFF

A journey of a thousand miles may start with a single step, but it continues with a gazillion more. Stumbles can occur at any step, not just in the early stages of the expedition. Insure each task on your provision and to-do list targets *daily existence*. Some cruisers gladden the chandlery cash registers preparing for the ultimate wave to cast you upon the shores of disconsolate wilderness. Many become enamored of cruise preparation itself. They only leave starting mode when they return. If you haven't cruised foreign before, get a reality check with a winter's cruise of the Bahamas **Far Out Islands**, then to Florida for a summer's realistic refit. The second time out you'll do it like an old hand.

CRUISING VS. SAILING

Much miscommunication comes from the word "cruising". We talk with our points of view from different cruising styles. Take the following exchange of letters in which my candid reply to friends never got answered. Cruising and sailing define matters of style.

One year we hand-brushed Imron onto our boat in a peaceful mangroved lagoon near Cumaná, Venezuela. While there, we received a three months' batch of mail in which I found a letter from an old friend. He had retired and now taught navigation for the Power Squadron in Florida. I opened the letter, and the miscommunication began.

He and his wife, he said, "were considering trying out the cruising life". He wondered if they could visit us to try out a *half day*'s cruise to see if they would like it. I wrote back with the truth. It might take several days of work to break camp, I told him. When we found ourselves harbor bound for more than a week the boat got cocooned in sunshades, spider webbed in lines and bedecked with all manner of half done projects. I told him I wouldn't undo all that for my own mother just for a half day sail. On the other hand, I wrote, if we had to make a passage, guests aboard could interfere with its routine and safe operation, especially in hurricane season. I proposed he visit next time we found ourselves in a short-term harbor while island hopping. That way they could enjoy staying aboard, have their half day harbor hops and get to visit nice tourist places which wouldn't shatter their vision of the cruising life. They could pick either the place or the time, I said, but not *both*. I meant that either notification would come extremely short, or the place might disappoint them extremely. Such as Castries, or a week in Laguna Grande, where we lay then, where they would dress with paint rollers in their hands and mosquito nets round their heads.

I thought this a marvelously honest and complete answer, as only a good friend deserved. I looked forward to his reply and to his sometime visit.

Some days later I sat at the bar in Cumanagoto Marina taking my Sundowner Gin and Tonic (**SG&T**, see Glossary). Next to me at the bar, Pedro asked if I knew of a fellow called Skeeter. I waved my gin and tonic toward Skeeter who just then began walking our way down the dock. "The cruiser there on the dock," I said.

"Which one?" asked Pedro. "The Carver or the Trojan?" Words indeed have meaning.

Boats differ as do the uses of boats. I did my share of racing on Lake Worth half a century ago on really fast scows. I've used my cruising boats in PHRF racing as well. But when a weekend sailor with a gofast boat asks me about cruising, I'm not so sure we can bridge the communication gap. Nevertheless, I try. I can tell them some false expectations I've known people to have while they planned to take up full time cruising.

RACING FOR THE CLUB

Cruising calls to mind teenagers who piddled along Main Street in otherwise high-speed dragsters to ogle the girls hanging around the drugstore. In the Navy, the same young men *cruised* the bars on East Baltimore Street, teased into lingering too long at each stop where nothing really exciting ever happened to them. Later in life, after a day at the office, they *cruised* the body exchanges until, finally snared, they moved to the 'burbs, raised kids, made the school board and joined a yacht club. Sailing tugged at their middle age like the freedom of wheels did in their teens. These guys finally retire and go *cruising*.

At cruising gams and breakfasts, dockside happy hours and marine store seminars, the message gets heard. You must sail far and wide. Then you may grow a beard, wear a Greek fisherman's cap, give advice rather than seek it and chair the seminar, not just attend it.

So they fit up and sail out. They begin their race for the finish at the club where they hope to win a cupful of bragging rights. They do long laps between yachting centers where, again, nothing really happens to them. They straggle home where they grow the beard, wear the hat and sit under the dockside umbrella handing out advice.

Others, however, have lost themselves out on the course and dropped out of the race. They piddle along in the little places. Something happens to them every day they *cruise*. Which of these types would you call a *cruiser*? Which do you favor?

GETTING STARTED

Whatever you expect, you won't get it.

Sailing out of Stockholm, I imagined myself languidly cruising the Mediterranean in endless summers. Boy! Did I learn fast! My work list grew three lines for every one I struck through. I find the same phenomenon holds in the islands of the trades.

Cruisers start out with lots of man overboard equipment, and little or nothing with which to receive original source weather data. They have full game shelves and book shelves, but few engine spares and supplies; lots of yogurt and sourdough starter, but no resin catalyst; colored cloth to make courtesy flags, but no fiberglass cloth or sheet rubber. They've got shot records and pet pedigrees, but no engine shop manual. In other words, many focus on preventing boredom and surviving disaster, both very unlikely.

Much cruise planning focuses on the terror of the *Ultimate Wave*. However, with the right investment in equipment and skills, even a neophyte cruiser can read the weather sufficiently to hop between Ultimate Waves. The last time anyone asked me for shot records I didn't have any. They pulled me aside in Hong Kong and gave me a free smallpox vaccination. No one has mentioned health certificates since, nor my sloppy flag etiquette. I've always had pets on board. Officials have only petted them — not that exceptions don't exist, or one's behavior can't provoke inquiry. Just don't ask questions.

Target your preparations more effectively with language lessons for the countries you shall visit. Replace thrillers and romances with references on the islands. The more remote from your experience, the more you shall need it. The differences between what you expect and what you find should liven your day, not frustrate you or even cause strokes.

Don't expect to evade the recessive ills of society. They often dominate in the tropics. Ineluctable authorities, unfair taxes, irreversible poverty, rampant greed, welfare amuck, little opportunity, low wages and you name it! Everywhere in the trade belt one or all of these flourish in the tropic sun, dwarfing more temperate varieties to the north.

CRUISING STYLES

An itinerant myself for half a century I can certify the old refrains "You can't run away from yourself", "The grass always looks greener...", etc. The newcomer to life aboard in the tropics, recently unchained from responsibility's chafe, often careers along blinded by childhood's "new puppy" malady, or the adolescent "new car" syndrome. Eventually that wears thin and everyone finds their own style of cruising or they give up the game. I have drifted through several styles myself and I feel another coming on.

GLOBETROTTER

I sailed as a GLOBETROTTER for years in Europe, but I metamorphosed. GLOBETROTTERS charge about the sea testing self and boat in persistent replays of sailing magazine articles. They become instant experts and write articles as the Old Hand who has done it all. If cruising of that ilk appeals to you, go for it, but drop this book before it changes your life.

CAMPER

While rearing children I could only cruise for long weekends, vacations, summers and while relocating to new jobs. Even though a liveaboard, I became a CAMPER when out cruising. When not adventuring at sea, I repaired ashore. I felt awfully alive but did not live a life. One cannot sustain long term cruising as a series of camping adventures, and it won't feel anything like cruising with the kids.

TOURIST

Cruising TOURISTS rarely leave the comfort of their nautical nests. They cruise as passengers in a safari park, noses pressed against the window glass, marveling at the dangers around them. They savor foreign life and lands as do Manhattan yuppies their cappuccino. These cruisers leave the boat at each rest stop from which they can fly home. They bunch up in foreign harbors and do land excursions in groups. TOURISTS need money, so I never tried it — though I wouldn't mind it.

MINGLERS

Some cruisers enjoyed so much the weekend potlucks and raftups of their boat lives at home that, when they go out into the world for a long cruise, they continue them. MINGLERS gravitate to each other like magnets. They see cruising as a continuous 4th of July barbeque. If you like this style, you shall change venues each time the egg salad sandwiches run out, the keg dries up and the stories grow stale — all good reasons to go.

AIRSTREAMERS

I call some of my favorite couples AIRSTREAMERS. They poke around marinas and sea parks scattered along the seaways, not unlike Mom and Pop who settle into RV parks between highway excursions in their Air Stream trailers. If this laid back road gypsy life becomes you, as it does me, make the whole trade wind crescent your I-75, and you'll never come home.

ISLAND HOPPER or PASSAGE MAKER

PASSAGE MAKERS always take the long shots. They want open water. Some stay with this style for good. I sailed many years as a PASSAGE MAKER, but I metamorphosed.

Like a good friend of mine who can't abide waiting for weather. At sea he takes long passages to avoid the anxiety of making entrances and exits. In port he finds a secure hole and hangs out for months, even years. When in port, he doesn't "waste time with the weather". When he prepares a passage he has no mental data base of the weather because he lacks the patience required to carefully accumulate one. He comes unglued after just two days of waiting and throws himself and his boat into the sea to get it over with.

Because of his habit of nonstop long passages, my friend has a ferocious reputation as a great navigator, a real sailor's sailor, and I often see cruisers consulting him on weather and sailing strategies. In reality, he has seen few ports, though the ones he's seen, he knows well. He's done little sailing and navigating among islands, though he's done lots of tossing in his bunk while reading bunches of books out on the open sea. To me, he confesses he simply gets "scared shitless" near islands and while making their reefy entrances. He says he doesn't understand their currents, their effects on wind and weather, and that it "drives him bananas" to even think about the weather, let alone focus his worse fears upon it day after day while waiting for a weather window. When he feels ready to go, or some woman makes it known that he must, he screws up his courage, roars an oath and makes a banzai charge onto the hazards of the open sea.

We have traveled the same routes, he and I — he in one fierce gulp, I nibbling away at it one harbor at a time. As a consequence, we rarely meet, though we like each other well. A good beer buddy, he once confessed to me his admiration for the quality of mind which enables guys like me to face the hazards of island hopping. "It takes a lot of guts", he says. No amount of explaining of weather forecasts, of land effects, of night lees or of diurnal variations can persuade him of my cowardice. I don't even throw my tea bags overboard for fear of hearing their tiny shrieks in the night.

If you do long passages to test yourself against the sea, you have to know you shall eventually lose the test. PASSAGE MAKER or ISLAND HOPPER, only the COWARDS survive.

Jalan Jalan sailing
home to Puerto Plata, 1986

Ever look forward to October's bracing chill and the smell of burning leaves? Bottle it. The tropics offer the mosquito mugginess of the autumnal troughs and the black rain from burning sugar fields. You may have already girded yourself for changes of latitude, but how about the accommodations you must make to differences in mores, tact, dignity, decency, body language and much more, among the different people you shall encounter?

INTRUDERS

On two occasions nighttime intruders have roused me from my bunk while I lay in a remote anchorage. The first time it happened I had not slept in two days.

When I finally made harbor, I doused the adrenaline level with a couple of **SG&T**s (see Glossary), then dropped like an anchor into my bunk. At four in the morning an unshaven, red-eyed, dirty and, except for old and holed jockey shorts, naked man shook me semiconscious. The hand not rousing me held an AR15 automatic.

In my befuddlement, I suspected that only Huk guerrillas, dope smugglers or officials of a banana republic, even while naked, carried a weapon like that. Smugglers can afford clothes. I hadn't heard about any revolution. The Philippines had all the Huks.

Fortunately for me, I sleepily guessed that he had a permit for the gun and that he represented some authority who had bought it for him, he not appearing to have the resources to buy one for himself. I mumbled, "*Buenos dias*". And so my day began.

The intruder identified himself as the local part-time representative of the Navy who had the responsibility to inquire at the boat which had surreptitiously slid into the bay that night. Out fishing all night with buddies in his little log canoe, he returned to port with the dawn. When they found my boat, they knocked on the hull, but to no avail. A serious man, he went the next step and stepped aboard. Still with no sign from me, he stepped inside.

Good thing I didn't grab my gun, a hand-sized automatic on the shelf over my pillow. Had I done so, we would both have drowned from water pouring through the holes he could make in my hull with his machine gun.

Instead, we had an amiable beer together the next day, and he warned me again not to go sneaking up on his beach like a Cuban fifth columnist. He suggested that if I really wanted a special reception, I might try night anchoring unannounced in Cuba under Fidel.

A TIP

In a "going south" meeting on the beach at Georgetown a lady expressed concern with the entrance charges in the Dominican Republic. I told her the charges for Immigration, Agriculture, Ports Authority and Customs. She appeared annoyed with that answer. She wanted to know the *informal* fees versus the *official* fees. She wanted a tale of corruption, and I didn't bite. I addressed the group instead.

Can you find corruption in the islands? You bet; the same as everywhere, but to a much lesser degree. By definition a small country has only petty officials, and therefore the corruption, by large country standards, has quite petty dimensions. Abuse of power in smaller countries more likely touches the individual. In the yachties' countries billions get wasted (stolen) daily, but it doesn't overly annoy them. If an island official makes a sly suggestion that one buy him a beer, however, some yachties become outraged.

The lady of the informal charges now asked about tipping. I told her Latin Americans generally tip only when something superlative merits it. They also enjoy doing favors for each other to express their appreciation more than do Europeans or Americans. Sometimes waiters' tips get put on the bill, and one leaves the small change. Taxi drivers don't get tips as a fast rule. A driver might not understand a tip, but he might understand "Keep the change". If not tipping a waiter makes you uncomfortable, then use 10 percent, plus or minus, as the Americans use 15 to 20 percent. Overtipping wins disrespect and larger charges next time.

She appeared incredulous. *Not tip?* Then followed a long harangue about her daughter making it through college from tips as a waitress. I worked my way through high school as a hotel bell hop. I think I know about tips: no begrudging someone who forgets, and damn any rules, you only get what you *earn*. She really lay into me, railing my selfishness. Trying not to respond to personal attack, I gave the point but warned the group that tipping too much, or when not expected to, could cause embarrassment. The waiter of a small *tipico* might own the place, proudly independent after a lifetime's struggle. Attempts to tip can insult — or classify you as a sucker. Watch what locals do, and when in Rome ...

THE PRICE OF STRESS

Signs of normalcy in one culture may cause alarm signals in another. For example, Latinos like to carry guns as a sign of authority. Why not? Sure makes good logic.

Sometimes, the smaller the authority, the larger the guns. Larger guns may cost less. Guns from the former Soviet Union come cheap in quantity, and because you haven't seen them before, they look all the more sinister. Unless quite well traveled, you might suppose you've stumbled into a revolution when you see poorly clad citizens roaming the streets with Russian machine guns and rifles — but you really only see bank guards.

Culturally transmitted visual stimuli and their culturally correct responses don't map easily from one culture to another. They can, in fact, directly conflict. The receiving organism — you — shall undergo stress depending on the extent to which responses expected by the two cultures to the same stimulus differ. If a mild and occasional conflict, you giggle. If strong and continuous you undergo a stress reaction called **Culture Shock**.

You may have a repertoire of cocktail stories of what happened to you on your tour of Thailand. In that case, you understand the phenomenon of culture shock, but you may never have experienced it in shock dimensions. If you lived on the local economy of another nation for extended periods, forced to use another language exclusively as, say, a member of the Peace Corps, you know well the phenomenon at shock levels.

Roaming around the Caribbean on a small boat provides greater exposure to local people and their customs than does jetting in and out of well protected resort complexes. If you haven't had the opportunity of experiencing Culture Shock before, you shall learn on your boat. When it gets unpleasant you can't simply take a cab to the airport.

Culture Shock has many symptoms with which you should familiarize yourself before leaving home. Your ability to communicate with or without language, your capacity to get what you want, say, an engine part, depend on your skill in cutting through the background noise of your culturally learned responses and creating a totally new set of responses which can achieve your goals.

The better your skills in creating useful new responses to confusing stimuli, the higher stress levels you may suffer due to the number of unsatisfied natural responses you have accumulated.

You may have success handling the customs guys, finding clean fuel, provisioning at fair prices, replacing a motor part, and so forth, but you shall build a head of steam that you've got to blow off. You pay that price for coping successfully.

I've blown my safety valve right in customs and got charged entrance fees others didn't have to pay. I've seen others air ship expensive parts from home with all the attendant hassles of telephoning, wiring funds, misdirections and delays, when they could have cut through the static of their learned responses and bought an equivalent, sometimes superior, part locally in two days for less money.

In other words, you can buy off **Culture Shock** with money or effort, and mute it with anger: take it in the purse or in the gut. You decide how you pay the price, but pay it you shall. Unfortunately, some people get others to pay it for them.

For example, the Albert Schweitzer in you might want to enfold the entire disadvantaged population of the Third World in his compassionate embrace. You settle for inviting a couple of homeless street urchins aboard for peanut butter and jelly sandwiches. Your finer instincts may be stroked by your behavior, but watch the kids don't walk in uninvited with their friends later on. Your behavior may appear bizarre to them, remember, and they might expect that you want to adopt them and take them off to New York to pick gold up off the streets. Why otherwise would you usher them aboard a thing as foreign to them as a spaceship? Obviously you shall take them to Mars, if not New York, right?

Many years ago, I witnessed an incident that illustrates the point.

SPACESHIP YACHT

Two American couples in a motor yacht moored next to me brought some kids aboard their boat with tragic results for the children. They gave the kids a tour of the yacht, an old classic motorboat, once belonging to a famous American. They then fed them peanut butter and jelly sandwiches on deck. A few days later the couples discovered the kids had come back aboard and some costume jewelry had gone missing.

Seeing themselves as having participated directly, and with great humanity, in the work of *Save The Children* by their charitable invitation to peanut butter and jelly, the cruisers, justifiably outraged that the children had come back to *steal*, complained to the police. The officials took a serious view of offenses against tourists in their fragile tourism sector. The state security police, the dreaded *Ton Ton Macoute*, took direct charge of the investigation. As a result of their inquiries one child got crippled and two badly and bloodily beaten. They sent one child home with a compound fracture, to find his loot. When asked if she'd got all her plastic bracelets returned, one of the women from the yacht, panicked by the sight of a child holding the flesh over his bone, cried, "No, but they don't matter, just, for God's sake, please stop beating them!" The beatings, of course, went on, since she said the property hadn't got recovered fully.

The child probably didn't want to give up his bit of brightly colored plastic, a link to the goddess-mother from the spaceship. She who had him experience motherly warmth, perhaps for the first time in his life, along with peanut butter and jelly. She who seemed to promise to carry him off to another and better star.

So they broke his arm. He and the other children paid the price of the yachties' inappropriate responses. The yachties, blaming it all on the police, rushed to their boat and vroomed out of the harbor for home. I got one of the dock lines they left behind.

PIRATES!

Returning to Georgetown from Puerto Plata, a beer buddy grabbed me in mock fright. "God, it's good to see you. I heard you had gone into Abraham Bay at Mayaguana."

After massaging the blood back into my arm I learned that the **SSB** nets buzzed with tales of piracy in Mayaguana. Rumor had it that three boats had anchored there off the town. One boat had got boarded by pirates in blue jump suits masquerading as Bahamas Customs officials. A fight ensued in which one of the boats disappeared.

Over the Regatta period the essentials of the story changed little, but the details, for no one actually knew for sure, ranged from gory to grisly. After Regatta I returned home to Puerto Plata, stopping, of course, at Mayaguana. This time I bypassed my usual reef anchorage and set anchor in the bay to visit the settlement and get the dirt first hand.

The two constables on the island, one twenty-two years old, the other twenty and just out of the academy in Nassau, wore blue jump suits. As Bahamian police they of course had no guns. I chatted various sea stories with them, including their recent unarmed arrest of eight Colombians with Uzzis who had gone aground in Horse Pond Bay. The unarmed constables stroked out to the ship in a little borrowed rowboat to make arrests. Pretty brave boys in blue. The islanders put the prisoners up in their houses until Nassau could send a plane down for them. That's how life goes in the **Far Out Islands**.

With a little conversational nudging on my part a story gradually emerged about a power boat that had come in one evening while two sailboats already lay moored in the bay. The boat didn't answer the constables' hails so they borrowed a rowboat and stroked out to say "hi".

The skipper looked tired, perhaps even intoxicated. A big florid faced man, he met their queries with growls of "I don't want any" and "get away".

Being good constables the two young men smelled something awry. They asked if he had any arms aboard, the next question in the rote they used. When he met this with a surly shout they decided this boat definitely didn't pass the smell test.

Instead of bidding the yachtsman a warm welcome to **Mayaguana** and paddling home, they started to tie their painter to the big gin palace and requested permission to come aboard. Not ever anticipating a negative response to such a pro-forma question, the younger, and less experienced, of the two climbed aboard, whereupon the owner skittered into the saloon and emerged waving a shotgun. With a foaming roar of curses he shoved the young constable into the bay, where, given the sudden appearance of this maniac with a gun, he gladly swam off.

The yachtsman immediately upped his anchor and blasted out through the cut in the reef into a setting sun and disappeared. Next morning's cruiser nets blazed with the story.

"Pirates masquerading as customs officials" probably got reported by the guy in the gin palace. The "fight" would naturally come from the sailboats observing from some distance away and hearing nothing but dim shouts, seeing the brandishing of a gun and a body going overboard. True, "three boats lay in the anchorage". That one boat "disappeared" might have come from releasing a mike switch too soon, untimely radio interference or simple embellishment.

The whole pirate story came about through the *klatsching* of the cruising community on their radios, sopping up their alienation and **Culture Shock** at the expense of two fine young Bahamian officers and the reputation of an island badly in need of visitors. For many years after that I still got approached at the Two Turtles barbecue with anxious queries as to piracy in Mayaguana.

Once, at the barbecue, I heard a fellow at the next table authoritatively replaying one of the scarier versions of the old story, but, like all good stories, the essentials hadn't changed. Two guys in blue, a fight, a lost boat.

I learned long ago that the price of correcting a know-it-all in public comes too high for me to pay. Instead of bringing them all down on my head, I ordered another Gin and Tonic. After all, no one likes a spoil sport and everyone likes a good story. Especially me!

THE REMEDY

Culture Shock accounts for the flocking syndrome of expatriates in any country. Latin Americans in America, for instance, or Americans in Latin America. While living in Paris I always noticed Americans *klatsch*ing with other Americans to whom they would never speak while on their native soil. Matrons from Old Greenwich would eagerly trade recipes with the wives of North Sea oil roustabouts from Louisiana. They clutched together for the sole purpose of hearing their native tongues bad-mouth the Parisians.

Grumbling about the environment producing your stress seems normal and even necessary. Frenchmen do it in America, Germans do it in Spain and Englishmen do it everywhere. But watch where you do your grouching. You don't idle in the private *salons* of Paris while sitting in a cheap restaurant in a small Venezuelan port. You sit on display for the locals. Bitching about the local environment while under the gaze of petty port officials, dock boys and small time secret police, doesn't rank as too *suave* by me. Doing it in a restaurant where the couple at the next table run the local grocery shall get you higher prices on your veggies tomorrow.

Find your own general remedy to the stress of Culture Shock, and apply it at appropriate times and places. Whether yoga, expatriate *kaffee klatsches*, or self flagellation, a personalized remedy should permit daily satisfaction of personal and boat oriented goals while increasing your enjoyment of the different scenes.

Some boaters crawl into a VCR-induced haze, not leaving their boats for days at a time. Others meet every evening for a happy hour where they massage each other's spirits with spirits. The **SG&T**, while a dandy motivation to be at anchor early and safely, makes a poor remedy to the stress of Culture Shock. The ports of Asia and Latin America teem with besotted expatriates who have taken this false remedy to their destructions.

Whether you go into frenzies of varnishing, practice meditation, write long letters to the kids or *klatsch* on the SSB, your remedy should work off the stress of learning new responses. You will reduce the costs of making inappropriate responses in the future and increase your enjoyment of the foreign cruising life.

Beware, though, that *klatsch*ing on the **SSB** may have far-ranging effects.

THE SIMPLE STUFF THAT DRIVE YOU CRAZY

The shift to living aboard in the Antilles from even the sleepiest rural town above 22° latitude may rival the move of a charged up urban yuppie ad man to a cave in the wilderness. The very basics of daily life change, and you won't relish it. Change causes discomfort, and you've got billions of years of evolution behind you with which to fight it.

To paraphrase Shakespeare: which thousand natural shocks shall *your* flesh inherit? Let's see . . .

CHANGES IN ATTITUDE

Failure to wait patiently for a good **weather window** (that time during which wind and wave favor your completing a leg of a passage in safety and comfort), in my experience, overwhelmingly contributes to unhappy cruises. Yet patience hardly hallmarks many cruisers. Most cruisers have strong independent streaks. Strong willed and self confident, most skippers tend to take charge easily. Those very traits lead many to seek the challenge and independence of life on the sea.

These so-called **Type A** people come in both gender flavors, and I commiserate with them for their jumpiness. I, like them, tend to stuff time. I listen to the news while reading the paper while carrying on a conversation (poorly). Take waiting for weather, for example. Getting all set to go, then having to sit in port day after day, unable to go out, unable to schedule anything — and boy! do Type A's like to schedule — just waiting on a bus that never comes, it seems. All enough to try a saint. When a window does open, most Type A's jump at it immediately. They take the first hours of a three day window, the swells still up, the winds not yet laid down. Then they sit in the next anchorage for the best part of the window. I don't wish to play psychologist, but a bit of my own experience might help.

In my first few tough trips on the **thorny path**, I recognized behavior in myself and others which I had seen many years ago as a full time air traveler. The first-in first-out queues of taxis, ticketing, and baggage checking drove me bananas. Waiting in line infuriates me. Shuffling along with the herd of travelers like cattle does likewise. It didn't take me long to learn to act contrary to the flow. I became the last on the plane, strolling through an empty waiting room. I sat in the plane doing some work when it came time to deplane, while most people crammed the aisles for 20 minutes or more. Then they rode busses crammed to overflowing. Then they waited at the empty baggage carousel for 20 minutes more. Meanwhile, I lolled around in a half filled bus and strolled up to the carousel just in time to lift off my bag. I had a hundred other tricks to air travel then, and I'm sure you know lots more and different ones today, but does that translate to cruising on a sailboat? You bet it does: Type A's can always find a useful way to pass time without *waiting*.

Sir Francis Bacon, father of the Age of Reason, patriarch of all modern science and mathematics, wrote, "Nature, to be commanded, must be obeyed." You can make Nature serve you only by knowing Nature's elements and arranging your purpose in accordance with them. To the cruiser with an education in the hard sciences, this does not come as news. To some others, perhaps lawyers, it may come as a *revelation*. I have good news to these unfortunates: there exists a way out short of an epiphany in monstrous seas.

You don't have to deny your Type A nature. *Use* it to outflank the forces that frustrate it. Get busy! Study the weather. Become a weather maven. Get equipment with which to gather **Wx** data. Sharpen your own deck level observations. The world holds nothing quite as fine for a Type A as *control* of a situation through knowledge, except perhaps the payoff of the smooth passage that results.

Think weather watching takes time? During my waits I spend a good *4 hours a day* on the weather. How so much? I listen to Herb and Chris, or whatever current weather nets, while doing some fixit project. I get the Offshore Reports, then satellite views, then the Tropical Weather Discussion. Morning, midday and evening I get the Tropical Prediction Center's weather charts. Add to those 4 hours a couple for meals, a couple of hours for swimming and diving, a couple reading and varnishing, and a nap — where did the day go? After decades at it I found each **wait for weather** full of accomplishment, while, as I grow older, the rounds of provisioning, potlucks and happy hours demand more patience.

SIMPLE STUFF

AIR

If you stayed in the Bahamas several months, as far as your allergic reactions go, you might as well have languished *at sea* several months. While at Hispaniola you bathe for twelve hours a day in air sliding down from the middle of the 250 kilometer (150 miles) wide, high mountainous island . This air brings with it all the pollens and allergens of practically every type of flora known and then some. You haven't seen a deciduous tree or grasses in several months. Keep your antihistamines handy and double your vitamin intake.

WATER

Most maladies reported by yachties arriving directly on Hispaniola from an extended stay in the Bahamas come from these effects of climatic and allergen change. But like the New Yorker visiting New Jersey in the summer, they blame everything on the water.

On the other hand, all developing countries have notoriously poor public sanitation coupled with poor or intermittent pressure in their town water lines. The H_2O from the mountains in the DR may run pure and delicious, but as in New Jersey, wait a couple of days after an outage before tanking up on the water. And, as in Florida, *always* treat it.

Jerry jugging can become a way of life. If you count on catching water, you can be sure it won't rain for weeks, so load up when you can. I have found it convenient to have several 6 gallon jerry jugs for water and diesel. Larger sizes become unmanageable and smaller sizes make for too many trips. You should equip for it. We take 1 or 2 showers a day (albeit "Navy" showers), and we wash dishes and vegetables in fresh water. That means at least 3 gallons a day per person, or a water jug run every 3 days with 2 people aboard. If you can afford it, I have a real back saver: use a large flexible tank with a 12 volt in-line pump with which to pump water aboard via the dinghy. Look, Ma, no hands!

WASHING FRUITS AND VEGETABLES

You shall use markets most places you cruise which differ little from the kind of markets your grandparents used, and perhaps your grandchildren shall again. Fresh lettuce, cabbage and tomatoes may have the dirt in which they grew still clinging to them. Eggs can have residue of that end of the chicken from which they exit. Rural communities in the Caribbean may have no major sanitary infrastructure. Anything you can peel must get washed thoroughly in bleached or limed water, or with white vinegar.

DOING WITHOUT MR. CLEAN

American products come clever and useful and well packaged. When they sell for the marine market they come clever, useful, well packaged and expensive, and, in the Caribbean, generally unavailable. You can port 50 bottles of each product and displace 10 cases of rum, or you can carry the following generic chemicals, refilling the product bottle with a substitute solution which may work better and more cheaply. Remember the first two principles of provisioning:

The Highest Utility for the Least Space, and *The Greatest Savings First.*

In other words, a boat full of small bottles of cheap, but high quality rum, and a year's supply of cleaning agents in a few chemical flasks means both a happy and clean boat.

Remember also to store and handle all chemicals with the care they deserve. I use sturdy, well-sealed plastic containers. I snugly wedge them into plastic milk cartons so they cannot move around and chafe. Never place plastic bottles directly against fiberglass mat or similar rough surfaces such as found in a lazarette. Stowage techniques which worked great while fattening the kitty from a mooring or a marina, suddenly can cause ghastly accidents on a passage. Think of a container of muriatic acid leaking into the bilge together with a bottle of ammonia. You'll have a clean and bug free bilge if you survive the gas. Soap flakes and chlorine can cause a fire when their containers chafe through!

DISH SOAP — I carry Joy dishsoap by the gallon. Others swear by other products, but I find Joy the one which foams most in salt water. Cheaper still, and as effective, you can try the non petroleum based industrial degreasers. The jug usually says *biodegradable* and it smells like soap, not oil. We used to make it even cheaper in chemistry class, but too long ago for me to remember how. I can't bring myself to use degreasers for the dishes, though.

Dish soap or non petroleum, biodegradable degreasers will:

—Clean the bilge.

—Degrease the engine and engine room.

—Prepare the deck around the deckfill for diesel spills.

—Emulsify any spills when squirted on the surface and spread with a hose.

—Keep dirt and grease from under your nails if rubbed there before starting a dirty job.

AMMONIA — Foaming **ammonia** strips the wax off woodwork with a soft scratch pad. I keep a squirt bottle on hand, good for any cleanup: water with 10 % ammonia and 5% Joy.

ALCOHOL — acts as a great astringent for skin problems, and it stuns fish for boarding and slaughter (see *Trolling*). Have quarts aboard. I used Aramis aftershave since the early 1960's. When I cruised back to America and found it expensive, I changed to a mixture of **alcohol** and witch hazel. Eventually I settled on only alcohol.

Stove alcohol, or 99% pure anhydrous (waterless) alcohol, thins epoxy beautifully, making thick roofing epoxy do jobs not worthy of more expensive stuff, and making the expensive stuff penetrate better. You find it in refrigeration stores or pharmacies.

HYDROGEN PEROXIDE — Pour over abrasions, cuts, wounds to disinfect before applying topical antibiotics. Have quarts aboard if you ding yourself as often as I do.

BORIC ACID POWDER — Sprinkled or "puffed" lightly in all unseen areas, (under drawers, beneath cabinets, or the lazarette), Boric Acid shall keep the boat roach free as long as it stays dry. Eggs that hatch after 6 to 8 weeks also get taken care of since the little fellows take it back to their nests on the hair of their legs. Then they explode when they groom each other!

Mixed with honey, boric acid also takes care of ants who carry it as a present to the Queen. See *Mauny's Cookies* in the recipe section.

MURIATIC ACID — ordinary **HCl**, or the stuff that's in your stomach. Don't add this powerful and dangerous stuff down there, though. You get it at hardware and swimming pool stores, and it's usually 20°. Don't dare breathe its acrid fumes, even at 20°. Always mix it with lots of water, pouring the acid into the water, not the reverse. It will:

1. eliminate rust stains and gelcoat chalking when mixed 1:10 in a spray bottle, costing a hundred times less than some identical products;

2. make your corroded 12 Volt deck sockets work instantly if sprayed into them (or your brass boat horn as I once had to demonstrate to the USCG boarders);

3. keep your coolers and heat exchangers bright and new inside when mixed 1:8 (stainless and copper only, not aluminum);

4. keep your head clean and unclogged by calcium buildups when mixed 1:6 (rubber and neoprene seals only — no leathers);

5. become Part B of two part teak cleaners when mixed 1:5 with water. Plain old lye crystals and water become Part A (NaOH). You can find lye in some toilet bowl or drain cleaners. Be sure you have *pure lye* and not some explosive mixture! You can still readily find lye crystals in developing countries.

First brush the lye solution onto your teak with a soft paint brush. Scrub the teak across the grain (never *with* the grain or you'll ablate the teak). Second, wipe dry with a cotton rag and brush on the acid. The teak will turn blonde almost instantly, and you can flush the teak with fresh water.

Of course, you should not allow acid to react too long without flushing it away.

CHLORINE— Swimming pool shock treatment which comes in rapidly dissolving granules or small pellets, and which has *only chlorine* as the active ingredient will provide you with a year or more supply of chlorine bleach for:

—treating the head

—pouring in the bilge

—doing your laundry

—killing black pin mold when sprayed on teak

—purifying your water

To get normal strength bleach put 1-2 tablespoons powder into a gallon of water. You've used too much if you can taste or smell it in the drinking water.

MINERAL SPIRITS — (if of good quality) will:

—burn more cleanly in your oil lamps than specially concocted products,

—thin your paints and varnishes,

—clean and oil your interior woods,

—start your BBQ fires and

—run in your diesel engine when you run out of fuel.

Besides all of that, mineral spirits sells cheaper than most of the products whose use it supplants. White kerosene makes a reasonable substitute, though it may have a slight odor in lamps that the purest of mineral spirits does not have. You'll find mineral spirits at hardware stores and general stores, sometimes called "thinner" (*not* lacquer thinner).

To thin varnish, even polyurethane varnish, use 25% mineral spirits on the first coat on teak, 15% on the second coat, 10% on the third coat, sanding between coats.

If you used polyurethane varnish for the first three "sealer coats" you can continue to add coats of a transparent linear polyurethane paint (Imron, Varithane, Awlgrip) *without sanding* between coats. Use brushing thinner and ultra violet (sunlight) protector as well. You need a dozen coats exterior and six coats interior, but don't fear: It brushes on like water and dries before you can come back for the second lap. I sold my ketch with the teak still glass-like *eight years* after varnishing this way. Eight varnish- and sanding free years!

CLEAN HANDS — and the best way to stay healthy in the Tropics? Wash your hands like your mother told you to. Don't worry that your Psychology 101 instructor said it showed your paranoia. After shaking hands with someone or handling money, keep your hands away from all bodily orifices until you can clean them.

MANAGING ALONE

The Emersonian requirement for self reliance, that which you always held in righteous esteem, translates to a fundamental of your biological survival on your foreign cruises. How? A wad of sour dough starter and a tray of bean sprouts? They may make you feel good, but self reliance leading to survival? Come on! Maybe after the Bomb, but not in an area of the world awash with cheap grains, organically grown (yes) fruits and vegetables and cheap tailors. Self reliance simply means to *rely first on yourself.*

If you can't do something, don't look for someone who can. Try do do it yourself first, even badly. You'll learn how to do it next time, and more importantly, what some "experts" don't even know, how *not* to do it.

TRAVELING IN GROUPS

Headed south from Georgetown I've often kept company with from 5 to 15 yachts. These trips weld friendships and make a delightful trip south even more enjoyable.

STAYING TOGETHER

I always make clear to sailing companions that I paddle my own canoe, do my own navigation, select my own anchorages, and when I grab a **weather window** and go, I've made my own decision for my own boat. I encourage everyone else to do likewise.

My boat and I, a little universe on a savage sea, function as a team completely different from any other vessel and crew. Barring an emergency at sea, I neither slow down to nor catch up with other boats which could compromise the teamwork between me and my boat, and perhaps force an unnatural rhythm to her functioning at sea. I suspect many problems on the path south precipitate from this phenomenon, and by the *subconscious* reliance on other boats. (*Well, if I miss the weather, one of the other guys must have it.*)

You also have a unique boat and crew. Proper respect for the sea and your vessel come first, demonstrations of camaraderie, second. Sailing in company, get advance permission to dawdle or to leap ports ahead. In other words, *sail alone*, even in company.

BUDDY CHANNELS

Many boats sailing in company stay tuned to buddy channels instead of VHF Channel 16. I have seen one yacht sink and many others suffer narrow escapes while the "buddy boats" blithely sailed on in ignorance of repeated warnings on Channel 16. Chatting on low power on Channel 16 while on the open sea shall not bother ships in the area. On the contrary, you both may gladly discover that you lie within two miles of each other and didn't know it. Using buddy channels while under way in or near harbors, with dangers like reefs and funneling traffic, rates the stupid prize. Always at least *scan* VHF Ch. 16.

FLEET OPERATIONS

With all consultations finished, each captain must make his or her own decision, sharing it with the others out of courtesy, but not for approval. Maintain contact by radio at sea if you can, or wait to meet up in port, but sail your own boat, not the fleet's.

If you must stay together, emulate the fascists whose emblem was the Roman *faces*, or bound bundle of spars. Appoint someone Navigator and someone else Admiral. Picture a fleet of neophyte cruisers at sea, all strung out like a gaggle of geese, asking each other on the VHF whether to reef or tack while assuring each other of their like-mindedness, regardless of each vessel's differences. Each boat thinks another boat leads. The one in the lead doesn't know he leads. Whinnie The Pooh, off to discover the north pole, organized better than most cruising groups I've heard on the VHF. Committee decisions, without a chairman to promulgate them, don't really get decided at all. Dangerous behavior in port, preparing for a storm. Deadly at sea.

MEET THE EXPERTS

Freedom seems the common denominator behind most people's choice of the cruising life. But freedom bears responsibilities not known in our modern socialist societies. Among the most cherished freedoms, those of carrying water, washing clothes by hand and trudging miles to the market in the dust and the heat, and all the neat stuff our ancestors got to do. The freedoms to act as your own blacksmith, carpenter, physician, plumber, weatherman and mechanic comes as a shock to most new Caribbean cruisers. Americans' ancestors had to do those things and more on their isolated homesteads. So can cruisers today. I sometimes don't face up to those heavy responsibilities. Instead, I prefer to jury rig until I get to a phone and call for parts. Then I practice component replacement, until all goes right again. But with help at hand, I still handle the problem myself. Usually anything you do yourself beats turning to the *experts*. You can more easily fix your own screwups.

Like the mule hand in the old Wagons West shows, I stand aside and chuckle at the game as people get stung year after year. Let me introduce you to some experts I see repeatedly on the Wagons South show. See if you'd rather trust *them* than yourself.

THE WEATHERMAN

Pained by days of waiting for a **weather window** in Luperón, I dinghied to the town dock to buy a newspaper and spend another day at the ready. As well, I waited to go *downwind*! I had not before waited more than a few days to go downwind. Everybody enroute north wore thin in patience. As I putt-putted through the anchorage I passed a fellow jubilantly hauling at his anchor rode. An airline pilot by trade, he looked like one of those clear eyed, straight toothed, solid men with the great airside manner and the calm, resonant voice. ("We've lost only two of our four engines folks, but, not to worry, they designed this aircraft to glide.") He read the weather to the more timid types on the VHF radio every morning. They trusted him. He became their *weatherman*.

"Cleaning the rode, Jack?" I asked.

"Heck no! Great window! We're off!," he puffed between pulls. He hadn't learned to let the catenary pull the boat, he was still using the coronary.

"Window? I heard there was 25 knots and a gale system coming NE across Cuba."

"No way! '*Northeast 15 behind the front*'! It'll be a *reach* the whole way." The anchor came up with a bang on the chocks, and, callused by years of gratuitous advice forcefully cast back in my face, I wished Jack a safe and happy trip. I dinghied on to town.

Back aboard, I threw aside the newspaper and reread my full transcripts of the Offshore Reports. As I thought I knew, but which Jack had made me unsure of, we had *three* gale systems. One pulled the front that had gone through the day before, another pulled a front down on us that should arrive the next day. A third gale center out of Cuba headed northeast right over Caicos to our north. I searched for the words "northeast 15 knots behind the front". I found them, just north of Puerto Rico, *behind the front that had passed us two days ago*. Jack would have a *beat* into 25 knots northwest.

Three boats pulled out with Jack. One went ashore in the Raggeds. The Bahamas Defense Force pulled off the mate who flew home to mother in Toronto from Deadman's Cay. The skipper of that one dragged himself into Georgetown *three weeks* later severely dinged. I left two days later. I had 10 to 15 knots at the most, clear skies, full moon, and I anchored every night without going to shore. I had 12 days of the finest fishing vacation while sailing to Georgetown. I had waited 11 days, and I got a window for the records.

Jack lay beached at Landrail Point when I got there, making a new rudder out of construction scraps. A gaggle of tourists and a few yachties surrounded him to hear his tales of *The Ultimate Wave,* and how cleverly his master seamanship and knowledge of the weather saw him through. You just had to admire him. When he finally reached Georgetown, he taught courses on celestial navigation for $5 an hour.

Do you think you need Jack for your *weatherman*?

THE MECHANIC

Ace was a "cruiser down on his luck", as people say. He ran a marine electronics fixit shop from his boat, which looked way down on its luck. Ace did pot. His girlfriend did other things. They got by. I call these guys dirtbaggers, but what do I know? Ace did fast work. In fact, he could get a rebuilt unit faster than Fed Ex could fly. He simply went to his warehouse, the fleet of boats he "boat sat" for absent owners. He always found a replacement part somewhere among them. He eventually got caught and spent a few days in jail. The police found $50,000 of stolen electronics tucked away on his boat.

Once a cruiser asked me if I could recommend Ace. "No," I said, "he's a thief."

Now, con men can convince and charm. If they couldn't, they wouldn't have the job. The cruiser liked Ace anyway. He went to Ace and told him what I said. Next day I had 20 gallons of water in my fuel tank. I found it while crossing the path of an incoming cruise ship. The motor quit with a clogged high pressure pump. The judas cruiser got his, though. The cops took the radio Ace had "fixed". Now he had none.

Do your own work. And don't expect me to recommend anyone but yourself.

THE SAILING MASTER

Many folks who think they know all about sailing may know nothing about the sea. In the old days of sailing they had a position of Sailing Master aboard ship. The captain looked to him to provide expert instruction to effect the maneuver he wanted to make.

For three years Dashing Dan darted all over the Caribbean. To the Med and back, in and out, up and down, damn the torpedoes, he played the star of the Herb show every night. If it blew 40 knots and he had to sail more than 200 miles, Dan blew away.

I take the south coast of Puerto Rico a few miles a day in morning calms, rather than wait out a 20 to 25 knot forecast looking for longer windows. Anchored at **Gilligan's Island** one year, I heard Globetrotter Dan calling a cruising couple anchored in **Cabo Rojo**. They had a small child aboard. Dan sailed down the west coast in the big island's lee. He cajoled the other boat to join him on a night sail to Ponce, around the corner to the east.

"You've got a *well found boat*," he hammered, "you're a *sailor*," he challenged, "I *know* this coast. It's not bad at all." Dan said he reached in 11 knots of wind in a flat sea. Of course. He sailed south down the west coast of Puerto Rico and had not yet turned the corner to the east into full trade winds and seas. Thoroughly intimidated, the father agreed to come out and play. I thought of the little girl aboard. I called repeatedly on the VHF, but he couldn't hear me. Maybe he had his squelch turned up.

I mixed a nightcap and stayed tuned to the unfolding drama on the VHF.

Within 5 hours Dan was ankle deep in motor oil, feeling the bilge for a dropped bleed screw without which he couldn't start his engine. "Comes with the territory," he croaked on the VHF. The smaller boat's skipper left the air for 15 minutes, then came back on groaning. He'd got tossed across the saloon. Luckily, he only suffered a few contusions. Wife and child had packed themselves between mattresses on the stateroom deck.

Both boats crept into **La Parguera** at 8 a.m. After 12 hours of vicious beating, they had made good only 9 miles. Earlier that morning I had put in my usual 10 miles in a 2 hour calm.

Don't listen to Dan. As the song says, "he's a devil, not a man".

THE LOCAL

A magazine article appeared detailing the drubbing the "*Argonut*" took. Early in the article the writer made clear that he had discarded my sailing directions in favor of *local knowledge* from a tired cruiser named "Sam" who had stayed at the same spot for 5 years.

I knew Sam well. A nice guy who, tired of cruising, took a local job and moored in that harbor for good, never to go any farther. Each time Sam had ventured out he went in forecast trades over 15 knots and against northerly swells. He never found a night lee along the coast in those conditions. In the daytime, he couldn't make headway against the winds accelerated by his own island. Because he got hammered every time he tried to move to windward, he stayed put. Over the years "Sam" had collected stories at the bar from passing cruisers. All Sam's *local knowledge* came from anecdotal evidence assembled from beginners passing through, newbies who had made tragic errors. Sam developed a simple theory: Forget the forecasts, just take your chances.

This book's advice comes from hundreds of coastal runs and dozens of long passages in the Antilles. It documents *local knowledge* gathered by me personally from all my successfully safe and comfortable voyages. Yet *Argonut* went with advice from Sam, the local cruiser at the bar, who must *know*. And *Argonut* got hammered. But the skipper had an epic tale to tell afterward. He won many admirers for his manly deeds. And he freely passed on lots of his and Sam's *local knowledge*, not stuff from some show-off writer.

Some cruisers with "local knowledge" remind me of the rednecks around the bait box on a fuel pier in Florida. "How deep is it at the dock?" I hailed. "Lossawada, lossawada!" they chorused. "Yes, but how many *feet*?" I persisted. "Big boats come in here allatime," they assured. Probably *Morgan OI 41*'s, I thought. "I draw six and a half feet!" I hollered. "*LOSSAWADA!*" they yelled, getting belligerent now that their expertise came into question. I spent the next 8 hours 14 feet from the fuel dock, hard aground. I got no fuel, but I got "lossa" dings from all the really "big boats" that came to fuel up beside me.

Passagemakers have the same problem travellers passing through New York have. The average New Yorker, when asked for directions, will send you first to his own bus stop.

Jalan Jalan
S a l i n a s ,
Puerto Rico,
1995.

COMMUNICATIONS

MAIL

Postal officials around the world shall more conscientiously look for your mail if you follow this simple routine the first and every time you ask for it. Face the clerk squarely and look directly into his or her eyes. Smile brightly. Say "Good morning. How are you?" Pause and look like you want to say goodbye, that you had only come there to make them happy. Then, with a shrug, remember you had minor business and, regretfully, wonder if they couldn't help you find your mail. Give them a card with your name written in large block letters. This gambit works miracles everywhere. Even in the US Virgins. If your name is Van Somethingorother, tell them sometimes it gets filed under *ess*.

In the **Dominican Republic** and **Venezuela** use Federal Express, not the mail. In **Puerto Rico** use "General Delivery" mail. The bilingual postal clerks in PR shall scan for General Delivery not *Lista de Correos* after they see your gringo face. In the US Virgin Islands you'll find it safest to use the address of a local business where they specialize in communications rather than identify yourself to the mail clerks as a cruiser.

HOW TO SEND THE MAIL

Never make letter mail in bunches look like a parcel! Tell your forwarder to separate the mail into 2 or 3 small envelopes so yours doesn't get shuffled off as a package to customs or parcel post for 3 weeks, especially in **Nassau**. You should know exactly how many envelopes to expect so you don't wait around for the third packet that never comes. Have Aunt Lizzy label large mailing envelopes "1 of 3", "2 of 3", etc, and even "1 of 1".

A tip about avoiding local taxes on parts shipped into **Puerto Rico**: send it *Priority Mail* or *Air Parcel Post* to *General Delivery* to small locations that presort in Miami, such as **Boquerón**, PR00622; **Salinas**, PR00751; **Fajardo**, PR00740; or **Culebra**, PR00735. Uncle Sam refuses to collect local taxes, but large traffic points like San Juan, Mayagüez and Ponce have resident PR tax men who whomp you with 6.6% and delay delivery.

Never send checks mail in a way the handlers can see the contents. *Anywhere.* If they can't turn the contents into cash themselves, they can always sell it at discount to someone who thinks they can.

Many places in the Caribbean transients deal with **UPS** only with great difficulty.

Federal Express bends over backward to help in any way. With FedEx you can call collect for pickup or with inquiries and get a *real person* who *can* answer your question.

It may sound nautical to address yourself at General Delivery as:

Captain John J. Courageous
Aboard the good ship S/Y Chicken Little

Your mail will almost certainly get stacked under Captain, or Aboard, or sent to the Little's household. Try this for better results: *JOHN COURAGEOUS*

Aside from the pretentiousness of such nautical addressing it makes you an easy mark for someone looking for rich yachtie marks.

As you paw through the mail boxes yourself at the various bars and hotels along your route, you will notice all those non-uniform yachtie addresses and the difficulty of sorting them sensibly. If you have problems, then think about the third world postal employees who might not spell as well as you, nor scan as well as you, nor have an inkling that addresses can get so complicated.

Latin Americans sort by the middle name. So delete yours unless it reads John X. Smith.

TELEPHONE

You can dial direct from any street booth almost anywhere in the Caribbean. But with the cell phone revolution you will find them disappearing rapidly. You might have a satellite phone aboard, but the cost may limit your use. I find it easiest and cheaper to call collect, to call with phone company **credit cards** or call with prepaid phone cards. If you stay in a country awhile it will make sense to either buy a cheap local cell phone, or to have a local dealer convert one of your old phones to local mode. You can then use prepaid phonecards for outgoing calls and get unlimited incoming calls for free.

Most Caribbean islands use the country code for North America, 1, followed by area code. For the **Bahamas**: 242. The **Dominican Republic**: 809. **Puerto Rico**: 787. In both the DR and PR if you start speaking to the operator in English they will answer you in English.

With the exception of Puerto Rico where everyone has a phone, Caribbean telephone companies have offices with phone, fax and internet services, and many permit you to hookup and send email via your laptop. When you strip your calls of all the howdy-do's you usually have only a message to transmit. *Email* or *telefax* makes for unequivocal communications and costs lots less. Internet services abound in the Dominican Republic. Buy your kids a fax machine or a computer for Christmas, and save on phone bills.

TELEPHONES IN THE DOMINICAN REPUBLIC

The DR has the highest per capita telecommunications usage in Latin America. Each teenager has at least one cellular. All towns have excellent telephone communications. In the cities, use any street booth to dial collect, direct (0 - area code - number), and, unless you speak Spanish, speak in English to the operator. Use any phone company office (*Centro de Llamadas*) if you want to pay. The country hosts many independent telephone companies with direct dial anywhere in the world. At their offices you just dial the full number. When you hang up a bill shall print out for you in English from their computer. Most harbors at which you shall wait for weather have **Internet** Café types of services.

LANGUAGE

Don't let the myth of **language barriers** undo the enjoyment of your cruise.

Most of us cruising the world see local people like two dimensional cardboard cutouts, unless, with luck, a local befriends us. Cruisers seldom read local newspapers. They seem uninterested in any subject outside their immediate yachtie environment. Local language newspapers, politics and so on lack reality and can't interest them. Yet even while in Dubrovnik I "read" the newspaper every day — and got something out of it.

In non-English speaking countries many cruisers excuse the lack of any but superficial interest with the old "language barrier". Many stay aboard waiting for weather rather than discover the local scene or traveling farther inland. Some pay too much for everything and later whine they got "cheated". They rarely get satisfaction out of the cruising life.

With most of my life spent outside English speaking countries I think I have a qualified viewpoint on the matter. Simply put, you erect your own language barriers. Take my experience. I have lived or worked in many countries where I did not speak the language. I have studied 7 languages, and came to live in 4 countries where I used the language well enough to make a living. Yet I always got along best in the countries where I didn't know the language!

If you don't do the local language, people expect less of you and help you more. They have more patience with you, going out of their way to guide you. People express more interest in you. As a visitor not able to use the language at all, you have privilege. As a visitor trying to pick up a few words, you have sympathy, and honor as well.

If you speak their language fairly well, you become more of an interloper in their society, not a visitor. Yes, humans practice prejudice everywhere. Parents show great interest when daughter brings the foreign exchange student home for dinner, but the excitement really gets big when she brings one home to marry!

If you seriously want to talk well in a foreign language, go ahead and make a serious try. Prepare for a mind wrenching, personality bending experience. Languages carry culture, and learning them requires personality change. Acquiring language often causes physical pain. It takes a long time and requires exhausting effort. Yet it never becomes 100% successful, despite what you've read in spy novels where the hero goes undetected while speaking rural dialects of Upper Volton. Science has long proved that language learning proceeds most imperfectly for humans beyond puberty, so don't worry when you don't sound perfect. And when someone mocks your accent, have as much fun as you do with ethnic humor back home. You shall, after all, have fun, and achieve great satisfaction. But it shall change forever your ability to seem an interesting visitor everyone wants to help.

Get out and see the world while cruising. Don't erect your own language barriers. Wiggle your eyebrows, wave your arms, point to things and words and have fun.

But don't ever say to me, "It's easy for you. You speak the language." The little I may speak came with great difficulty, even agony. And using it often creates more of the same.

Finally, a word of advice from a friend of mine, Guillermo Goudreau, a Puerto Rican criminal trial lawyer in Salinas: Always speak your native tongue to policemen. That way you leave no room for later equivocation and misquotes, perhaps intentional.

fishing boats called *piñeros* or *yolas*

Tales of Caribbean rape and pillage have titillated youngsters since the 1600's when the maraudings of L'Olenois, the **Corsaire**, and Morgan, the **Privateer**, first hit the British bookstalls. Most long distance cruisers have adventurous and, to some extent, childish hearts. Their titillation runs wild upon occasion and their stories of piracy and skullduggery on the thornless path are among many false dangers. Like cloud shadows on the banks, if you spend your time trying to avoid them you risk running into a real danger.

PERSONAL SECURITY

One encounters bad actors all over the world. Pirates, just bad guys potting at targets of opportunity upon the wastes of the sea, or in the alleys of the waterfronts, really do exist. You don't cruise in the Sulu or the Red Sea, however. Your chances of running into a pirate in the Caribbean runs even less than your chances of stumbling into one off Key Biscayne. Ask any European and you'll discover that most of the civilized world sees America (the U.S.) as among the most violent nations on the planet. Unfortunately statistics substantiate that opinion. The thornless path exposes you to personal assault, on your boat or ashore, less than almost any yachting center in the United States. Having said that, I yet have some caveats which may make for a more pleasant cruise.

AFLOAT

Avoid pickup crew. The Caribbean crawls with hitchhikers both American and European, especially in the large yachting centers. Some simply want to do what used to be called *Le Grand Tour* between college and the start of a career. Others simply want to *do you*. If, after thorough investigation, you do take someone aboard, hold the person's passport and enough of his or her money to fly them back to their native country from your boat's destination. An even better filter of their real intentions: do as some Europeans do and charge the crew for their room and board and the trip. Let the leeches pay or go get their own boat! Unbelievable folly has been met with pickup crew.

Avoid casual tours of your boat. What a thrill for that nice school girl to see a yacht. But she goes to school with not so nice school boys. A yacht presents a remote concept for them, unassailable as the homes of the local rich. Innocent talk at school, God forbid a fullblown *Show and Tell*, may make your snug little home familiar and assailable.

In anchorages without much VHF traffic, leave your hailing channel on at night. Your neighbor may frantically call warnings you need to hear. Don't let anyone board your boat at any time for any reason unless they present indisputable documentation of their right to do so. Have interior deadlock bolts below, and lock yourself in when you feel you need to.

Beware of *asymmetrical* cruisers: hustlers in the Caribbean without apparent resources and with hollow stories that don't fit neatly with accent, age, physiognomy, boat's and personal appearances. Yachties took turns inviting to dinner a good looking young fellow who had run out of funds. "And just imagine!" they gushed at me, "He's off around the world with no charts, no navigation aids and hardly a dime. What spirit! A real nice guy." He looked like a leech to me. After he'd left for the wide world, a rash of burglaries occurred while everyone attended a potluck dinner. They blamed it on the locals. One yacht claimed a $10,000 loss and quit cruising. Mr. nice-guy turned up in Central America fully equipped, saying he'd got the stuff cheap in Manzanillo. *Manzanillo?* I met rafts of cruisers down islands who still thought he was a great guy, and they sincerely delighted in his finding the right equipment to go round the world. Lesson? ***All con artists appear trustworthy.***

Ashore

It hasn't always looked grim. Times change. In the early 1980's in Puerto Plata and Belize City, a naked sixteen year old virgin with fistfuls of dollars would attract only admiration. And you should have seen the alleys of Belize City at night in 1981. Times have got hard here and there in the developing world. Skullduggery rises and falls. Until you know for sure, act as prudently as you would at home. No more nor less.

City waterfronts everywhere lie close to rundown sections with poorer, sometimes desperate, inhabitants. Don't walk alone down unlit streets with flamboyant tourist garb, a bulging hip pocket and half a bag on from some happy hour. In **Cumaná**, Venezuela, or **Port of Spain**, Trinidad, you may become dead meat. Yet I consider Cumaná my favorite port south of the Greater Antilles. Leave behind bracelets and necklaces. You may know you only wear costume jewelry, but does a 12 year old gutter snipe with a razor?

Travel light when out and about. Dress plainly and inexpensively, and not like a yachtie. Use flapped pockets, and sew in body pouches *inside* clothing.

If you have to carry a lot of cash, don't flash a roll. Keep it in separate pockets, and pay beers, meals, transport, etc., out of a "petty cash pocket". Don't use purses, backpacks, "fanny packs" and "belly bags". They may get ripped off with a razor. I know of one man who lost a kidney in Caracas. Instead of a wallet or purse that can get snatched, carry a **datasheet**, a sheet of paper with every number you ever needed, credit cards, telephones, citizenship, clearances, passports, whatever. Then wrap your folding walk-around money over your credit card and slip it into a flapped pocket.

A stolen passport can make a royal mess. Don't carry yours. On the other hand I've known respectable senior citizens who have spent a night in the pokey because they couldn't show a passport. Instead of a passport, carry a photocopy of your passport and visa stamp where you keep your projects list on the flip side of your datasheet.

BOAT SECURITY

You can count as few anchorages on the *Thornless Path* where you feel you must lock up your boat as you can count towns in America where you can leave your doors open. Most places, if a local inhabitant breaks through your locks he'll cause more loss through damage to teak joinery than he shall through the trinkets he likely walks off with.

Only boaties take boaty things. Remember that when you anchor next to the dirtbag boat full of hippies in a lonely cove. Such "cruisers" do exist in the Caribbean. Avoid these boats and their crews. If they need a snatch block they'll snatch yours. Unfortunately for world unity, some nations more than others tend to spawn boats like these.

In countries with acute economic stress petty theft by locals can occur. How and where you moor the boat shall give you more insurance than any company can offer. During extended absences, unless you can put up in a guarded marina, securely anchor the boat in a weather safe anchorage, far enough from young swimmers from the shore, but in amongst other yachts whose owners you know and trust. Leave them instructions for access to the boat as well as for charging the battery, feeding the parakeet or what-all else.

Alarm systems, like those in suburban America, may turn in more false alarms than real. But if you like to gadgeteer and have the money, by all means, have the fun of installing them and spoofing your friends with all the hooting of horns and strobing of lights. One boater I know has a neat switch over his bunk. When he throws it, a brilliant flood light mounted high forward in the saloon blinds anyone in the cockpit, the companion way, or messing about inside. Like a stun grenade: effective, simple and cheap.

GETTING HELP WHEN YOU NEED IT

In 1996 Frank Zachar on *Vagabond Tiger* founded the Caribbean Safety and Security SSB Net (8104 USB at 1215 UCT) in response to a rash of thefts and boardings in Venezuela. Frank and the yachtie community worked with local officials and marine industry interests to bring the problem under control. They came up with the good advice that any kind of emergency (medical, boat or security) should be met with noise and light.

Blow a horn, whistle or burglar alarm as long as possible, and fire flares.

Scream and keep screaming while waving arms or, say, a towel.

Get on the hailing channel and hail away like hell

Cruisers in the anchorage (or marina) should respond by illuminating the distress scene and by getting to the person in distress immediately. Keep a light on any bad guys and make noise — beat on pots and pans if you have to.

In the case of theft and boardings, making noise up the bureaucracy also works: coast guard, police, newspapers, tourism and business groups. Scream and keep screaming. Make them do their jobs. Wringing hands — "It's not my country. What can anyone do?" — guarantees more attacks. Nothing impresses officials more than a passel of arm waving, angry *gringos* milling about in their office, shouting unintelligibly. Wakes 'em right up.

FIREARMS

Firearms can cause hassles clearing in and out. (*Boat Stuff: Customs and Immigration*).

If you have firearms, train in their use and know when to use them. Never brandish a firearm. If you take one in hand, kill with it immediately. Pretty serious stuff. The problem lies in threat assessment. You need sober, nonprejudicial judgment. But you rarely have it in a strange, poverty stricken land, where people speak a different language with excited jabbers and seemingly ominous overtones. Hardly possible in a dirty town where they all stare at you, point and whisper. You become paranoid. It becomes more difficult when you get roused out of a sound **SG&T** induced slumber after a long, hard, adrenaline drenched beat to weather by someone who looks like a Huk guerrilla. Impulsive resort to a firearm invites tragedy. Probably yours.

FIREARMS ABOARD IN PUERTO RICO

Puerto Rico has full jurisdiction over all its waters. This means that *the Puerto Rico Marine Police have a 6 mile zone in which they can board any flagged vessel* to make any search they wish without presence of U.S. Federal officials who, if around at all, shall stand off.

This has baleful meaning to all yachts transiting the area. If boarded, you should know they require *all firearms within Puerto Rico territorial limits to have Puerto Rican registration, and all arms aboard to have carry licenses assigned to an ON BOARD Puerto Rican resident.* If you have arms, don't give them cause to board you.

The PR Marine Police may confiscate weapons which fail to meet these requirements. The weapons may get returned to the owner after hearings for violation of the Arms Law of Puerto Rico. Those hearings typically can take up to 6 months, during which time the vessel may get impounded and the owner not permitted aboard. I've seen vessels impounded for 6 months in Puerto Rico. Believe me, you should gladly surrender your firearm if asked. Curiously, U.S. Homeland Security (Customs, etc.) recognize your Constitutional right to have arms aboard your boat. What can I say?

DINGHY SECURITY

If you haven't learned **dinghy security** in your home waters, these tips may help you from **Nassau** onward. Locals won't steal a yacht dinghy or motor where it would stand out like a dugout canoe in a Connecticut yacht club. Theft occurs where the thief has a ready market, or the thief can stuff it aboard his own boat and take off.

First, use chain, minimum length twelve feet, minimum thickness 3/8". Padlock or permanently secure the chain to a permanent steel fitting attached to a hard surface of the dink (transom, for instance), *not* the towing eye of an inflatable dinghy — thieves will simply cut them off. Lock your motor securely onto the transom. Finally, lock the chain to some permanent fixture ashore with an eye to tide and current. You may want an anchor out to keep from sawing against a pier or going under one at low tide. If you don't, you may come back to an outboard motor badly dinged on the dock by a rising tide.

Lock your dinghy to your yacht's hip, coiling excess chain in a bunch on deck so it doesn't go overboard unless pulled upon. The thunk, thunk, thunk of the links going over the rail makes an alarm system and enables you to catch the varmint in the act and while still in the water. Depending on the sternness of your response, you won't have trouble at that anchorage for the rest of your stay. I've found flare guns neatly scare everyone in the anchorage as well as the varmint, and they certainly light up the scene of the crime well and call the attention of any law enforcement around pretending not to notice. Flares also continue to burn in the water, catching the crook in a ring of light.

If I'm concerned about a dinghy thief in the night, I leave my stern light on (it's separately wired), a cockpit anchor light on, and I have a cutlass and a flare pistol handy. Once I squeezed intersecting streams of muriatic acid and ammonia from their squirt bottles. The effect was devastating to the machete wielding bandit in the water. A friend prefers a "wrist rocket" sling shot with ball bearings. One fellow I know brought back a blowgun from South America with some pretty serious darts. I've thrown rocks from the cat toilet.

If you have big motorized davits, use them to haul up your dinghy and motor every night. Another method: arrange a three point bridle with its lifting ring centered to keep the raised dinghy and motor level as you haul the rig up to the rail with your halyard. Make the bridle out of heavy stainless cable, or it may readily get chopped with a machete.

Plaster your dinghy and motor with reflective tape so you can find it when it drifts away at night. It also becomes a less attractive target for thieves. An inflatable in the Virgin Islands becomes less attractive to thieves (other boaters) when you plaster it with multicolored patches and caulk. One of my best dinghy trades was a flawless Avon RIB that looked like it had been through the battle of Trafalgar. I never had to lock that one up.

The yacht's name on the dink at a dock advertises your absence from the yacht.

Finally, at crowded dinghy docks, leave your dink anchored well off with thirty or so feet of painter run to the dock. Neophyte cruisers often snug their painters to the dock and tip their motors up. As the tide changes their props become bucking and slashing scythes which can cut your bow section to ribbons. I usually approach a dinghy dock with a stern anchor out, actually an undeployed grapnel. A rock can do as well.

I plan my landing perpendicular to the dinghy dock (see #1 in the figure at right) a good distance down from where I want the painter tied (#2). The dinghy then lays off roughly that same distance, well free of the crowd (#3). I retrieve it at any point on the dock by dragging, since the anchor, or rock, isn't grabbing hard.

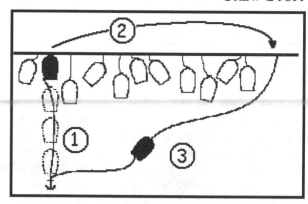

INSURANCE

Insurance helped me when I rammed an uncharted subsurface rock in the Skagerack. It came through when Hurricane Elena took off my bowsprit and taffrail. Then, after many years of self-insured bliss, I went with the Seven Seas Cruising Association's recommended agency. Despite A.M. Best ratings, platoons of government inspectors and $1100 of my financial support, the underwriter went belly up three months after I signed up. That accounted for 11% of my net income that year. I went self-insured again.

Like the stock market, invest in insurance only what you can afford to lose. With all the boats around, and all the scams the insurers let by, rates have gone through the ceiling.

The companies increase profitability by policy restrictions only a New York actuary could come up with. Some refuse coverage between latitudes 12° and 22° during hurricane season. Others demand you get below 16° before June.

I challenge the wisdom of chasing Mom and Pop through the islands and across the sea to places with little storm protection and crowded harbors. Feeling pressed to get south, they bust their gear and propulsion systems, if not themselves. One fairly young fellow I knew made it 30 miles into the "safe zone" only to die of a heart attack the next day. His "risk" amounted to a doubling of his deductible if he got totalled by a named storm. Maybe he died by letting an accountant in a Manhattan tower do his navigation for him.

DOCK BOYS

Throughout the Caribbean the loafers on the docks and in the harbors will hassle you for work which they may not do or errands they may not run. Some will ruin your laundry if you let them and gouge you in the bargain. The bad actors of the breed have got spoiled by "ugly Americans", mostly paid delivery crews in town for a crack at the red light district. These crews push out their absent owner's dollars like Bible tracts at the airport. Therefore some of the dock boys respect neither your common sense nor your wallet. So sailor beware! Meanwhile, there are people who can do useful chores. Some dock boys want to sell courtesy flags, and I don't deny them the business if I don't have one. If you employ someone for chores or errands, especially dock boys, specify short, specific tasks with firm, fixed prices. Have each task finished and paid for before going on to the next task, assuming you still want him to work for you. Finally, if a dock boy thinks you've agreed for a service from him, *never* change dock boys before you have paid and discharged the first one. You may find yourself in the middle of a labor dispute right out of Marlon Brando's *On the Waterfront*.

BOAT STUFF

ANCHORING IN THE CARIBBEAN

I spent some time interviewing a family who had sailed 15,000 miles of a planned three year round the world cruise to end it all on the edge of a cut through a reef. A simple lack of proper GPS procedure cost them everything but their lives. How can it have happened to seasoned "round the worlders", to seasoned seamen like these?

Well, it didn't happen to seasoned seamen. These folks had no more sea seasoning than the bright brass of their port lights. They had many years winning races at their home yacht club, though, and the skipper had even done the Whitbread world race. I wondered if their anchoring techniques matched their bad piloting skills.

After talking with them for a couple of days I learned that they had anchored less than a dozen times since learning to sail many years before. Their round the world blitz cruise — my friends all took 8 to 10 years — went from dock to dock. They took long legs and hung out for long periods for work to refresh their kitty. They gave talks at yacht clubs along the way. This family unfortunately typifies many cruisers. Many people who have sailed a bunch have not anchored much. They may not realize they lack such elementary seaman skills. They might have completed their round the world, but in doing so, they would have added little more to their seamanship store than they had when they left.

Sharpen your anchoring habits before you leave. Don't learn the hard way enroute.

THE GOOD NEIGHBOR

Good neighbors remain silent while you anchor or weigh anchor. Let the new boat anchor in peace. I sometime get gratuitous complaints that I'm too close to someone's boat while I start to lay my first anchor. Then the guy sees the second anchor deployed and my boat lays on a wide vee 100 feet off his quarter. He thinks I did it for him.

Anglophones particularly worry about Francophones who have a much shorter sensitivity radius. I personally prefer Latin closeness to Anglo aloofness. Anyway, Anglos have a perception problem. The French may anchor closer, but I notice they usually do a good job of it, if not better. All should fear Charterphones, and with good reason.

A good neighbor does not call you on the radio nor dinghy over to talk to you while you work your anchors. Often I would go to the shortest possible scope, hoist the mainsail, then haul anchor while the bow paid off the way I wanted her to go. People often dinghied over to chat just as a gust took the sail and the boat started to move. I try to stay civil at times like these, busy maneuvering under sail in a crowded anchorage. I suppose I sound rude by shouting, "Couldn't you have come by at a better time?"

A good neighbor doesn't offer help or advice unless asked. I take my time. I don't strain myself or my boat. Sometimes I do a "two-cupper": two cups of coffee to let the chop unglue the anchor while I flake the chain out to dry. I don't need anyone's help.

BRIDGE COMMUNICATIONS

This subject ought to come under a heading of Marriage Counseling. Mom and Pop on their retirement cruise have never worked so close for so long in forty years. Now they stand farthest apart only while anchoring. Only 30 feet or so.

Pop stands at the wheel for his supposed technical skills, while Mom stands at the bow anchor because she has stronger hands from years of manual work. Some prefer to reverse roles. One or the other signals and the miscommunication begins.

It can take another forty years to develop hand signals and the divided responsibilities needed to choreograph the delicate ballet of anchoring successfully in all conditions and in front of the usual audiences who pretend to look the other way. If you can't do it alone at least follow these rules.

The bowman (-woman) should do all signaling from the same position always and with the same hand always while holding the forestay with the other hand to ensure its immobility even more than to ensure Bowman's stability. Signals needed?

**left ï hard left ï right ï hard right ï center wheel
ahead ï astern ï more power ï less power ï stop ï @^$*%>#!!!**

Treat the last command as optional, since it might destroy harmony in the more untested relationships. And to avoid nasty equivocation, keep all fingers together.

Boats under 50 feet handle best with one person. You haven't the Queen Mary. Knowledge of what got done while anchoring should not reside somewhere between the wheel and the pulpit with neither station having all the facts. This can save marriages as well.

The person who selects the sandy spot and lays the anchor should prepare the boat to fall off in the proper direction, not someone who stays at the helm and doesn't quite know where the spot lies nor how the anchor may soar to it. It also calls for knowledge of the boat's characteristics of way, its momentum, and how easily she faces or crosses the wind.

While anchoring single-handedly, maneuver to station the slowly swinging bow over the spot selected such that the walk forward from the helm to the pulpit goes with a certain seaman-like decorum, rather than a headlong, cursing rush.

LAYING ANCHOR

Yachts that drag into you in the tight anchorages invariably seem to pay more attention to sailing than to seamanship. Any idiot can make a boat go. Ninety-five percent of seamanship lies in the art of keeping the boat from moving. The below aphorisms, when taken together, go some distance toward describing the art of anchoring in the trades.

Don't anchor near boats with damaged topsides. (No explanation necessary.)

Don't anchor near boats with performance hulls or rigs.

Likely these five-percenters have only five feet of chain. They dance all over the harbor in any breeze. I watched one hull-sailing full circles all night long. He had two anchors, thank goodness, and the boat would wind itself up like a cuckoo clock and then take off on the other tack for another fifteen circles.

Set anchors by wind and current first (when you have them).

Not by someone behind 80 horses unable to see the tension on the rode. Burying types such as Bruces and plows, dig in by wiggling and worming with the action of the sea and tug of the chain. If you apply full tractor power to them before they've set, they will revert to kind and plow a furrow. Watch for drag by picking a range from two in-line objects on shore perpendicular to the extended rode. Also, a grasped rode can telegraph dragging to your hand.

It may prove difficult to set any anchor in mangrove mud in windy conditions or hard marl. Arrive in those harbors early, before the trade wind comes up, or after it dies. Otherwise, you have to motor into the wind at low revs so as to maintain slow enough *straight* sternway to permit the anchor to set. And not too many can do that.

35

Anchors like to get *laid*, not dropped, thrown or swung.

All anchors benefit by proper *laying*, but especially Fortress and Bruce types. *Laying* an anchor implies touching its crown to the bottom, gently *laying* it biting side down, shank to leeward, and controlling a smooth backward drift in the direction of the expected wind or current, while *laying* the chain in a straight line behind the straightly *laid* anchor.

Lay out the chain. Don't let the anchor pull it out. Lay enough chain to ensure that any pull on the anchor will direct itself along the bottom, which you gently hook. Pay out more rode and dig it in again. Pay out 30% - 50% more rode than your final scope, and test with motor, gently at first. Sailors who routinely talk about *dropping the hook* often do have little hooks instead of proper anchors, and they usually simply *do* drop them, heavily trussed in a bundle of rope and chain.

Let the yacht come to rest before setting scope.

Snug in to your final scope only after securing the yacht and tidying up the deck. That will ensure more time for her to reach rest condition. Don't hurry so you'll look proficient to the other yachties glaring at you. The seaman who takes longest to get his yacht settled on her anchors probably does the best job of anchoring.

Dive on the anchor, if possible, to check it.

If necessary, set it by hand. While down there check your neighbors' as well. I cruised in company with a good friend, a professional diver on the oil rigs. In deference to his skills (and my taste) I started on the **SG&T**s while he dived on our anchors. He found a neighbor's CQR lying sideways on the bottom. "Impossible!" shouted the salty-whiskered downeaster while posed cross-armed and bantam-like on his taffrail. "I set that anchor with 55 horses!"

Select your anchors for bottom and boat.

Later in this chapter I provide tables which show the holding power of some anchors along with ground tackle strengths and the loads generated on your ground tackle while riding out a Class 1 hurricane in a protected hole. The data may surprise you.

Use about a pound of anchor for every foot of the boat. A 45 pound Danforth would suit a 40 foot boat. Danforths, while capable of tremendous holding power, do not reset themselves well and the stock can easily foul. Heavy burying type anchors such as the CQR or Bruce work well on most all bottoms and tend to reset themselves. Use Danforth types, CQR or Deltas in mud or grassy bottoms, making well sure the points dig in. In a blow, Danforths hold best pound for pound, but no matter what the Danforth folks say, don't use a short length of chain. It may function in theory, but in the tropics nylon rodes can chafe through on the bottom, if not by coral, then by broken rum bottles.

For rocky bottoms use a heavy prayer.

In coral rock, whatever you put down may just break off a bit of coral and come loose during the night. If you mange to set an anchor on smooth, hard rock, it shall scrape and bounce across the bottom as soon as wind or current changes to dislodge it. In boulders you may ride safely through the night but lose your anchor in the morning.

Use enough chain: long enough and big enough.

Consider first that the chain's catenary must never reach the anchor itself so as to exert upward drag on the shank — even in the most violent conditions — especially in the most violent conditions. Second, ensure that any fiber rode attached cannot come into contact with the seabed or obstructions on it (coral heads, rocks, wrecks and broken rum bottles).

Take care that chafe at deck level does not occur, or consider using all chain. The catenary of a chain rode makes a good shock absorber. If you use all chain, attach a half inch 3-strand nylon snubber as long as necessary to quiet the action. Use absolute minimum chain length of five feet for every 16th of an inch of chain size, i.e., 25 feet for 5/16 chain, 30 feet for 3/8, etc. Another rule of thumb: use a boat length. These rules assume you anchor in water no deeper than triple your keel depth.

For full displacement boats, add a 16th of an inch in chain size for every 10 feet of boat's length above 20 feet. Thus, for LOA's 20-29 feet use 5/16 inch chain, for 30-39 feet use 3/8 inch, for 40-49 feet use 7/16 inch, and for 50-59 feet use 1/2 inch.

FOR ALL CHAIN *lie* to a scope of three to five times the depth of water *added to the distance from sea level to anchor roller*. But *set* the anchor with a scope of 7:1 in mud.

FOR CHAIN AND FIBER RODE lie to a scope five to seven times the depth *added to the distance from sea level to anchor roller*. But set the anchor with a scope of 10:1 in mud.

To reduce the amount of scope required in tight anchorages, consider extending your anchor snubbers from a rugged bow eye built in at the water line.

Use two anchors when in doubt.

Other than creeks in the Bahamas you'll find few actual uses of the Bahamian Moor, one anchor against each expected change of current direction: tidal bays, coves, creeks or rivers, places where currents can become strong and regularly reverse with the tide. Most anchorages don't have these effects, so why else use two anchors?

Because everyone around you does, and if you don't you'll find your bow poking into someone's bedroom in the middle of the night.

Because you expect a switch in the wind or a front to come; or worse, because you don't expect it and it comes anyway.

Because the harbor goes absolutely calm at night and you want to prevent the boat from walking around your lone anchor, doodling chain all over and under it, so that when the morning wind rises you drag onto the beach, towing a ball of tackle.

Because you come first in a harbor used by the charter companies, and you expect 40 partying bareboaters to plunk balls of chain all around you in the middle of the night and you want to keep your elbows tucked in.

Because you don't want to wind your rode around a coral head.

Because you're leaving the boat unattended.

BUT, if everyone else swings to one anchor, go with the flow and set only one yourself so they don't bash you.

Below 22° north *always* set your anchor to the direction of the trades.

Do this egardless of what direction the boats lay to when you arrived in harbor.

WEIGHING ANCHOR

The following may seem old hat, but sit any morning in harbor and watch the scene while folks up anchors. Before observing too long, you'll want a tot of rum in your coffee.

When weighing anchor, keep the chain vertical.

Doing this ensures two things. First you shall approach the anchor along the chain's lie and at a pace commensurate with the proper stowing of the tackle. Secondly, you unlay the links of chain right up to the anchor's shank, ensuring that you don't dislodge the anchor until ready and it won't skitter around and roil the seabed fouling things like other people's rodes. Keep the chain vertical under the bow by never powering beyond the catenary. Instead let the catenary pull the yacht forward, not the coronary. If you use a windlass, use it only to pull up slack in the catenary, not to pull the yacht.

Keep station until the anchor clears the water.

The bane of all anchorages, the morning clod who, upon sensing the anchor has broken loose, turns his head aft and yells "She's up!", and off the yacht drifts downwind, with a giant grappling hook beneath her soaring a few inches off the bottom, headed almost surely for *your* rode. Even bane-ier: the knuckle head who powers about the anchorage with an acute angle of chain stretched behind the bow while the crew tries to wrestle up the taut chain and anchor before they snag — you guessed it — *your* rode!

Schedule cleanup when you use mud anchorages.

Mangrove anchorages have a colloidal mud bottom which makes the anchors-up drill a messy, sweaty job. Best you should, as noted in the section on **staging**, do the cleanup the day before leaving. Wherever possible, depart fresh and rested from a clean, short rode. Ground tackle cleanup should never have to upset your departure timing or your crew.

Set or weigh anchor before or after the trades blow, never *while* they blow.

OPEN ANCHORAGES

Often cruisers on downwind passages among islands get so enamored of their progress they continue right past ideal sandy beach anchorages on the lee sides of the islands, then find themselves sailing among reefs and islands in the dark. It only would have taken a few minutes to have loosed sheets and rounded up into these well protected lees, and anchor in their deep sand bottoms. The idea that the boat would lie open to ocean on three sides haunts the skipper new to the trades. So they don't stop. Nor do the trades in their relentless westward flow, making such lee-side beaches ideal in settled weather.

Know your criteria for choosing anchorages while passage making. If your weather window starts to close on you earlier than you thought it would, you may get stuck in your anchorage for a considerable time doing another wait for weather. One wants a good hangout. Ditto, fishing and diving. Temporary anchorages have different criteria.

No one wants to suffer a rolly anchorage, but you don't always find landlocked anchorages while harbor hopping. Tuck into anchorages *enroute*, don't set up winter camp. Open anchorages in the lee of an island, such as **Plana Cays** in the Bahamas, or a reef or a headland can make daysails out of overnights in settled weather. Trade wind direction

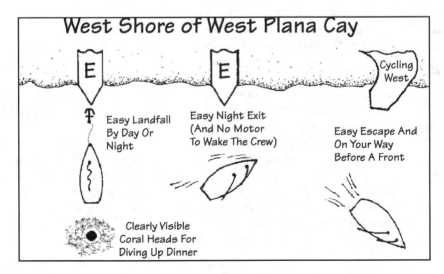

West Shore of West Plana Cay

E — Easy Landfall By Day Or Night

E — Easy Night Exit (And No Motor To Wake The Crew)

Cycling West — Easy Escape And On Your Way Before A Front

Clearly Visible Coral Heads For Diving Up Dinner

stays rock steady. This makes for minimum roll in even wide open lee anchorages.

Ideally, a lee anchorage on a weather shore should have deep sand with lots of productive coral heads or rocks under keel depth. The skipper can anchor to windward of a good fishing spot and let out rode until the stern sits over his dinner. Plans for an arrival during favorable light conditions should of course consider the light needed underwater to skindive up your dinner from the bathing ladder, usually before four p.m. The dinghy can stay in the davits. Such anchorages as **Santa Maria** (Long Island), **Conception Island, Pittstown Landing** (Crooked Island), **West Plana Cay**, **Betsy Ba**y and **Start Bay** (in Mayaguana). Those roll-free anchorages so often sought out by the mate may turn to deathtraps. The landlocked harbors of **Attwood Harbor** (Acklins), for instance, in a northerly, or **Calabash Bay** (Long Island) in anything but east. Besides, who can sleep without some rocking?

ANCHORS AND GROUND TACKLE

You may come from the Chesapeake Bay or the Los Angeles area. Though capable of holding your 38 foot boat quite happily at home, a 12 pound Danforth Deepset and a half inch nylon rode with 6 feet of chain, as recommended by Danforth himself, will not suffice in the coral strewn tropics. If the sun doesn't melt such thin fiber rode then chafe from the bottom or the bow will surely set you adrift some night.

I've seen many cruisers with too light and too few anchors. And they spent years of recognition as knowledgeable sailors at their home ports. They usually use no swivels and favor undersized nylon rode behind too little and too small chain.

But when they turn for home and leave the trade belt, they've all got big anchors and heavy chain.

Use Danforth type anchors for grassy and mud bottoms. Heavy burying type anchors work better on coarse sand bottoms or hardpan, clay and shale. Both types of anchors can hook or wedge fast in rock and coral bottoms, but a heavy plow type will dislodge the easiest when you go to get it up in the morning, and it will have less chance of getting bent if a you get caught in a high chop. I've come to prefer the Bruce for all but grass, and there I use the CQR. Both heavy, the Bruce with a lot of chain.

My Fortresses wait for hurricane season in the bilge and lazarette with all my old used chain. I use a 20 pound Danforth as an occasional lunch hook to keep the boat comfortable in swell when out for the day with friends. Counting the dinghy grapnel, I have at least five anchors along with a few sand screws. I have had as many as nine. You can never have too many anchors or too much used chain, because if you don't use them for moorings, you can always make money selling them in hurricane season to the goofs that have too few.

Below I've listed some facts from my logbook, gleaned from too many sources to recount. I give them for the reader who, like me, can't easily find the data compiled in one place. When time comes for refurbishing my ground tackle, I make my purchasing decisions for my boat from these notes and calculations. But, like all statistics these numbers can tell different stories to please the tale teller.

The following table shows pounds of cable tension necessary to drag different anchors when set with a 5:1 scope in soft mud before getting well silted in (which could take weeks). Note that this differs from some holding powers which may imply breaking strengths of the gear. Multiply by 5 to obtain figures for hard sand.

Safe Working Loads in pounds for Ground Tackle

Diameters in inches--	1/4	5/16	3/8	7/16	1/2	5/8	3/4	7/8	1
BBB CHAIN '3B'		1700	2320	3160	4120	6300			
PROOF COIL 'G3'	1250	1900	2650	3520	4500	6800			
HIGH TEST 'G4'	2600	3900	5400	7200	9200				
STAINLESS CHAIN	2000	2850	3550	4300					
GALV. FALSE LINKS	1400	2000	2800	3720	4750	7250			
GALV. SHACKLES	1000	1500	2000	3000	4000	6500			
GALV. SWIVELS	850	1250	2250		3600	5200	7200		12500
NYLON 3-STRAND		240	340	470	520	620	1380	1880	2460
DACRON BRAID		230	330	500	640	700	1600	2300	

—Safe Working Loads (SWL) for chain runs about 40% of the load under which chain links begin to elongate prior to breaking. If you find elongated links, chop them out and splice with false links, also called connecting links.

—You may exceed SWL of galvanized chain during shock loads without permanent damage, but the chain should get replaced when elongation begins to occur. All galvanized chain will elongate up to 15% before breaking.

—You should never exceed SWL of shackles and swivels.

—Proof Coil chain has already had tests to 200% of SWL.

—High Test chain may have from 2 to 3 times the SWL of Proof Coil, but High Test chain breaks in a shorter time after elongation than does Proof Coil and BBB.

—Ultimate Breaking Load (UBL) of Proof Coil and BBB chains run 4 times the SWL.

—UBL of High Test chain runs about 3 times SWL.

—UBL of galvanized shackles and swivels run up to 6 times their SWL.

—UBL of stainless shackles and swivels run double their SWL.

—Dacron Braid has no stretch and its UBL runs up to only 5 times the SWL.

—Nylon 3-strand will stretch up to 33% and its UBL runs up to 10 times the SWL, making it ideal anchor rode.

—Don't use nylon 4-strand. The strands criss-cross, and under shock loads they can effectively cut each other. Nor does it avoid chafe by rolling when stretched.

Lbs. Cable Tension to Drag in Soft* Mud at 5:1 Scope

WEIGHT OF ANCHOR IN POUNDS	10	20	30	40	50	60
BRUCE	110	180	230	280	330	370
CQR (plow)	160	250	330	400	470	530
DANFORTH TYPE	460	730	960	1160	1350	1500

* Not the harder stuff underneath (marl, caliche, packed mud, clay). Remember to set in mud with a scope of 7:1 all chain, 10:1 chain and nylon. And let it set in harder bottom.

Effect of Knots on Nylon Rode

TYPE OF KNOT	% REDUCTION IN UBL
EYE SPLICE (4 tucks, 3 tapers, unfinished)	15
CLOVE HITCH	30
ROUND TURN and TWO HALF HITCHES	30
ROLLING HITCH	40
BOWLINE	50
OVERHAND KNOT	60
SQUARE KNOT, or REEF KNOT	60

The above values show the percentage reduction in Ultimate Breaking Load (UBL) in 3-strand nylon rope tied with the indicated knots.

In addition, the strengths of nylon ropes reduce by up to 15% when wet.

Lbs. Wind Drag on a Yacht in a Category 1 Hurricane (up to 80 knots)

Pounds of drag in 80 knots of wind		TRAWLER				CENTER COCKPIT			
		DBL. CABIN		SEDAN		SLOOP		KETCH or YAWL	
feet on deck	feet of water line	wind on the BOW	wind on the BEAM	wind on the BOW	wind on the BEAM	wind on the BOW	wind on the BEAM	wind on the BOW	wind on the BEAM
28	23	1578	3595	2623	5246	1150	2890	1610	3520
30	25	1812	4122	2978	5991	1310	1310	1830	4020
32	27	2046	4692	3351	6786	1490	3770	2070	4560
34	28	2280	5262	3723	7582	1660	4220	2300	5100
36	30	2558	5890	4146	8478	1860	4740	2560	5710
38	32	2835	6577	4586	9426	2070	5280	2840	6360
41	34	3274	7600	5263	10882	2380	6110	3260	7340
43	36	3595	8375	5771	11965	2620	6730	3570	8070
45	38	3946	9178	6295	13082	2870	7380	3900	8830

The table above shows pounds of drag exerted on various yacht configurations in 80 knots of wind, both on the bow and on the beam while the yacht sheers.

—Sailboat data includes spars, standing/running rigging, stanchions and lifelines.

—Trawler data includes radar spar, stanchions and lifelines.

—Data assumes you stowed all canvas below.

—Data assumes hull streamlining efficiency of 20% (30% = maximum for a yacht).

—Data does not consider the effects of seas or shock loads while sheering.

—Data assumes you put the yacht in a secure hurricane hole with no wave action.

So-called "Hurricane Mooring"s

Load increases with the square of the velocity of the wind, and wind will gust to 50% of its sustained velocity. Therefore, you should notice the complete futility of riding out a Class 3 to 5 hurricane at anchors. "Hurricane moorings" exist only in fiction. If the mooring holds, either it or other boats shall beat you into the bottom. If the pennants hold, they'll saw your bow off. If your bow holds, your bulkheads will flog loose from the hull.

Making a long rode from shorter ones, or when you scarf together several dock lines, tie each loose end into the eyes splice or bowline of the next using double sheet bends.

GETTING OFF GROUND

This simple exercise performed all alone in the wilderness of the tropic islands has Zenful beauty. But it outdoes a Keystone Cops episode when cruisers rush to help. If you've done a public grounding, you can practice the art of centering amidst the grand huzzah of a fleet of cruisers who "only want to help". Pretend with all your might you stranded solo on Hogsty Reef. First, run a heavy anchor from the bow to some boat lengths out into deeper water *aft of the beam*. You can't easily push or pull any boat aft or forward over ground, but all boats like to *pivot*. Second, set up *strong and constant* tension on the anchor. Deploy chafe gear on your bow as needed. If you have bow eyes, go through them. With a chain hook on Dacron line — *not* nylon or poly — led to your windlass, or halyard or sheet winch, take in *a link or two at a time* with each sag of the catenary. Strong and constant tension means a bar taut chain, or stretched nylon rode. Third, if you haven't any chop, make some, in order to get bights of slack to sweat in from the taut rode. Set up rocking of the boat, even a 20 tonner, by madly running the beam back and forth, or churn about with your dinghy in snowplow mode.

If your eager salvors still mill about in their dinghies like Dodg'em Cars, they'll love the exercise of making chop. If you hear snatches of sage counsel from them between the oaths and alarums they bandy during their collisions, ignore it, stay cool and carry on.

Tremendous forces hide in wave, time and tide. Go look at your tide tables *after* setting the kedge. Reckon both the tide and any expected change in current or wind. If you draw a falling tide, assert tension in the slackening rode *every inch* you get. At low tide, go below and read a book. When the tide again rises you shall gradually pivot toward deeper water without lifting a hand, provided you kept the rode humming tight while it went down. If high tide doesn't get you off, redeploy the kedge and go again. You'll read two books and get that much smarter for next time.

When finally laying fair to wind in good water, take an icy gin and tonic and go to bed. Deduct the day from eternity. Never try to recover it by hurrying on or planning a larger leg the next day. That probably answers why you went aground in the first place.

PROVISIONING AND REPAIRS

Except for the Dominican Republic and Puerto Rico, provisioning a yacht gets expensive and often difficult in the Caribbean.

KNOW VALUE

Inflation and debasement of currencies (including the US dollar) can cause prices to fluctuate within only a few months. Generally speaking, one can buy goods made locally in the Dominican Republic for export to the US market (e.g., Libby's, Victorina, Linda, Campbell's), for a percentage of the prices charged for the same items in standard US retail outlets.

The prices you will find depend on many economic and political factors. For example, a can of Campbell's soup may come imported from the US and as well as from local canneries. Hatuey crackers, though usually quite cheap, skyrocketed when the United Nations bought them all up to give to Haiti. Knowing value before you ask the price will keep you out of a lot of trouble (e.g., *always* get an estimated fare before entering a taxi).

First you have to establish a known value such as your favorite bottle of catsup. Then find out what that item costs locally. You now have a percentage to apply to anything.

Victorina catsup costs the equivalent of 40 cents US and you paid $1.00 in the US for Heinz. Ergo: 40/100= 40% of US prices for locally manufactured products.

If you got a beer and a pizza in the US at a not-too-swank place for $8.95, then you should expect the same to cost a Victorina Catsup percentage in the DR, or, 40% of $8.95 = $3.58 equivalent of pesos.

This percentage shall be more or less good to use in pricing almost anything of local origin. Restaurants, pizzas, Coca-Cola, etc., but cars. Cars on islands may cost more than double the US price because of import limits.

BEERONOMY

I have practiced an economic theory based on beer since 1970, and it has worked all over the world. In any country in the world you can appraise the "oughta-be" value of goods by ratio-ing against the price of a *standard cold beer in a workingman's bar*. If a beer at a tavern near the station costs a buck at home, and a good suit costs 250 bucks at home, then a good suit at your island should cost you 250 cold beers bought at a workingman's tavern there. Guys can learn a lot from the window of a shoe store, too, but I'll keep that for when we meet down island.

CASH AND CREDIT OR DEBIT CARDS

You can get **cash** from **credit cards** through ubiquitous automatic teller machines. Never exchange on the street where you may run into fast change artists. Keep your shopping roll in a deep flapped or interior pocket, and your petty cash, or transportation and meals kitty, in a handy front pocket.

Use credit or debit cards whenever you can to avoid carrying lots of cash. I have lived a checkless and nearly cashless life since my first VISA card from Societé General in Paris in 1973. I keep a small balance which I refresh from a savings account as needed. You can bank by Internet so you can instantly check amounts and conversion rates when you use your card and, if needed, arrange another transfer from savings.

FUEL AND WATER

Take on **water** whenever available. Always bleach water with 1 tablespoon bleach per 30 gallons of water. Always filter the fuel with a **Baja Filter** (see Glossary) if you have one, tee shirts if you don't. One year I had FIVE motor stops at sea due to fuel filters clogged with microbes and water. In **Abraham Bay** I bucketed out all the fuel from the tank and gleaned 4 pounds of sand and gravel.

Between Georgetown and Venezuela I tank up at **Luperón** in the DR, **Ponce Yacht Club** in PR and **Crown Bay Marina** in St.Thomas. Each of these places usually has clean fuel, and a singlehander can easily make the docks at Ponce and Crown Bay. At Luperón you can jerry jug fuel from the town's station, have it pumped from barrels at the marina, or order a fuel tanker to the city dock. Always treat fuel with **Biobor** or equivalent.

Treat your water, and never tank after a recent loss of line pressure.

IN THE DOMINICAN REPUBLIC

You can save a lot by large-scale provisioning in the Dominican Republic. Skippers kick themselves all the way down islands because they didn't make room to buy in the DR. Refer to the sections on Puerto Plata and Santiago for how best to shop in those cities

TRANSPORTATION WHILE PROVISIONING

Steer away from the group of yachties all chartering a bus or a van to provision. You need to take a private shopping tour on public transport. Explore on your own, without suffering group consensus. You shall find unbelievable bargains the group never does.

SAMPLING BRANDS

You should therefore forego restaurants for a couple of days *early in your stay* and shop single items from the *mercados* to find out what you like before getting case lots. Make a separate buying trip to get individual items to sample for both quality and price. Local products differ unevenly between brands, so try them all. *Buy only locally made goods.* You'll find some good prices due to Spanish and Latin American trade concessions, some of which get bulk shipped and bottled locally (olives, wine, mushrooms).

Sample several individual products before deciding what to buy by the case.

BUYING INDIVIDUAL ITEMS

You must ask for what you want. One fellow complained to me that the DR had no bacon. It's called *tocineta* [toe-see-NAY-tah]. Too shy to ask, he assumed it would come in a vacuum packed package like Oscar Mayer's, with the slices of bacon splayed out like a poker hand. In the smaller stores in the DR, called *colmados* [coal-MAH-dose], meats usually get wrapped in white butcher's paper and stored in packages in the cooler. It comes whole and needs slicing. For that reason, it usually also tastes better.

Ask to taste everything. Sample cheese and salamis before buying.

WHAT TO BUY

I love French cut green beans. I use them with mushrooms, onions and mayonnaise for great salads when I can't get fresh. You may hate French cut green beans and mushrooms. Have a dictionary handy to find what you do like (see also *Spanglish for Cruisers*).

44

Here you have a list of DR products which usually represent high quality at low price: powdered milk (*MILEX*), espresso grind coffee (*MONTE REAL*), Worstershire sauce [*Salsa Inglesa*] , vanilla extract, all kinds of fresh spices, pounds of fresh shelled Spanish peanuts (*maní crudo*), soy sauce [*Salsa China*], jams-preserves-marmalades (*Bon* brand), Rum (the *Añejos* at 8 years, specials at 12 years), Gin (Bermudez), local McAlbert's Scotch (*caveat emptor*), Creme de Cacao and other liqueurs. For Advocaat buy *Ponche Nutrititivo* (*CREMA DE ORO*), cooking wines, cigarettes (Marlboro), world's finest cigars (the DR makes Cohibas for Fidel), *MasMas* chocolate bars for watch snacks, salamis (*taste first!*), cherizos and sarano hams (*El Cid*), large loaves of cheese called *QUESO DANES*, red ball Gouda cheeses (white cheese only). Leaf cheese (*QUESO DE HOJA*) makes superb pizza, especially on the big round garlic casabe breads (*CASABE AL AJILLO*). They make casabe bread from yuca the same way the Taino Indians did.

Foreign products get displayed alongside the local products, such as Dutch Gouda cheese, but try the local brand first. You can find all sorts of European cheeses. Buy a *greca*, the hourglass shaped aluminum or stainless coffee pot, to make espresso. Control the strength by controlling the amount of grounds.

BUYING CASE LOT GOODS

After you have tried out the brands, make a list of labels of what suits you and what can save money with power purchases. Many wholesale warehouses give you the same prices they give the grocery stores. *Almacén* [alm-a-SANE] means warehouse. Take a look in any walk-in coolers in the *almacenes*. Remember they have a furious trade with the fancy foreign tourist hotels. You may get surprised by fresh asparagus and artichokes for dinner.

Usually you can find a broken case lots section. Here you can buy items which you won't want in full cases and at the same time you get to see pretty much what they have in all those cases stacked outside. If you don't see what you want, crawl back into the alleys of the boxes and look. If you don't understand what's in a case, ask them to break it open and show you. If you can't find something, ask. Shy people make bad purchases.

Cans: I have fished cans out of the forward bilge after 3 years aboard in the tropics and found them still legibly labeled and delicious inside. Don't waste your time varnishing cans if you have a basically dry boat.

Eggs: I've had unrefrigerated eggs aboard as long as 2 months and found them delicious, although they don't foam as much when whipped. Of course, you must buy only unrefrigerated, fresh eggs; refrigerated eggs go bad quicker. You can easily spot unrefrigerated eggs. They have chicken poop on them. Instead of waxing your eggs, try turning them once in a while, as you would champagne bottles, to keep the yolks centered.

Chickens: A word about eggs and chickens in the DR. You may see a scrawny barbecued chicken for sale, and chicken eggs more like bird eggs. You probably have found *huevos criollos* [WAVE-ose cree-OH-yose], or criole eggs or chicken (*pollo* [PO-yo]). Snap it up. While more expensive, you'll find out what chickens and eggs tasted like in your great-grandmother's time, before factory conveyor belt methods.

Fresh Fruits and Vegetables: I can say the same for fresh veggies as I said for fuel and water: Buy them whenever you see them available. And wash them before putting them aboard. Take away all cardboard. Cardboard brings aboard cockroach eggs.

You must get to the fresh produce markets early. In Luperón a vegetable and fruits truck makes a call at the Marina Puerto Blanco 2 to 3 times a week. It gets announced on the VHF standby channel 68. Try out the different root vegetables that fed our ancestors before the Idaho white potato and mass production methods drove them from North America.

Dry Staples: You can find rice, sugar, flour, beans, wheat and meal readily available almost everywhere and at reasonable prices. Have smallish dry staple containers aboard. Trying to store too much flour or rice will have you throwing it away when the insect eggs hatch, that is, unless you have pounds of Laurel (bay leaves) to put in your canisters.

Parboiled rice will have no eggs. You may need to clean the rice and beans of small stones and stems. When visiting Florida I found myself cleaning a bag of beans, still in my Caribbean habit. After discarding more than usual the amount of small dirt clods and sticks, I saw I had bought the beans in the U.S. So much for superior food standards.

In the country towns you shall find that flour does not always come "enriched", rice not always "polished", sugar not always "refined", and not much says "new and improved". But it just might favor your health and taste good as well.

avocado	*aguacate*	banana	*guineo*	breadfruit	*buen pan*	key limes	*limones*
plantain	*plátano*	cashew	*cajuil*	chayote	*tayota*	cocoa	*cacao*
coffee	*café*	grapefuit	*toronja*	guava	*guayaba*	manioc	*yuca*
mango	*mango*	passion fruit	*chinola*	orange	*naranja*	papaya	*lechosa*
peanuts	*maní*	pear	*pera*	pineapple	*piña*	potato	*papa*
sapodilla	*zapote*	sour sop	*guaya-bana*	sweet potato	*batata*	tomato	*tomate*

Bread and Dairy Products

You find bakeries, or *panaderias*, everywhere in Spanish countries, where they make fresh *pan del agua* ("Cuban" or small French breads) twice a day. The presence of middle eastern populations, from the great exodus at the turn of the century, ensures that the DR and Venezuela have excellent *yogurt*, cheap and by the gallon! Ask for *yo-GOOR*.

Meats and Sausages: The DR has the oldest *beef* culture in the western hemisphere. You will often get tough and tasteless beef in restaurants and in stores, and you may conclude that DR meat is awful, a complaint often heard from yachties who just didn't know what to order and how. Beef filet is often only sold by the entire filet, but at a price that you can't believe. Good filets get prepared the European way, aged and blue. Other cuts of good beef also come European style and look lean to North Americans. If you can, get a *Sarano* ham, the Spanish version of the Italian Parma ham, to hang aboard. It may cost you ten times as much in Spain as in the DR, but the masters that make it in the DR all come from Galícia.

They call cheap beef *res* [race] and it needs tenderizing with papaya. The secret to buying good meat: Do not go cheap. Buy the most expensive filet, *filete* [fee-LAY-taye] *lomillo* [low-ME-yo], and it shall certainly please you. Local *solomillo* [SO-low-ME-yo] sirloin, smoked ham, boiled ham and *smoked pork chops* usually make great buys.

Pharmaceuticals: Refurbish your medicine chest without prescriptions, often cheaply. The DR does not tie disease curing drugs to doctors' prescriptions, nor can the people afford to buy drugs abusively. Therefore you'll find pharmaceuticals available without prescription, if you know what you want. The pharmacist will gladly show you the book (*diccionário*) so you can translate your antibiotic, or whatever, to generic, and back to product name as available locally. They sell the English seasickness pill, **STUGERON**, in the DR. It always works, and without side effects. Have it aboard!

Drugs needed commonly for public health might get subsidized. Exotic items can cost more than at home. But if you need to replace drugs used up during treatment aboard, then do it. And stock up on Stugeron. Also, pharmacies traditionally handle dangerous chemicals such as acetone, muriatic and stove alcohol, but in quantity only at certain stores.

Siesta [see-ACE-tah]: All family operated stores close for a two hour siesta. Plan to take your lunch during these hours near a park. Every park has a flavor all its own. Watch the parade pass by while you breakfast or lunch or, in Puerto Plata, pig out in the Austrian ice cream parlor on the park; and eat cheap hamburgers called *Riki Takis* from the street vendors; read world newspapers available at a *Libreria*; get your shoes shined.

Street food: I know I've got it coming to me, but four decades abroad in the strangest of places, I've rarely got ill from street food. I got sick at the grand restaurant of the Palace hotel in Biarritz, but not once on street food in India. In India, one would expect to become ill from the *nazi* balls (rice balls) the peddler rolls in his hands and pops into ancient hot grease. Not so. Perhaps the super hot oil does it. Latin countries have superb little puffed, stuffed pastries (*empanadillas* in PR, *pastelitos* in the DR, and *empanadas* in Venezuela). The baritone vendor in Puerto Plata sings his wares. He says that the meat-filled ones have "mice meat" in them. But he means "mincemeat", I'm sure.

FINDING FOREIGN PRODUCTS IN THE DR

Having spent all this space telling you how to survive on the local economy while provisioning, I must hasten to tell you that the DR has supersize modern shopping available. Santiago and Santo Domingo have stores that put the best American supermarkets and hardware stores to shame (La Sirena, Nacional, Carrefour, Ochoa, Bellón). They have delicatessen counters where you can stuff yourself just taste-proofing the offerings that come from Spain, Italy, and France, since all those countries contribute heavily to the DR population. For instance, the Gallicians, the Celtic Spaniards who specialize in sausages and smoked meats, seem to dot the mountains in the DR with their smoke houses. Try the El Cid brands. They have American products, of course. In Puerto Plata try Supermarket Tropical or José Luis.

IN PUERTO RICO

Puerto Rico hasn't as large an industrial base as the Dominican Republic, but the Virgin Islands and onward until Venezuela have *none*. What does that mean? It means any industrial strength boat repairs or refit should get taken care of in the DR or PR. In Puerto Rico, the south coast has the harbors, the supplies and repair shops boaters need.

Temptation shall draw you to **Mayagüez** as soon as you make landfall on the west coast of Puerto Rico. It hasn't the variety nor the price advantage of **Ponce**, and Mayagüez lies as distant in time and transport as Ponce, PR's industrial city, does to **Salinas**, the best yacht harbor on the island. And you must pass Ponce to get to Salinas. When you get your price sticker shock down island, you'll also get the sorries that you jumped the gun by dabbling at your provision/repair tasks from Boqerón instead of from Salinas.

Salinas makes the most sense for shipping stuff in by 800 telephone numbers. By the time you've arrived in Salinas, you've had a chance to see what you can get locally on the island, before going to the expense of shipping gear in.

Shop in Ponce, not Mayagüez, then do any installation work in Salinas.

NAVIGATION AIDS

Most cruisers consume themselves with getting to a certain place at a certain time. For this they heavily invest in all sorts of navigational equipment. The real art of navigation, however, lies in staying out of the wrong place at the wrong time. Use that as your criterion for choosing navigational aids.

CHARTS AND GUIDES

The problem of too much information confronts modern skippers as more devices come on the market. Years of cruising in the Third World with few documented navigation aids, and Europe, where they have too many, have led me to make the following recommendations, listed in priority order.

YACHTING GUIDES

Guides, this one included, become out of date before they get printed. Look for guides that give you less tips on where to do your drinking and more detail on anchorages.

You must have guides like Monty and Sara Lewis's very accurate *Explorer Chartbooks* in the Bahamas, Stephen Pavlidis' *The Turks and Caicos* and his *Guide to Puerto Rico*, Nancy and Simon Scott's *Cruising Guide to the Virgin Islands*, Doyle's *A Cruising Guide to the Leeward Islands*, Doyle's *A Sailor's Guide to the Windward Islands*, Doyle's *Cruising Guide to Trinidad & Tobago,* and *Doyle's Cruising Guide to Venezuela and Bonaire*.

The more guides, the better, since each author has a slightly different viewpoint.

Both Simon Charles' *The Cruising Guide to Cuba* and Nigel Calder's *Cuba: A Cruising Guide* proved excellent for the uses I put them to: Nigel at the chart table and Simon at the wheel. Nigel's chart reproductions proved quite helpful for planning purposes. Simon had more hands-on poop from behind the reefs, and his chartlets contain those indispensable curving arrows one follows through entrances.

MEDIUM SCALE CHARTS

These **charts** get you between cruising areas. For instance, if you already have guide-books, you only need a single chart each of the **Leeward Islands** and the **Windward Islands**. You only need the single chart covering all of the **Virgin Islands** that comes with Scott's guidebook. You only need a single chart of **Hispaniola** if you have **Wavy Line Graphics** chart of that island. I use **Waterproof Chart #16** which shows Florida to Puerto Rico and on its back the **Mona Passage** with **Cabo Engaño** on one side and **Puerto Rico**'s west coast on the other. For Puerto Rico I use **Waterproof Chart #53**.

The scope and shallows of the **Bahamas** requires good charts. You have the best available with Monty and Sara Lewis' lat/long corrected **Explorer Chartbook** series.

For the eastern Caribbean the **Caribbean Yachting Charts** series, verified by Chris Doyle, beat **DMA** charts because they offer the scale a yachtsman wants. They show landmarks of interest to the small boat skipper making for small harbors. They also have a format which better fits small boat nav tables, and they have excellent color contrasts.

Along with Pavlidis' guide to the Turks and Caicos, you shall want **Gascoine and Minty**'s navtable sized, double sided chart showing routes on Caicos Bank. Also, their **Great Exuma** chart rates superb as does their work in and around Luperón which appears as insets on their Hispaniola chart. Watch for more of their careful work in the future.

PILOT (ROUTING) CHARTS

The U.S. *Pilot Charts of the Central American Waters* have a chart table size page for each month showing 150 years of average conditions for every patch of sea. I kept a pilot chart on my chart table at all times. I used it only occasionally for plotting Caribbean crossings, tracking **Tropical Storms**. and planning passages with the current and wind data it provides. However, it got used every morning in the winter to plot the **Cold Fronts** and every morning in the summer to plot the **Tropical Waves**. Covered with pencil marks and coffee rings it became the single most used chart aboard. Now, on my trawler, I have the Wx chart behind plexiglass on my refrigerator door, right next to my navtable. No coffee rings anymore, just tracks and doodles of 3 colors of dry-erase pens.

LARGE SCALE CHARTS

These charts cover small geographic areas. Except in the Bahamas, you need these charts only where you intend exploring areas not shown in available guides. *Explorer Chartbooks* give all the detail needed for areas they cover in the Bahamas. For the eastern Caribbean see the **Caribbean Yachting Charts** series verified by Chris Doyle. For Great Exuma detail see **Wavy Line Graphics'** (Gascoine/Minty) chart.

SMALL SCALE CHARTS

These charts cover large geographical areas. They make great wall decorations at home. At sea, I have only those needed to plot crossings and major passages. **Waterproof Charts #16** gets me from Florida and across the Mona Passage to the Virgin Islands. A weather chart of the entire Caribbean, such as a Pilot Chart, does nicely for the rest.

ALMANACS

Of great use as reference works aboard. (Who knows the breaking strength of 5/16 BBB chain, anyway?) I have found that a single copy of *Reed's Nautical Almanac* from any year provides more useful information than *Chapman's* and *Bowditch's* combined.

TIDE TABLES

In the English Channel I never sailed without my **tide** tables and current guides. The tides, after all, went to 34 feet at my moorings, and the currents reached 9 knots! In the Caribbean you need nothing outside the information on the Pilot Charts which doesn't vary year to year. In the Bahamas the daily tides get broadcast several times a day on standard AM broadcast radio. The tidal differences on **Nassau** rarely exceed one half hour in the open anchorages, and tidal anomalies, such as on the banks, all call for local knowledge. I've found both Hans Pieper's Shareware *Tide Prediction Program* or **The Captain** software accurate for all anchorages near the sea.

Near open ocean you can assume *high tide at 8 o'clock* **local time** *on the day of a full moon.* **Aadd 52 minutes a day thereafter and do without tide tables forever!**

NOTE: The south side of the Greater Antilles and the Virgin Islands have diurnal tides with a higher high and a lower low instead of two lows and two highs.

THE BARE MINIMUM

COMPASS

I sailed for many years with only a **compass**. After a while I found even the log a luxury. Knowledge of your boat's speed settles into your bones after only a few weeks of cruising. You can navigate surely and safely forever with only a compass by careful and frequent position plotting, attention to leeway, current and tidal currents, and by *introducing intentional errors* in order to ensure which side of a feature you make your landfall. Even the compass needn't be all that accurate, since who can hold a perfect course anyway, what with all that bobbing around?

Old fashioned binnacles look nice and can get used as a pelorus for taking bearings of ships, but you can't see them from comfortable seated positions. You should mount your compass where you can see it comfortably from your sailing position on either tack while cruising. You rarely sit bolt upright behind or beside the wheel. The cruising steering position has a little more Zen in it. For instance, I sailed scrunched up in a ball in the same corner of the cockpit on both tacks, never behind the wheel. Therefore I used a bulkhead compass. And I use any convenient fixed gear on the boat as the sight vanes of a pelorus.

The compass should have a rapidly damped large, legible scale, well illuminated, not just bright. Some compass lights illuminate everything but the card's scale.

Swing your compass from time to time, even though you compensated it, to adjust your compass' deviation table, and make sure you are using this year's variation.

LOG

Use sumlogs, taffrail logs, or any device which keeps a digital track of miles run only as a double check on the navigator. They all fail, and the skipper ought to know intuitively how fast his yacht goes through the water.

Before the impeller gets tangled in seaweed or a shark eats the rotor, take the time to calibrate your sense of the boat's speed by the old chip log method. Select a fixed length of deck *viewed from your usual sailing position*. Time bits of foam passing between perpendiculars of that length, checking results with actual speedo readings. Then use:

SPEED IN KNOTS= 2 x METERS ÷ SECONDS

Count seconds the same way you do to determine a light's characteristics. You can use either "one-Mississippi, two Mississippi ... " or "one-thousand-one, one-thousand-two...", whichever works for you. But either way, you must *speak* the words to have them work, and you must revert to "one" when you get to ten.

Practice makes perfect and eventually you can tell with a glance how fast you go in any condition. An old principle of navigation says that the more regular and frequent you plot your position, the more sure your course. If you have no sumlog, you should plot in shorter intervals. Shorter intervals average out errors in speed estimates. Thus, the more frequent your plots, the more accurate your position.

SEXTANT

It seems sextants have gone the way of the slide rule. The last time I used my **sextant** I crossed the Atlantic in 1979. Even so, I discarded it the moment I heard a Caribbean rock station on the AM band. If you really know how to use sextants on clear and starry nights, then you might use one crossing the Caribbean. I have a friend who could pull off a 3 star fix faster than my Satnav did one. He couldn't beat a GPS, however. Solar and lunar sights don't usually provide the kind of precision required to navigate among islands. Island hopping short distances in the Caribbean you have unmistakable and inevitable landfalls. On the other hand, if you cross the Caribbean Sea, masochistically beating up to St.Thomas, great accuracy isn't really called for, but the sextant can confirm drift.

In the passages described by this guide, you better spend your time and money on chart work and a good compass. You don't want to be like the *professional* delivery crew who gave up their charge on East Reef, Mayaguana, having spent all their time playing with their sextants and none of it plotting to avoid a lee reef. The day after the *paid crew* of three men deserted their ship, by the way, it was taken off the reef whole by one salvor using the boat's own ground tackle. He turned the key and motored off with the boat.

ELECTRONIC NAVIGATION AIDS

You can't buy safety at sea with expensive equipment or fancy calculations. As Eric Hiscock loved to say, "The price of safety at sea is *eternal vigilance*".

If you only really need a chart and compass, then why spend the money on fancy electronic navigation aids? Well, the older I get, the mistakier I get. Once I missed the Dry Tortugas entirely. A pair of pliers left under the compass gave me a deviation of 17°.

December 19th, 1984, the **NWS** called for continuing fine weather. We up-anchored and sailed for Georgetown from the north shore of Caicos. They came back 6 hours later with a hurricane warning for *Hurricane Lilly* which they placed exactly 90 miles off my stern and blowing me northwest into the islands. *Lilly*, a small, tight 'cane, came out of season and bearing no telltale feeder trails. She broke up early but spawned several days of gales throughout the area. Only a hiccup for Mother Nature, but a major surprise to small boats.

When I received the forecast I already had the boat on the run before it, surfing down ten footers with the log pegged at eight knots, and me, between curses, wondering what the heck was going on. For 36 hours we slowed our progress toward the **deathtrap** of Exuma Sound, with its raging cuts to leeward, by zigzagging down breaking waves in continual darkness. My oval of navigational uncertainty became so big, I still don't know if we passed the Plana Cays and the surrounding reefs on the west or the east. On the trip back south I had a Satnav on board.

In general, the more navigation aids, electronic or not, the better. Bless you for being affluent enough to afford them, clever enough to select the right ones from the welter of black boxes on the market, and patient enough to keep fixing them. Which devices will serve you the most on the way south? This list follows, like the last one, in priority order.

DEPTH SOUNDER

The **depth sounder**, or **fathometer**, gets much under-used among yachties. I rate this navigation aid only second to the compass. You need a reliable digital depthfinder in the cockpit for coasting. Tack in to 10 fathoms, tack out to 20, and so on. Additionally, some evidence exists that sounders left on, even when off soundings, deter broaching marlins and whales from coming up under the boat.

Use the **chain of soundings** when lost off a coast where everything looks the same. I use this method of navigation unconsciously while coasting in order to confirm the boat's position. With chart in hand, keep mental track of the soundings shown on the fathometer. If the readings of the fathometer do not agree with your expectations gained from the chart, you have reason to wonder about your position.

By sailing a straight line and taking soundings at regular intervals one can arrive at a "signature" of the bottom which usually identifies only that line over that bottom. For a somewhat complex, but unequivocal, way of doing it, plot the readings to scale on a piece of clear plastic or tracing paper. Then move the tracing about on the chart until you have a match. Of course the bottom must vary, and sometimes you get a long line, and you have to get it all done before you've left the area and become lost again. As long as I am on soundings I prefer to just make mental note of the fathom lines as I cross them and never lose my chain of soundings in the first place. While coasting I follow a fathom line anyway.

VHF

Required. Only one will do, but you'll like having a handheld in the cockpit or dinghy.

GPS

Review the cautions on the GPS given in the Introduction chapter of this book.

AM/FM

Of course you have an AM/FM aboard with cassette or CD player. You should also have a hand sized portable with a rod type extendable aerial in the emergency locker. If you have to abandon ship you can listen to all the religious stations that dot the Caribbean. But more important, you can use it as a highly reliable **radio direction finder**, homing in on island rock stations. Reception will be loudest with the aerial perpendicular to the rhumb line to the station. Perhaps the combination of direction and religion shall save you.

AUTOPILOT

I believe exhaustion has caused more accidents at sea than any other human factor, and like the "rapture of the deep", exhaustion takes its toll before you notice it. The **autopilot** has become an absolutely necessary piece of equipment on any cruising boat. The trip to windward can tire one enough without having to face the tyranny of the wheel. You can buy autopilots today for ampere-poor sailing craft, which have minimal current requirements: 3-5 amperes on duty, negligible current draw on standby. Most ketches and yawls can sail themselves close hauled with a lashed helm and balanced rig, but the autopilot handles motorsailing better than a crew could. For long distance trade wind sailing you might want to snap on a self steering device such as the *Aries* wind vane.

SSB RECEIVER

For receiving the **National Weather Service** reports and the various cruiser nets you must have a radio capable of receiving **Single Side Band**. You can use a cheap portable with a "BFO" switch. Before you pay $300 for a Sony look at more professional gear which may even prove cheaper in the long run and give much better reception. I had two small Sony units which corroded. One of the older Radio Shack models, however, lasted for years. To talk to the forecasters (Herb or David) you need a transceiver.

COMPUTER WEATHERFAX FROM SSB

The best solution for the cruiser combines the fax with a computer (as if your life hasn't enough complications already). You can receive and store weather charts, satellite pictures, and even get the telex of the verbal **NMN Offshore Report** to eliminate copying errors. Miami's **Tropical Prediction Center**, a branch of the NWS, broadcasts weather charts covering 10° to 32° latitude by 55° to 100° longitude via the USCG's **NMG** out of Louisiana on 12788, 8502 and 4316 USB (adjusted), at 0700, 1300, 1900 and 0100 EST. They broadcast the schedule at 1530 and 0130 EST. They also simulcast NMN audio reports. Needless to say, the computer can do email, charts, keep records — you need one.

Weatherfaxes represent some of the source materials of the Offshore Reports you hear on the radio. The analysts that make the Offshore Reports studied for years and went on to earn an incredible buck reducing these macro plots of micro data to a carefully considered verbal report with which mariners can make decisions within local areas. To second guess their analysis seems dangerous. Don't exclude the **Offshore Report** for only faxes.

SSB TRANSCEIVER

A transmitter helps you keep in touch with your friends while sailing in company and leapfrogging each other. It also helps you keep up with the rumor mill which grinds between the cruisers on your path so you don't feel such a stranger when you arrive. Take care with weather information received, however, as well as talk of piracy, revolutions, the sky falling in, and so on. You may use either the more powerful **Marine SSB** radio or a less powerful **HAM radio** which you can get modified to transmit on the marine band.

RADAR

As with all electronics, think of your ampere usage and make sure you can handle it. Some components, such as a water maker, can suck juice. The Caribbean has no fog. The radar gets used for confirming landfalls, finding seabuoys and, 'lordy, lordy', plying a windward coast so close you can shake hands with the natives. For the singlehander, a well tuned eight mile radar with a "fence" function may help keep watch on crossings.

RADAR REFLECTORS

Marginally more effective than a *tiki* in avoiding collisions. Better to keep a good watch. *Yachting Monthly* showed the futility of anything but welded radar reflectors and the Japanese "goat's eye" solid type in a study done in 1978. We repeated their tests in Antibes the next year and got equally dismal results. Even the manufacturers produce reflectors that you can not mount in the proper "catch water" attitude. I had used a fender full of aluminum chaff once until I discovered my mast steps offered a better target. A fairly recent Norwegian tube type seems to work well.

Radar transponders depend on the ship's officers looking at their radar within the time you've got between acquisition and collision.

To calibrate your boat as a target, talk to seagoing tugs. They usually keep a good radar watch, they will enjoy helping you, and they will talk with you quite a while.

RADAR DETECTORS

They work, but ships often don't use their radar in the open sea, and if you're coasting or in a shipping lane, you better darn well keep your own lookout. These things chirp at such distances the alarm goes off constantly despite no ships in sight. If you squelch them to eliminate ships over the horizon, with the controls (pots) so cheap and rinky-dink you may squelch out the guy about to run you down.

RADIO DIRECTION FINDERS

Though fine for simple homing, unless you have a double loop, mast-mounted antenna tunable to any frequency, forget it. Any fix available from three shore based senders will have a cocked hat larger than the gap between you and the shore. I buried my last RDF in the North Sea. Better use a portable AM with whip antennae on rock stations.

HAM Radio

It certainly gets you invited to a lot of hamfests, and whether a *Rowdy* or a *Good Citizen*, you will find a team to root for on the various *Radio Nazi* shows HAMsters run. During emergencies the Marine SSB nets have proven more helpful. Also, Marine SSB supports email without the hoo-ha and uproar over commercial correspondence.

Electronic Charts

All the debate notwithstanding, this gets my lowest priority. Simply changing chart media does not make them more accurate. The medium of today's computer screens does not suit the sunny tropics. The current cruising helm stations and screen technologies often give legibility below safety requirements at just the wrong moment.

A computer screen rarely displays a properly scaled chart from which to make transits on distant points of land. The small screen won't display the scale you need to see both an off-lying reef and the island features with which to strike a good range.

But, if you've got the wherewithal to play the game, and a shady and weatherproof bridge why not play? Have backup on the navtable. Use a paper guide book in the cockpit.

In my home port of Luperón just about all the strandings occur by skippers steering a cursor into the harbor instead of their boats. In the Bahamas I've often heard irate explanations like "That rock's not supposed to be there!".

South of U.S.A. coast and waterways official charts usually have *WRONG* lats & longs

Satellite Phone

This only appears at the bottom of my priority list because I can't afford one. Ideally I would have a duplex of those big white eggs the Saudi boats have with omni-directional satellite antennaes capable of giving me broadband phone, internet and television 24 hours a day. But then I'd have to have a different kind of boat, certainly larger, and perhaps with professional crew, chef, engineer and medical staff. Ain't gonna happen.

If you have elderly parents or not so independent dependents, you may want to have one aboard. But watch those costs spiral if you do all your Wx with it on the internet.

USING THE RADIO

VHF

FM Radio Telephony, or **VHF**, has reached an interesting stage of development. Rules for using the VHF got developed for poor reception. When Alpha wants to call Bravo, Alpha should say "Bravo, Bravo, Bravo; Alpha, Alpha" and Bravo should reply "Alpha, Bravo; *nn*", where *nn* means the number of a working channel to which they both repair.

Now that VH F provides high quality reception at a cheap price, every boob has one into which he speaks as would Thomas Alva Edison into the ear of Victorola's dog if he had expected the dog to speak back to him. Worse, today's Bravo has invented a lottery in which he asks Alpha to "Pick a channel". If he doesn't, then Alpha asks Bravo to do it. Although they call each other several times a day, they will usually pick channels which neither has. Then they talk in International Signals Code over the telephone. These guys also call themselves "*THE* Bravo", or worse, "This is the sailing vessel Alpha". Sheeesh!

These same guys play CAPCOM MCC (Capsule Communicator, Mission Control Center) and say "Affirmative" and "Negative" and "Roger That" 3 times each to a boat two hundred yards away. Deke Slayton took endless ribbing when he slipped up on acknowledging a complex transmission from space with "Roger ... uh ... that". He never repeated it. But today a whole new generation of Captain Videos repeat it and other airwave eating clichés — endlessly. Myself, I like to play Glenn Ford at the controls of his screaming Saberjet calling to his wingman . . . In other words, *keep it brief on hailing channels.*

In congested situations, while coasting or at anchor, some choose to turn off their VHF or go to so-called private contact channels, and that can cause them to miss emergencies that may affect them or others whom they could have helped had they kept the standard hailing channel. In most anchorages VHF users lay in good hail of each other on low power. In **Providenciales**, with 200 land stations and 50 boats, or worse, in **Georgetown** with 50 land stations and 400 boats, just keep it brief and on *low power!*

DOs rarely DONE	DON'Ts DONE frequently
turn your power down	call yourself anything but your name, Red Ryder
find an idle channel before calling	talk HAM or CB, good buddy
talk normally, and out of the wind	eat your microphone
wait thirty seconds for Bravo to answer before calling again	repeat everything twice
get off the hailing channel with minimum chatter	use channels permanently assigned (e.g., Coast Guard, hotels ...)
use your mother's language	sit on your handheld's transmit switch, blocking all traffic for hours, while the whole harbor listens to your muffled grousing about your spouse
make each transmission brief and use a minimum of words	chastise non-English speakers without understanding them
repeat only if asked	deputize yourself a Radio Nazi

Radio Nazis sit by the radio and bust in with chapter and verse of the *Law of the VHF*. They take up more air time than casual abusers because their dictates get followed by storms of support from the Good Citizens around and Bronx cheers from the Outlaws and the Rowdies in the harbor. Unless duly authorized officials of the country whose air they use, you can tell the Radio Nazis to take their Barstool Regulations and . . .

VHF BUDDY CHANNELS

I recall the two yachts off Montecristi which crossed the steel cables of a 1500 foot tow at night, while the tug's skipper bawled on Channel 16, and I desperately dialed around to find their buddy channel. The hawser could have sawn the boats in halves, sintering fiberglass and flesh in a heartbeat. It took instead a small bite from a skeg.

The two yachties had sailed blithely in the night unaware of the approaching guillotine.They stood tuned to buddy channel 66 without a dual watch or a scan to 16.

CAUTION : *NEVER* use "buddy channels" to the exclusion of Channel 16.

SSB, or HF

I took a weather window that I knew had a certain risk of collapse. Enroute I heard a yacht radioing a friend that he intended to use the open anchorage of Rio San Juan. I had that intention as well, until I heard the 6 p.m. weather. Herb said the window would collapse. A stalled front had begun to move quickly. I sailed directly to Escondido, thinking to rest and look again at the weather. If the front continued, I had just enough time to boogie around into Samaná for refuge, something I couldn't do from Rio San Juan.

Silly me, I did what one must never do. I offered gratuitous help. I called the yacht behind me and advised the skipper of the weather changes and of what I intended to do. He said he hadn't listened to weather all day or the night before. Silly him.

I arrived in Escondido and promptly went to bed, knowing I might get chased early from the anchorage by a bad weather report. The alarm woke me at the appointed hour and I turned on the SSB. The other guy now lay next to me, gabbing on a close by band. I stayed awake for the next 6 hours trying to get weather. Each time I began to get a report the guy started blabbing with relatives on nearby HAM frequencies or with cruisers over marine SSB. I couldn't raise him on VHF. His was off though security precautions would have it on. I finally got pieces of a report. The advancing front had slowed. My normal departure time now only 2 hours away, I just couldn't get back to sleep. While I raised anchor, the guy doubled the insult. He popped up and wanted to know what I'd heard on the weather!

**If you use a manual tuner, tune up low power 6 KHz away from a used channel.
If you use an automatic tuner, tune well off a net frequency, not right on it.
Please don't use a frequency half or double that of an in-use weather net, like 8104.**

EMERGENCY PROCEDURES

Use VHF 16 for all emergency traffic as well as for initial contacts. Leave your VHF on channel 16 when not in use. Use these levels of safety broadcasts on whatever radio:

SECURITÉ (say-CURE-it-TAYE, French for "safety") Broadcasts of navigational hazards come after the word *securité* said 3 times. For example, a sea mark out, or off position, or a tow restricting passage in a channel.

PAN (PAHN, Greek for "everywhere") Broadcasts of lookouts for personal safety follow the word *pan* said 3 times. For example, the Coast Guard uses PAN when it has lost contact with an overdue boat, or you could use PAN when you have lost the ability to maneuver, but life threats do not exist.

MAYDAY (MAY-day, kind of French for "help me") Broadcasts of imminent danger to life proceed from the word *mayday* said 3 times. Use *mayday* if sinking, if on fire, if someone has gone overboard, or for any immediate threat to life. Do the following:

1. Set the VHF to 16, and the SSB to USB 4426, 6501, 8764, 12788 or 13089.

2. Clearly and slowly pronounce, "*MAYDAY, MAYDAY, MAYDAY*".

3. Say your boat type and name, "[sailing vessel, trawler, motor yacht] *Boatname*".

4. Clearly and slowly give your position: "latitude 1804, longitude 6528".

5. Repeat the emergency simply, "sinking, sinking", or "man overboard" or "fire".

Speak all numbers with single digits. For instance, *fifteen thirty* gets easily understood as *fifty thirteen*, and vice-versa. Say, "One five three zero", instead.

If you can't stand by your radio, repeat the *mayday* several times, hammering on position and type of distress. Force yourself to speak clearly, slowly and with a *minimum of words*. Everyone shall understand "man overboard" even with bad reception. No one can grasp the nature of a rapidly shouted "my husband was looking over the stern and fell in the water and I can't find him". See also the chapter on *Security Afloat*.

RADIO MARINE FREQUENCIES

Hailing Channels	2182	4125	6215	8291	12290	16420	-	TPC Miami Wx faxes on 4316, 8502, 12788 USB 1200, 1800, 2400, 0600 UCT
Legal ITU Marine USB Working Channels	2065	4146	6224	8294	12353	16528	22159	SJ, PR NAVTEX Offshore Rpt in FEC SITOR on 516.9 USB
	2079	4149	6227	8297	12356	16531	22162	at 1000 UCT then each 4 hours
	2638	4417	6230	‡	12359	16534	22165	Miami NAVTEX Offshore Rpt in FEC SITOR on 516.9 USB
	2738	†	6516	‡	-	-	22168	at 1200 UTC then each 4 hours

Expanded Ship to Ship Working Frequencies for Marine SSB:
† **4 MHz:**　　　*from* 4000 to 4057 *every 3KHz.*
‡ **8 MHz:**　　　*from* 8101 to 8110, 8116-8125, 8131-8191 *every 3KHz.*

WEATHER BROADCAST TIMES AND FREQUENCIES

EST	Station Call	Freq. 1	Freq. 2	Freq. 3	Freq. 4	Marine Weather Broadcasts
0930	NMN	4426	6501	8764 13089	17314	NWS Offshore Forecast, USCG, also at 1600, 2200 and 0330 UCT
1000	NMA	516.9	USB FEC (NAVTEX)			Offshore and Puerto Rico Reports
1030	WVWI	1000	AM also on Wx3 VHF			VI Radio Sailor's Report (MTWTF)
1035	Arthur	3815	HAM - LSB			West Indian Wx Net Barbados
1100	WOSO	1030	AM			San Juan, after hourly news all day
1115	George	7241	HAM - LSB (±3 KHz)			George (St.Croix) rebroadcast Wx
1130	Chris	4045	USB			Chris Parker's Caribbean Wx Net
1200	NMG*	4316	8502	12788	USB	MIA TPC Wx Faxes each 6 hours
	BASRA	4003	USB			Bahamas Air Sea Rescue Wx Net
	ZNS1	1540	AM			Nassau after hourly news all day
	NMA	516.9	USB FEC (NAVTEX)			Offshore Reports out of Miami
1215	SSB	8104	USB			Caribbean Safety & Security Net
1220	HAM	7096 (or 3696) LSB				BASRA Bahamas Wx on HAM radio
1230	Chris	8104 then 12359 then 16531				Chris Parker's Caribbean Wx Net
2000	Herb	12359	USB			Southbound II Wx Net
* NMG also simulcasts the Offshore Reports of NMN. See fax schedule at 0325 and 2025						

USING THE MOTOR

SAIL	POWER AND SAIL
Switch the motor on when you need to maintain the minimum average speed you assumed in planning your landfall.	Trim ship for comfort and accept the easier destination.
Keep the jib up only if it helps you point better. Don't strike sails until in harbor in a safe lee. Raise reefed sails before leaving a harbor (i.e., navigate all entrances with sails up).	With the engine up to temperature & RPM, do a flashlight tour of the engine room. Look for spotting from oil or water leaks or fog from exhaust leaks, check bilges and repeat every hour.
Always have the main up, usually reefed, while motorsailing. Tack a bit to fill it if running dead into the wind.	Heeling: air can suckthrough the raw water intake causing an airlock in the cooling system which will overheat the engine. Sea water can siphon into the engine after you switch off if the anti-siphon valve stays under sea level.
Ensure the exhaust outlet stays above water while the engine cools. Following seas or heeling may cause sea water to get drawn into the exhaust, flooding a cylinder and seizing the engine.	Let the engine idle to lowest operating temperature before killing it.
For downwind passages install a ball valve at the exhaust outlet. Remember to open it when the engine cools! Tie the key to the valve handle.	Ensure a goodly air supply to the engine by opening hatches if you have a tight installation. Ducted fans may not carry enough air to the engine.

MOTOR MAINTENANCE

If you can't maintain your own diesel motor, stay home. You shall find few marinas and most of the "help" available might leave you worse off than if you had done it yourself reading a shop manual. You have a shop manual, of course?

BEFORE YOU LEAVE HOME

If you have accustomed yourself to leaving the car for maintenance at the corner garage because you never had the time to do your own maintenance, you now have the blessed opportunity to change. If you really want to travel the *Thornless Path*, you've got nothing but time. Get a shop manual before you leave home, and do your own maintenance. When you screw up, you at least learn something and won't do it again. If you let someone else do it, you will pay for the same screwup time after time. If you do use a mechanic, have him help *you* do the job, so you have that one under your belt.

Take a course in diesel mechanics. Manufacturers such as Ford and Detroit (Perkins), offer simple short courses, as does your local adult education center. Think of it! You can get independent of mechanics simply by going to your local high school one evening a week for 8 weeks. Some courses last only a single day. If you don't incline mechanically, don't think you can't do it. Nothing simpler than a diesel engine. Patience and logic, assisted by a new part or two, can follow down and cure any problem.

The SAD Syndrome

An engine simply running out of fuel gives a resigned *puff-puff-klunk* and dies, just like when you use the kill switch. An engine killed by something stronger than it stopping its rotation, like a huge cargo net wound up in the propeller, dies with a squawk and a bang, and perhaps the sound of rushing water.

The infamous **Surge And Die** syndrome (**SAD**) occurs when a diesel gets air into its fuel lines because the desperately sucking fuel pump succeeds in breaking their seals. When this happens the engine surges (fast RPM-ing), making a panicky scream. Engine death inevitably follows.

The vast majority of engine problems on the *Thorny Path* come from contaminated fuel. You can finesse most of these problems by using a **Baja Filter** (see Glossary), using a good fungicide (not too much), and by preparing your installation with adequate filtration. Adequacy at home turns to insufficiency between the tropics. Besides the manufacturer's engine mounted canister filter and the engine's lift pump screen filter, you should have at least one other filter and a water separator mounted between the tank and the engine.

You can mount a switchable fuel pump to get a few more hours of engine life when clogged fuel filters starve the engine of fuel, or air in the fuel llines causes SAD. This also gives you a way to bleed your fuel lines without getting spasms in your thumb from the lift pump lever. It also gives you a way to clean your fuel tanks without having to bucket out the fuel and strain it through tee-shirts.

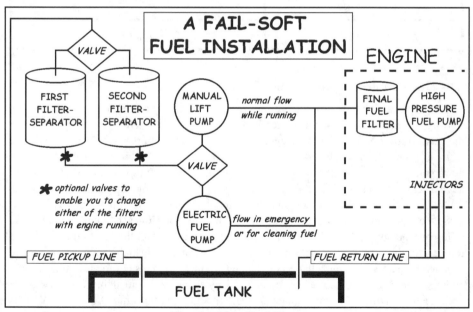

Keeping Your Fuel Clean

This installation gives you better filter reliability, and the electric fuel pump gives you the ability to overcome clogged filters in order to make port. When you hear the engine start to surge, switch on the fuel pump and put it in-line. Once in port, you can also use the installation to clean your tank.

SPARE PARTS

If you have recently installed a new engine you may consider saving key elements of your old engine for spares: head, high pressure pump, water pumps, injectors, delivery pipes, exhaust elbow, starter motor, alternator and instrument senders. However, the following minimum spares should be aboard before leaving home. Replace questionable engine parts with new ones, and place the worn ones in spares.

Sail and Power	Also for Power
VEE BELTS (3)	ALTERNATOR
COMPLETE GASKET SET	HEAT EXCHANGER
STARTER	OIL COOLER
FUEL FILTERS (6 EACH)	RAW WATER PUMP
OIL FOR 6 CHANGES	FRESH WATER PUMP
FUNGICIDE FOR 1500 MILES FUEL CONSUMPTION	SHORT VEE BELT TO GO BETWEEN THE CRANKSHAFT AND THE FRESH WATER PUMP (A MOCK ALTERNATOR)
OIL FILTERS FOR 1500 MILES MOTORING	FUEL LIFT PUMP
FULL GASKET KIT	2 MOTOR MOUNTS

THE DIRTIEST JOB IN THE WORLD

Nothing beats changing oil on a diesel engine for nasty. Thorough preparation before starting makes the job somewhat easier. In other words, flip the settee cushions looking for the new oil filter before your hands get covered with black goop.

Invest in a filter wrench and lots of 3-ply garbage bags. Also have a good stock of old newspapers. and save those plastic gallon jugs with which to dump the old oil. If you don't have a scavenge pump, have a funnel standing by (a cut off plastic bottle top works) to catch the black goop. Even better, install a petcock in place of your pan's drain plug.

Scavenge pumps get most of the old oil out but they don't get the gunk in the bottom of the pan. Accumulation of this stuff can ruin your engine. Get the last of the old oil out through the drain plug in the bottom of the pan. You can also flush the engine from time to time with diesel, if your installation has an angle which prevents complete drainage.

Flush the sump each time you change oil by using more oil than necessary. After draining the old oil, and before replacing the filter, add a quarter sump of fresh oil. With the engine kill switch *on*, run the starter for 20 seconds, pause a few minutes and do it again. Drain the engine again, change filters and add the new oil. This procedure costs you a little oil every time you change, but it may add thousands of hours to your engine's life.

As with many engine jobs, you have an easier cleanup if you start the job with a little **Joy** dish soap rubbed under and around your fingernails.

MOTOR FAILURES

Skippers have their own styles going to windward, and every boat performs differently. Some sailboats motor more than others. Some trawlers motor faster than others. Some crash into it or corkscrew down from it, others tack and wear. Broken engines litter the trail south, because their skippers didn't wait for good conditions. They bucked right into short, steep seas for dozens of hours with the throttle wide open. The boat manufacturers generally do not anticipate this use of engines when they install them. Neither do boat owners generally ask much of their engines until they meet trade wind conditions.

I've listed below the usual engine failures one finds on the **_Thorny Path_** south. You can make it _Thornless_ for your engine by either modifying your installation before leaving home, or not leaving port in the conditions for which your engine has not come prepared. A truly **leisure sailor** will do both.

FUEL SYSTEM

Motoring into heavy chop emulsifies whatever the fuel tank has in it besides pure fuel. It also gives your fuel pump a good gulp of air between sloshes in a near empty tank.

The **SAD** syndrome described earlier will come from air being sucked into the system. Clogged filters and water in the fuel will produce the opposite of surge: a deceleration.

If running dangerously low on fuel, you can supplement diesel with mineral spirits from your lamp oil supply. You can throw in some transmission oil to thicken the brew if you use more than a couple of gallons. I know a German ship's engineer who made port on his yacht with a mixture of cooking oil, engine oil and gasoline. Shake well before using. And don't forget the oregano if your engine's Italian.

You can buy dirty fuel in the Caribbean, so plan on having it. Put in a fail-soft fuel installation as discussed earlier, and use a **Baja Filter** and **Biobor** when adding fuel.

COOLING SYSTEM

Your engine can overheat for hundreds of reasons, but motoring to weather in tropical heat exposes you to all of them. When it happens, which it shall eventually, check:

—weed clogged raw water through-hull fitting

—gulping air with raw water while heeling and pitching (airlock)

—clogged raw water strainer

—raw water strainer too small for flow volume

—water pump impeller going or gone (salt or fresh)

—water pump belt slipping or gone

—heat exchanger clogged

—thermostat jammed

—water pump bearings gone

Some raw water pumps have a weep hole in the shaft housing between the pump seal and the engine oil seal. Some manufacturers make weep holes small. Salt and corrosion will seal them up, and they won't weep. If you don't have one at the _bottom_ of the housing, bore a quarter inch hole to permit weeping. This will prevent water from getting through your oil seal and ruining the engine. They designed the seal to keep oil in, not water out.

Powering off sandy ground in the Bahamas can etch pump shafts and undermine the seals. Volvo motors have high pressure raw water pumps guaranteeing an effective sand-blasting of the shaft. Water in your engine's oil, due to blown pump seals or gaskets, will show up as milky streaks in the jet black dirty diesel motor oil. If it just started, look for drops of condensed steam clinging to the inside of the oil filler cap after running.

If you waited until you had a gully washer pouring into the oil galleries, watch for a fountain of hot gray oatmeal-like stuff to come foaming out of the blown oil filler cap. Better you check for the water droplets on the filler cap before this happens.

EXHAUST SYSTEM

Intrusion of the sea through an open exhaust port into a cylinder can ruin the engine. Water gets into your exhaust manifold several ways, not limited to those already discussed above. Corrosion in the exhaust elbow's water injection jacket will not be noticeable from the outside, and with some installations, water can drip back into the manifold this way. Know how your elbow is constructed and check it before leaving.

If you have a water muffler such as the wet exhaust Verna Lift type, make sure it has a tank large enough to hold all the water from a full exhaust swan neck. The volume of water in your swan neck is the length of hose to maximum rise multiplied by half the inside diameter squared (Vol = Length x πR^2). Make sure you have a high enough swan neck to motor heeled in high seas and your outlet won't spend a good deal of its life under water.

Throw away those bronze anti-siphon valves and replace them with rugged plastic ones. While you do it, raise the anti-siphon valve and its U-fitting higher than the level of sea can conceivably come without your boat turning turtle.

The bane of the windward yacht, **chafe**, can hole your exhaust hose. While not mortal, it sure makes a mess.

Always idle your engine until the operating temperature bottoms out before cutting it off.

If you attempt to start your engine and it doesn't budge, count your blessings. The attitude of the stroke when it stopped was such that the flooded cylinder compressed before another one fired. Water being basically incompressible, your starter can only sit there and hum a tune. Had a dry cylinder fired, you'd have scrap for an engine.

Many of these problems occur on yachts on their first real sea trials motorsailing the thorny path. If you elect to bash into it and cause these problems, they shall happen by the time you reach the **Dominican Republic**. Get new parts out of **Santiago**, and fix it before going on. If you continue in the same style, the next 280 miles to Puerto Rico will be the *coup de grace* for your engine. You can find anything in the DR and they have cheap and good labor.

For many years I have trusted Felix Juan Barros, of **Mercantil Antillana**, the Lister and Perkins dealer in Santo Domingo on Máximo Gómez 174 (tel: 809-566-3141 to 43). Mercantil Antillana has more than 70 years in the diesel business in this agricultural, industrial and fishing country. Felix Juan went to the University of Michigan. Trust him to give you straight skinny on any make engine — if he doesn't know, he'll find out for you.

Water in the Cylinders

If you have seawater incursion do the same thing you did when you dropped the outboard motor overboard. If you haven't done that yet, not to worry, you will soon.

1. Take off all the injectors (sparkplugs) to expose the flooded cylinder(s).

2. Crank to expunge the water through the injector (sparkplug) holes.

3. Pour in some diesel or mineral spirits through the holes, and crank again. If the water got to your oil supply as evidenced by gray streaks on your dip stick, drain the oil, pour in a quarter sump of diesel oil, crank briefly and drain again. Now add oil, crank lots, then change oil a final time.

4. Put back the injectors, bleed the fuel system and get underway.

ELECTRICAL SYSTEM

This guide does not intend to provide a treatise on boat electrics. You can find many fine reference works readily available to thoroughly confuse you. I intend to only give you warning of pitfalls unique to **passage making** south. You will for sure have charging problems and more charging problems. You can have wind generators, solar panels, automated battery charging systems and generators separate from the engine with which you get propulsion. You'll still have charging problems. Especially if you have an electric refrigerator with less than 6 feet of insulation and more than one cube's ice making capacity. The wind won't blow, the sun won't shine, all your charging connections will corrode and generate more heat than they carry electricity. Certainly your diodes will blow.

Law of boat electrics: Consumption expands beyond the boat's capacity to supply it.

Carry a spare alternator and get the burned out one fixed or rewound in the Dominican Republic. Anywhere else this procedure costs dearly, if it can get done at all. Go to the Yellow Pages and look up *Taller de Alternadores*. Don't ask the dock boy or taxi drivers.

Chafe and corrosion cause most electric failures. Before you leave home do a thorough review of all wiring runs. Invest in good metal jawed cable ties and tie them everywhere. Make a wiring diagram of the whole boat including motor and instrument panel.

Have a good multimeter and know how to use it to debug the system. If you rewire anything use one or two gauges of wire heavier than called for, and use tinned stranded wire. Label everything and turn square corners with the runs. In short, failures shall happen. Have a system that you can quickly debug.

A gift: While cleaning up your engine's wiring, install a momentary switch on the hot line to the starter solenoid where it runs through the engine room. You'll use this for bleeding the fuel system at the injectors.

Another: Use solderless connectors, forks, not rings, for most jobs regardless what the boating standards experts say. They will save you from cutting back and scarfing up shortened wires, thereby introducing more points of unreliability. You can easily remove and replace solderless connectors. Even twist-on wire nuts have their uses.

CUSTOMS AND IMMIGRATION

The customs and immigration officials of the world meet every February in Den Hague to formulate plans for confounding guide writers. They get merit points for attending seminars in changing procedures rapidly. Find a good bartender or a cheap gourmet café and they'll last at least six months, long enough to make the final proofs. Then the bartender shall run off with the cook the day you go to press. Customs, however, has a plan. They change it every ten boats that enter. If someone tells you, "Here's how you clear customs in Gerfunknik", better do the opposite. Only *general* guidance follows.

TIPS ON CLEARING CUSTOMS EASILY

In general, your experience with clearance officials depends on you. Have your boat and yourselves presentable. Have your papers in order: ships papers, passports and clearance out (*despacho* or *zarpe*) from your last port. Crew lists help in Spanish speaking countries. Most other countries ask you to fill out their forms for crew lists.

Smile, answer honestly, friendly and courteously. *Don't ask questions! Look bored.* Never bribe. Never lie. You may get in trouble, and once started, it never stops.

The customs guys all over the world get trained to use their sixth senses. If the trip tired you, and the hassle of mooring got you all harried, you may give odd responses to them. You can anchor around the corner with your yellow Q flag flying, and get a good night's sleep before entering. Always try to clear at ports which specialize in yachts.

In places where they don't have many yachts you must realize that you intrude on their management of a port, and you give these low paid working men a pain in the neck.

FIREARMS

All countries can hold onto your arms and other bonded stores while you use their port. They may decline to check your arms depending on their own criteria such as the length of your stay, the length of your hair, security of your bonded locker and so on. The U.S., where military assault rifles get hawked on every street corner, doesn't bother.

If you sit long at a dock where gun-checking goes on, you shall see how some yachts carry enough arms to look like mercenaries out to overthrow the local government. Some places boats have their fancier weapons turn up missing when they go to clear out. I've never heard of that happening in the Dominican Republic nor in Trinidad. The best insurance against this piracy? Have crummy guns, and check in at yacht-only ports.

Insure the accuracy of your serial numbers and ammunition counts. They may check again on your way out. If you had a mistaken number on the way in, you shall have a major bureaucratic nightmare getting out. Bullet counts easily get off by one, and corroded serial numbers get misread . Long ago in Port of Spain, while digging out ammo for the police to impound during my stay, I came up with a block of corroded 0.22 bullets all stuck together. I tossed them over the side kind of nonchalantly. The boarding officer had a fit. Now he couldn't get an accurate count. The upshot of the whole thing, however: They awarded me a police car with a good looking policewoman at the wheel to run me about town for two days while they checked me out. We had lunch at her place. Talk about punishment!

Puerto Rico requires a special warning. Puerto Rico Marine Police can board vessels of any flag to make any search they wish without presence of federal officials who, if around at all, shall stand off. This has baleful meaning to all yachts transiting Puerto Rico, especially considering their frenzy of nationalism. If boarded, stay polite and look bored.

Puerto Rico requires Puerto Rican permits for all firearms within their territorial limits. They further require arms aboard to have *carry licenses assigned to a Puerto Rican resident aboard the vessel with the firearm.*

Unless surrendered, the police will confiscate the weapon when one fails to meet any of these demands. If surrendered, the weapon may get returned to the owner after hearings for violation of the Arms Law of Puerto Rico. Those hearings typically can delay up to 6 months, during which they may impound the vessel and not allow the owner aboard.

I have seen yachts after 6 months impoundment in Puerto Rico. I advise anyone caught in this trap to gladly surrender their weapons. You should know that a large number of Puerto Rican Marine Police have themselves got caught engaging in the narcotics trade. If they take your firearm, get an official receipt and carefully vet its accuracy. You don't want it turning up later in a murder investigation and having your name on it.

BAHAMAS, CAICOS, HAITI, DR, PR, AND THE VIs

THE BAHAMA ISLANDS

They have made clearing into the **Bahamas** simpler: just pay $300. And it includes a fishing license. Coming from the south you can clear easiest at Mayaguana.

TURKS AND CAICOS

The procedures in these islands vary with the official. See the sections on **Sapodilla Bay** and **South Caicos**. In both cases you just dinghy into the freighter dock.

HAITI

You can use ports of entry Cap Haïtien and Fort Liberté, on the north coast. Four or five officials shall board you. In other harbors officials shall board you to check the papers you got when you cleared in, One must firmly allow only one member from each bureaucracy aboard, else the whole town shall roost on your settees all day. Both **Cap Haïtien** and **Fort Liberté** can clear you in or out. Recently many yachts have ignored clearances and gone directly to Acul Bay, **La Badie**. Cruise ships call here, and yachts provide security for each other. See American Norman Zarchin at his **Coco Beach** hotel for local guidance.

THE DOMINICAN REPUBLIC

U.S. vessels needn't have U.S. clearance out papers from U.S. ports.

The DR clears foreign vessels in and out of every port with customs facilities and, *theoretically*, they allow you to go ashore only in those ports. If you haven't gone to the Caribbean before, learn in the DR to ignore bossy dock boys hopping about the dock in their khakis, frantically waving, hoping to get a job. I saw a yachtie present one of these with a fifth of Scotch, then go about bragging that he had the '*comandante*' in his pocket.

You should arrive in all the north coast harbors in the *early morning calm* when you can easily make the piers, if you want, and easily get your anchors set in the mud bottoms. I always anchor *where I want*, then dinghy in to find the officials if they don't first dinghy out to me. The Coast Guard and Customs shall handle you immediately. Immigration may not come immediately, but don't sweat it. The little cards they gave you when you came into the Bahamas work as Bahamian clearance out devices while entering the DR.

The DR charges vary from time to time. Just get an official receipt or don't pay them.

To extend your visa simply take it to the immigration officer who will extend it without question as often as you like, unless you have become an undesirable.

PUERTO RICO

Non-US vessels, and vessels with nonresident *aliens* aboard (what Americans call foreigners, I fear), must check into Puerto Rico at official ports of entry, even if they already have a valid U.S. cruising license.

US pleasure vessels can clear Customs in Puerto Rico from their landfall by any means of communication including telephone. The operator of the vessel (or designated representative) must report to a Customs officer at the first place the boat comes to rest after entering U.S. territorial waters where telephones exist. Only the reporting person may leave the boat. No persons may board the boat and you can do no loading or unloading until Customs has given clearance. You must also contact local U.S. Immigration, sometimes even Agriculture. Customs will give you directions on how.

Usually Customs just requires a current sticker for U.S. boats arriving in Puerto Rico. If you don't have one, they'll tell you where and how to buy one, and they'll give you provisional clearance pending your purchase of the sticker later.

I have never had anything but professional and courteous reception by Puerto Rican agents of the U.S. Federal Government (versus local PR Marine Police).

Coast	City	Location	Phone Numbers
west coast	Mayaguez	commercial pier	831-3342,43
south coast	Ponce	Playa Ponce	841-3130,31,32
east coast	Fajardo	Puerto Real Customs House	863-0950, 4075
north coast	San Juan	Muñoz Marín Airport	253-4533,34,38
Vieques	Isabel	airport	741-8366
Culebra	Dewey	airport	742-3531
St.Thomas, USVI	Charlotte Amalie	ferry dock	
St.John, USVI	Cruz Bay	ferry dock	
St.Croix, USVI	Christiansted	dockside	
Outside hours 0800-1700, Mon. thru Sat., call Customs in San Juan at 253-4533/34/38			

US VIRGIN ISLANDS

US vessels coming from Puerto Rico don't need to clear into the US Virgin Islands, but they do need to clear going back to Puerto Rico, because of the USVI's free port status. Do not expect courtesy, especially in St. John. Just go in, shut up and get out.

HAULING OUT

THE DOMINICAN REPUBLIC

The DR has good manual labor. Possibilities to haul exist, but I generally can not recommend them. Of course, real do-it-yourselfers can get by with anything, if they have all materials and tools onboard and the skipper supervises everything. Multihulls and bilge keels can use the beaching facility at **Manzanillo** with good effect. A railroad lift exists in **Bahía de Carinero** (careener's bay) in **Samaná,** Columbus's old careening spot.

You'll feel quite historical if you haul there, but quite hysterical when you launch. In an emergency you can use the railroad haulout in **Puerto Plata**, but only in a real emergency. You can purchase the tin-based Ameron paints in the DR, the same as sold in Trinidad, as well as Dupont Imron at quite reasonable rates. See Brian at Luperón Marine Store.

Club Nautico in Boca Chica, just east of the capital Santo Domingo, has a 77 ton Travelift. Forrest Rodriquez' Centro Marino marine store lies just across the street, and the club has a good bar and restaurant. Perhaps of interest to the single-handers, Boca Chica constitutes one of the prime sybaritic tourist poles of the Caribbean. On the down side, the functionaries at the Club Nautico somewhat disdain outsiders.

PUERTO RICO

Puerto Rico has many boatyards. You shall have no trouble finding one for a quick haul and paint. For more extensive work, as always, shop around by fax and phone.

If leaving your boat for the summer hurricane season, consider leaving it on the hard at **Palmas del Mar** (852-4530), near **Humacao,** or **Puerto del Rey** (860-1000), in **Fajardo.**

Puerto del Rey has Travelifts of 35, 77 and 170 tons, one of which must surely handle your beam if you have a multi-hull.

The following yards, listed counter clockwise around the island, have little or no facility for long term storage but can give you good and fast haulouts:

> **Villa Pesquera** (851-5690), in Puerto Real near Boquerón,
> **Ponce Yacht Club** (842-9003),
> **Isleta Marina** (384-9032), in Fajardo,
> **Villa Marina** (863-5131), in Fajardo,
> **Varadero de Fajardo** (863-4193), in Las Croabas.

Las Croabas, a government fisherman's cooperative, makes the cheapest haul if you don't need to dry grind or spray paint. Bring everything with you. Villa Marina specializes in motor yachts and has good chandleries, engine and canvas shops next door. I've hauled in Venezuela, Trinidad, BVIs, USVIs, but Ponce and Croabas, in Puerto Rico, come to mind as my happiest hauls. Great country cantinas surround the Croabas yard, while Ponce's boardwalk cafés face Ponce Yacht Club.

Each year I fax all these places and more to get their prices and hauling conditions (do you have to buy everything from them, electricity, water, live-aboard, pressure wash, do-it-yourself, labor rates, blocking, ladders, etc., etc.). Surprisingly, Ponce Yacht Club usually comes out as best haul in the Caribbean. But, you must have insurance, and members, of course, get preference. When there, see Jose Becerra (Ho-chi) for any work.

VIRGIN ISLANDS

The Yards in **Tortola**, Tortola Yacht Services, at **Roadtown**, and **Nanny Cay** Marina do quite professional work. Many cruisers lay up for hurricane season at Virgin Islands Yacht Harbor in **Spanish Town, Virgin Gorda.** The **USVI** has Haulover Marine on **Crown Bay**, in **Charlotte Amalie** and Independent Boat Yard, on **The Lagoon** on the south shore.

LEEWARDS AND WINDWARDS

Farther down island you will find Bobby's Marina in **Phillipsburg, St.Martin**, the Rodney Bay Marina in **St.Lucia**, Castries Yacht Service in St.Lucia and Prickly Bay Marina, in **Grenada**. Use Arch Marez's **Rodney Bay Marina** for equipment and convenience.

ISLAND WEATHER

I don't pretend to be a weather guru nor to produce a weather text book. If you want either, you can't do better than Admiral Kotsch and his US Naval Academy textbook, *Weather for the Marinaer* (ISBN 0-87021-752-6). I learned to forecast at deck level from Alan Watts' books, *Insant Wind Forecasting* and *Instant Weather Forecasting*. They use extensive color photography and illustrations. Chris Parker (aboard *Bel Ami*), the Caribbean cruiser's personal weatherman, has produced a well respected primer, *Coastal and Offshore Weather*, and I also like David Jones' *Concise Guide to Caribbean Weather*.

Now let's take a look at specific tropical weather features by season.

WINTER COLD FRONTS

Many northern yachties arrive in the tropics still applying the term **norther** to a **cold front**. A cold front in the southeastern extremity of the continental weather pattern has little similarity with blue northers up north. Don't let use of terms such as norther inhibit you from seeing cold fronts as useful friends.

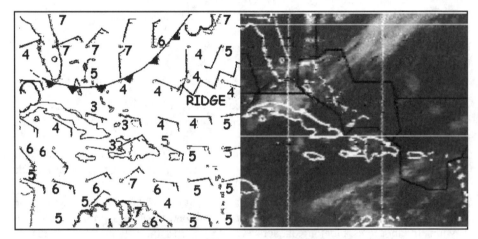

Tropical Prediction Center charts show a stalling front killing the trades.

Unlike western European and North American waters, the building grayness of wind and sea during the passage of a front in the lower southwest North Atlantic and the northeastern Caribbean never build to **storm** conditions (Force 10 Beaufort), and they rarely build to a gale (Force 8). More likely they collapse on their south ends, exhausted into several minor frontal lines or a broad, weak trough. Don't always run for shelter. Get out your dividers and plot your progress south. It rains warm if it rains, and you can sail with or without a bathing suit, though you may need a sweater when the front passes and it blows clear and cold. A poncho perhaps, never a slicker!

If a front doesn't stall north of you, but continues through your position, it typically veers the wind from southeast through south, continuing clockwise all the way around to northeast. When the northeast wind has blown itself out it will usually *soften and dip a bit below east*, before returning to the winter pattern of ENE, a very useful fact to know.

When leaving **Georgetown** I often take a full clock of the wind over to **Salt Pond** in Long

68

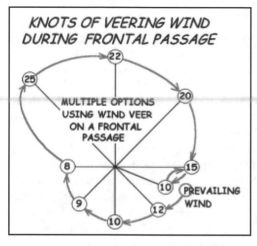

KNOTS OF VEERING WIND
DURING FRONTAL PASSAGE

MULTIPLE OPTIONS
USING WIND VEER
ON A FRONTAL
PASSAGE

PREVAILING
WIND

Island, then I stage myself up to **Calabash Bay** via **Simms** and **Joe's Pond** in the lee of the island, while it continues to blow northeast. When it begins to soften and dither below east, I sail to **Conception**. That strategy beats hiding from the front in Georgetown, then beating into it after it has passed.

Some fronts blow strong from the southwest, but a mild front will follow something like the pattern shown in the diagram — certainly most fronts in Georgetown, because of the chains of islands and banks that shield the harbor.

Late in the season, on a *mild* front, you can trim for a broad reach and leave her there all the way from **Rum Cay** to **Mayaguana**, scribing a long arc down islands with the wind's veer. Early in the season the northeast winds may persist for several days after passage of a strong front. South of 22° latitude fronts *rarely* fully clock the winds.

If you want to go only in sunny weather, take a plane. Clear weather in the winter usually means 20 knots on the nose and hobby-horsing into 6 to 8 foot short seas. By including fronts in your winter strategy you can cut weeks off your trip south and at the same time insure yourself a good three days to a week of leisurely fishing while doing a **wait for weather**. Take care, however, not to ride a bronco of a strong front.

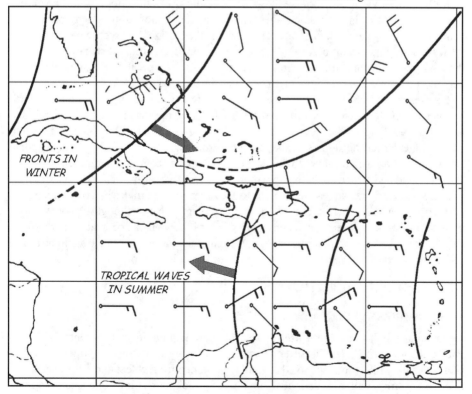

FRONTS IN
WINTER

TROPICAL WAVES
IN SUMMER

BETWEEN SEASON TROUGHS

October to late November boats go up on the beach practically every year in **Bonaire** from unexpected west winds. They should expect them. Fronts begin to make it as far as the western Caribbean in the fall, albeit weakly, and **tropical waves** (see the Glossary now for each of these weather feature terms as I present them) still make it to the western Caribbean, albeit old and frail. The combination of stalled, weak fronts and stalled, dying waves often become **troughs** (see Glossary) which can stretch from the Andes mountains in South America to Georges Banks off Canada. Imbedded storm cells, if not the troughs themselves, can spawn west winds at the unprepared anchorage on Bonaire. It caught me more than 200 miles to the east at Blanquilla, in the Venezuelan islands, one October.

In the other 'tweener season, May to June, the dying fronts and early weak waves can create similar titanic troughs. Learn to see these as opportunities, not necessarily threats. From Luperón east, these 'tween season, large, stationary systems give great protection.

You can use these systems to make progress down islands from the Bahamas as well, when you have a settled period of yucky weather, but with predictably mild conditions. East and south of these seasonal troughs, from Turks & Caicos to the Mona Passage, the trade winds gets quashed, and you get opportunity for easy easting in fine weather.

SUMMER TROPICAL SYSTEMS

In the summer months one watches the east for a variety of **tropical systems**, the nomenclature of which may sound randomly chosen to the cruiser new to the Caribbean. The names of these Wx features follow a simple progression of severity, and therefore the cruiser, especially if uninsured needs to know them all well.

Rather than continue to confuse these terms, refer now to the Glossary for the definition of each. Learn about these weather features and know how to use them, rather than confuse and dread them all. First on the scene come the **troughs** and **tropical waves** out of Africa crossing the Atlantic. A tropical wave may spawn a **tropical disturbance**. One of these may begin to whirl from **Coriolis Force** to become a **tropical depression**, which can become a **tropical storm**, which often becomes the dreaded **hurricane**. So it goes.

One season I left **Salt Pond** to take advantage of the weak circulation around a north bound **tropical depression** well to the east of us. It helped me make my usual leisurely sail to Puerto Plata. The words *tropical depression* had alarmed most of the Bahamas fleet into staying put. Upon the depression's passage, strong winds returned and stayed for a while. I heard on the HAM net that one couple had got discouraged with their "Wait for Weather" and had turned back, that two more had given up waiting and, now out of synch with the Wx window, had terrible beats to **Rum Cay** where full trades had come up to their northern limit and had them cornered. One of them, Captain Nogo, thought a good **weather window** looked like a breezy, sunshiny sailing day, as shown in the beer ads. Ugly looking days he stayed at anchor, regardless of wind strength and direction. Once again he didn't go. He didn't know a *friendly* tropical depression when he saw one.

USING HURRICANE HOLES

BASIC REQUIREMENTS

Land must lock a **hurricane hole** close enough to run lines to shore against dangerous wind directions. The hole must offer unrestricted entrance at all times and tides. Unless in a bay or estuary likely to empty on the wind, look for depth a few feet under the keel at low tide. **Storm surge** will raise your boat, not lower it. Look for shallows and island shelving to weather of the hole in order to reduce storm surge. If in the path of the storm's right quadrant and holed up near deep ocean (e.g., eastern Antigua) you may suffer the storm's full open ocean surge. Your boat can rise fully exposed above reef and mangrove.

THE BEST HOLES

The perfect hole does not exist. Nowhere gives you 100% safety, but you can get close. The boat wants good holding and soft shores to wash up on.

Mangroves make the softest shores. They grip the ground with myriad springy roots. The brittle dead wood snaps and breaks easily, but live wood bends like a palm. A tight bark covers the hard wood like an easily broken skin. A thick mucous layer lies underneath. Strike the tree and it first bends, then its skin breaks. The mucous slides the striking object upward, where smaller and more plentiful branches continue the same action. An impinging boat slides up the mangroves harmlessly as onto a Teflon bedspring. Absent overwhelming storm surge, the boat slides back when wind and water abate. Don't clean off the red mangrove stains. Sunshine melts them away. Furthermore, despite the power-game claims of academics and bureaucrats, the process does not hurt the mangroves.

East of **Morocoy National Park** in Venezuela, you shall find precious little protection. Yet between Tucacas and Trinidad, yachts will eventually stack sardine like in deep, exposed and rock sided anchorages. With the insurance companies chasing boats south, **Chaguaramas**, in Port of Spain, with its currents, tides and deep, scoured bottom, begs to polish your boat with Trinidad's perennial summer southwesters.

Throughout the Virgin Islands charter boats and boats with no skippers aboard plug up the harbors during a threat, making the crunch of boats around extremely dangerous.

Salinas, on the south coast of Puerto Rico has nearly two square miles of deep mangroved rivers and bayous in a wetlands national park. The park lies far enough from charter fleets and megamarinas that few boats come. Vieques and Culebra, PR, lie squarely on the fleet evacuation routes from the Virgins and Fajardo, so they get chock-a-block.

Samaná has a great hole across the bay in the **Bahía San Lorenzo**. (See *Los Haitises*.) Samaná has never had much of a hurricane problem anyway. A careful look at the geography will show why: surrounding land masses and mountains combat the winds even with a direct hit. The dangerous semicircle can scarcely penetrate Samaná bay undiminished. The same holds even more true for **Luperón**, on the north shore of the Dominican Republic.

Luperón's two mangrove bays lie vulnerable only to a *southbound* storm. It has a small village with a large tourist hotel and good communications. Hurricanes crossing the island lift over the high mountains and disorganize, producing much destruction on the south coast and only rain on the north coast.

Manzanillo, farther to the west in the DR, ranks high in protection but poor in civilization, despite the ever present and ice cold Presidente beer. **Ft.Liberté**, farther west still, in Haiti, scores well on protection, but bottom on civilization. Yet the Barbancourt *rhum ancien* can acculturate even the heart of wilderness.

WHAT TO DO

Run! Run every time, and run early. Don't dither. Don't cavil at false alarms. Don't listen to the jerks with the jokes, the hardies with their parties. *Run!* Getting an early jump means forsaking commitments, not letting friends or job distract.

Never run from a 'cane at sea as the bar myths say, unless you can do 30 knots in heavy seas as carriers and destroyers do. Run to a hole, which you should already have scoped out. Stake your claim before the 36 hour **Hurricane Watch**, then begin to act slowly and deliberately in order to get your nose pressed into the ground all during the **Hurricane Warning**, the 24 hour period before storm landfall. Stay put until the warning lifts.

Always have your boat sea-ready in hurricane season. Storms sometimes rise out of nowhere, practically skipping the Tropical Depression stage. Have a clear plan for a hole *downwind* within timely reach. If you decommission your engine for any reason, do so tied into mangroves at a hurricane hole.

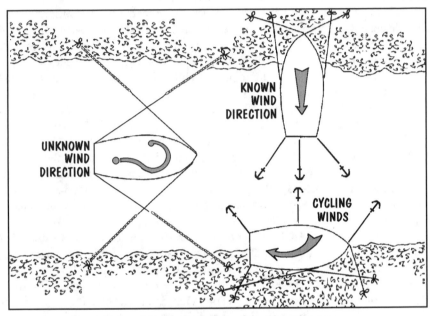

Tying into mangroves for a hurricane

Rumors and grousing to the contrary, named storms, with rare exception, follow the instructions of the Miami Hurricane Center. With each report, plot the storm's approach and tie in another line, leaving open the most options possible. Between reports, the work of stripping the boat will loosen the knot in your guts and ease the pain of waiting.

STAY ON OR GET OFF?

No absolute answer exists. If you penetrate deeply into mangrove rivers for ultimate protection you can't leave the boat. To leave the boat you must use a hole within dinghy reach of civilization, but not surrounded by drooling looters. If you can make the boat safe, then you can safely stay with it, can't you? But have you made it safe?

THE DANGEROUS SEMICIRCLE

Beware the **dangerous semicircle** of a **tropical storm**, the half of the rotating system which has its winds moving the same direction as its forward speed. Typically, the winds in the dangerous semicircle can blow fifty percent higher than the winds in the other half of the storm. If encountering the storm at sea and caught in the dangerous half, the direction of the winds tend to sweep you into its path rather than knock you aside. For example, if you fell in the path of one of those street cleaning machines which has rotating brooms, which side of its rotation would you rather fall? The side which will squinch you forward and into its maw, or the side which will only maul you and shove you aside?

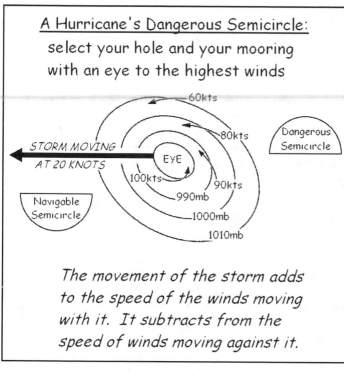

A Hurricane's Dangerous Semicircle:
select your hole and your mooring
with an eye to the highest winds

60kts

80kts

Dangerous Semicircle

STORM MOVING
AT 20 KNOTS

EYE

100kts

90kts

990mb

Navigable
Semicircle

1000mb

1010mb

*The movement of the storm adds
to the speed of the winds moving
with it. It subtracts from the
speed of winds moving against it.*

Although you may watch the formation of the 'canes in the Atlantic and you may plot their probable paths two to three days ahead, they can still steer most erratically. If a storm heading west will pass your anchorage to the south, then you don't care if the anchorage is open to the west, and you can put your nose in the mangroves of the eastern shore. If a 'cane passes north of you heading west, almost any good hole may do. The permutations become, of course, endless and you must choose from the holes you have available. All of these "What If?" **hurricane games**, like war games, must be played well in advance of a crisis. You must act instinctively when it becomes apparent a hurricane makes its final approach and may not veer. You won't have time to dither.

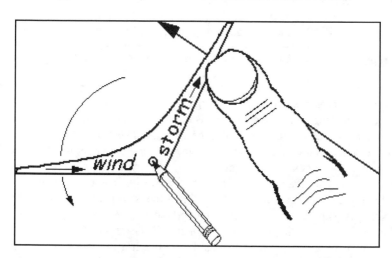

Cut a boomerang shape (115° angle) from an old credit card. Label, as shown, one end *storm* and the other *wind* and punch a pinhole in the center. Hold the center on a chart of your hurricane hole with a pencil point, and push the *storm* point along the probable storm path. The *wind* point will scribe the progress of the wind on your boat as the storm passes.

For more on storms see *Neat Stuff: When You Can't Get Forecasts.*

WEATHER WINDOWS

The word *window* got applied in the manned spaceflight program to indicate a favorable conjuncture of complexly interacting variables, the solution to which required detailed analysis and great precision. It began with familiar concepts of windows for launch, orbit insertion and reentry, but soon spread to all the esoteric disciplines of that great endeavor. I may have aided its currency in the cruising world, and it annoys me to find it most often used with shallow understanding, handling only one or two simple factors.

In or near the **trade wind** belt, weather becomes cyclic and regular. Periods of low, or altered, activity in the trades create *windows of escape* from normally strong windward weather. **Weather windows**, therefore, need the conjuncture of favorability in the cyclic wanderings of *six* different elements:

wind velocity and direction,

height and direction of wind driven waves (or chop), and

height and direction of swell.

How do you cruise to windward without beating your brains out or performing marathon stunts when any of these elements go against you? Wait for a miracle.

Miracles come in the form of certain weather features which upset the status quo of trades conditions. In combination with these weather features, a window may both widen in favorability and lengthen in time. Short windows accommodate short hops. Long windows can harbor *several* short hops. Reserve long hops for windows both long and wide.

This comes when winds lighten up and **back** or **veer** off your nose. If you must beat, do so in trades moderated to less than 15 knots *maximum* and seas less than 4 feet.

A **weather window** starts *only after swells have abated*, but when it starts, take the leading edge of it and *don't delay*. If you really want to attend one more beach bonfire, or one more dance at the Peace and Plenty, or you already invited the boat next door for cocktails, then enjoy yourself and wait for the next window so you can sail in leisure. Don't drink up half the window in harbor and bank on the second half holding up for you. Take a new window rather than risk getting the current one slammed shut on your tail.

Depart only when favorable conditions shall last for a day longer than you need to make safe harbor.

A **wait for weather** means taking advantage of the periodic switching of the prevailing easterlies between northeast and southeast as the **trade wind**s wander, in winter, by the passage of a **front**, and in summer, the passage of **tropical waves**.

If you feel you haven't got time to wait for an appropriate weather window, if you feel pressed to make your next cruising ground as soon as you can, closely examine your motivation and play it off against your reasons for cruising, and more importantly, your safety. If you press on in 20 knot trades and 5 to 8 foot seas in a 35 to 40 foot boat with a small auxiliary engine, you beg disaster to overtake you. When it doesn't, you haven't cheated it, but you've got that much more of a disaster next time.

Some waits may last longer than a week, but rarely. It may seem that a window will never open. Both in 1991 and 1994, for example, the **Christmas Winds** came late, and they stayed into hurricane season. Even in those tougher than usual years, cycles of moderation appeared regularly, if less frequently, and shorter than usual.

Even in those years the **Offshore Report** showed 2-3 day windows of 15-20 knots, 4-7 foot seas at least twice monthly. More usually windows of 10-15 knots, 3-5 foot seas, come twice a month, more often in the summer. In 1997, a vintage year for short Wx windows, many went unrecognized. I found myself passaging alone more often than not.

The weather you wait for may not always look that good to you at first glance. See *Grim and Gray Can Go Great.* Good sailing days come around like good lovers, I guess. My mother told me: "They're like buses. There's another one right around the corner if you're looking for it." And if you don't look for it, or worse, don't know what to look for, you'll spend your life getting neither. You must *know* what to look for.

KNOWING WIND AND WEATHER FEATURES

The path travelled, the island harbors selected, the safety and comfort objectives of the thornless path described in this book each singularly depend on the skipper's knowledge of, observation of and use of the effects of wind and wave *at the margin of land and sea.*

Can you identify the wind and weather features around you, such as the **sea breeze,** the **nocturnal wind, land breeze, gradient wind, surface wind, inshore wind, coastal fronts, troughs, ridges, depressions, tropical waves?** If you can't, look each of them up in the Glossary now. Don't only *think* you know, but *know.*

Do you know all the ways the observed surface wind can differ from the forecast gradient wind at sea? How much it can differ in inshore waters, and why? Do you know all the reasons why the wind in harbor differs from the **inshore wind?** Do you know how banks affect the weather? You shall never find **weather windows** threading the chain of islands without taking advantage of **island effects,** which *you must know cold.*

HARBOR TELLTALES

Don't try to guess the weather from harbor anywhere but the Bahamas. Even many harbors in the Bahamas have massive banks and land areas to weather of your boat, and you can't feel the real wind; such harbors as **Landrail Point, West Caicos, Providenciales,** and **Rum Cay's Flamingo Bay.** You can't even get the real gradient wind in **Georgetown** in anything but north through east, because southeast and west from there lie 60 to 90 nautical mile fetches over land and banks. On the north and south coasts of the Greater Antilles, in prevailing conditions, the harbor wind can blow at times greater and at times much less than the wind *just a half mile offshore.* In **Boquerón,** Puerto Rico, it can blow 15 knots from the west, while, only five miles away on the south coast, it blows 20 knots from the east. In **Salinas, PR,** the wind will go to zero at night, while outside the reef, only one mile away, it will still blow 20 knots. Each anchorage and harbor has unique and complicated variables which contribute to its diminishing, increasing or changing of the direction of the real wind. Therefore:

Ignore all harbor wind from Georgetown south, except for the telltales of the cycling of the trades.

Watch the cycling of the wind's direction and strength and take your exit only on a down-tick of a cycle, taking advantage of reduced wind speeds and southerly trends. On the north coast of the Dominican Republic, for instance, moderated **prevailing conditions** means less than 15 knots and south of east, to ensure you get shielded from the eye of the wind by the bulk of that great island. Even then, you need to go in the **night lee.**

To watch the winds, you should construct a table such as the one presented in the section on *Crossing the Mona Passage.* This technique tracks the winds and establishes a baseline from which to discern "up-ticks" and "down-ticks" in the strength of the trades. Always use the **NWS Offshore Report** winds. Average the forecast winds for both zones if you find yourself on the borderline of two forecasts, or near a significant weather feature in one of them. For example: if you lie near 73° with a forecast of

W OF 73W WINDS E 15 TO 20 KT and E OF 73W WINDS E TO SE 20 TO 25 KT

then assume you shall have winds of east by south 20 knots. You shall not normally lie so simply equidistant from different forecast areas. Normally you'll have to use weighted averages, favoring the nearer area but giving *English* to the farther one. Though a little complicated with 3 areas at play (e.g., the **Mona**), you can still do it, more or less the way you do it by eye when studying up to 4 differing wind arrows around your position on a surface analysis chart. Always, of course, leave harbor on the *beginning* of a downtrend in the wind strength cycle, never at the middle nor near to its end.

Some examples follow of harbor telltales I've found to work. Coupled with your tracking of the cycles in the NWS's report of the **gradient wind** outside the harbor, the additional information you receive from these telltales give you a sure indicator of your position on a cycle. You can confirm both *when* your weather window opens and for *how long*.

On the south and north coasts of the Greater Antilles, in normal trade weather, and in the absence of perturbing weather features such as fronts and waves, the daily progression of the time at which the morning winds rise in harbor indicates the trade cycles.

In **Puerto Plata**, one friend suggests watching the mountain. If the clouds haven't crowned the mountain by 11 a.m., he says, you can go. In **Salinas**, PR, watch the clocking of your spreader flags from northeast to southeast in the morning. It will start earlier (or later) each day and take shorter (or longer) to finish clocking.

Telltale: harbor wind down to Force 3 by 3 p.m.

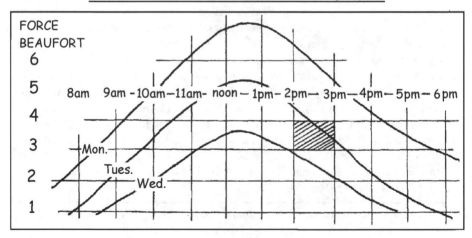

In **Luperón** observe the clocking of the winds each day and the cycle of their strengths day to day. The prevailing easterlies come back down to earth along about 9 in the morning along the coast, much earlier at sea, and farther out, they never lift. They reach a maximum between 1 p.m. and 3 p.m., tapering off to a calm as early as 5 p.m. or as late as 10 o'clock at night. If you read maximum strength during the day as, say Force 5, and it goes down to Force 3 by 3 p.m. (having raised to no more than Force 3 by 9 am), get going! The rule, then, says: "Force Three by Three".

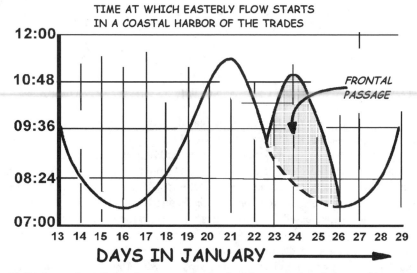

TIME AT WHICH EASTERLY FLOW STARTS
IN A COASTAL HARBOR OF THE TRADES

DAYS IN JANUARY ➤

Telltale: what time the nocturnal wind loses out to the seabreeze

One can also watch cycles in the endurance of the **nocturnal wind** over the daytime **seabreeze**. I constructed this plot in Luperón. It clearly shows the regular cycle of the winds which become masked, but not ultimately deformed, by a **front**.

You can make your own plot as simply as I did. When you hear your chain rattle against the bowsprit each morning, as the boat turns to face the rising wind, chunk the time into a spreadsheet on your computer. You can make it as simple as a keystroke with a macro.

FLYING WINDOWS

The trade winds blow for thousands of miles. They amount to a river of air that follows the Canaries Current southwest, bend with the **Coriolis Force**, and sweep into the Caribbean through the Windward and Leeward island chains. Just as a river does, this fluid stream meanders a bit and eddies some. Like turbulence in a river, the trade winds have some memory of upstream events. Watch the reports closely and regularly, and you shall begin to see the stream of air switching a bit like a cat's tail: east to east-southeast, to southeast by north, then back up to east. This might happen for just a day, or even less. Often I see these switches moving toward me, but they don't endure. Then again, occasionally they do happen, as the following tale tells.

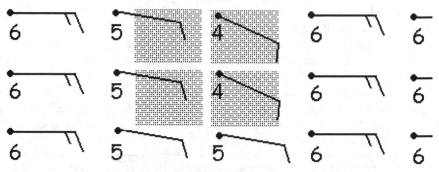

A narrow window moving in the river of air.

My waits for weather keep me busy. Radio weather schedules keep me bound to the boat for 4 hours a day at least. Not for others. Occasionally a bored Type A with nothing to do hangs on my rail during my breakfast, or worse, while I copy a weather report. He usually starts with, "Charlie says it looked pretty good today. Whatcha think?" I should answer, "I don't know because I'm talking to you instead of copying the weather!" I try to harness my tongue. So normally I answer that I don't know, because truthfully, despite all my attention to looking for a window, I don't know for sure I've got one until I've left.

The more we know, the more questions we can think of. The more variables at play, the more confusing it can get. At the end I commit or I don't.

For some time I had waited in **Samaná** to cross the **Mona Passage**. A 12 hour period of 10 to 15 knot winds appeared in the NWS **Offshore Report**. It stayed there for 24 hours, or for 4 reports. It then moved up to the 12 hour section for Thursday with forecasts of 15-20 knots straddling it for the 12 hour periods of Wednesday and Thursday nights. On a chance of shooting it, I cleared out, shifted to a clean, short rode and waited for the 6 p.m. report. It still came on. I left to meet it 90 miles to the east, midway in the Mona Passage.

Two skippers, experienced sailors as it turned out, dinghied up beside me while I raised anchor. (Why always then?) They wanted to know what I knew about the weather. I couldn't press my five days of study into a few minutes for them.

I told them I wanted to shoot a *flying window*, leading it much like you lead birds with a gun. I had little time for them. I had to work against the sun and against a moving 12 hour window that I wanted to catch just in the Mona Passage.

If the window evaporated by morning, I planned to hole up in **Punta Macao** at the edge of the Mona. I urged them not to go. They'd not done the Mona before. They had no knowledge of Punta Macao. They had not put away their boats. They hadn't cleared out. Nonetheless, all enthused, they raced off to clear out and get under way.

I followed my usual ploy, motorsailing the **night lee** of the Dominican coast. In the morning I dawdled as usual outside Punta Macao until the 6 a.m. report. The window had not evaporated! I rode a truly gorgeous starboard tack, flanking the evening thunder storms west of Puerto Rico, in not more than 13 southeast knots. Then, as usual, I drifted down the Puerto Rican **night lee** to a morning arrival at Mayagüez, playing my favorite tapes, singing all the way, and arriving 32 hours after anchors up. The two behind me spent 60 hours getting hammered. For that story, turn to the passage notes on the Mona.

PICKING WINDOWS

The criteria for good weather windows changes for every harbor and each destination and, of course, every boat and crew. That said, I do try in the passage and harbor notes to provide as solid guidelines as possible which applies to most all boats under the most common conditions. I'll give you the conditions *worse than which I won't go.*

Common sense must prevail. For instance, I stress my sailing tactic for sailboats on the Mona Passage because that solid advice applies to all sailboats in the most commonly available weather window. Does it mean you can't motor across in a dead flat calm? Duh.

Some absolutes do exist, however, and you shall find them throughout in subsections entitled *Picking Windows*. For example, you should not stop in any Dominican north coast harbor between Puerto Plata and Samaná with any kind of northerly swell running. Nor should you do that coast in an onshore wind.

Like fish, large windows appear rarely, but little ones swarm in their multitudes. They get you here to there in short hops sooner than you can find a rare big one.

ISLAND STRATEGIES

This book intends to help cruisers plan *windward passages* on the way south, *not* to give the cruiser a precise road map and timetable for the cruise.

Descriptions of the islands, and the anchorages themselves, are provided to support the sailing directions, not to rehash information adequately covered in the guides for the Bahamas, the Virgins, the Leewards, Windwards and South America. Use those guides to cruise those areas. Use this book to transit between them.

When you have tired of cruising one area, and you want to move on to the next, you must have a specific strategy in mind while planning the passage: a strategy to move you to windward from point A to point B with *safety* and *comfort*: a **thornless passage**.

This section provides cruisers with the planning strategies essential to creating their own **Thornless Path** between their chosen landfalls. These rules of the **Leisure Sailor**, when inflexibly adhered to, create a delightful cruise. Sometimes seeming just rules of elementary seamanship, which we all should know, all of the disasters I have met while going south have generated from the failure to obey any one of them.

If I tell you, as on the north coast of the DR, 5 rules to follow, and you choose to follow only 4, you may do so with moderate success 9 out of 10 times. By at least the 10th time, however, you will lose your boat. Simple? If you don't understand why I recommend a course of action, study up on the rule again. Don't do 4 out of 5, 9 out of 10.

WAIT FOR WEATHER

It always amazes me that retired cruisers, who, with nothing but time, and having piddled around in harbor for weeks, even months, suddenly break into hives if they can't go *right now*! Others insist on going "next Tuesday", or "on the 22nd". Year upon year, like the *Tortoise and the Hare*, I pass them where they hole up with repairs, breathing hard.

These folks, whom earlier I watched go stir-crazy waiting for a break in the weather, give up their wait and go to sea because, as they say,

"It's rolly here."

I change to a less rolly anchorage.

Or they say, "it's best to take bad medicine all at once."

I refuse to take any bad medicine.

Seasoned salts say, "We've got a strong boat."

I've got a strong boat, but it has a weak me inside it.

The stoic downeaster usually says "We've seen worse!"

I remember all my worses all too well. I won't repeat them.

And everyone uses the "well, we sailed with a group and ..." excuse.

If you want good passages rather than good excuses, learn to interpret the **weather forecasts**, the **sea conditions** and the **island effects**. And thoroughly understand the concept of **weather windows**.

THINK BEAUFORT

FB	knots wind	descriptive term	SEA CRITERIA	waves in feet
0	0	calm	sea like a mirror	0
1	1-3	light air	ripples, but no foam crests	¼
2	4-6	light breeze	small wavelets with glassy crests	1
3	7-10	gentle breeze	crests begin to break, glassy foam	2-3
4	11-16	moderate breeze	fairly frequent white horses	4-5
5	17-21	fresh breeze	long waves, many white horses	6-8
6	22-27	strong breeze	extensive foam crests, some spray	9-13
7	28-33	near gale	sea heaps up, foam blown in streaks	13-19
8	34-40	gale	spindrift forms, clear foam streaks	18-25
9	41-47	strong gale	tumbling crests, dense foam streaks spray may affect visibility	23-32
10	48-55	storm	long, overhanging crests; great patches of dense foam streaks; surface of sea appears white; tumbling of sea heavy and shocklike.	29-41
11	56-63	violent storm	sea completely covered with long white patches of foam; everywhere the edges of the wave crests blown into froth; bad visibility.	37-52
12	74	hurricane	Air filled with foam and spray; sea completely white with driving spray; visibility very seriously affected.	45+

The Force Beaufort Wind Scale

Work in **Force Beaufort**. It accustoms you to consider overall sea conditions including recent or pending changes.

The **Beaufort Wind Scale** encompasses both wind and wave. The Beaufort ratings assume relatively stable conditions. For instance, you can't call a nice 10-15 knot breeze in the morning after three days of 25-30 knots a Beaufort Force Four. The wind driven waves of 3 to 5 feet roll over residual swells heaped to 8 to 10 feet!

PREVAILING EASTERLIES

In the winter months the prevailing easterlies run between northeast by east and east-southeast at Force 5 to 6. In the summer, May through October, they run east-northeast to southeast by east at Force 4 to 5. If the **Offshore Report** for the eastern Caribbean forecasts either a southeast or a northeast wind, look for a significant weather feature such as a **tropical wave** in summer, a **front** in winter, or an unusually strong **high** or **low** to weather of the zone. The trades *never* blow true northeast or southeast.

Swells from the 3000 mile fetch of the Atlantic Ocean litter the route south. They get superimposed with swells from distant storms and, of course, waves from local wind and chop from currents. These all slow windward progress and make for uncomfortable sailing when compared with similar wind strengths at home. Cutters and spoon-bowed sloops may carve through these conditions better than clipper or schooner bows. The going can get extremely rough. Cutters may have their expected way cut by 20%, clippers by half.

Here's a good Beaufort rule of thumb for all hull configurations in these waters, assuming settled conditions for the next 36 hours. Starting with a rhumb line dead to windward, add one Force Beaufort for each compass point working aft from the bow until reaching Force Six. For example, if you have a forecast for 48 hours of light airs with a few ripples on the sea, you may motor to windward. If it shall blow 17 to 21 knots aft of your beam, with a few white horses, you'll have a good sail, but not a good trawl.

The jocks in their yellow slickers eating cold beans from cans go in Force 5 forward of the beam. The **Leisure Sailor**, whether power or sail, sails in swimsuit and eats pate from china (Corningware unbreakable?) plates.

Expressed in degrees (**D**) of the wind off the bow, the **Force Beaufort** (F_B) you want should not exceed:

$2 + D/30$, max. $6F_B$, or, for the purist, **half the square root of D, max. $6F_B$**.

Never start out in a Force 6-7, but if one develops on the quarter, ride it all you can and don't shelter. Unless you missed something major, it won't grow stronger. Finally, if you need a slicker and you can't sail in a bathing suit, you should not have left harbor.

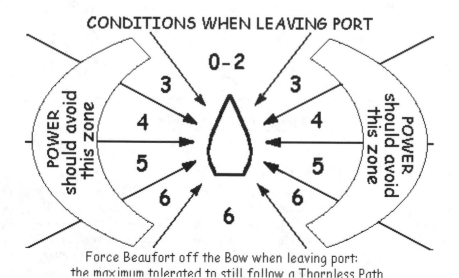

CONDITIONS WHEN LEAVING PORT

0-2

3   3

POWER should avoid this zone   4   4   POWER should avoid this zone

5   5

6   6

6

Force Beaufort off the Bow when leaving port:
the maximum tolerated to still follow a Thornless Path

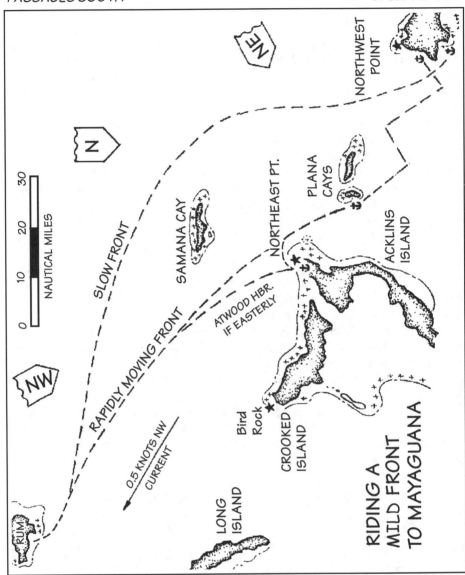

Riding Mild Fronts to Mayaguana

GRIM AND GREY CAN GO GREAT

In the winter months you may ride *mild* **front**s down to the Caribbean. A new front makes up every week in early winter, every few days in midwinter. By April you'll be lucky to get two good ones all month. They not only get less frequent but they get slower and weaker late in the season. With luck they'll slow and stall as they sweep down on your little boat, giving you days of pleasant, if somewhat gray, reaching and running. Even luckier if the stalled front backs up as a warm front giving you two rides for your money.

PLAN YOUR ROUTE FLEXIBLY

This rule, and the next three, deal with the strategy for choosing anchorages while wending the Thornless Path under continuously changing conditions. The bottom principle to this rule: avoid the *idée fixée,* or what the French see as foolishly stubborn.

One acquaintance left the sanctuary of **Salinas** just before Hurricane Dean to sit in its path at **Fajardo**. His logic, as such, said that Fajardo was "closer to St.Thomas" which, *in his mind*, meant some sort of terminus, or cusp, in his cruising plans. His *idée fixée* nearly did end it all for him at Fajardo. He got nailed by Hurricane Hugo. The last boat to shelter at the overflowing hole, he'd dithered about because he didn't have fallback plans.

THINK TWO MOVES AHEAD

When planning your next leg consider what conditions shall prevail at each destination, and what steps you might have to take when you get there. Like moves in chess, your maneuverability at your next position (and your next...) should be thoroughly considered.

Sometimes stay: Sailing to **Clarence Town** from **Rum Cay** might end your frustration of waiting day after day for the wind to change from dead east, but it might guarantee you two days of motoring against wind, wave and current, while slogging from Clarence Town to **Landrail** to **Attwood Harbor**. Take two more days of the world's finest snorkeling in good companionship at Rum in exchange for those two days of the wham-bangs spent in mutual disgust. When you roll at Rum, jibsail down the bay and round the corner to anchor in flat calm on the white sand beaches of the western shore. Or to Flamingo Bay on the northeast corner of Rum in a prolonged southeaster.

Sometimes go: If the wind goes light to 12 knots but doesn't change to the direction you want, you may leave harbor anyway, exercising an alternate plan to go off on the other tack to a different anchorage, at a more stately, close-hauled pace than you had wanted. Or you could motor flat-out to your original goal. Either choice shall alter your original plan. Landfall or arrival times have changed. Therefore other contingent conditions have changed: the angle of light for reading the water, the distance to the next comfortable harbor when your **weather window** closes, and so on.

In other words, plan flexible landfalls, even while enroute. And never, of course, *ever* set a schedule or a deadline. Don't hang up on a particular destination as though you had a pot of gold under only one particular rainbow.

PASSAGE ELAPSE TIMES

To estimate the time required to make a specific passage while using the strategies in this book, you must add *time underway* to *time waiting for weather.* When planning a cruise consider the time of year since winds shall vary depending upon season. Consider your mode of passage making. If a blow-boater, do you motor, or motorsail, at the slightest contretemps? Or do you follow the purist way and sail in whatever? If a stink-potter, do you blast into it or tack and wear with the seas?

I have had to whiz down islands to make business schedules associated with my ketch *Jalan Jalan,* chartering in the north, building a house in Puerto Plata, and refitting each year in Venezuela. I sailed down several times a season to work on the house between charters. Single-handed and uninsured, I traveled as fast as feasible with the welfare of both my boat and myself in mind. Many trips I made for pleasure, or just aimlessly wandering, which the expression *Jalan Jalan* means after all.

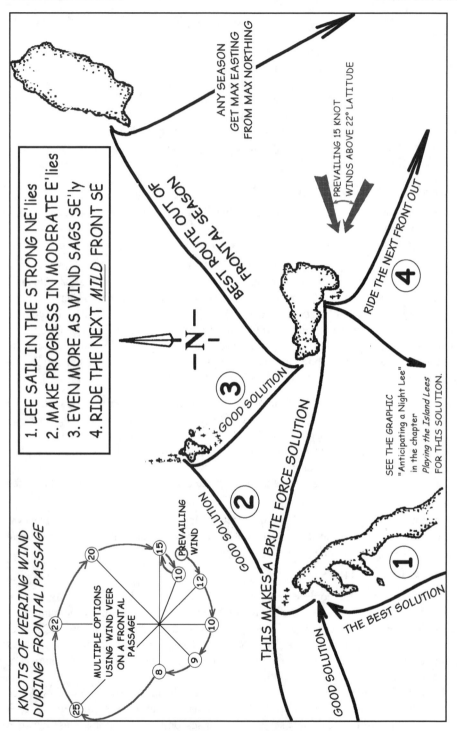

1. LEE SAIL IN THE STRONG NE'lies
2. MAKE PROGRESS IN MODERATE E'lies
3. EVEN MORE AS WIND SAGS SE'ly
4. RIDE THE NEXT *MILD* FRONT SE

ANY SEASON GET MAX EASTING FROM MAX NORTHING

PREVAILING 15 KNOT WINDS ABOVE 22° LATITUDE

BEST ROUTE OUT OF FRONTAL SEASON

RIDE THE NEXT FRONT OUT

④

③ GOOD SOLUTION

THIS MAKES A BRUTE FORCE SOLUTION

② GOOD SOLUTION

SEE THE GRAPHIC "Anticipating a Night Lee" in the chapter *Playing the Island Lees* FOR THIS SOLUTION.

KNOTS OF VEERING WIND DURING FRONTAL PASSAGE

PREVAILING WIND

MULTIPLE OPTIONS USING WIND VEER ON A FRONTAL PASSAGE

20 15 10 12 22 10 9 8 25

① THE BEST SOLUTION

GOOD SOLUTION

Alternate routes may take longer in distance but pass shorter in time and go easier on boat and crew.

We tacked directly to windward only under Force 4, accepting a 3.5 knot average. Despite those that claim tacks of 35° to the real wind (C. A. Marchaj, *Sailing Theory and Practice*, ISBN 0 229 64253 5, says you can't come under 37.5°), *Jalan* persisted in giving me a fat 50° on the passages described in this guide. I guess a 35 foot sloop with a 30hp auxiliary and a retired couple aboard should do about the same. With 50° tacks at 5 knots, you shall put 14.4 miles under the keel for each 10 miles on a windward rhumbline. With minimum of half-knot Equatorial Current against you, make it 16.6 miles. To make 5 knots you've got to have a Force 4-5 with seas 4 to 7 feet. You will lose way with those seas. You shall lose about one degree of course for each Beaufort number. So! A cruising boat should get *1.75 keel miles to each rhumbline mile* while tacking. Less than 2 knots!

Despite all this many cruisers ask me exactly how long a particular leg will take *their boat* with *them* making *their* decisions. Well, calculate the speed you make under full motor, against 20 knots of wind, three quarters knots of contrary current and short 8 foot seas. Add thirty percent for leeway and optimism. That ought to work!

Cruising takes time. Each stop you make will require rest and recuperation, perhaps some touring or local cruising, and get-togethers with other cruisers. For example, novice cruisers try to make Rum from Georgetown. Experienced crews go through **Conception**. I sometimes do those 60 miles to **Rum Cay** from **Georgetown** by following the clocking winds of a medium front to **Long Island**. When the northeast winds blow themselves out and flag briefly south of east, I go to **Conception** for diving on **Southampton Reef**, then I take the leg to Rum at the end of the **weather window**, where I again wait for weather.

DAY	LOCATION OF FRONT	WIND DIR. AND SPEED	ANCHORED THAT NIGHT	ACTIVITY
1	NO. FLORIDA	E-SE 15-20	REDSHANKS	Partying
2	CEN. FLORIDA	E-SE 15	FOWL CAY	Staging
3	SO. FLORIDA	S-W 10-15	SALT POND	Cruising
4	NASSAU	NW-N 20-25	SALT POND	Waiting
5	OUT ISLANDS	NE 20-25	SIMMS	Cruising
6	HISPANIOLA	E-NE 20	JOE'S SOUND	Cruising
7	PUERTO RICO	E 15-20	CALABASH BAY	Cruising
8	DISSIPATING	E-SE 10-15	CONCEPTION	Diving
9	DISSIPATED	E-SE 15	RUM-PT.NELSON	Partying
10	NO. FLORIDA	E-SE 15-20	RUM-FLAMINGO BAY	Snorkeling
11	CEN. FLORIDA	E 15-20	RUM-WEST COAST	Fishing
12	SO. FLORIDA	E-SE 15	RUM-PT.NELSON	Staging

Find the log in the table below· *Five pleasurable miles a day* folks!

If you haven't partied out when a good **weather window** opens up, or your favorite serious child flies down to visit the wastrel parents fiddling her inheritance away in the Caribbean, and you miss the leading edge of the first window, then *add more time on your total cruise.* In fact you the best plan would have you wintering in the Bahamas, spend hurricane season in DR and PR, the next winter in the Virgins, Leewards and Windwards, the next summer in Venezuela and the third winter in Trinidad. Now you've got lots of time.

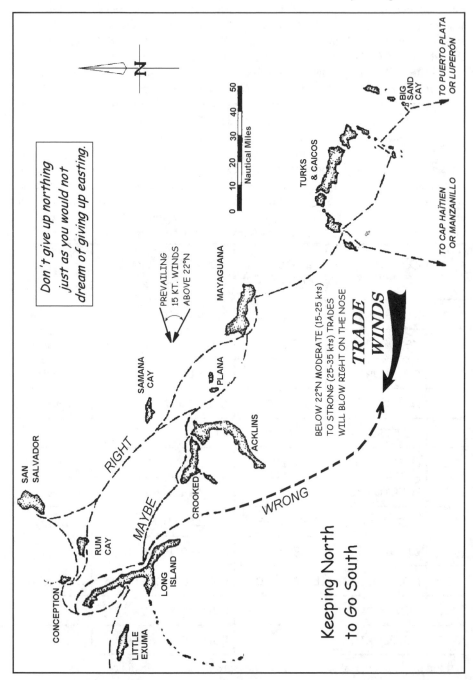

KEEP TO THE NORTH TO GO SOUTH

Given a choice of routes, you should give weight to the *northernmost* to preserve any windward advantage. The Caribbean lies to the south*east*, not to the south. Consider that the "collective eye" of the **prevailing winds** blows east to east-southeast. In order to maximize your possible **weather windows** you have to widen your angle on the wind. Either you must get *over* the eye of the wind to sail south-southeast, or you must sail *under* it to sail east-northeast. To do the latter requires fitting wheels on your boat to cross Hispaniola, an expensive procedure. I recommend gaining easting by using the prevailing southeast-erly flow while sailing through the islands up north, then spending the windward advantage accumulated by sailing south-southeast.

You play the **island effects** and the slight switches in the wind. If you find yourself in Great Inagua and your windward rhumbline plots east-southeast, the wind will *never* switch enough for you to lay it. So, when you choose your routes each day, have upper-most in your mind that you *don't give up northing*, just as you wouldn't give up easting.

Only masochists take the **Great Inagua** route, lured by the easy 65 south-southeast miles of **Long Island** early on in the trip. I have sat in Georgetown and seen a 120 foot charter schooner, with English crew, leave for that route. A contingent of yachties followed. After all, didn't those big boat *professionals* know best?

The answer? "*No!* They had never done it before."

But, anyway, the cruising couple in their sixties with a 35 footer and a 25 hp engine, let alone the 50 foot ketch with the 120 hp diesel and bow-thrusters, cannot compete with a passel of temporary hires behind 1200 horses dragging the bottomless purse of some foundation. They invariably find themselves slogging directly into the eye of the **trades**, more prevalent farther south. They also must buck into the mainstream of the **Equatorial Current**, which runs three quarters of a knot NNW in the **Crooked Island Passage** and up to *one and a half knots* WNW along Hispaniola (though normally three quarters knots). And in their wake drifts the broken flotsam of retired cruisers with the jetsam of their broken marriages and relationships. Think I jest? When you get as far as the Dominican Republic, start interviewing yachties that took this mistaken route. You will hear their stout denials: "it wasn't at all a rough trip, it was a good trip, really — glad we came that way, because Rum Cay was too rolly ... ", etc. "Why didn't you wait it out in Flamingo Bay on the northwest corner of Rum?" "Well, we were with a group and ... well ..."

In Luperón, notice how the Great Inagua group preoccupy themselves with quite major repairs, compared to your *to-do* list. See Great Inagua on the road back, along with **Hog Sty Reef.** To "go south", unless you want to go to Jamaica, *keep north.!*

LET LANDFALL DETERMINE DEPARTURE

In the Bahamas plan your departure to make landfall in favorable light, arriving with *several hours* of daylight left. The way south has many windward shore anchorages (i.e., entered to the east) where you will need the sun high and over your shoulder. A 3 p.m. landfall may dictate a 4 a.m. start. If you like to wake at 7 a.m. and have your Wheaties before addressing the world, and you don't want to break that custom, then sell the boat and move ashore. Almost every leg of the *Thornless* Path requires an early start, even a start in the dark, in order to benefit from **island effects** that reduce headwinds.

Have a variety of departure plans ready for different breaks in the weather and for different landfalls. Prepare to cancel all your commitments and haul anchor at the first opening of a **weather window** meeting one of your plans. Similarly, never plan a last minute chore, such as one friend who wanted to buy cold milk when the store opened at 8 a.m. That bottle of milk caused him to miss an earlier departure. When the situation altered, he tried to use the change in the weather despite a later start and got pinned down in Long Island. I reached **Mayaguana** before he left **Long Island**. Two weeks later, while I dined in **Puerto Plata**, he had a window slam on his tail and suffered some delamination problems from all the pounding he took. He returned to Georgetown. The lengths of the windows and the lengths of the legs just didn't go together for him. The morals to this story?

Plot several routes contingent on breaking weather.

Depart at the earliest time called for by your contingent routes so that you can alter course in response to changes in the weather.

Every delay in departure creates a risk upon arrival.

If in **Calabash Bay** at 11 a.m. expecting to lay **Rum Cay** on a wind north of east, and it instead goes to the south of east, *go anyway!* But go to **Conception Island** and depart earlier. Why? You won't **lee-bow** the currents and you must take an extra tack or two giving you a low light entry at Rum. So you have a motorsailer or a trawler, and you'll motor it? Well, even if you don't have to take sailing tacks, you'll still benefit from motoring tacks and shall cetainly make slower progress while pinching wind to Rum than reaching and rolling for Conception.

Reckon on 20% less speed to windward than you normally get. If you get more, great!

Contingency Planning

Most of us plan adequately when planning contingencies along the route. The discussion above illustrates a contingency of over-the-shoulder light on landfall. Many other contingencies exist, so *leave yourself enough time.* When most cruisers quote how long it took them to make a passage they usually talk about offing to offing, ignoring the time taken with departures and arrivals. I quote hours of a passage from ready to up anchor to anchors down and set (e.g., Georgetown to Rum Cay: 60 nm including 8 nm getting out and in of the two harbors). When planning your route, add in contingencies both for getting underway and for getting settled at your new anchorage.

Contingencies Getting Underway...

the office hours at the customs shack for clearing out,

the light needed to wend your way out of a reef anchorage,

the anchors-up drills with lots of mangrove mud to clean off oneself and the boat,

getting the dinghy and motor aboard,

and on and on.

One wonders sometimes how one ever escapes some harbors. Different factors should worry you on the landfall side:

Contingencies of Landfall...

any reefs to navigate in over-the-shoulder light,

time to nose around selecting a safe and shallow spot in which to anchor,

getting the dinghy and motor down before shoreside closings,

properly put the boat to bed in a new anchorage with an eye to 2 a.m. anchor drills.

Passage planning must consider timing of arrival at capes as well as at landfalls.
See the section on *Playing the Island Lees: Cape Effects.*

Tally the time taken by the above lists, then add a couple of hours of safety margin. You shall discover that navigating some hours in the dark seem inevitable for most passages. I've learned to **stage** (see below) my departures to reduce contingencies. I've also learned to benefit from the night to make safer passages and safer landfalls.

NEVER MISS A SUNDOWNER

A leisurely gin and tonic at sundown, with the boat all squared away and ready to move again, should end every Bahama landfall. Not a frivolous rule, to *never* miss a **Sundowner Gin & Tonic** you've got to plan your navigation with lots of margin for engine stops, adverse currents and so on. In order to make your landfall in time to get down secure anchors, square away yourselves and the ship, and make yourselves comfortable with a drink by sundown, you must make your anchorage several hours before. The **SG&T** (some of my friends leave out the gin) reward you for good planning. Never miss it.

IF IN DOUBT, STAY OUT

A two million dollar, 92 foot ketch lay on the rocks outside Puerto Plata for three months. It stranded there only one month after launching in Ft. Lauderdale. They went aground early on a clear night at the foot of the light house at the *fortaleza* San Felipe.

Even after scrupulously following all the rules, Murphy's Law eventually will catch up with you. If you can't make the tidy daylight landfalls suggested here, or you just feel uncomfortable with an entrance under some conditions, stand way out to sea, set the boat to an easy jog in open water, or heave-to and go below in watches. A properly hove-to boat makes you snug as a baby's cradle. Of course you make coffee your **SG&T** at sea.

STAGE YOUR DEPARTURE

The most common fault while planning a passage poses the gravest threat to the boat: underestimating the endurance of the crew. Not planning sufficient reserves of stamina to satisfy **Murphy's Law** guarantees you shall need more. We often make judgments based on our younger selves. You can shorten every leg on the way south by several hours in time, and a bucket or two of adrenaline, by one simple practice:

stage to a departure anchorage the day before leaving.

Get away from the crowd. Get near the sea. Get your dinghy up. Go to one shallow hook. Clean up all your rodes. Make sea-ready on deck and below. Take in a reef while at anchor. You'll easier shake out a reef than tie one in later. Take a swim and a snorkel. Eat a candlelight dinner, listen to music, read a book. Turn in early. Turn out an hour before anchors-up. Watch the dawn, or listen to the night. Hoist a cup of coffee or two. Then hoist sail, bring aboard that shallow single rode, fall back on the wind, and slide out. You'll shorten the first leg by an hour or more, sometimes much more. Why do all that work just before departure, then sail out of the inner harbor with muddy decks and sweaty crew?

In Georgetown, you get four miles ahead of the game if you stage at the **Fowl Cay** exit.

By going to the **Martín Pinzón** anchorage in **Luperón**, you save a mile and perhaps several hours, or a whole day if the *comandante's* people have wandered off while you cursed the muck on your anchor in the inner harbor.

In **Samaná**, the afternoon winds caroming off the coast can create a terribly heavy chop in the 8 mile entrance channel which usually doesn't lay down until after dark. Stage in the morning to the sand anchorage behind **Cayo Leventado.** There you can make a safe night exit after the seas have subsided but still with time to make **Cabo Engaño** by 8 a.m. If you stay in harbor, at least go to a clean, short rode to avoid delays on departure.

In **Salinas**, Puerto Rico, stage yourself onto the tough slog to **Punta Tuna** by taking the relatively short leg to **Puerto Patillas.** But first stage yourself to **Boca de Infierno** by taking those 5 windward miles in the shelter of the reefs. Many elect to stay awhile in those peaceful anchorages. The advantage only becomes apparent to those that don't do those stages: the motorsail around the archipelago of cays east of Salinas can take several hours, and the motorsail over to Patillas, though only 13 miles, becomes miserable more than a couple of hours after daybreak. In this area Puerto Rico sticks out the most into the onshore **Equatorial Current** with shoaly, hard to read water, and with a rough chop.

In **St.Georges**, Grenada, whether bound for Venezuela or Trinidad and Tobago, stage over to **Morne Rouge Bay** and leave from there.

Stationing yourself on the harbor nearest the pass you want to cross in the **Lesser Antilles** will get you in to the next island before the lunchtime squalls.

Cleaning up and waiting for weather in **Trinidad's Scotland Bay** or **Tinta Bay** on **Chacachacare** gets many miles behind you, and makes a relaxing interlude.

I could go on forever with examples. If you haven't started staging your departures already, spend a few years *cruising*, not *sitting*, in the Caribbean. You shall quickly learn to spend your last day on an island staged at a lonely cleanup anchorage on every step of the path, however insignificant.

Staging into harbors to rest and clean up before clearing in also makes a lot of sense.

DON'T FEAR THE DARK

Caribbean cruising calls for 8 to 15 hour passages, anchors up to down. When one considers all the conditions and requirements upon getting underway, a 6 hour sail easily becomes 9 hours, and even that short leg to windward may cause a night landfall.

For instance, I leave **Grenada** for the Venezuelan **Testigos** Islands after sunset to ensure a well lit mid-morning landfall. Rather than push out of the **St.Georges** crowded lagoon and busy harbor in the dark, I stage the day before to an easy night departure site in **Morne Rouge Bay** just outside. I moor off the windward beach with a clean rode and a short scope. At nightfall I hoist sail in the gentle breeze, lift the shortened anchor aboard and, making coffee below, I ghost out beyond the island's lee where I take up my course for Testigos. No rounding up in 25 knots of wind to raise sail with sheets flogging and snarling on the pinrails. No sweating and cursing over fouled and muddy ground tackle.

Bound for Turks and Caicos from the Bahamas, I stage myself in **Mayaguana** to the beach at **Southeast Point**. Leaving at midnight I have a pleasant 15 knot apparent wind close reach of only 35 miles to **Providenciales** instead of a 50 mile close hauled beat into 20 knots apparent wind from **Start Bay** or **Abraham Bay**.

To sail from Caicos to **Cap Haïtien** or to **Manzanillo**, in the Dominican Republic, I first move from **Sapodilla Bay** over to a **West Caicos** mooring, or depending on conditions, to the entrance of the Caicos ship channel. Before dawn I hoist my reefed sail and fall back on the light night wind from the banks. After I've breakfasted underway, the lee of the reefs gives way and I'm reaching in midmorning trades. That night the loom of either **Monte Cristi** or **Cap Haïtin** lead me into Hispaniola's night lee where the land breeze warms my cheek and crowds my nostrils with the scents of cows, grasses and charcoal fires. I anchor near the customs dock in a flat calm even before the officials arrive, and of major importance, I clear in and motor off into the mirror calm **Estero** before the trades come up.

You can make many anchorages in the dark also. I have often sailed into **Pittstown Landing**, Acklins, or **West Plana**, both in the Bahamas, by only starlight. **Gros Islet Bay** outside **Rodney Bay** in St.Lucia and **Isabela**, just east of Luperón, also make fine night landfalls. In most of these cases the windward beach gently slopes with a long shelf of sand without keel hinder. From a mile or more out one can luff into the mild **night lee** until the sounder shows just a few fathoms. From that point on you can idle dead to windward, the clear sand below visible by only starlight. I creep into the wind until the bright white sand beach is off the bow, gently fall off in silent **nocturnal wind** and slowly feed out the anchor. A much easier exercise than making anchorage in full afternoon trades.

I've seen countless cases of the fear of night sails leading a cruising couple into problems. Take the **Mona Passage** for example. Not everyone has the patience to wait for a rare calm in order to transit the Mona in 24 hours, so many cruisers try to make it in two days and one night, because they "don't like night sailing". That may compromise their landfall to late in the second day. Just one pause to replace a blown raw water pump impeller, or slowing down to coddle an overheating engine, puts them precisely where they didn't want in the first place: close to land in the dark. I've seen several incidents where crews turned back exhausted after forty eight hours jilling around in the Mona under full trades precisely because they departed **Samaná** in the morning rather than the evening. No other factors differing, they could have had a delightful passage.

In **prevailing conditions,** a night departure from Samaná permits a lee motorsail down the Dominican coast, a slack northeast tack during the day, and a southeast tack in the lee of Puerto Rico on the second night. Two nights and a day often equals 24 hours of lee sailing and 12 hours of close reaching compared to 36 hours of beating and bucking full trades during two days and a night. Furthermore, potentially dangerous thunderstorms often cut loose from the land and drift westward off Puerto Rico in the late afternoons and evenings. Taking my tacks, I slip around and behind these colossal systems. Even more, while they weaken out at sea, their convections provide me some shifting and moderating of the trades even before I feel the lee of Puerto Rico, further reducing my exposure. Again, I have a dawn arrival with plenty of time to clear and get sorted out before the winds get up.

Every time I cross the Mona I meet boats who start out to do two nights and a day, but in the afternoon they find themselves irresistibly pulled by the direct rhumbline to Puerto Rico. They usually break faith and rev up for a run at the land, often darting into a wall of thunderstorms before arriving at 2 a.m., their landfall navigation aids obscured by a blaze of shore lights. Nerves frayed by the storms, they pick their way into harbor and tumble below exhausted at 4 a.m. They remain asleep while, rested, I trundle out the dinghy to go clear in only 3 hours later. What did they gain for those 3 hours?

Certain night passages often become mandatory, such as coasting to windward along the north shore of the Dominican Republic, along Puerto Rico's south shore and along the **Paria** peninsula in Venezuela. Besides being a required cruising skill, nighttime navigation has many benefits. You make earlier landfalls, leaving more time to investigate and enjoy your anchorage. You avoid sunburn and glare. Along with quieter watches you get cleaner radio reception and better visibility at sea. At night lights loom over the horizon, then stand out sharply while still many miles away with ship type, size, aspect and course instantly apparent. In daytime, everything blends into a vague blur on the hazy, headachy horizon. Far from a scary enemy, cruisers meet their best friend in the dark.

HUG THE SHORE AT NIGHT

The wise navigator, like **Columbus**, takes advantage of the **night lee** on the windward coasts. Modern sailing yachts sail well to windward under these light conditions and in calms they can proceed under auxiliary power instead of behind a rowed longboat like Columbus had to do. This technique applies to the north and south coasts of Hispaniola and Puerto Rico and the north coasts of Venezuela.

How Far Off?

My rule for coasting a hazard free coast: Steer by fathometer only, *not* GPS, and stay between 60 to 100 feet by day, or between 80 to 120 feet by night. Tthe **night lee** will give you a strip of really calm water that can stretch out 1 to 3 miles like an asphalt road. You'll even gain time by following the minor ins and outs of the fathom lines.

A Stress Test

Some cruisers find coasting at night stressful. Fight that stress with this test. Normally I steer a good watch on an inshore tack and go below to read or catnap on the offshore tack, relying on the rougher water to shake me out of the bunk so I can head her back inshore again. One year while reading below on an outward motor tack on the coasting run between **Cabo Macoris** and **Cabo Francés Viejo,** on the north coast of the DR, an incident occurred which, unfortunately, happens commonly among cruisers passaging south.

I heard a barely intelligible call on the VHF. Cruisers I'd met in Georgetown supposedly followed my advice to hug the coast with me. I marked my book place, heaved the cat off my lap and ambled back over the upright deck to the navstation.

My friend's voice over the radio reminded me of an old Charles Laughton movie where the terrified helmsman, lashed to the wheel during a survival storm and backdropped by mountainous seas, gets whipped by buckets of sea water and horizontally flying foam on the screaming wind while the ship groans onto her beam with every wave.

At any rate, that seemed the condition of his vessel and crew to judge by the sound effects coming over the VHF and the strain with which he spoke.

"Where the heck ARE you?" I asked.

"A-ABOUT FOUR...MIIIILES...OOOUT!" he cried stoically from the heart of the gale.

"Why not come inshore?" I asked after rescuing my peanut butter sandwich from the cat who almost dumped my coffee cup in her backward scurry.

"We ... WE'VE ... SEEEEN ... WORRRSE!" crackled the speaker.

Earlier, this same guy had insisted on punching on through the day rather than waiting for evening behind the Cabo Macoris headland at **Sosua** because *"people were saying we couldn't anchor there."* I had anchored off Sosua as usual and, after a refreshing four hour nap and a hot supper, I had continued on. Despite his earlier start I overtook him that night motorsailing inshore of him. And, even though I spent most of the next night anchored at **Escondido**, while he went on, he made **Samaná** only a few hours earlier than I.

Totally zonked out, he didn't clear customs until the next day while I, fully rested, cleared in immediately and went out to lunch with an old friend. Later, when I asked him again why he punched on in the daytime and why he didn't sail further inshore, he told me that his wife didn't want to sail at night, which they had to do anyway. He also said he worried about the rocks along the shore, which his chart told him didn't exist. You figure it.

If you get stressed hugging a windward coast at night, then I propose you take a stress test. Convinced you sail as close inshore as you dare? Talked yourself into accepting conditions as tolerable? Take this stress test. No matter how calm you may think you already have it, nudge the boat still closer inshore, keeping the depth over 100 feet. Nudge it again, then again. With each shoreward nudge you shall discover a strange paradox. Relaxing sea conditions and better boat speed and stability overcompensate the stress of nearing shore. With a good fathometer, you can forget your fear and stay inshore.

Don't make cruising either an Outward Bound course or an endurance contest for retireds. Navigating coasts that stretch along the trades requires good sense and planning, not a high tolerance for pain. I find the passage along the DR's north coast (your first test) a good trip, and I rarely see a white cap. If you round the capes in midday, or fail to coast close inshore at night, you shall indeed have an evil trip, and shame on you. Double shame if you venture out into 15 knots or more of forecast **gradient wind**, or wind which blows north of east, or in northerly swells coming from far away storms.

Hugging the shore pays a bonus by putting you inside the boundary layer ripple outside of which most trash floats. Whether a rock in a stream or an island in the trades, the same phenomenon that makes ducks fly in vees shall fend off most of the feared flotsam.

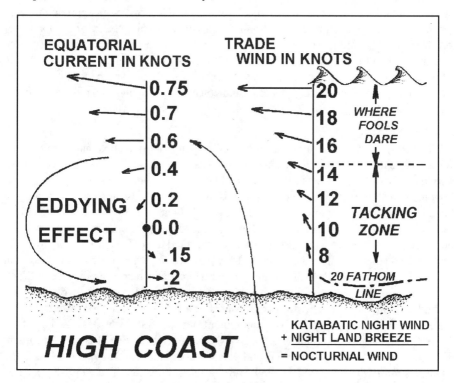

STRENGTH and DIRECTION OF WIND and CURRENT as a function of the DISTANCE OFFSHORE

COPYING THE WEATHER

THE OFFSHORE REPORT

Don't get fooled into using any other official report than the **Offshore Reports** of the **NWS' Tropical Prediction Center**'s **(TPC)** in Miami. The wind strengths and sea conditions given by this report, and this report only, form the basis of my directions. I have copied many thousands of these reports, *in situ*. I can certify their sufficiency for the routes and the harbors covered by this guide. (For Europeans, the Offshore Reports have their equal in the **Shipping Reports**.) Offshore Reports get read on VHF and HF by amateurs including HAMs. *Listen to rebroadcast Offshore Reports at your peril!*

You should use the Offshore Reports for the **Southwest North Atlantic** until Puerto Rico. From Luperón to Boquerón, use *both* the **NWS Offshore Report** for the **Southwest North Atlantic** and for the **Eastern Caribbean.** Stitch them together with averaging techniques and with attention to **island effects** on both sides of the **Mona Passage.** In Puerto Rico you can get fair **Coastal Reports** on NOAA VHF Wx channels, and from San Juan NAVTEX. From Salinas, PR, to Virgin Gorda, BVI, you get all the Offshore Reports plus the **Tropical Outlook** and the **Tropical Weather Discussion** on VHF Wx Channel 3.

The NWS's Offshore Report uses an internationally standard lingo with little variance. You can easily take shorthand notes each day and compare forecasts. The *changes* in the forecasts should interest you. For instance, if you have a forecast of an approaching cold front with a thunderstorm reach of 180 miles, moving at 20 knots, and with 20 knots of northwest wind behind it, you better batten down for the passage of a reasonably sized front. If, on the other hand, the previous report of this same front gave only a 100 mile radius and a forward speed of 15 knots with only 15 knots of wind behind it, you now know you've got a Grand Daddy of a blow and you must make condition red preparations. That thing's growing like *The Front That Ate Tokyo!* Watch the *changes.*

YOU NEED HARD COPY

When copying verbal reports I use the 3M Company's Post-It slips that I can stick up on the bulkhead over the radio. Because the forecasts get repeated in the identical format every day, my shorthand notes fill the slips in the same way and I can rapidly scan them, showing a weather picture developing, or disintegrating, just as those still pictures you flicked through with your thumb as a kid made the lady take her clothes off.

If you didn't have that colorful a childhood you may wish to employ another method such as recording the broadcast. People who do this tend to not have it written down and can't find it on the tape when they need it. They play you the whole rotten rigmarole from Georges Bank to Texas while they mutter about which day's recording they've got. You can't flip cassette tapes to get the change picture. If you record, *write* anyway while you listen, then replay immediately to correct your shorthand. And erase the blasted tapes!

You can get hardcopy right into your computer from your SSB by **NAVTEX.** NAVTEX on 516.9 USB (adjusted) broadcasts the SWNA and Caribbean Sea Offshore Reports in FEC code from Miami at 0700 EST, and every 4 hours thereafter. San Juan NAVTEX broadcasts *unreliably* at 0500 EST and every 4 hours thereafter. You can use your text editor to format these reports on your computer in such a manner that you can again flip through several reports on your screen and "see the lady take her clothes off".

DON'T LISTEN TO YOUR "BUDDY"

If you know the formats and lingo of the reports, you can separate the wheat from the chaff (nicely said) put out by some fellow yachtie on the SSB or VHF. For example, if Captain Hornblower gets on the horn and knowingly declaims the Offshore Report for the Eastern Caribbean as east 15 knots with swells 3 to 4 feet and waves 1 to 2 feet, you know he's full of it! The **Eastern Caribbean Report** does not give swells and waves, it gives sea conditions in overall heights with notable exceptions. He probably repeated the in-shore waters section of the Puerto Rican coastal report, about as useful as the beach report from Miami for a skipper crossing the **Mona Passage**. One yacht I know crossed the Mona, hearing on the Puerto Rico Coastal Report that waves ran to only one or two feet, forget the swells. When he returned to Samaná he adamantly insisted the NOAA report had gone wrong, and Hornblower continued as an accurate source. With forecasts on the path south, you may find your worst enemy in your best friend.

LEARN TO BE YOUR OWN WEATHERMAN

Study well the chapter on *Making Sense of the NWS Offshore Report*. Know your reports, the lingo and the area covered. And always listen to the same reports every day at the same time so as not to louse up your sense of progression -- remember, the *changes* count. Get hardcopy. Get it right from the **NWS**. Soon you'll *smell* the weather windows.

When you read reports and weather faxes, or listen to the nets, *don't confuse the map with the territory*. The gradient melodies they play on their smooth earth models don't include themes local land effects can play. Only you hear the terrestrial counterpoints.

REGULAR LISTENING

If you think you do a good job of tracking the weather because you catch the reports *most* of the time, as when not out to dinner, or because you listen to the **Offshore Reports** *almost* every morning, filling in with the evening report when you miss it, try this: record a piece of music leaving out one note per measure, change the key on one chord per measure, then delete the introduction, and the refrain. Now ask anybody to name the tune.

That's exactly what 99% of cruisers do, and they wonder what happened to all the windows. Be smart. Write up NMN offshore reports, or download and format them on your computer, *every* morning. Listen to several nets, Chris, Herb, George, Arthur, Maurice — whoever — every day. And, another gift, *listen to the entire net!* You'll get fills.

USING OTHER REPORTS

Even within the Offshore Report I've seen horrendous mistakes made in choice of report to use. One *professional* captain I knew insisted on taking the Northwest Caribbean forecasts while in the Bahamas. He earned the nickname Captain Nogo, because he made decisions based on conditions prevailing in Jamaica. Nonetheless, he read the weather on the Georgetown net, and everybody loved it. After all, as a *professional* sea captain ...

Start with the Offshore Reports. Don't accept rebroadcasters such as HAM nets if you can get the official source. Then fill in details and get experienced counsel from qualified forecasters such as **Herb** Hilgenberg (*Southbound II)*, or **Chris** Parker (*Belami*) of the **Caribbean Weather Center**. They give forecasts and routing tips for individual yachts interactively on Marine SSB. I've used their reports for many years. They know their job, and they make great teachers, *if you listen to the whole show*. With these as a basis, you now do *your* job and putty up the cracks with local conditions and land effects.

See page 57, *Boat Stuff: Using the Radio: Wx Broadcast Times and Frequencies*

COASTAL NOAA REPORTS

Use *only* on the coasts of Florida, the west and east coasts of Puerto Rico, and the Virgin Islands. On the west coast of Puerto Rico, the **night lee** off the land makes it *calm* at night in mild easterlies. Off the east coast of Puerto Rico there lies an 80 mile fetch to windward with islands and shallow, heated banks that provide a land-like night effect. Conditions on both east and west coasts of Puerto Rico usually conform to the San Juan Wx VHF **Coastal Report**s, which San Juan sends out on NAVTEX along with the Caribbean and Southwest North Atlantic Offshore Reports. You will find this referred to by HAMs and others as the "Puerto Rican Report". When crossing the Mona Passage, you can play off this report's sub-zone "out to 68°" against the Caribbean and the Southwest North Atlantic Offshore Reports. But in no case use it *in lieu of* the Offshore Reports.

HIGH SEAS REPORTS

Do *not* use the **High Seas Report**. It has no detail and gives maximum conditions for large areas. While the Offshore Report might home in within a degree or two of your position, this report gives you max conditions between you and Central America.

MAKING SENSE OF OFFSHORE REPORTS

For following the National Weather Service reports and the various cruiser nets, you must have a radio capable of receiving **Single Side Band**, Upper Side Band (SSB-USB).

In the Bahamas, the Caribbean and the Gulf of Mexico, listen to the NWS's **Offshore Forecast.** The Coast Guard's NMN station at Portsmouth, Virginia updates and broadcasts these reports every six hours. The Offshore Zones have the name because they report on zones lying off the *continental* shore. They include the Bahamas and all the Antilles. Even if you lie only 5 miles off the shore of one of these islands, you come under the heading of *offshore* (the *continental* shore).

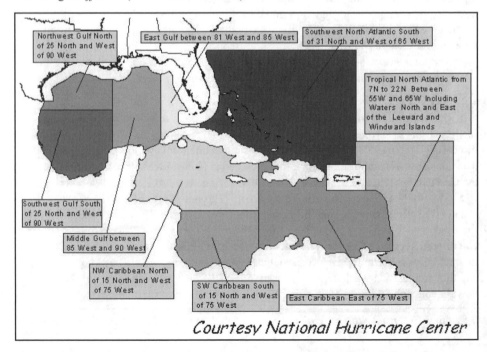

Courtesy National Hurricane Center

If in harbor awhile, I begin listening to the Offshore Reports *ten days* before leaving harbor. That ensures my listening and my shorthand get properly exercised before going to sea. Those ten days also let me develop a sense of rhythm and progression about the weather. In tropical trade wind areas, where the weather ardently pursues periodicity, one develops a prescience for its cycles. I get the early morning reports with my coffee. That way, since I live aboard, I never miss a report. I've seen no end of grief for cruisers simply because they listen to broadcasts at more convenient times like 1700. Then they eat dinner in town and miss the forecast one evening and catch up the next morning. They lack a sense of progression since they listen at different times of the day and not every day. Or worse, they rely on the guy anchored next to them. It boils down to just plain discipline.

The offshore reports use a fixed format and jargon which you shall understand only by repeatedly listening to the report for the same zone at the same time of day. The Boston and Washington, DC, offices of the NWS give forecasts for the zones under their responsibility, followed by the Southwest North Atlantic and Caribbean reports from the Miami office. Last, they read the Gulf of Mexico forecast from the New Orleans office. Each

U.S. NATIONAL WEATHER SERVICE		
MIAMI'S NATIONAL HURRICANE CENTER AND TROPICAL PREDICTION CENTER		
OFFSHORE REPORT		
TIME STAMP	time and date report issued (e.g., 0915 UCT 2/28/06)	
SYNOPSIS	positions and movements of fronts, lows and highs for the next 4 to 10 forecast periods	
FORECAST PERIODS	**MONDAY**	the next 12 hours (e.g., 0600-1800) *my* reliability score: 100%
12 hour periods of decreasing reliability rolled over in each 6 hourly broadcast starting at 0500 EST (0600 AST)	**MONDAY NIGHT**	the next 12 hours (e.g., 1800-0600) *my* reliability score: 95%
	TUESDAY	the next 12 hours (e.g., 0600-1800) *my* reliability score: 85%
	TUESDAY NIGHT	the next 12 hours (e.g., 1800-0600) *my* reliability score: 75%
3 TO 5 DAY OUTLOOK	up to 6 more successive 12 hour periods, perhaps with diminishing detail	

office's report begins with a time stamp, the time and date at which they released the report. But if technical problems arise, the Coast Guard may replay an old report in the absence of a new one. During Hurricane Hugo this went on for 17 hours. Some thought Hugo was stalled, and they began to venture out! If a yeoman screws up badly, you may get a report from last January. *Always* note the report's time stamp.

Refer to the diagram. They divide the Caribbean forecast into three sub-zones which get reported in sequence: northwest, southwest and eastern. Another zone, the Tropical North Atlantic extends east of the Lesser Antilles island chain between 7° and 22° degrees north. **NOTE:** the Caribbean Sea zone ends at the shores of land surrounding it, *not* at 22°.

The forecast begins with a synopsis of significant weather features in the zone, followed by at least four 12 hour periods beginning with the time on the time stamp. Then comes an "outlook", or longer range forecast, for a 24 to 96 hour period following the 48 hours already covered. The forecast for each period has wind (strengh and direction), sea heights and precipitation, *relative to the weather features given in the synopsis.* Swell gets reported when significant. All told, a minimum set of four 12 hour periods gets forecast every six hours for each wedge of territory defined by the Wx features. You interpolate wedges, just as you would eyeball a position between several wind barbs and wave heights on a Wx chart, and come up with a unique report for your boat's position.

BEAR IN MIND . . .

BOUNDARIES OF THE REPORT ZONES HAVE *IMPLICIT* COORDINATES.

The NW Caribbean Offshore Zone lies west of 75W and north of 15N. If, in the report for that zone, the analyst says "North of the front wind NE 15 knots", that does not mean you have NE 15 knots at 20N. That zone stops at the south coast of Cuba. The analyst works as a surgeon with an opaque sheet around the square of the operating zone. Nothing outside the zone gets mentioned. An impinging frontal system, if not affecting the zone during the forecast, shall not get mentioned. If you want to know about impending weather features, copy the zones to weather of you (east in the summer, north in the winter).

EAST TO SOUTHEAST DOES NOT EQUAL SOUTHEAST TO EAST.

Nor does it equal east-southeast. If the analyst has gone to the trouble of telling you "southeast to east", a movement counter to the diurnal flux of the trades, you can bet he means it. He means the wind shall more likely **back** than **veer** (see Glossary), usually a sign of strengthening trades. A veering trade usually portends weakening of the wind.

WHICH WEATHER SOURCE GIVES THE BEST RESULT?

Answer? All of them. I use Offshore Reports, Tropical Prediction Center Charts, and forecasters Herb and Chris. Yachties often compare the value of different sources, missing the *stereo vision* value of taking all of them together. All sources access the same data, but weight them differently. The U.S. Navy models get high marks from Herb. NWS' Tropical Prediction Center has consistency. And each one tells of developments at different times during the day, thus creating differences. In any case, get the *official, original* source, not a rebroadcaster. Beware of yachties, and HAM net operators, who just repeat "Thursday" instead of "*by* Thursday" or "*through* Thursday", losing you 8-16 hours on calling a front. *A 160 to 320 nautical mile mistake!*

On the south coast of Puerto Rico, you shall find near gradient wind, *Offshore Report conditions, immediately* **outside at night,** *not* **the Coastal Report conditions.**

SHORTHANDING THE OFFSHORE REPORTS

Consider this example: "south of the front and west of 70° west, winds east to southeast 15 to 20 knots, seas 4 to 7 feet; elsewhere (meaning south of the front and east of 70° west to the end of the zone at 65°) winds east 20 to 25 knots, seas 5 to 8 feet. Scattered thunderstorms west of 75° west." In shorthand this might look like the following:

$$S_F \text{ W70 } E\text{-}SE \text{ 15-20 } 4|7 \quad \exists \text{ E20-25 } 5|8 \quad S\theta \text{ W75}$$

Note that I use subscripts to indicate "of". Thus R_α means *remainder of area*, E_F means *east of the front*. Shorthand of voice reports beats garbled RTTY telexes. Compare my actual shorthand below that picked up "a second cold front will move SE from the Carolinas in the afternoon", which got garbled by the RTTY. Listen to later rebroadcasters to double check your copy from NMN, and you'll see how your shorthand improves.

CF cold front	**WF** warm front	**F** front	**R** ridge; remainder
Fl frontal line	⊙ center (low)	**S_F** south of front	**N_R** north of ridge
2d today	**2n** tonight	**2m** tomorrow	**SMTW θ F δ** (days)
am morning	**pm** afternoon	**ℓ_g** late	△ little change
nr near	**fr** from	**bt** between	**fw** few
lg large	α area, along	∃ elsewhere	θ through, T-storm
stn stationary	→ moving	**bld** building	**bc** becoming
v decreasing	∧ increasing	<> less than, etc.	≤ up to
W widely	**O** Outlook	**D** depression	**S** scattered, showers
G gale	**GW** gale warning		

Legend for My Shorthand System

RTTY NAVTEX vs. Shorthand

OFFSHORE MARINE FORECAST NATIONAL WEATHER SERVICE MIAMI 0915 UCT TUE FEB 11 1992
CARIBBEAN SEA AND SW N ATLC BEYOND 50 NM FROM SHORE.
. SW N ATLC S OF 32N AND W OF 65W
...GALE WARNING N OF 29N E OF 73W TODAY...

.SYNOPSIS...GALE CENTER ABOUT 150 NM SW OF BERMUDA EARLY THIS MORNING MOVING RAPIDLY NE. COLD FRONT WILL EXTEND S OF GALE CENTER TO __ MVOE TO NEAR 65W TONIGHT. ANOTHER COLD FRONT _ W EJ_CARLOINAS WED AFTERNOON.
.TODAY...N OF 29N E OF 73W WIND NE 35 TO 45 KTS. SEAS 12 TO 18 FT. E OF COLD FRONT WIND SE TO S 15 TO 25 KTS. SEAS 6 TO 9 FT. REMAINDER OF AREA WIND NE TO E 20 TO 30 KTS. SEAS 7 TO 10 FT WITH LARGE NE SWELLS. SCATTERED TO NUMEROUS SHOWERS AND TSTMS OVER THE NE PART.
.TONIGHT...E OF 75W WIND NE 20 TO 30 KTS. SEAS 7 TO 10 FT WITH LARGE NE SWELLS. W OF 75W WIND NE TO E 15 TO 20 KTS. SEAS 4 TO 6 FT WITH LARGE NE SWELLS. WIDELY SCATTERED SHOWERS.
.WED...WIND NE TO E 15 TO 20 KTS. SEAS 4 TO 6 FT WITH LARGE NE SWELLS. WIDELY SCATTERED SHOWERS MAINLY N PORTION.
.OUTLOOK FOR WED NIGHT AND THU...LITTLE CHANGE.

EXAMPLES OF WEATHER REPORTS

I have modified actual NAVTEX transmissions to show both the content of the reports and the formatting I usually do in order to easily compare reports day to day.

THE SOUTHWEST NORTH ATLANTIC OFFSHORE REPORT

```
OFFSHORE MARINE FORECAST
NATIONAL WEATHER SERVICE MIAMI FL
1030 AM AST SAT APR 22 2006
SW N ATLC S OF 32N AND W OF 65W
.SYNOPSIS...
    A FRONT WILL BECOME ABOUT STATIONARY NEAR 29N 65W
        TO THE FLORIDA STRAITS TODAY THROUGH SAT.
    WEAK LOW PRES WILL FORM ON THE FRONT OVER THE
        BAHAMAS TODAY...MOVE NE ALONG THE FRONT
        TONIGHT...TO BEYOND FORECAST AREA BY EARLY SAT.
.TODAY AND TONIGHT...
    WITHIN 200 NM N OF FRONT WIND NW 15 KT BECOMING N TO
        NE 15 TO 20 KT LATE TODAY AND TONIGHT. SEAS 5 TO 7 FT.
    ELSEWHERE N OF THE FRONT WIND NW TO N 15 KT...EXCEPT
        N30N TONIGHT WIND BECOMING W 10 TO 15 KT. SEAS 5 FT.
    S OF THE FRONT WIND S TO SW 15 KT. SEAS 5 FT.
    SCATTERED TSTMS ALONG AND WITHIN 200 NM N OF FRONT.
.SAT...
    N OF 28N WIND BECOMING SW TO W 15 TO 20 KT. SEAS 5 TO 7 FT.
    ELSEWHERE N OF FRONT WIND NW TO N 10 TO 15 KT. SEAS 5 FT.
    S OF THE FRONT WIND SW 10 TO 15 KT. SEAS 3 FT.
    SCATTERED SHOWERS AND TSTMS WITHIN 200 NM OF THE FRONT.
```

THE CARIBBEAN OFFSHORE REPORT

```
OFFSHORE MARINE FORECAST
NATIONAL WEATHER SERVICE MIAMI FL
1030 AM AST SAT APR 22 2006
CARIBBEAN SEA AND SW N ATLC BEYOND 50 NM FROM SHORE.
.CARIBBEAN SYNOPSIS...
    NO SIGNIFICANT FEATURES.
NW CARIBBEAN N OF 15N AND W OF 75W.
    .TODAY TONIGHT AND MON...
        WIND E TO SE 15 TO 20 KT. SEAS 4 TO 6 FT.
        ISOLATED SHOWERS.
SW CARIBBEAN S OF 15N AND W OF 75W.
    .TODAY TONIGHT AND MON...
        WIND NE TO E 20 TO 25 KT. SEAS 6 TO 9 FT.
E CARIBBEAN E OF 75W.
    .TODAY TONIGHT AND MON...
        WIND NE TO E 15 TO 20 KT. SEAS 4 TO 6 FT.
        ISOLATED SHOWERS.
```

THE PUERTO RICO COASTAL REPORT

This quite complete, five sub-zone report can cause trouble for passage makers who haven't got experience with it. Start getting this report regularly while in Luperón, comparing the sub-zone below which covers half the Mona Passage with both the Caribbean and Southwest North Atlantic Offshore Reports. If understood in the context of the Offshore Reports and the near coast land effects, you can use this report to good effect..

1030 AM AST SAT FEB 09 2002

PUERTO RICO AND U.S. VIRGIN ISLANDS WATERS
SYNOPSIS FOR PUERTO RICO AND THE U.S. VIRGIN ISLANDS WATERS-
1030 AM AST SAT APR 22 2006
SURFACE HIGH PRESSURE WILL CONTINUE TO EXTEND FROM [and etc.]

ATLC WATERS FROM PUNTA CADENA TO MOUTH OF RIO GUAJATACA THEN E BEYOND 100 FATHOMS TO ANEGADA PASSAGE N TO 19.5N BETWEEN 68W AND 64W-
[and includes the next subzones]
ATLC NEAR SHORE WATERS FROM MOUTH OF RIO GUAJATACA E TO CABO SAN JUAN CONTINUING E-NE TO ANEGADA OUT TO 100 FATHOMS-
1030 AM AST APR 22 2006
.THIS AFTERNOON...WIND MAINLY EAST AROUND 15 KNOTS. [and etc.]
CARIB WATERS FROM PUNTA VIENTO TO CABO SAN JUAN S TO 17N AND E TO 64W INCLUDING THE CARIB WATERS OF CULEBRA VIEQUES AND THE U.S. VIRGIN ISLANDS [and etc.]

CARIB WATERS FROM PUNTA VIENTO TO PUNTA MELONES AND THE WATERS OUTSIDE 12 NM FROM PUNTA MELONES TO PUNTA CADENA W TO 68W AND S TO 17N- [i.e., the Mona Passage]
1030 AM AST SAT APR 22 2006
...A SMALL CRAFT ADVISORY MAY BE REQUIRED SUNDAY...
.THIS AFTERNOON...WIND EAST AROUND 15 KNOTS. SEAS [and etc.]

NEAR SHORE WATERS OF W PUERTO RICO FROM PUNTA CADENA S TO PUNTA MELONES W TO 12 NM- [i.e., the west coast beach report]

1030 AM AST SAT APR 22 2006
.THIS AFTERNOON...WIND VARIABLE...MAINLY EAST AROUND [and etc.]

See page 57, *Boat Stuff: Using the Radio: Wx Broadcast Times and Frequencies*

PLAYING THE ISLAND LEES

One reviewer cautioned me on including this material. "Too text booky," he said. But when major yachting magazines published it, I knew I'd found the form to explain my decades of observations, something to answer simply the unremitting question, "But why?"

On the north coast of Hispaniola, I advise cruisers to go east only on **gradient** forecasts south of east, less than 15 knots and no northerly swell. "But *why*?" they often grouch. Unsatisfied with brief answers, off they go. Had they taken time to study the complex set of simple answers to *why*, they wouldn't have to accost me down islands for their rum run.

New to the tradewind belt, most yachties can't shuck the idea that the wind will eventually back or haul around to get them where they want to go. Well it won't. For that reason they call it a **trade wind**. If you bring your boat through the islands, you must use *island* sailing tactics. All good things come with a price. You must learn to play the island lees. You must understand and predict them. You must learn to modify forecasts of **gradient** open sea conditions and make your own *local* forecasts.

Islands, reefs and banks change the trade wind conditions passing through, over and around them. Playing these effects in series, a sailor can make safe, comfortable and pleasant progress against normally impenetrable trade winds and seas. After decades observing and using these effects under different forecast conditions all along the thorny path, I can assure you that you *can* predict these effects. Now you have something to study.

Good interpreters, like **Herb Hilgenberg** and **Chris Parker**, unravel daily the system of thermodynamic chaos called Weather. They cut through its riddles using high-tech models, fairly accurately predicting gradient conditions several days in advance.

Gradient forecasts assume a smooth billiard ball of an earth. But physical obstacles such as islands, reefs and banks, and their thermal radiations, present upsets to these smooth earth forecasts. You have to assess the effects of a nearby headland, a rapidly shelving bottom or a strong but offset coastal front. Herb, David and the NWS won't have them.

Looking at the many effects, each of which inhibits you from obtaining an accurate local forecast, you may conclude that you just have another jumbled and chaotic puzzle. Not if you understand each of these effects, learn to predict them by your own observation and listen, with pencil in hand, to the *entire* broadcasts of both Herb and Chris.

Given a settled weather forecast, you can overlay the effects discussed here to come up with your certain local forecast. With an unsettled, or rapidly changing forecast, forget going out anyway. Need a simple definition of "settled weather"? Look for an **Offshore Report** with the same data for each of the Today, Tonight and Tomorrow sections.

If, after careful study of this exposition of **island effects**, you still can't create a *local* forecast from the *gradient* forecasts on your radio, you can sell the boat and buy back the farm. But if you just begin from the top, as elementary as it appears, it quickly gets complex.

UNDERSTANDING WIND	air pressure • isobars • wind • gradient wind night wind at sea • day wind at sea • trade wind
ISLAND EFFECTS ON WIND	capes • channels • seabreeze • landbreeze reed switch effect
ISLAND EFFECTS ON SEAS	groundswells • shoals • reflection • refraction trench effect
ISLAND LEES	lee of wind • night lees • lee of *garbage!*
INTEGRATING EFFECTS	Mona Passage • Gulf Stream

Rhumbline sailing the GPS in the trades has caused hundreds of crews to hang it up and go home after just a few miles on the Thorny Path into the Caribbean. Inadequate answers to other questions cause turnabouts as well. But navigation? Come on! Haven't they solved that problem? Many cruisers deceive themselves that they have -- with GPS!! Even after the inaccurate lats & longs of old tech official charts put them aground.

Islands give the sailor shelter from the relentless dead ahead onslaught of trade seas and winds. They also radiate special effects which the skipper can use as pivots, or hinges while threading the islands. A to C to B might take less than just A to B.

Islands change conditions in many ways. Most of these effects operate **diurnally** in accordance with the sun's day. These shifts from the conditions forecast for the open sea can favor or disfavor the sailor. Even in the Bahamas, where the tradewinds don't quite reign, sailing rhumblines and ignoring the effects of islands and banks on sea and wind shall for sure get you there slower. And with more wear on boat and crew. Among the hundreds of low lying, light-colored Bahamian islands, only a relative few exhibit strong resistance to open-sea wind conditions. Banks, on the other hand, often make prime examples of the effects of daytime heating. They store heat then radiate it back.

I used to run charters in the Bahamas, dashing back to Hispaniola between guests because I had a house going up there. With little time to waste I learned to flit in and out of the island lees in combination with forecast wind shifts. Fleets of sailboats out of George-town would often punch directly into it on long inter-island passages. I would leave Georgetown at the same time as they did, but I'd already have lain at anchor several days in Puerto Plata to watch them, broken and bent, limping into port. In my case, I had already leisurely reprovisioned, and I stood ready to up anchor and sail back again when they came in. Today, I watch the same drill from Luperón.

Before looking at how islands alter the winds and waves that the weatherman de-scribes, you must understand the wind and wave forecasts. For instance, all but inshore marine forecasts predict the *average of the upper third of wave heights*. Wind forecasts give the sustained **gradient wind** expected 33 meters above the surface in open sea. The predictions come from quite accurate models which take input from measurements of wind and wave and air pressure at fixed points. Most weather models describe the atmosphere in terms of isobars, or the set of points of identical air pressure at specific altitudes. At the risk of boring some, I shall present the case for island effects from the very beginning.

AIR PRESSURE

Scientific purists will tell you that minute collisions of the atmosphere's gas molecules cause us to feel pressure from the air we breathe, kind of like adding up the impacts of a gazillion teensy billiard balls in what they call Brownian motion. But you can think of **air pressure** as the weight of air molecules stacked vertically above the place at which you measure it -- between

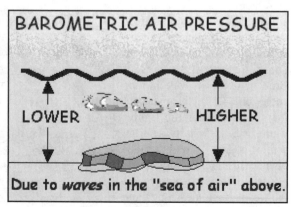

BAROMETRIC AIR PRESSURE

LOWER   HIGHER

Due to *waves* in the "sea of air" above.

your ears. I think of myself walking around with a 400,000 foot wobbly stack of air on my head. Air, weighing only .07 pounds per cubic foot at sea level, when stacked high, presses down on you with about 14.7 pounds per square inch.

Take a look at the island in the figure. As you move around on the ground, the weight of air over your head goes up and down as fewer or more molecules appear above you. The upper reaches of the atmosphere churns with molecules at the end of the collision chain. Some punch back into the mess below after a precipitous rise, others actually escape into space. The earth's atmosphere acts like a colossal sea. We really crawl around on the seabed of an airy ocean. Way up there on its surface it has waves and troughs just like the real ocean. These stack more or less air molecules over your ears, making the weight you feel, or the *pressure*, lighter or heavier.

ISOBARS

If you look at any arbitrary pressure surface above the island, say 200 millibars, it clearly looks like the surface of the sea does from your boat, but in *titanic* scale. Weather scientists navigate these mountains and valleys, hills, cliffs and inclines of our sea of air the same way Girl and Boy Scouts, orienteering enthusiasts, army generals and surveyors do the dry land. They use *terrain*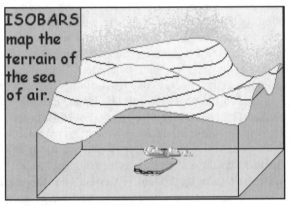

maps. Instead of lines of equal altitude in feet, they use lines of equal pressure. In the diagram, the island lies under a dome of air with a long, tapering **ridge** leading away from a steep cliff face. Next to this ridge and across a valley lies a round dome of air almost as high. Nowadays they call the valleys **troughs**, in recognition of the fluid nature of the atmosphere. Until the 1950's, weathermen still used the word "valley". Ridge has remained in use, however. (I hope you didn't expect consistency from weather scientists.) They call bowl shaped valleys **low pressure centers**, and dome shaped mountains they call **high pressure centers**, of course. Now how does this help me understand wind?

WIND

A thermodynamics professor argues that wind comes from temperature differences between large masses of air as the more energetic hot mass tries to Brownian-bash its way into the cooler one. Or the heavier cool mass slides under the lighter warm one. It all starts with the sun, of course. Don't get spellbound with chicken-and-egg arguments. You need to know what the weatherman means by wind

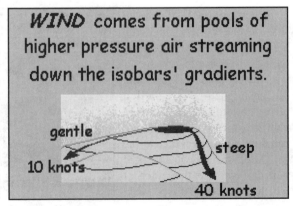

because, as goofy as it may sound, you must use his definition in order to know how his forecast gets affected by your island.

The weather guy thinks those waves and troughs he describes with isobars really act as a fluid. If air molecules heap up too high in one place, they start to slide downhill to another, lower place, just like water, albeit on a much grander scale. This avalanche of air molecules starts the wind. If the hill comes with a steep grade, then the molecules really whiz on down. If the hill makes a gentle grade, then they sort of stroll their way down. As a military strategist might view the battle on a terrain map, so the weatherman watches the atmosphere's troop movements on the isobar charts. Air masses stream fast across tightly spaced isobars (showing steep grades), and wander slowly across widely spaced ones.

Not surprisingly then, the differently *graded* slopes depicted by isobars get called **gradients**, and the wind that slides down them has the moniker **gradient wind**.

GRADIENT WIND

The National Weather Service gives the **Offshore Forecasts** in gradient wind near the surface of the open sea. When discussing forecasts for any but local areas, you should use the gradient wind as the frame of reference. If you don't, the discussion falls into the apples and oranges class and no one knows what anyone means.

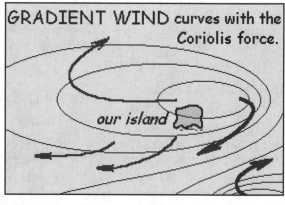

GRADIENT WIND curves with the Coriolis force.

our island

We use the word *gradient* to describe the wind whooping down the ridges and high pressure zones of the atmosphere, always headed toward the nearest lower pressure zone, such as that of a **wave**, a **trough** or a **low pressure center**. Gradient wind turns always to the right in the northern hemisphere, due to the **Coriolis Force**, an incredibly small force around the neighborhood, but incredibly large when applied across the large distances that the wind blows. Because of Coriolis, wind wants to spiral clockwise off its mountains and counterclockwise into its valleys, always veering to the right nonetheless.

Unless something gets in its way, **gradient wind** should blow over your head (33 meters above sealevel) just as forecast. But it rarely strikes your sail as forecast except at night, and then only if you navigte many miles from nowhere. Why it doesn't make it to your sails unchanged, only the sailor at the island can know. The weatherman tells you what wind shall get shipped to you, not how it looks when it gets delivered and unwrapped.

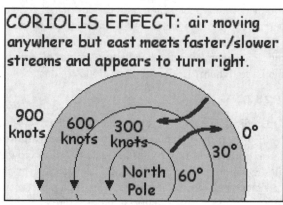

CORIOLIS EFFECT: air moving anywhere but east meets faster/slower streams and appears to turn right.

900 knots   600 knots   300 knots   0°
30°
North Pole   60°

NIGHT WIND AT SEA

Most cruisers I meet prejudice their navigation with the presumption that the **night wind** blows softer than the day wind. Not so. Night wind, with only friction of the sea surface to slow it down, has the nearest to maximum gradient conditions. Lighter gradient winds, 5 to 15 knots, can curve as much as 10° to 15° toward lower pressure as they brush the surface. Stronger winds bend much less. The sailor

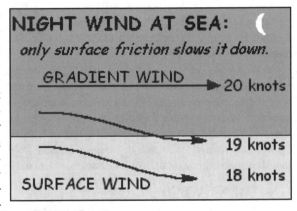

below 33 meters of altitude may see a light night wind in the sail which varies from the weatherman's forecast as much as a compass point. The sailor of a large boat pinching a light wind at night can get fooled by masthead instruments which deviate significantly from what strikes the sails lower down.

DAY WIND AT SEA

The day's wind gets complex as the day wears on. As the surface of the sea accumulates heat from the sun, it gives back progressively more of it to the air it touches. This convective transfer of heat to the lower layers of the atmosphere causes a vertical heat gradient. Then when pieces of air of different temperatures mix, as with humans of different tempera-

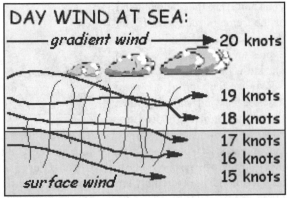

ment, a bit of jostling goes on. This turbulence causes the otherwise orderly troops of the gradient wind to stumble. In the ensuing riot the wind trades in some of its energy to produce water vapor which rises to a level cool enough to condense into **clouds**. All this energy expended to make clouds, the wind has to get slower.

From either sea or land, clouds mark rising heat. As you approach an island think as an old time general had to when he lost sight of his troops in the confusion of battle. Where did he find them? Under all those clouds of dust.

TRADEWINDS

Gradient winds which run permanently like rivers over the earth got dubbed tradewinds by the traders that depended upon them. In the **tradewind** belts daytime heating of the sea forms uniform ranks and files of fluffy **cumulus** clouds at altitudes up to 2000 feet. High altitude pilots see them as looking like a broad river of neatly crisscrossed city streets.

Tradewinds flow as do rivers, from high pressure areas of the tropics to the relatively low pressure areas of equatorial regions, rarely getting above 22° latitude on the western shores of the oceans. **Northeast Trades** of the Atlantic bend with the **Equatorial Cur-**

rents, the North Atlantic highs and, of course, Coriolis. *Easterly* by the time they pour over the Lesser Antilles into the Caribbean, they continuously switch like a cat's tail between poles of northeast and east southeast at 15 to 25 knots in the winter, and between east northeast and southeast at 10 to 20 in the summer. Wind blowing any direction not *within* those limits during those seasons has bent from island effects or significant weather features in its way, such as a **tropical wave,** or the rare **cold front** or **warm front**.

Islands in the stream of the trades make them appear stronger along the coasts in the daytime and weaker, even nonexistent, at night. Growing up near the beach in south Florida, I had nothing but mosquito screens between me and the wind as it soughed through the 60 foot casuarina trees above my little porch. I thought it as natural as sunrise and sunset that the **night lee** of the land would kill the strong sea breezes and reverse them with a 10 knot land breeze. Finding these effects and more in the Caribbean came as no surprise. Yet most yachties I meet must hail from inland cities. After several years cruising the islands they still haven't noticed all these different breaks from wind and sea that the islands give them to employ toward their comfort and safety on their passages. Let's count them.

ISLAND EFFECTS ON WIND

Islands present themselves as obstacles to the **gradient wind** which would sweep otherwise unhindered across the wastes of the sea. Given the gradient wind from the weather forecast, the sailor must take into account a number of often conflicting effects, mostly diurnal, with which the islands change it. Any course plan based solely on the prevailing background conditions shall go wrong within up to 30 miles of a substantial island. The best course planning tries to benefit from these effects, not just mitigate them.

CAPE EFFECT

Any bay, river or lake sailor can tell you how to take advantage of wind off a point or a headland during a race. For example, as you round a headland, the breeze always seems to come directly from the point until you get well clear of it.

But sailors in the tropical trades seem to forget everything they learned dinghy racing in the rivers and lakes of their temperate homelands.

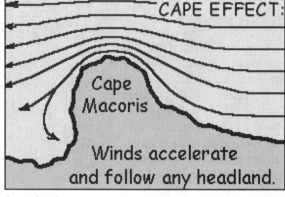

The sailor who rounds a headland by keeping parallel to the shore finds the wind on the nose all the way around despite nearly 90° of course changes during the beat. The mountainous capes of the Caribbean islands act as the camber of an airfoil, squeezing the wind blowing by them. The same volume of air passing a smaller space must go faster, or the air behind would stack up clear back to Africa. This occurs even in light night conditions. Don't despair, the real wind is less than what you see at the capes themselves. The wind around **Cabo Macoris**, in Hispaniola, can get to a fierce 30 knots on the Cape in the daytime, while it blows only 15 to 20 knots beyond the cape to the east or out farther to sea.

CHANNEL EFFECT

When plowing to windward through a cut in the Exuma chain in the Bahamas, or transiting the channels between Lesser Antilles islands like Dominica and Martinique, both the wind and the sea squeezes between the ends of the two islands. The resulting effect can stymie the sailor who hadn't snuck up to the channel prepared to use the squeeze to advantage.

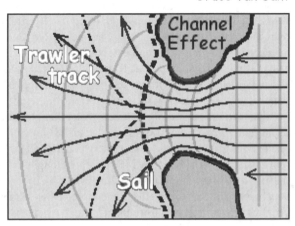

The sea's parallel waves broadcast in concentric patterns on the lee side of the channel. So trawlers do better approaching the cut from offshore, keeping the seas at a comfortable bow angle, while sailboats have to sneak up on it, playing the spreading wind in a continuous reach.

The **channel effect** has a cousin in the optics business known as diffraction. In fact, the chain of islands in the Lesser Antilles makes up a diffraction grating, whose wave interference patterns you can see in the Caribbean swell up to 100 miles off. Once I played Polynesian Navigator by ignoring my instruments and calculating my landfall by the swell patterns. Since sea and wind states gradually altered as I closed the islands, I turned off the pilot and trimmed sail and rudder to follow the pattern. The **diffracted wave** train brought me right to Martinique without touching a sheet. Once again, I found that trimming ship for *comfort*, not rhumbline, also made for a faster trip. But more on sea changes later. Let's stick with the wind effects for now.

SEABREEZE

Daytime heating of the land creates the **seabreeze** just as rising thermals made the sea's daytime surface wind. The sun heats the land. The land heats the air above it. The warmed air rises and must get replaced by cooler, heavier sea air. A circulation begins which can create wind of up to 20 knots with effects distin-

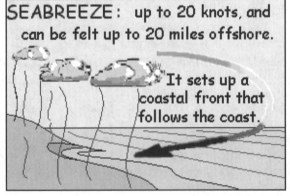

guishable as far inland as 10 miles and as far at sea as 20 miles, depending on the terrain. In the tropics, seabreezes run year around, but they blow strongest in the spring and summer.

The seabreeze in the islands of the Caribbean and in the Bahamas, makes up the prime **diurnal effect** with which the sailor must contend. Seabreeze can reinforce a light tradewind. It can even outright cancel it. Even a strong trade of 25 knots, gusting to 30, can get significantly bent by seabreeze. A forecast breeze of 10 to 15 knots *along* the coast can become 25 to 30 knots *onto* the coast by 2 pm. Nevertheless, I often see sailors rushing to the harbor entrance to look out at the sea in mid afternoon to correct the weatherman's forecast. They take the seabreeze for gradient wind and retire to the bar. Can't go tonight. Nor the next, nor the next. Some never catch on. They just follow their buddies out.

NOCTURNAL WIND

The **nocturnal wind** begins after sundown and dies before dawn, reaching its strongest between midnight and 2 a.m. It asserts itself by combining **landbreeze** and **katabatic wind**. Landbreeze reverses seabreeze. It occurs at night with a much milder circulation than its daytime sister. Since seawater holds the heat it absorbed during the day

Nocturnal Wind: is the sum of cool mountain air sliding downhill, and the opposite of seabreeze, the nighttime landbreeze.

better than land, which quite quickly gives it up, the land becomes cooler than the sea at some point. A nighttime circulation starts from the land and feeds updrafts over the warmer water. On high islands the land breeze gets an assist from the katabatic, a wind that flows down slope, bringing cooler upper level air which, heavier than its coastal cousins, slides downhill.

COASTAL FRONTS

Turbulence of the seabreeze fluffs up cottony balls of cumulus clouds which mark the beach below them where the colder sea air pushes in. These mini cold fronts map the island's shoreline. Depending on the colors and textures of the land below, they can show you a mirror image chart of the coast before you see the coast itself. The island's colors and the water behind it often reflect in the lower surface of these clouds, particularly in the Bahamas where the islands have fairly uniform colors and textures.

A curious effect of the coastal cold front, it produces a mild convective circulation up and down its length, just like its big brothers. Perhaps not surprisingly then, the circulation runs counter clockwise. This results in the seabreeze always turning to the right as the day wears on. Its onshore vector gets rounded out by the front's circulation vector which grows as the sun's day proceeds.

The heat of the sun nails the coastal fronts in place over the coast. The seemingly tranquil pillows of coastal front cumulus in reality move inland at quite a clip, but they don't get far before evaporating. A stop action motion camera shows these clouds furiously making up on their seaward leading edges, while their trailing edges break up and drift off. When the sun sets, the front dissipates unless the island supports the manufacture of really huge amounts of vapor. In that case they can build high enough during the day that the temperature gradient due to altitude causes an internal *vertical* circulation. That gives birth to **cumulo nimbus** clouds which can live on awhile as evening thunder storms.

On the larger islands, look for strong gusts and showers coming from storm cells spawned by the large coastal fronts in the late afternoons. Don't make the mistake of forecasting sea conditions based on conditions in harbor beneath a strong coastal front, especially over an irregular coastline (e.g., Ponce, southern Puerto Rico, Exuma, Bahamas).

The **coastal front**s normally get pushed around somewhat by the trades. They usually get shoved farther inland. In some circumstances they can get offset *out to sea*. The next figure shows a coastal front that got set up when the heated south shore created a southerly seabreeze. Then the light northeast gradient wind catches the costal front and shifts it southwest which obscures the clear and sunny bay to sailors offshore.

A Real Life Drama

When I sailed into the Bahama island of Mayaguana a while back, I encountered quite a VHF drama with two buddy boats, one in the harbor at **Abraham Bay**, the other in the offing, waiting to take the southern reef entrance. A light gradient wind blew from the east northeast, which shifted the southern coastal front to the south and west, where it ob-

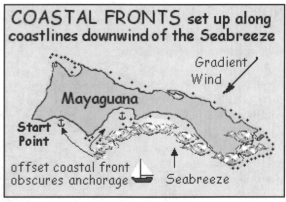

COASTAL FRONTS set up along coastlines downwind of the Seabreeze

Gradient Wind

Mayaguana

Start Point

offset coastal front obscures anchorage

Seabreeze

scured the entrance with rain. Bound for a short overnight by Start Point, west of the bay, I passed the western entrance. I could look behind the coastal front into the clear waters of Abraham Bay where the sun shone on the buddy at anchor inside.

On the VHF, the boat inside assured the boat hove to beyond the curtain of rain, that he could see the "size of the storm" on the radar, and that it should pass through in 20 minutes. Each 20 minutes he gave the same advisory to his weary friend. Both marveled at how the "storm" seemed to make up from the east as fast as it moved to the west. I finally got on the horn to advise them that they sat on either side of an afternoon coastal front, and that the boat wanting to enter should go around it through the western entrance. They curtly informed me they had the "storm" on radar, that they "knew what they were about" because they had sailed the whole Caribbean, and coming from the east, they didn't feature going around to the west entrance. I hung up, But the VHF radio theater ran into late afternoon while I soaked up the sun at Start Point, along with a gin and tonic.

BANK EFFECTS

Cruisers need to understand the effects produced by shallow banks such as Caicos Banks, **Great Bahama Banks**, Exuma Banks, the banks between Long and Great Exuma Islands, between Crooked and Acklins Islands, and even the 90 mile bank upon which the Spanish, United States and British Virgin Islands lie. These banks act like land. In other words, they store heat dur-

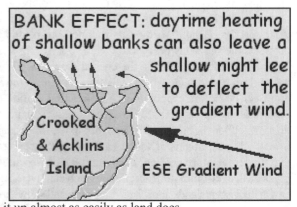

BANK EFFECT: daytime heating of shallow banks can also leave a shallow night lee to deflect the gradient wind.

Crooked & Acklins Island

ESE Gradient Wind

ing the day, and at night it gives it up almost as easily as land does.

The 60 mile wide Caicos Bank stops moderate winds at night, but lets it rip in the daytime. The 180 mile long sea mount between the Mona and the Anegada Passages holds the islands of Puerto Rico and the Virgins. On the east end of the big island of Puerto Rico, in the center of that bank, light to moderate trade winds drop dead at night, even though you can look uninterruptedly east clear to Africa. Often you get a **katabatic** there as well.

COASTAL ACCELERATION

Gradient wind will try to follow a coastline upon encountering an island. Even a wind truly parallel to the coast will accelerate as it bunches up over land toward the lower elevation of the sea and, in the daytime, away from the warmer gradients over land. Let the **gradient wind** strike the coast at an oblique angle and the surface wind will accelerate even more as it bends to the coast, similar to what happens as it rounds the capes. You can't turn the wind without it accelerating someplace. An east-northeast wind on the north coast of the Dominican Republic can accelerate up to 10 knots. On the south coast of Puerto Rico, a gradient forecast of east to southeast 10 to 15 knots in the daytime can deliver 20 to 25 knots to you on the coast.

The sun heats the land and the seabreeze sets up. By 2 pm the combined effect of **coastal acceleration**, **coastal front** circulation and **seabreeze** can get to 30 knots, *ferocious* compared to the wind forecast. Now add the acceleration on the capes ... *And* I haven't yet told you about coastwise circulation you can add from island lows.

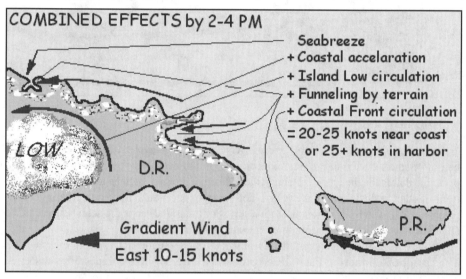

COMBINED EFFECTS by 2-4 PM

— Seabreeze
+ Coastal accelaration
+ Island Low circulation
+ Funneling by terrain
+ Coastal Front circulation

= 20-25 knots near coast
or 25+ knots in harbor

LOW

D.R.

P.R.

Gradient Wind
East 10-15 knots

ISLAND LOWS

Mountainous islands produce their own weather systems scaled to the size of the island. Trade winds penetrate the island and lose their moisture on its slopes. This convection activity gets aggravated by daytime heating of the island's central portions. By late summer afternoons terrific aggregations of cumulus nimbus can span the interior of the island creating a regional low pressure center. Check your weather fax's satpics of the island of Hispaniola at 8 a.m., 2 p.m. and 8 p.m. and you shall *see* it.

Significant winds can begin to circulate around island low pressure systems formed in this manner. For example, in the hills north of Ponce, Puerto Rico, near Coamo, a storm cell up to 40,000 feet may form. Talk to the captains of the big jet airliners that have to avoid them. Early evening, such towers drift westward into the Mona Passage along with the rest of the western coastal front. See the section *Crossing the Mona Passage.*

In Puerto Rico circulation around the Coamo **island low** shifts the coastal front north of the Lajas Valley and that in turn may diminish the cape effect at Cabo Rojo. On the high cordillera in the north central part of Hispaniola a vast island low can develop. It can grow large enough to keep strong winds circulating around it and parallel to the coast long past sundown, long after the sea breeze dies and well after accelerated coastal trade winds should have abated on the night lee. In the harbor of Luperón it can appear daunting for yachts wanting to leave on the night lee. Before midnight, however, the low has dissipated, the coastal front vanishes or tumbles out to sea, and a belated night lee asserts itself under a star bright sky. The midafternoon squalls of the high islands of the eastern Caribbean chain may unload the minor lows of those small islands, but in the summer months they can stay until quite late, cooling the yachties in the lee harbors. See **David Jones'** *Concise Guide to Caribbean Weather* for some detail of their makeup.

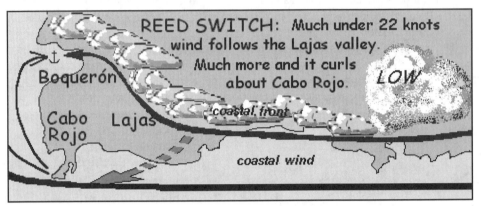

THE REED SWITCH EFFECT

Some decades ago the Scientific American had a wonderful article by scientists who had built an air driven digital computer based on the **reed switch**. They used the same principle that made the reed in Glenn Miller's clarinet produce such beautiful music. Variations of wind intensity cause the reed to deflect from one side to the other, creating a non-electric, air-driven binary switch. With a series of tubes and reeds the scientists created a sophisticated binary digital computer operated by wind flow.

Real geographical instances of this physical phenomenon help sailors everywhere. The harbor of **Boquerón**, Puerto Rico provides a case. When the trades blow under 22 knots out of the east, but not south of east, the midday wind forks at the keys and bayous around La Parguera. The north fork circulates around the **island low** up the **Lajas Valley** to spill out over the harbor of Boquerón. While doing this it shaves off the corner of the **coastal front** that builds with the land heating of the day. The coastal front wraps the island's western end, bypassing Boquerón. Under these conditions it rarely rains in Boquerón in the summer, but **Puerto Real** just to the north gets horrendous tropical downpours.

Let the trades blow out of true east at much more than 20 knots, however, and they stream right on by **Cabo Rojo**. Under these conditions the coastal front can build south to Lajas which will create a seabreeze from the west into the bay of Boquerón. The **cape effect** around Cabo Rojo further helps the **seabreeze**, and you've got 15 knots of a good fetch west wind into the anchorage setting the yachts to pitching.

At this point the yachties all shout "Hooray for a west wind!", let their genoas fly and head off for Cabo Rojo for an expected run to Ponce. If they actually try to round Cabo Rojo, some blow out their head sails in 25 or 30 knot easterlies at the cape before giving up the attempt. That evening, as the unchained coastal front moves out to sea, they sit back in Boquerón under a downpour, grousing about the weatherman.

ISLAND EFFECTS ON SEAS

Islands interfere with the sea's fluid dynamics as they do those of the atmosphere. You usually want to predict an island's effect on the sea in order to avoid their consequences. Salt water weighs about 850 times more than air. It should not surprise anyone that changing the movement of good hunks of water can have crushing results on a small boat.

When the sea vibrates in periodic vertical motion, we call that which we see **waves**. Waves actually reflect the minute movement of molecules of water which, acting like a jillion closely packed billiard balls, nudge each other to transfer energy put into the sea by an external event like surface wind. Or maybe *Krakatau* (see Glossary), which caused a titanic tsunami. When the nudging reaches the surface it goes around again to the bottom, since the air above doesn't nudge much, and the energy has to go somewhere. A wave, really a tall, oval vibration of water, hasn't much movement at bottom where great pressure gives great resistance, but a bunch at the top.

Whether from the launching of a boat or a thrown rock, the energy imparted to the water starts a vertical vibration of its molecules. Small energy inputs, like a child doing a cannonball off a yacht, create small vibrations that don't reach too deep nor propagate too far. A large one, like Krakatau, the volcano that emerged in the Samudra Straits between Java and Sumatra, creates vibrations which go to the deepest bottoms. While its explosion got heard in Africa, Krakatau's waves created less surface disturbance than a cannonballing child in the deeps of the Marianas Trench. However, when it reached the shoaling waters of some Pacific atolls it created surface waves much higher than the islands themselves. Sounds like stuff we ought to know about if we sail through the islands.

GROUNDSWELLS

Even small vibrations of a ripple or a wavelet, when moving into shallows shall heap the water up on the surface. Waves move great quantities of water in great depths, albeit each molecule of water gets moved only a tiny distance. When the wave enters shallow ground it has less water to move, but it still has most of the energy. The flatter trajectory of the oval oscillation now literally throws the water forward as well as up. Hundreds of tons of it in the space of your boat, whereas before, nothing.

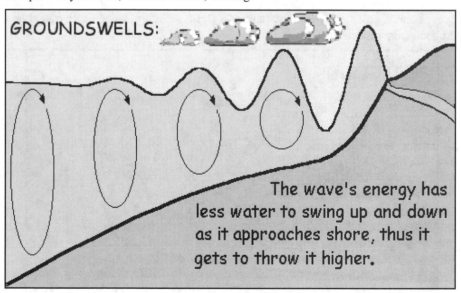

GROUNDSWELLS:

The wave's energy has less water to swing up and down as it approaches shore, thus it gets to throw it higher.

SHOALS

Many cruisers don't anticipate shoals on their charts because they run several hundred feet deep, and that does not, in their experience, mean shoal. However, when the water these shoals try to contain comes from the Equatorial Current, the shoals must dissipate a lot of water and a lot of energy. You don't want to take part in it. Pay attention to the fathom lines of your charts, even though they read in the hundreds. Take care for any area much more shallow than another if it lies downwind of sharp bottom gradients.

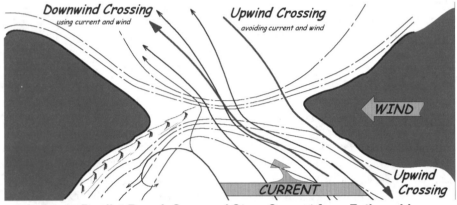

Learn to Predict Rough Seas and Stray Current from Fathom Lines

Often an undersea land bridge connects islands. Any current between the islands must climb this wall. Cross the passage so as to avoid the confused seas down current, and to get a lift from the current while it tries to slide along the contour of the bridge.

REFLECTION

Confused waves, like those you see on an oscilloscope when you speak the word "spaghetti" into its audio input, come from waves reflecting off steep shores. The convexity of the island's shore as it lies athwart the onslaught of the seas, and the concavities of its seaward bays, cause the sea's waves to behave just as waves of light do when they hit convex and concave mirrors in the funhouse. But it ain't fun for the sailor caught in a drubbing from **reflected waves**.

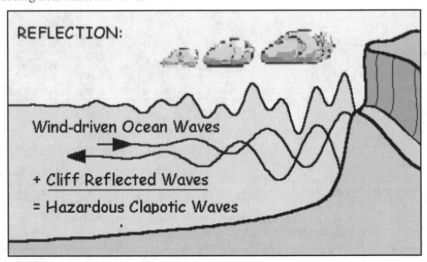

114

REFRACTION

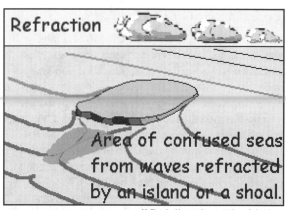

So island passes diffract the seas, and their coasts reflect them. What about **refracted waves**? Similar to light through a lens, wave refraction occurs at a critical angle of incidence of the wave onto the shore. (Perhaps 37°.) Above that angle, the wave's energy gets reflected. Below that angle, the wave continues to move forward, but in a

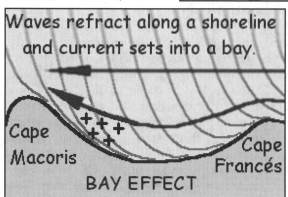

Area of confused seas from waves refracted by an island or a shoal.

Waves refract along a shoreline and current sets into a bay.

Cape Macoris

Cape Francés

BAY EFFECT

modified direction. The friction drag of the shoaling shore acts on the wave, causing the seaward parts of the wave train to stumble on the shoreward parts, dissipating energy. These wave parts now travel at different speeds. The wave appears to turn, and it wraps the island. Similarly, waves and current refract along the shore of island bays. A westbound sailor can get set onto the reefs in the diagram.

TRENCH EFFECT

Many islands show on the charts surrounded by elongated forms of closed fathom lines. These describe elongated deeps, or **trenches**, along the coast. Ride these trenches like a bowling ball does the gutter. You'll have a safer and smoother ride in its quieter water. The trench effect particularly works well from Cabo Engaño to Punta Cana, in the DR, and from Puerto Patillas to Punta Tuna, in Puerto Rico. You can often find them, but you've got to look for them. When you find one, you can just slide over a few hundred yards, and the going gets really easy, and your speed increases.

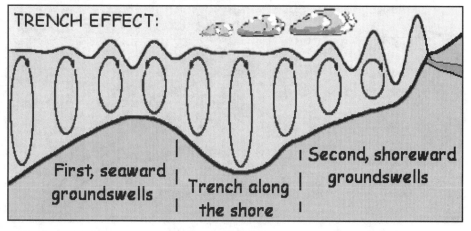

TRENCH EFFECT:

First, seaward groundswells

Trench along the shore

Second, shoreward groundswells

THE GARBAGE LINE

High seas flotsam, whatever can fall off a ship, will wash around islands in a predictable way. It has dangers beyond the sea grass and dead fish of tide lines and dixie cups and palm fronds of river outflows. Next time you find yourself seated by a brook with nothing to do, have a fistful of pine needles with you. Pick a rock, the kind that looks like an island in the stream. Throw your pine needles way upstream of the rock and watch what happens.

You'll notice the rock has folds of ripples on its upstream side. The pine needles rush down stream and divide themselves either side of the rock, bunching up on the ripples, following them around the sides of the rock and sliding out into the troughs behind.

More than pine needles float out there. Crossing from the Virgin Islands to Venezuela my cruising buddy called back on the VHF, "Wow! We're looking down on a whole city of pipes!" Having more curiosity than sense, I cut the autopilot and guided the boat gingerly toward the spot he had just crossed. I soon found myself, the best way I can describe it, flying low over an oil refinery. A forest of pipes, flues and chimneys thrust out in all directions, the nearest of which jutted out within 8-10 feet of the surface.

We sailed along in a gorgeous 10-12 knot beam breeze with hardly a surface chop. But if my 6½ foot draft fell into a trough of a 6 foot sea while the jumble factory below bobbed upward at the same time, it easily could have impaled my ketch with untold tons of force.

I associate that plumber's nightmare with a ship's boiler system and all its attached tubes and capillaries. The sea floor crawls with corroded, broken wrecks whose tankage, upon breaking free, can reach neutral buoyancy and present itself just as whatever I saw.

Avoid the **garbage line** by hugging the shore. Normal cruising configurations — long keel, full displacement, keel-hung rudder with shoe — should have no problem with tidelines and river outflows. But bottoms with shaft struts, spade rudders and some centerboards may snag an occassional piece of plastic or net fragment in the rainy season. No big deal.

But a fleet out of Luperón one year thought it a big deal when one of the boats with a racing configuration caught a bit of what they called "drift net" in their strutted prop outside Puerto Plata. After that, they all sailed 4 miles offshore to avoid "drift nets". They sailed right down the high seas garbage line. Only one of the five boats reached Puerto Rico without incident. Two turned back spooked. All for a bit of yarn.

A "drift net", by the way, has tough steel cables, floats deep and runs up to 7 miles long.

All vessels are at risk for high seas flotsam along a line 1-2 miles off the capes and 3-5 miles off current-wise coastlines. Thinking to stay off a bit to avoid rare inshore hazards, you may instead encounter a semi-submerged container or a full size tree from the Orinoco.

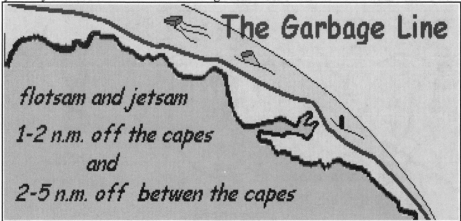

The Garbage Line

flotsam and jetsam

1-2 n.m. off the capes

and

2-5 n.m. off betwen the capes

Sailors benefit most through the reduction of wind or wave in an island's lee. Using **island lees** from adjacent islands, or the cascade of diurnal effects from a chain of islands, one can navigate from the effects of one island to those of another, much as astronauts might use the focus of the planets' gravitational fields to swing around the solar system.

LEE OF THE WIND

The diagram's island doesn't have the height to trouble the wind much, nor the breadth to block the seas. The seas shall meet on the lee side and some confusion shall result. But there shall exist a sweet spot up to 10 times the island's height somewhere to leeward where the seas remain regular, reduced by refraction, and wind favors your tack.

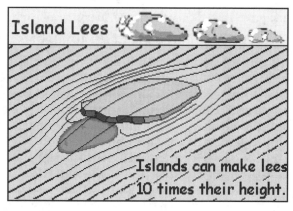

Island Lees

Islands can make lees 10 times their height.

NIGHT LEES

The greatest benefit of all, the **night lee** creates distinct calms which follow daytime heating of land, or **banks** (land under shallow water). Land cooling faster than nearby deep water creates a thermodynamic anomaly which lifts or deflects the tradewinds. An offshore nocturnal wind, the combination of **land breeze** and **katabatic** wind, increases the shield against the trades. The bigger and higher the land mass, and the stronger the daytime heating, the more assertive the **night lee**. Usually the effect of the night lee collapses under assault by gradient winds at 15 knots or more. Along the mountainous shores of the North and South American continents night lees extend many miles, and they can block relatively stronger gradient winds.

A strong night lee shall result when trades become depressed, perhaps by incipient weather features such as **fronts** or **tropical waves**, or by strong heating of the island due to either its topography or surface colorations.

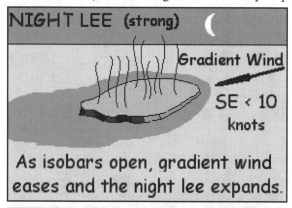

NIGHT LEE (strong)

Gradient Wind

SE < 10 knots

As isobars open, gradient wind eases and the night lee expands.

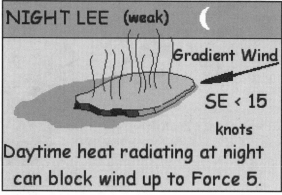

NIGHT LEE (weak)

Gradient Wind

SE < 15 knots

Daytime heat radiating at night can block wind up to Force 5.

In the Caribbean the strength of the night lee also depends on the seasonal declination of the sun and even whether the atmosphere has **Sahara dust** cover. Rocket science?

Forecasts available today from the **Tropical Prediction Center**, and interpreters of the various forecast models who provide consulting services via Marine SSB, such as **Chris Parker** from the Tortola **Caribbean Weather Center** and **Herb Hilgenberg**, in Ontario, have made gradient wind and its near term progressions known quantities. The sailor can know the rest simply by first copying the TPC's forecast, then listening closely to the interpreters and then practicing good observation of local conditions.

EXAMPLE OF USING NIGHT LEES FROM BANKS

I got a three day leg up on a gang of boats waiting for weather at Rum Cay by using a trick I learned while sailing years before between Menorca and Mallorca in the Med.

A strong stalling front just to the north of us kept everyone at bay. The forecasters agreed that the front had equal chances of moving forward again, or of stalling hard and dissipating in place. I knew that the north shore of Crooked and Acklins Islands had a good night lee in the conditions forecast for them 24 hours ahead: east-southeast 10 to 15 knots. By sailing *away* from my rhumbline for the safe harbor at Clarence Town, Long Island, I could put myself in a position to use that lee the following night if the front stalled. If the front continued to move, I had fat time to make the safe harbor at Clarence Town from which to wait for the winds to clock and weaken. I set sail for Long Island.

All night I watched the fireworks in the skies to the north, while downloading every forecast. When the front did stall, and the wind backed, I tacked into the lee of Crooked and skipped comfortably over to Mayaguana using the night lee now on Acklins' north shore. The gang behind me, if they left now, faced 90 miles dead into the Force 5.

These same tactics would work as well for my trawler.

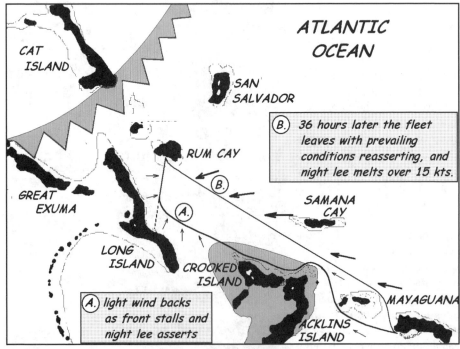

Anticipating a Night Lee

The real payoff of threading the islands south comes in *integrating land effects*, and you can practice it on your first step! The diagrams below show the Gulf Stream between Miami and Gun Cay looking north. With a gradient wind forecast of easterly 10-15 knots, you could expect daytime winds up to 33 meters above the surface more or less as shown.

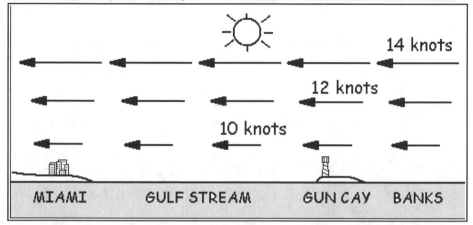

By midnight the radiating heat from the land of Florida and from the shallow banks (5-10 ft.) east of Gun Cay, part of the Great Bahama Bank, will stop or reverse the gradient winds near the surface. The Florida land breeze will set up and blow out to sea for quite a distance. The calm reigning on the bank side shall spill miles westward over the sea.

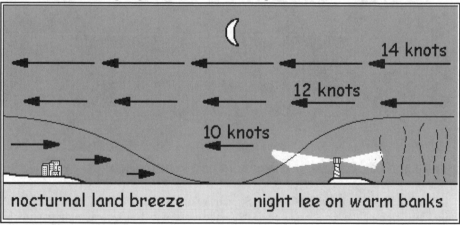

The effects will begin to assert themselves shortly after sundown. A smart skipper will begin to work into the Stream behind the shield of the lee as it spreads seaward before the boat, cross the now gentle middle and arrive at Gun Cay early morning while the banks lee still rules. The more forecast wind, leave later, but always when less than 15 knots forecast.

If bound to Florida from the banks, follow the night calm out to arrive Miami early morning while the land lee still holds. The land breeze will have quit some time before dawn or earlier, but a calm will still prevail until the sun gets high enough to heat the land again.

The banks lee and the Florida lee, like God and Man in Michaelangelo's Cistine Chapel ceililng frescoes, reach each other to finger touching distance in a forecast of 10 knots.

Deeper banks (15-30 ft) north or south may not radiate nearly as well. Go for Gun Cay.

As my run from Rum to Mayaguana using the Crooked/Acklins night lee shows, the longer sailing route through islands can sometimes beat rhumblines. I gained several days with just one overnight! And my backup landfall would have worked out just as well.

When I step off various routes for the conditions I've got, I often wish my dividers could lay out the miles in light and dark colors for daytime and nighttime sailing. Then I could bend the routes near different islands and slide the day and night strips back and forth until I knew exactly where I would sail and when, such that each island's diurnal effect got used to best advantage. Maybe someone can do a computer program that lets me drag day and night denoted routes around like elastic Bezier curves. Don't you wish?For another easy to understand example of this technique, see the diagrams below of a **trawler crossing** of the Mona Passage between Hispaniola and Puerto Rico. Assume that the trawler does 8 to 10 knots, and that it leaves Samaná on the northeast corner of the Dominican Republic. The forecast calls for under 15 knots for the first night, dipping to 10 or under the second night, returning the following day to normal trades. The trawler uses two night runs in calms and a day in port while the wind blows.

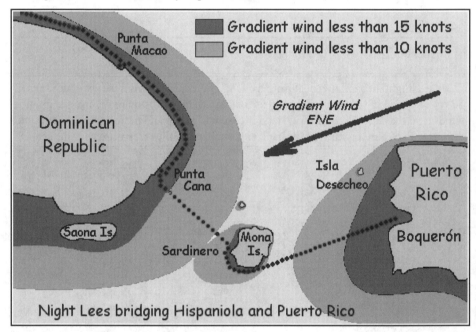

Night Lees bridging Hispaniola and Puerto Rico

The first night the trawler sails from Samaná to one of the east coast ports in the weak night lee, hugging the big island's coast to get the most of it. The second night the trawler runs in the much larger night lee, following it out into the Mona as it spreads eastward from the big island. She then gets the most out of Mona Island's shelter from seas and wind, and continuing, scoots into Boquerón in the morning with the Puerto Rico night lee just evaporating behind her.

A slower trawler might make four steps of it, resting at **Mona Island** to see, as the weather reports unfold, if it gets another night added to the window.

Most motorsailers can follow either the fast or the slow trawler routes.

Sailboats that can't do the quick stepping needed here can use an ESE wind under 15 knots. In ESE light wind on the night run down the DR coast the night lee extends quite a bit more than it does with ENE wind. At daybreak a sailboat should take a sailing tack northeast from **Punta Macao**, getting off the coast before the daytime accelerated winds and heaping seas begin. Later that night the sailboat can outflank any storm cells which might blow out to sea from the collapsed Puerto Rican **coastal front**. Finally, they tack down through the Puerto Rican night lee to a calm and peaceful early morning arrival in Mayagüez or Boquerón. See more details in the chapter on crossing the **Mona Passage**.

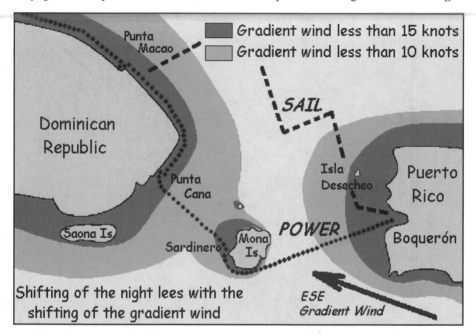

It should not need saying, but I continue to find people who do want to hear it:

if you draw a sure 2 day forecast of flat seas and no wind, then you should of course drive straight across the Mona and damn the tactics — but don't wait for it to happen.

FIRST PRINCIPLES

The **Thorny Path** had almost no traffic until the age of steam. Commercial sail owners who valued their ships avoided the windward route to the islands. Now today's yachties brave the **Thorny Path** that those heroes feared to tread! Notions of iron men on wooden ships shame them to navigate on the "take whatever comes" principle. They punch the rhumbline from island A to island B like they imagine the iron men of old had. Despite their brave and knowledgeable talk at the bar, I've noticed some curious behaviors. For example, the deeper the water, like the Mona Passage, the quicker they seem to want to go and get it over with. Few actually take my sailing route across the Mona during light **prevailing conditions**. Halfway across they crank up the revs and bash straight east like I zipped by graveyards in my childhood. Many seem to fear the dark as well. They start out in the morning and take 2 days and a night to cross, crashing and banging into trade seas.

Somewhere between quitting the job and casting off, many cruisers have lost their first principles of cruiser navigation: *safety, comfort* and *pleasure*. I profoundly hope the above discussions will enable you to return to those three basic principles.

THE BAHAMA ISLANDS

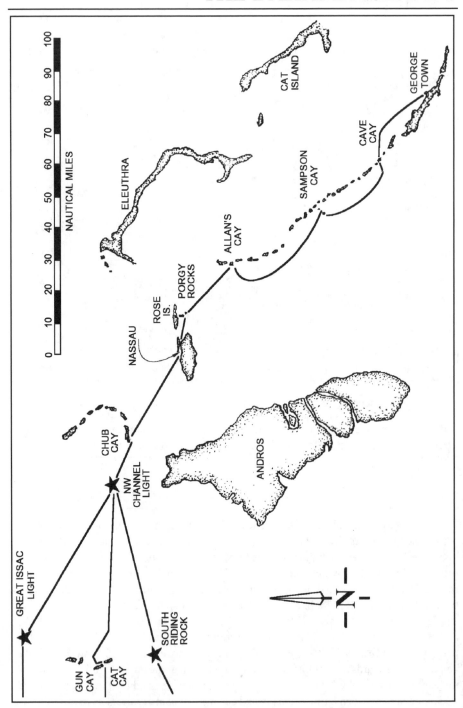

Florida to Georgetown, the critical path.

Pavladis' *Off the Beaten Path* and the *Yachtsman's Guide to the Bahamas* more than sufficiently cover the route from Florida to Georgetown. The charts you *must* have: Monty and Sara Lewis' **Explorer Chartbooks** series for the Bahamas. These give excellent scale, precision and the accurate lats/longs needed to properly gunkhole these myriad islands.

Also, Jane Minty and Bob Gascoine (Wavy Line Graphics) have an excellent correc5ted chart for all of Great Exuma.

From Florida to Georgetown the cruiser has such vast choices of wholly separate cruising grounds that cruisers could, and should, occupy themselves there many months. However long, and wherever you choose to cruise the upper Bahamas, your best plan would make Georgetown, Exumas, by early March.

Cruising the Exumas and the near out islands can easily exhaust the months of November until March. The Georgetown Cruising Regatta in early March and its Family Island Regatta in late April give plenty of reason to putter around the central Bahamas until early May. Visit the **Far Out Islands** during the more settled month of May and early June, but get nose down for the summer in the hurricane holes of Hispaniola or Puerto Rico by the end of June. Start east and south again after the hurricane season to enjoy the chichi cruising grounds from the Virgins to Grenada which best occupy a full winter's cruising.

THE GULF STREAM

The Great Bahama Banks produce a **night lee** almost as powerfully as does the great land mass of Florida. Whether going east *or* west across the Stream I use the night lees on both sides, departing late at night and arriving on the other side in the early morning. Departing Florida you have a calm sea and a land breeze at your back, and calm conditions with which to get settled on arrival. Review *Playing the Island Lees: Integrating Effects*.

Make your **wait for weather** in any safe hole south of Palm Beach. Where you start makes little difference except in heading and departure time, but wait *close* to the ocean. Count the hours of a trip from anchors up to anchors down. Getting out of mainland marinas, crossing the intracoastal bays and threading the barrier cuts in the dark, shall add hours you may not have thought of to your Gulfstream crossing. For example, waiting at **Dinner Key** Marina can put hours on your trip compared to **staging** at the marina inside **Government Cut** or **Hurricane** or **Noname Harbor** on Key Biscayne. Review the strategy section on *Staging*.

You may get a gentle southwesterly ahead of a stalling front that lasts a full day. Don't count on it. Under **prevailing conditions**, wait until the **Offshore Forecast** says south of east winds of less than 15 knots and seas less than 3 feet. Leave at night from the **Miami** or Ft.Lauderdale area. Never cross the **Gulf Stream** with wind against current, blowing northwest through northeast. If you take a southerly or westerly wind, don't get caught in the northerly winds that usually follow it. Against the Stream, they heap the seas up terribly. And never cross in conditions over Force 4. An average set of one and a half knots at 10° True from anchor to anchor works fine. Plot a course for an 8 a.m. arrival at **Gun Cay**.

If you anchor west of Gun Cay, check out the ledges on the shore for lobster. The weekenders from Miami assume someone already picked it clean and don't bother to look.

I've found it all round less hassle to clear at **Cat Cay** while waiting for weather, or go straight through to Nassau and fuel up while you clear in.

To take seven feet onto the **Great Bahama Bank,** proceed NNE from the **Gun Cay** light until the clump of trees on the north end of the Cay comes abeam. Then turn east to a point one mile east of the trees and northeast of the Gun Cay light. Now go to a course of 125° Magnetic for 4 miles. This gets you back on the rhumbline to **Russel Beacon**.

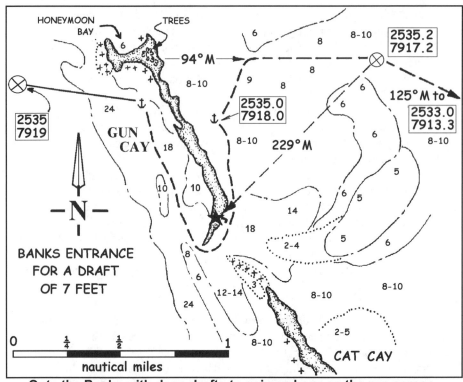

Onto the Banks with deep draft: to gain an hour on the run across, anchor *east* of Gun Cay the day before and leave at first light next morning and motor hard.

THE GREAT BAHAMA BANKS

You can wait for a totally calm day and motorsail lickety-damn (see the section on Motorsailing in the *Boat Stuff* chapter), or you can cross at night in any Force 3-4 forecast, using the calming effect of the **night lee**. If you opt for a daytime crossing, you can make the anchorage south of **Northwest Channel Light** before dark by leaving from the east side of **Gun Cay** well before dawn in southerlies or westerlies.

Staging yourself to the east side of Gun Cay the previous afternoon saves an hour, shortening the trip by 5 miles, and it makes it easier to start out in the dark.

My 6 and a half foot draft always took the route from Gun Cay to **Russel Beacon** with minimum 2 feet still under the keel. To navigate the shoal area east of Gun Cay with a 7 foot keel, leave on a rising half tide and follow the sketch above. If you worry about draft, take the northern route around **Isaac Light** in the ocean, or across the top of the banks from north of **Bimini** to Northwest Channel Light, passing a few miles north of the (unreliable) **Mackie Shoal** beacon. This route never has less than 10 feet of water.

Don't underestimate the high chop that can set up on the banks even in relatively light air. If forced to anchor on the banks, do so a good mile south of the lane you are traveling, and put on a long anchor snubber. Set out a bright light, and hope you don't have visitors.

The tide floods onto and ebbs off of the Banks from and to the nearest and largest access to ocean.

CHUB CAY

Anchor off the beach in front of the private club and marina. You'd find better anchorages at **Bird Cay** or **Whale Cay**, where you also shall have a better angle on the wind when sailing to **Nassau**. Each of these anchorages permits easy night exits. Set out two anchors

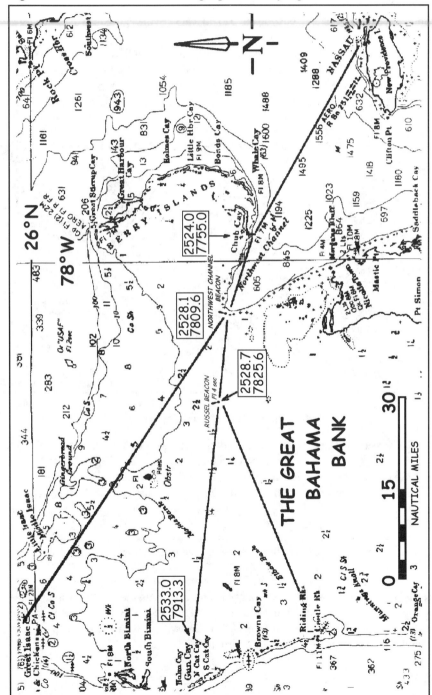

The Great Bahamas Banks to Nassau (SOUNDINGS IN FATHOMS)

for security from strong westerlies in squalls or thunderstorms year round. Leave around 3 a.m. to get to Nassau mid-morning which shall leave you plenty of time to fuss around getting a secure anchorage or to go shopping and tour in the afternoon.

NASSAU

Some love it, some hate it, but you have to do it at least once. If you arrive at a large port early in the day, you shall have lots of time to fool around changing anchorages as may become necessary. And you generally get a better handle on the town, than if you arrive late in the day. It makes much more productive whatever time you spend in port thereafter by arriving before lunch the first day. (See *Dinghy Security*).

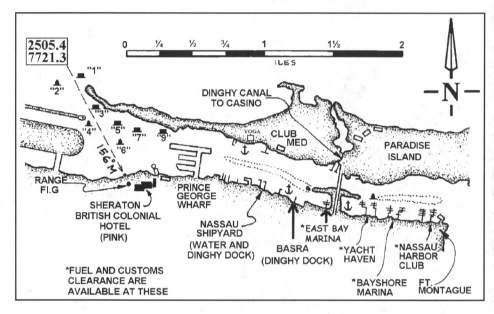

Transient anchoring in Nassau

Leave **Nassau**, for the **Exumas** shortly after daybreak on a day when the wind, if easterly, blows less than 15 knots. Take the direct deep water route to either **Allan's Cays** or **Highbourne Cay** from a point 2 miles east-southeast of **Porgee Rocks**. This route passes between **Middle Ground** and **Yellow Bank**. Deeper than charted, this channel has few and distinctive heads. Leave Nassau early so that you have the high light of late morning to early afternoon while enroute.

Stage **from Nassau to Bottom Harbour, then jump off from Porgee Rocks.**

To get a leg up on the passage, if the winds don't go light enough for you, **stage** in **Bottom Harbour** on **Rose Island**. To leave Bottom Harbour, motor west at sunup, close to shore, to the entrance to the salt pans, then head True South 0.8 miles until **East Porgee Rock** bears west, whence you turn onto 149° magnetic for 1.6 miles to the departure point east southeast of **Porgee Rocks**. See chartlet.

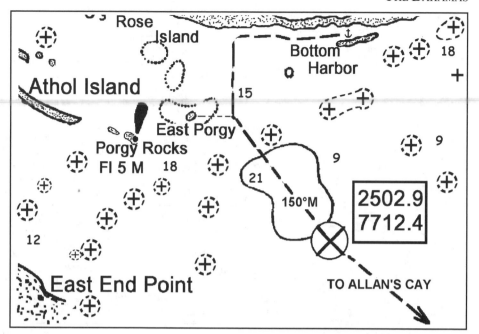

EXUMA CAYS FAST PATH

Westbound Boats who wish to shortcut the Bahamas can enter the Exumas at Galliot Cut, take the Decca Range out of Pipe Cay to the Tongue of the Ocean, then cross the Great Bahama Banks to Gun Cay on the Gulfstream, or sail non-stop to Ft.Lauderdale in deeper water via Isaac Light. See next page.

You should cruise the **Exumas** slowly and enjoy every anchorage available. You shall find no better cruising in all the Bahamas (some think the *world*), although the **Far Out Islands** offer better diving. The following notes assume you have already done your touring and gunkholing, and you want to now make a rapid and easy passage down to Georgetown.

For drafts to 7 feet the fastest, safest and simplest passage, take the **Exuma Banks** all the way down to **Cave Cay**, one of the easiest and deepest cuts and the last cut going south for vessels of draft. A draft under 8 feet has no reason to take the outside route. The banks will give you 10 feet or more most of the way, with convenient cays at which to luff upwind and anchor for the night. Drafts over 7 feet should exit the banks at **Conch Cay Cut**, just north of Staniel. Even so, playing the tides with close attention to the *Explorer Charts* deeper drafts can go farther. While worthy stops for the cruiser, **Staniel Cay** and **Pipe Creek** don't provide convenient waypoints on a banks passage. Drafts over 6 feet may have difficulty entering or leaving the banks at those points.

On the passage down the banks behind the Exumas you'll close reach on twenty knots of wind without a ripple on the water. The 10-15 feet deep water, clear as a swimming pool's, runs unobstructed with coral heads the whole way. *Even with a deep draft, don't shy from taking the Banks route behind the Exumas.*

Use this passage to learn to read the banks water of the Bahamas. Too many cruisers spend all their time in Georgetown at one anchorage, then, at the end of their festivities they start the 300 miles of Far Out Islands without the least skill in reading the water.

Fast Path Down the Exumas: take it slow (SOUNDINGS IN FATHOMS)

	WAYPOINT	LAT.	LONG
1	Porgy Rocks Jump-off	2502.9	7712.4
2	Entrance to Allan's Cay	2444.8	7650.5
3	Clear the shoal SW of Allan's	2444.0	7651.5
4	Clear Norman's Spit	2435.7	7652.0
5	Round Elbow Cay Light	2431.0	7649.2
6	Clear Cistern Cay Spit	2425.95	7646.8
7	Clear Fowl Cay Spit	2415.8	7635.3
8	Round Twin Cays	2412.5	7630.5
9	Round Harvey Cay Light	2409.0	7629.3
10	Entrance to Channel from banks to Galliot Cay	2355.3	7619.3

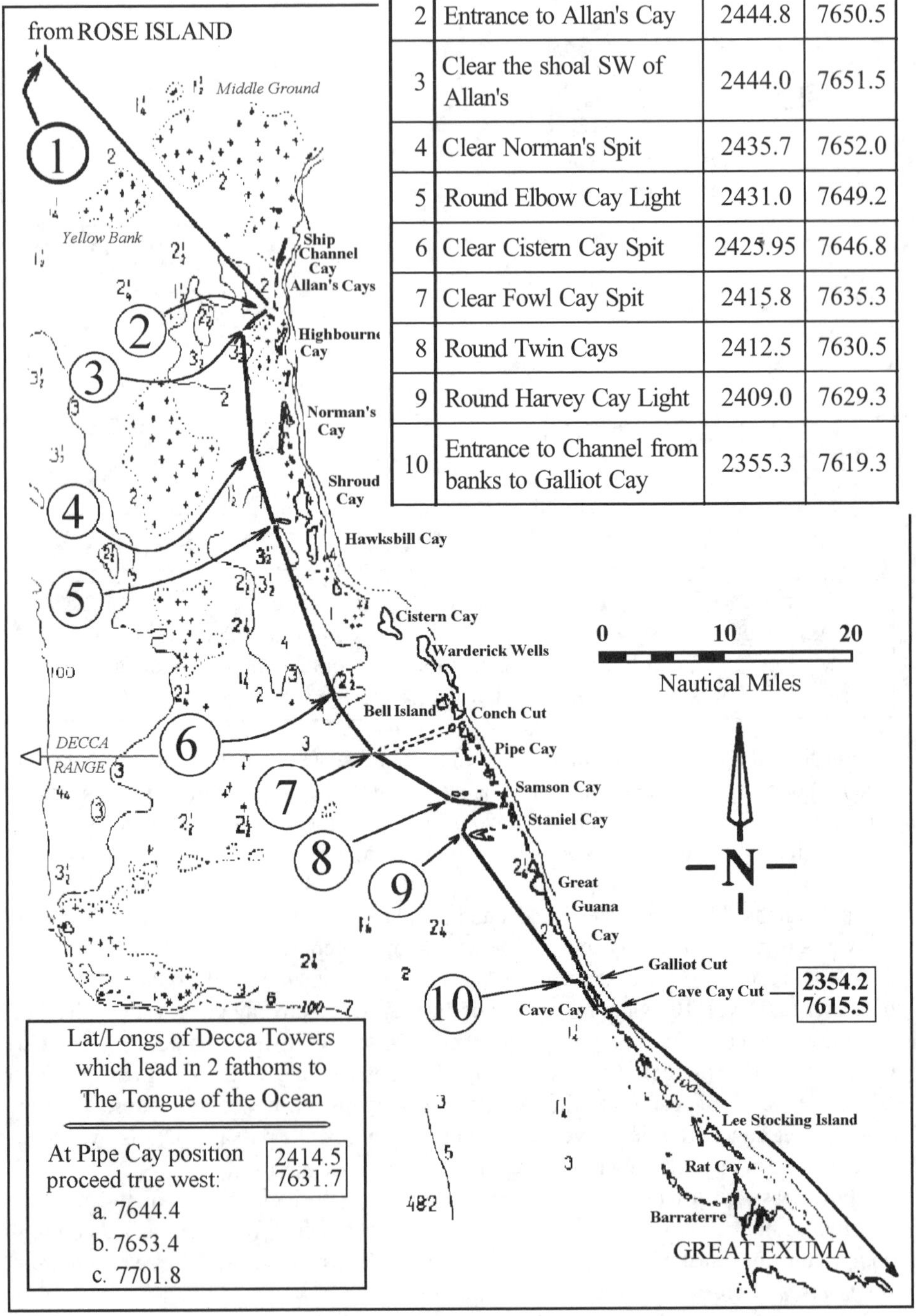

from ROSE ISLAND

Middle Ground

Yellow Bank

Ship Channel Cay

Allan's Cays

Highbourne Cay

Norman's Cay

Shroud Cay

Hawksbill Cay

Cistern Cay

Warderick Wells

Bell Island   Conch Cut

Pipe Cay

Samson Cay

Staniel Cay

DECCA RANGE

Great Guana Cay

Galliot Cut

Cave Cay Cut

Cave Cay

2354.2
7615.5

Lee Stocking Island

Rat Cay

Barraterre

GREAT EXUMA

0   10   20

Nautical Miles

—N—

Lat/Longs of Decca Towers which lead in 2 fathoms to The Tongue of the Ocean

At Pipe Cay position proceed true west: 2414.5 / 7631.7
    a. 7644.4
    b. 7653.4
    c. 7701.8

ALLAN'S AND HIGHBOURNE CAYS

Stay a day or two at the anchorage at **Allan's Cays**. If you want to make better time by going farther, take the anchorage off the beach at the middle of **Highbourne Cay**. It makes a good, calm waypoint in settled easterlies

SAMPSON CAY

Get fuel and water here. You shall also lie central to an abundance of little anchorages, each one suitable for easy starts to **Cave Cay.**

CAVE CAY

A draft of 7 feet can approach from the banks during mid-neap tide on 90° magnetic on the northwest tip of **Little Galliot Cay**. One may also use a transit with the beach on **Big Galliot Cay** just opening on the northwest tip of **Little Galliot**. When in deep water west of Galliot Cay, turn southeast to anchor behind **Cave Cay**. As almost always in Bahamas current, anchor in shallow water over deep sand. Set out an anchor light. Mail boats may take this pass at night.

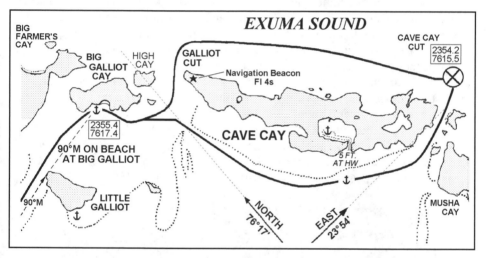

Exuma Banks to Exuma Sound via Galliot or Cave Cay Cuts.

Near slack tide in the morning, charge out the wide **Galliot Cut**, favoring the south side, or the deep **Cave Cay Cut**, favoring the north side, and sail off to **Georgetown** in a north of east wind of 15 knots. If you haven't got it, wait for it. Better yet, wait for a stable prefrontal westerly and reach down to Georgetown in Exuma Sound in calm water.

Stay and fish awhile if it has blown hard east or northeast for several days. You don't want to enter the Georgetown cuts in what they call a **Rage**, where a combination of wave over swell can catch you wrong and broach you onto the reef inside the cut when you try to make the turn. With the Explorer Charts trawlers and center boarders can continue further on the banks, coming out at Rudder, Adderly or Rat cuts.

Check out the underside of the fallen rocks on the south shore of **Little Galliot Cay** for yellowtail snapper, or try further south behind **Musha Cay**. The rocks on the south side of Cave Cay Cut (out of the current) also can produce for you.

GEORGETOWN

February through May **Georgetown** acts as the terminus for the apprehensive, who go back home, and for the adventurous, who strike out for the Caribbean. Mid-March Georgetown hosts the **Cruising Regatta,** started by then Georgetown dentist Joel Fine in 1981. Cruisers themselves put on this event to raise funds for the **Family Island Regatta** in April. It has drawn 500 yachts near the end of their Bahamas winter cruise.

The Family Island Regatta, the America's Cup of all the classic Bahamian workboat races, and one of the few remaining old time "Camp Town Race" type of expositions in North America, takes place the week after Easter. The **Salt Pond Regatta,** a similar, though smaller and, some think better, event, gets held 6 weeks after Easter across the banks in Thompson Bay, Long Island.

Between all these events you have access to the miniature cruising ground of **Elizabeth Harbor** itself. You can sail over to **Conception Island** or **Rum Cay** or **Long Island** for a week's getaway from the partying at Georgetown. You may, like myself, settle into a habit of Georgetown in the spring and Venezuela or the DR for the worst of the hurricane months. A wholly satisfying cruising life with lots of safe, short, *thornless* passages to keep crew and boat in condition, and you can provision cheaply for 6 months at both ends (Dominican Republic and Puerto Rico up north and Venezuela at the south end).

Georgetown earns the moniker of "Chicken Harbor" every season. Cruisers gab about stopping off at Conception on the way to Puerto Rico, or sailing to Rum Cay in one shot, as though they were just stopping by the convenience market before ramping up onto the interstate. Their biological clocks still set high from the hassle of getting the boat ready, the bustle of provisioning in Florida, even from the social whirl among the yachts at Georgetown, one after another finds an excuse to return to Florida and "go south next year".

Cruisers that take the plunge unprepared have their clocks quickly cleaned. Then they slow down to island time. They begin to see the wisdom of my constantly drummed advice: *wait for weather, leave early, get in early,* and *hit all the stops on the way down.* Some never get the message. They write the whiny letters to the **SSCA.**

The monument anchorage at Stocking Island

130

REDSHANKS

Georgetown abounds in fine anchorages, but unless you go into one of the holes in **Stocking Island** or **Redshanks**, you will move from one to another in the winter months as fronts shift the winds. They call it the Georgetown shuffle.

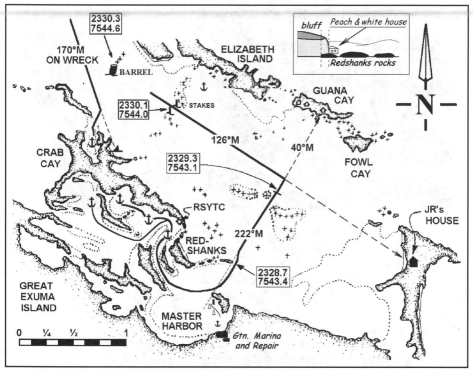

Georgetown anchorage at "Redshanks Yacht and Tennis Club".

Though a little remote, you only have an 8 minute ride to town in a gofast dinghy from Redshanks. And why don't you have a gofast in the Bahamas? To enter this landlocked harbor with a 7 foot draft, run down Elizabeth Harbor on a line 126° magnetic on JR's house on **Man of War Cay**. This shall carry you by the reef off **Sand Dollar Beach** anchorage and through the gap in the reef off the **Elizabeth Island** anchorage.

When abeam of the house on the middle of **Guana Cay** turn onto 222° Magnetic until able to distinguish a **transit** of the easternmost of the **Redshanks** and the bluff which bounds **Master Harbor** to the northeast. Keep these 2 features just closed, and you will pass a large coral head to starboard which stands in the center of a 100 yard gap in the reef beyond. Leave the last of the Redshanks forty yards to starboard and steer to the bluff, rounding slowly to starboard so as to leave the bluff 200 yards to the southwest. Then steer west until you see the entrance to Redshanks anchorage and pick up the darker colors of the entrance channel's deeper water. Anchor southeast of a ridge-like shoal which runs the length of the harbor in a northeast line. Here deep draft vessels will find from 9 to 14 feet of water in good sand. Enter 2 hours before high tide with drafts 6 to 7 feet.

Drafts under 6 feet may round the northern extremity of the shoal close to **Crab Cay**. Vessels under 5 feet may try the anchorages even farther to the west. The narrow and shallow entrance hides an anchorage of 3 fathoms with extraordinary protection.

The Club's Bar at the RSYTC

For many years the **Redshanks** anchorage has had fame as the locus of cruisers noted for their **Leisure** style. Whereas the **Stocking Island** anchorage has its *Volley Ball Beach*, and the monument anchorage has its *Hamburger Beach* at which yachts in the anchorage carry on their community activities, Redshanks has the *Redshanks Yacht and Tennis Club*. The RSYTC stands on a half moon of beach fronting a cliff with many shelf-like outcroppings, where cruisers hold nightly happy hours with hors d'oeuvres. Many of the same yachts return every year to enjoy the unique isolation in civilization available here, and a loose sort of club does prevail. With no founding member present, one of the yachts acts as Club Commodore, welcoming yachts on the VHF radio.

Past editions of this guide reported the *Redshanks Yacht and Tennis Club* with tongue in cheek, in the spirit of the Redshankers themselves, even reporting the Club's intentions to install a lawn tennis facility. Unfortunately for the game, a German megayacht squeezed into Redshanks after getting reluctant but official clearance from the Commodore. His outrage at finding only a few yachts and ragged rocks inside echoed clear to Nassau.

If you like to dive, or you have naturalist or libertarian tendencies, you'll love the Redshanks Yacht and Tennis Club. Check your tides when you dress for happy hour. The bar might get ankle deep at spring highs.

Georgetown Marina and Repair has its haulout facility in nearby Master Harbor.

EAST FROM GEORGETOWN

The **Leisure Sailor** following the **Thornless Path** may find it advisable to do **Long Island's** west coast, in order to get a leg up on the wind during the winter months. (See the example under *Island Strategies: Plan Your Route Flexibly: Passage Elapse Times* above). In any case, to leave Georgetown headed south you should position yourself at **Fowl Cay** first. Why? Review the section on *Island Strategies: Staging*, and *Island Weather: Winter Cold Fronts*.

132

All miles shown are miles under the keel, anchor to anchor, for sail.

Trawlers may experience up to 20% less depending on swell direction.

East from Georgetown: many options exist, take the one that suits the weather windows available.

If the dawn brings an evil blow with it while waiting at Fowl Cay, retreat to **Redshanks** for a day and attend the Redshanks Yacht and Tennis Club happy hour. Next evening wait back at Fowl Cay anchorage again.

A course of 35° Magnetic through a point 50 yards to starboard of the last of the rocks which stretch NE from Fowl Cay will carry you outside to **Exuma Sound**. The **North Channel Rocks** exit puts the sun in your eyes in early morning light. The **Fowl Cay** exit makes an easy off-light transit. Take a course of 62° magnetic for **Cape Santa Maria**.

The Fowl Cay exit from **Elizabeth Harbor** puts you a few miles nearer Cape Santa Maria and has a better angle on the usual winds than the **Conch Cay Cut** exit. It also has a better angle on early light conditions than the North Channel Rocks exit. You may shorten a **Conception Island** landfall by several hours if you have already anchored at Fowl Cay rather than in the middle of the harbor and then taking Conch Cut out into the Sound.

The North Channel Rocks channel angles directly against the sun for anyone leaving Georgetown in the morning and directly up light for anyone entering in the evening, usual departure and arrival times of sailboats and slow trawlers, and you must run it blind with

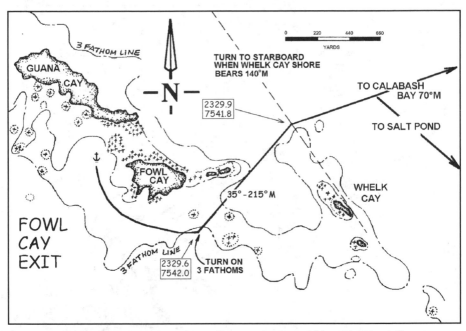

the GPS. North Channel Rocks makes a fine entrance at midday. The **Fowl Cay** entrance does not angle against the light, has landmarks close at hand with which to maintain a sure position while transiting and takes only a few minutes. A two fathom entrance with good visibility, you can *pilot* this entrance on a white sand road. *Pilot* your vessel. *Don't run my waypoints.* They're too close together.

Pilot this short leg. Don't run the outer and inner waypoints by GPS.

You should always try to have positive, near-at-hand landmarks navigating dangerous cuts. One season, we all listened to the breakup of a large ferrocement yacht which, with two other yachts following her. She wandered too far from the channel while going out the North Channel Rocks channel, against the light, early in the morning. He just didn't have enough positive identification of whereabouts in that channel. The water looks all the same, and a little drift you don't catch can finish you, especially if you use a buddy channel while JR bellows warnings to you on channel 16 (the actual case).

USING LONG ISLAND'S LEE SIDE

If you want to leave **Georgetown,** yet the wind continues to blow briskly northeast, then don't hang around Georgetown gathering commitments. Take a sparkling sail over the banks to Salt Pond, Long Island.

Leaving **Fowl Cay Cut**, watch set and leeway doesn't drift you onto Whelk Cay Reef as you round it going southeast. Get well beyond the **Whelk Cay Reef** before turning to a course for **White Cay,** on the banks. The course to White Cay is about 120° M, splitting the difference between **Black Rocks** and **North Channel Rocks**. You head for waypoint #1, two miles north of the east end of **Hog Cay**. Turn eastward to waypoint #2 where you shall enter a blue water trench bordered on the south by a white bank. Follow the white bank on your starboard hand at 118°M to its end at waypoint #3, then continue on course to waypoint #4 at **Indian Hole Point.**

134

Round **Indian Hole Point** closely and proceed directly northeast to the **Thompson's Bay** anchorage.

	LAT	LONG	ACTION
1.	2325.5	7529.0	turn east at **White Cay**
2.	2325.5	7524.0	enter blue trench
3.	2324.4	7520.0	leave white bank
4.	2321.0	7510.0	arrive Indian Hole Point, Thompson's Bay offing

PLAY THE TIDE FOR SPEED AND DEPTH

For drafts of 6 feet and more, you had best start onto the banks with an early morning low tide. You should try to catch the slack high tide half way across. Not only shall you get deeper water on the banks, but the stream shall carry you both onto and then off of the banks. The bank tides between the **Exumas** and **Long Island** run east-west in the west and north-south in the east. Reckon on one knot at full ebb. Tides at White Cay shall be about 1 hour 20 minutes later than Georgetown. Salt Pond tides shall be about 1 hour 40 minutes later.

USE THE LIGHT

If you leave from **Fowl Cay** (not Redshanks or the Monument) around one hour after sunup you will have fair light on the banks. Paralleling **Hog Cay** and **White Cay** you will again have good light at midday. Then the sun sits over your shoulder when you make for **Indian Hole Point**, the largest and darkest headland visible far to the southeast.

GETTING OFF THE BANKS

To leave the banks, sail north in the lee of **Long Island**. From **Salt Pond** north to **Simms** run from point-to-point about 200 yards off each point. From Simms to Calabash Bay stand well off **Ferguson Point** (waypoint #1 below), nearly a mile, and sail directly for **Dove Cay** (waypoint #2) until you can see the sandy bar west of it.

A fifty foot wide channel carrying 7 feet at low water will border the bar 280 yards west southwest of **Dove Cay**. Follow it 2 miles to deep water a mile southwest of **Hog Cay** (waypoint #3). Deep draft vessels can take the **Dove Cay Channel** with an incoming tide.

	LAT	LONG	ACTION
1.	2329.2	7516.1	clear Ferguson Point
2.	2332.6	7520.1	enter Dove Cay Channel
3.	2335.3	7521.6	leave Dove Cay Channel

CALABASH BAY AND SANTA MARIA

Calabash can roll in winds north of east or if they have forecast large northeast swells for the area. With east or south of east winds you shall have a fine, smooth anchorage. If it looks like the northeast wind shall go east, tuck in under **Cape Santa Maria** for an early takeoff to **Conception Island**, or fish the point in the morning and go in the afternoon. It takes just three hours to get there.

After entering Calabash Bay through the reef continue east to a grassy shoal which stretches blackly north and south in front of you. Turn to the small lighthouse built at the west side of the inner basin entrance, turning in toward the houses slightly to a point which bears 325° magnetic to the point of land to the west, 030° to the lighthouse and 200° to the point of land to the south. Here you have 8 1/2 feet at low water. Get out of Calabash if it blows anything but easterly. The chop and swell can get ferocious and will slam you on the bottom.

The reef entrance on the northwest corner of the anchorage can take 9 foot drafts.

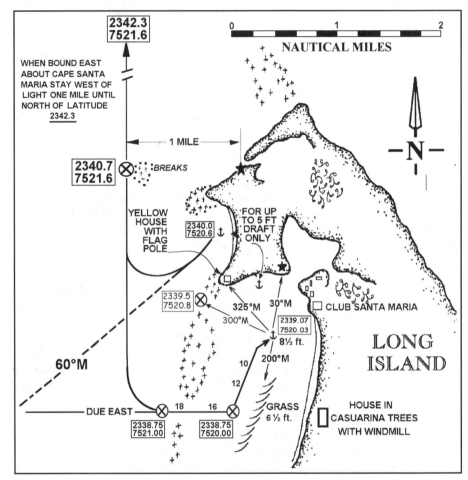

Calabash Bay and Santa Maria Anchorages

CONCEPTION ISLAND

If you have easterlies of Force 3 or less make your landfall at **Conception Island** on **Southampton Reef**, anchoring in 20 feet of rock and sand around two and a quarter miles north of **West Cay**. Dinghy over the reef for some of the most spectacular reef and wreck snorkeling available in the Bahamas, second only to **Rum Cay**. You shall find several square miles of reef diving here. With heads towering 20 feet or more over white sand bottom, you'll feel like Superman flying between the skyscrapers of Gotham City. The bad guys on the streets below are 10-20 pound groupers, snapper and 5-10 pound lobsters. Look long enough and you'll spot relics of the old wooden ships wrecked on this three mile reef which ships can't see from windward. Conception has gone into the Exuma land/sea park which has quite stringent rules for taking of shells and wildlife. Hone up on actual enforcement policies at the time of your visit. You neither want to despoil this island and reef, prettiest of all the Bahamas, nor do you want to limit your enjoyment of it based on *rumored* restrictions or out of date publications.

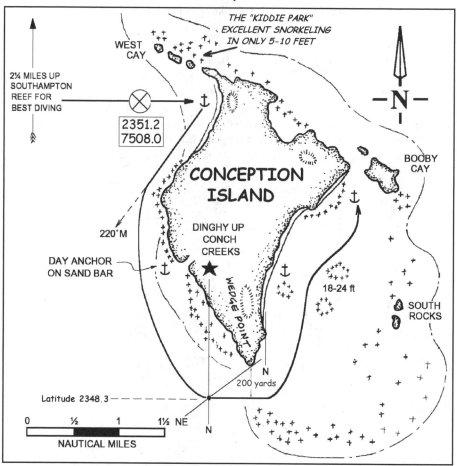

Conception Island: use the east anchorage in a westerly.

Other guides notwithstanding, the eastern anchorage has 18 to 24 feet of deep sand bottom and makes an excellent refuge in westerlies. Coral shoals are few and easily seen. Anchor in the corner between **Booby Cay** and Conception. You can move from the northwest anchorage to the east anchorage and back again during passage of a **front**, staying at Conception as long as you like. Enter the east anchorage from a point south of the light and southwest of **Wedge Point**, proceeding due east, 80-120 yards off the Point, and until the north-south line of beach is visible on the eastern shore. Proceed by eye even to the top of the harbor if you wish. Normally the water reads quite easily.

Many think Conception Island the loveliest of islands in the Bahamas. Unfortunately, I meet folks every year who, having left **Georgetown**, feel themselves *en marche* and zip right by Conception, or use it only as a waypoint. In such a hurry to get to paradise, they rush right through it, never knowing they had it under their keel. You can stay at Conception indefinitely, fronts and all, until a **weather window** opens which gives you a lay on **Rum Cay** or **San Salvador** as a **Leisure Sail**. Dinghy around the rocks to the shoal pocket east of **West Cay** and north of Conception. You shall find the snorkeling there absolutely outstanding. This extensive area of sand and coral has shallow and safe water for even nonswimmers in tubes. If you don't want to dive with the pros way out on **Southampton Reef**, then don't miss this snorkeling kiddie park.

RUM CAY

Rum Cay makes the best spot east of Georgetown to **wait for weather** — if tucked well in. It has the finest snorkeling, fishing and diving you can expect, a friendly little community of well under a hundred souls, and good local restaurants and bars. It can roll a little unless you shelter well under **Sumner Point**. When I tucked in with a 6 and a half foot draft we didn't roll much here (see anchorages on chartlet). You can always jibsail over to the west coast beach or beautiful **Flamingo Bay** if your wait for weather becomes extended, or you can use the marina in foul weather. See diagram *Swell Bridle*, below.

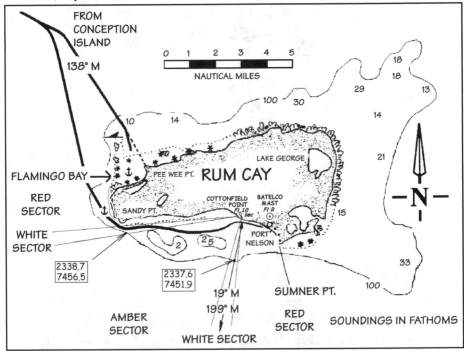

Rum Cay: best spot to wait for a front.

You should make your first time entrance here from west in afternoon sun, or from south with high sun. For the experienced, a light with 8° white sectors on safe entrance sits atop **Cottonfield Point.** Red sectors designate dangerous reefs while an amber sector covers an area with many coral heads. As often occurs in the Bahamas, it may not work.

Approach Cottonfield Point on either heading shown. About 800 yards off Cottonfield Point take up a 110° Magnetic heading on houses on the only hill north of the marina between the town dock and **Sumner Point**. The **Sumner Point Marina** project will see more homes sprout along the point. The hill north of the marina, with its houses, should nonetheless continue to stand out as a guidepost. When the Dive Club ruins' main house bears 10° magnetic turn to it and proceed to a clear white sand anchorage in 8-10 feet.

A larger anchorage, slightly less sheltered by the point, can be had by continuing several hundred yards on the 110° course instead of turning to the Club. A hole of about 8 feet can be found nearer the beach by holding the 110° course even farther.

Visit Kay's Bar and talk with Kay's mother, Doloris Wilson, a writer and local historian. Kay sells her mom's book, *My Rum Cay Home*, used by the Bahamas school system at *The Last Chance* general store just around the corner.

If you have an Ely 10-15 knot forecast, don't believe the SE 20 knot wrapping around Sumner Point. It made a guy I know keep his fleet in harbor here through three windows!

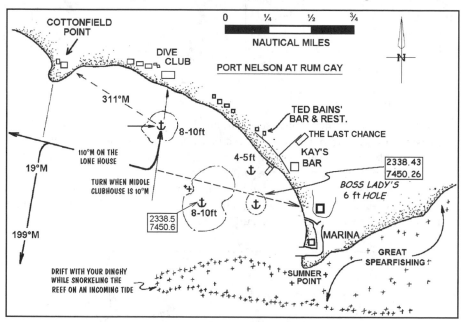

Anchorages at Rum Cay

Flamingo Bay, a beautiful anchorage on the northwest corner of the island, becomes a **deathtrap** in west and north winds. If you wait there, get out well in advance of any front. To enter Flamingo Bay enter at 138° Magnetic on **Pee Wee Point**, which appears from sea like a rock island, leaving the wreck at the tip of the northwest reef one half mile to starboard. Once inside the bay pick your way through the heads which only become numerous shoreward of a line between the points.

The Haitian wreck northwest of the entrance to Flamingo Bay carried a load of Salvation Army clothes to Haiti. They say the skipper ordered the Dominican helmsman to turn left to avoid the reef, which he did. Since the order stayed without countermand, the helmsman held it left in a broad, circling sweep that ended back where he started but slightly south — where you see it today. We used to renew our cruising wardrobe here, and not too shabbily (Ralph Lauren). Visiting the wreck may help you understand **Haiti** better before you actually go there. Thinking how it supposedly got up on the reef in the first place may enhance your enjoyment of the **Dominican Republic**: if you can empathize with the helmsman's "*no problema*" mentality, you shall *love* the DR.

Swell Bridle

Rum Cay lets you demonstrate a swell bridle to those fortunate sailors who never needed one in their home waters. From Georgetown to Luperón, and at odd points south, you shall anchor in open harbors where swell can sweep around the points. If roll annoys you, don't dash out into a full gale to avoid it, but fetch a boat's length of line and tie a rolling hitch to your rode at the bow. Cleat off the other end to your stern, then let out scope until you face the swell. Now you shall pitch a bit instead of rolling. You may also need some vernier adjustment at the stern.

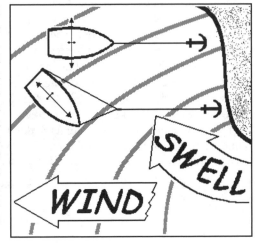

Sumner Point Marina

The marina makes a safe haven in severe fronts. The style and position of buoyage may change due to storms. If you haven't entered recently, you may want to call to have the marina staff talk you in. Answering VHF channel 16, they gladly furnish a free pilot to take in up to 7 foot drafts at high tide. The beautifully designed club house has a restaurant and bar, open daily for happy hour, with many artistic creations of the owners. The restaurant boasts gourmet dinners. You have to wait until Gorda Sound in the BVIs to enjoy both meal and ambiance that meet their standard.

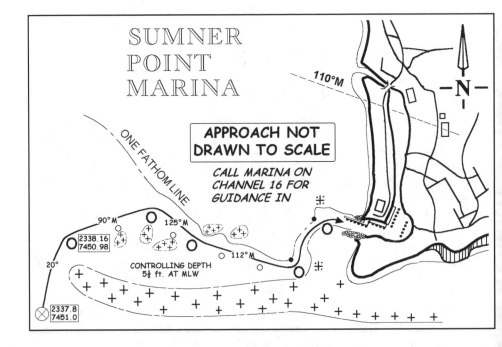

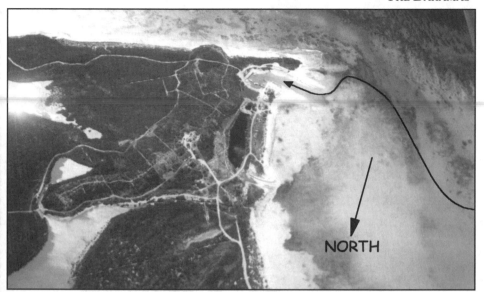

Aerial view of Sumner Point Marina looking south

RUM CAY TO MAYAGUANA

From **Rum Cay** you can strike various routes south. Bearing with the strategy to *Keep to the North to Go South*, you can make **Mayaguana** [*may-GUAH-nah*] direct with a *mild front* in winter, or **Attwood Harbor** and **Plana Cays** in up to Force 4 in summer.

Following a *mild* front to Mayaguana from Rum, take off on the first breath of southerly wind. By the time you get to **Samana Cay**'s longitude you could possibly broad reach north of Plana Cays then reach down the **Mayaguana Passage**. I've managed that several times, and at least one skipper reached from Rum to Grand Turk without touching a sheet!

Later in the season, with the more rapid veering of the front's winds, you might not turn the corner down the **Mayaguana Passage** before the wind goes east. In that case veer off to **West Plana Cay** or **Attwood**. In no case try to ride a *strong* front down through these reefy islands. Imbedded storm cells may cause you severe trouble.

You might jump up on a window by detouring to **Clarence Town** or **Landrail Point** (same as **Pittstown Landing**, or **Portland Harbor**), but only if the Offshore Report's outlook shows east to southeast under 15 knots 2 to 3 days out. You can use these light conditions on **Crooked Island**, to motorsail along the north coast at night to Attwood. Review the section on *Bank Effects* in the chapter *Playing the Island Lees* for details of a way to use Acklins' **night lee** if going by way of Clarencetown.

SAMANA CAY [suh-MA-nuh, not sah-mah-NAH as in the DR]

Once, when I approached **Samana Cay** from the south, conditions gave us a mirror image of the island, in color, on the bottoms of the clouds of the **coastal front** above the island. It began for me a series of discovery trips to this nearly unapproachable isolated jewel. If you want to know all about **Samana Cay**, read the November 1986 issue of the *National Geographic* (Vol.170, No. 5), an intriguing piece which proposes Samana as the real landing site of **Columbus** in the new world.

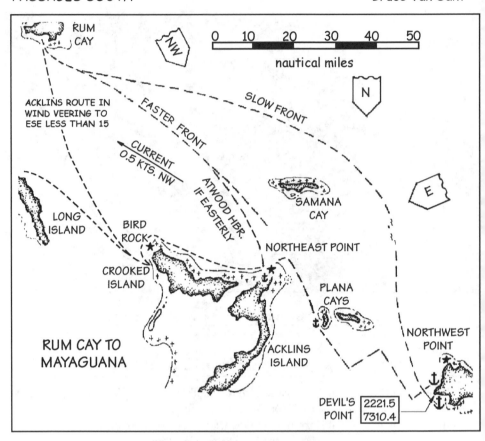

Riding a mild front to Mayaguana

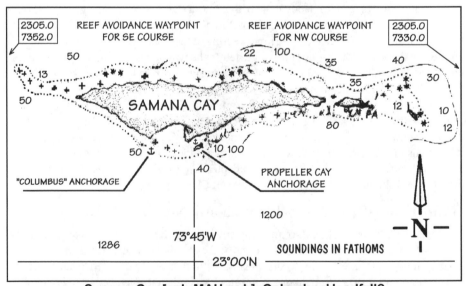

Samana Cay [suh-MAH-nuh]: Columbus' landfall?

Even in **Columbus'** day, Samana Cay got used for temporary fishing camps, where the **Arawak** inhabitants of **Acklins Island** to the south, could get away for awhile (for not always innocent reasons). They would hang out at Samana Cay, drying conch, crabbing and fishing until things cooled off at home and they could return to their settlements — or, as today, make a high speed outboard run over for cigarettes.

Anchor well tucked in at the supposed **Columbus** anchorage on the southwest and dinghy into the choppy bay anchorage on sand over rock. Have two anchors down and dive on them for inspection. With a draft less than 5 feet, you might make it into the bay where the fishing camps line the shore. Lead yourself in with the dinghy, however, and keep a kedge ready! And use the **Explorer Charts** here.

Pronounce Samana Cay SAM-uh-nuh or sah-MAH-nah, unlike the Dominican Republic harbor, **Samaná**, which you pronounce as the **Tainos** said it: sah-mah-NAH.

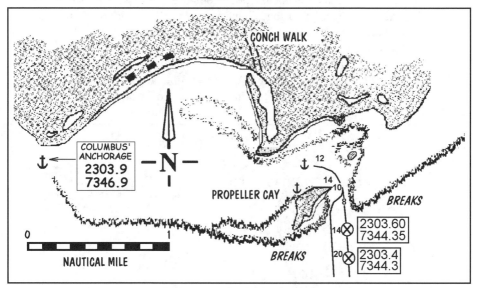

Anchorage at Propeller Cay

PROPELLER CAY ANCHORAGE

The 45 foot steel ketch *Steelaway* weathered a direct hit by Hurricane Klaus in the good holding behind **Propeller Cay**, in deep sand, but surrounded by perilous rock. If you take this anchorage, enter in light wind only with little chop (Force 3) and in good light (10 a.m. to 2 p.m., sunny). Stay on the white sand, 15 foot wide, 8 foot deep, zigzag channel. The current runs east and west *across* the channel.

Piloting directions:

1. Head magnetic north to the eastern most rocky point of Propeller Cay.

2. 100 yards south of the point, round east then north until 50 yards east of it.

3. Continue to round into the anchorage staying equidistant between the point and the isolated rock to its northeast.

With a GPS, head magnetic north from the waypoint shown until 50 yards east of the eastern most point of Propeller Cay, then follow step #3 above.

PLANA CAYS

Sometimes a fast moving **front** will outrun you and the winds go too far east to continue on comfortably. In that case, head for **Attwood Harbor** or **West Plana Cay**. The anchorage at Plana can roll a bit in southeasterlies but gets snug enough in stiff easterlies.

Proceed east to the middle of the sand beach. When over 20 feet of white sand bottom round to port to anchor at the northern end of the beach, south of a large coral patch.

As you coast to your anchorage, keep an eye on the heads beneath your keel. You want one not too deep and big enough to support a dinner sized grouper and a lobster for appetizer. Anchor about 150 feet dead to windward of the head you choose. After you have the boat snug for the night let out enough scope to bring the bathing ladder over the coral head. While the mate sets out the **SG&T**s, the skipper can harvest a bountiful dinner.

If forced to wait a while at Plana, the beachcombing on the windward shore gets as good as **Big Sand Cay**. You'll find good diving and fishing by dinghy, or off the beach, on the north end of the island. You can take your boat between the islands in a deep passage.

When the wind moderates, take a sparkling and sporty ocean daysail over to **Betsy Bay** for a good lee over grouper rocks and a tour of the small and friendly village there. As you round **West Plana Cay** on the south, the swells may intimidate, since the west northwest set of the deep ocean current spoils on the Plana shelf. But once out and away you've got a delightful daysail in clear weather and under Force 4 conditions.

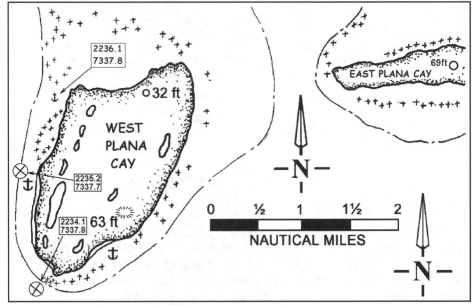

West Plana Cay Anchorage

ATTWOOD HARBOR ALTERNATE

For an alternate harbor try **Attwood Harbor** downwind from West Plana. Not a good spot in northeast wind, and a *deathtrap* in anything more northerly, Attwood otherwise makes a beautiful white sand Out Island anchorage. Enter Attwood only in good light from a point one half mile north at 2243.9-7353.2. Proceed 180°M to 50 yards west of the umbrella rock on the east side of the entrance. Round to the southeast since the harbor shoals to the west, and anchor in 8 feet of sand at 2243.22, 7352.80.

MAYAGUANA

When rounding Devil's Point (Southwest Point), take it close (40 yards) or the current may whip you out to sea again, and start a long tacking process around it.

Anchor over grouper rocks at **Betsy Bay** in southeast wind, **Start Bay** in east to northwest winds. Otherwise use **Abraham Bay**. If only overnighting, you can easily make the anchorage at Start Bay, and easily leave it as well. If the next day you decide to stay awhile, move into Abraham Bay via the west entrance. Take care to enter only in high afternoon light, and avoid the shoals and coral extending more than a mile south of **Start Point** to the edge of the western entrance to the bay.

Follow the reef to the blue water entrance channel a mile or more south of Start Point. Proceed northeast for one quarter mile inside the reef entrance, then one mile east to a position just behind the protection of the reef in 2 fathoms of water. To avoid all chop you must snug up to the reef. That also makes it easy to snorkel and dive the reef. Don't fear snugging in tight to the reef. I've sat here in 25 to 30 knots quite comfortably while more timid companions pitched wildly in the chop only 100 yards behind me. Park so that you have either breakers or bare reef to windward of you at high tide.

If you wish to visit the settlement you can take a 7 foot draft up the bay on a rising tide. From the anchorage behind the reef, steer toward the buildings to the north for 3 quarters of a mile, then steer for the settlement's radio mast, avoiding easily seen heads and rocks.

Bound for **Turks and Caicos** from Mayaguana, sailboats can *stage* to the beach at **Southeast Point**. When the winds go light easterly or north of east, take an afternoon sail over to Southeast Point. Arrive well before 5 p.m. in order to select a patch of deep sand in 12 to 20 feet at which to temporarily anchor. Do *not* snug up to the reef and coral heads to avoid roll. Leaving there at midnight, you shall have a pleasant close reach of only 35 miles to **Providenciales** instead of a 50 mile close hauled beat into 20 knots apparent from Start Bay or Abraham Bay. As an added benefit, if you arrive early enough near Provo, you sail into its night lee before it dissipates as the sun rises. You get another bonus if you can finish the **Sandbore Channel** before 9 a.m.

Leave **Mayaguana** only in settled weather (when the morning's **NWS Offshore Report** reads the same for "today", "tonight" and "tomorrow" — see *Making Sense of the NWS Offshore Reports*). Trawlers should look to swell direction before choosing a point of departure. It can make sense, in a persistent east southeast wind, for a trawler to break the trip into two legs by staging also at Southeast Point, but gauge the swell and any cross swell out beyond the island before deciding.

Whether you depart from Abraham Bay or Southeast Point, have your **SG&T**, read a little and catch a nap after dinner. Up anchor and depart so as to make a landfall at the Sandbore Channel entrance to **Caicos Banks** by *shortly after daybreak*.

I have had no trouble leaving my Abraham Bay reef anchorage in the dark with my deep draft sailing ketch, even before GPS, in order to go out the west entrance at night to make a good early morning landfall at Provo. But I *go slow*, and I have confidence of a minimum 2 fathom depth. You may want to stage out in deep water close inside the west entrance if you want to leave from the bay but have the willies about doing it in the dark. Boats have wrecked here, sometimes due to navigational error, but *all the time* for going too fast.

NOTE: Use Southeast Point in a window, *don't wait there for one.*

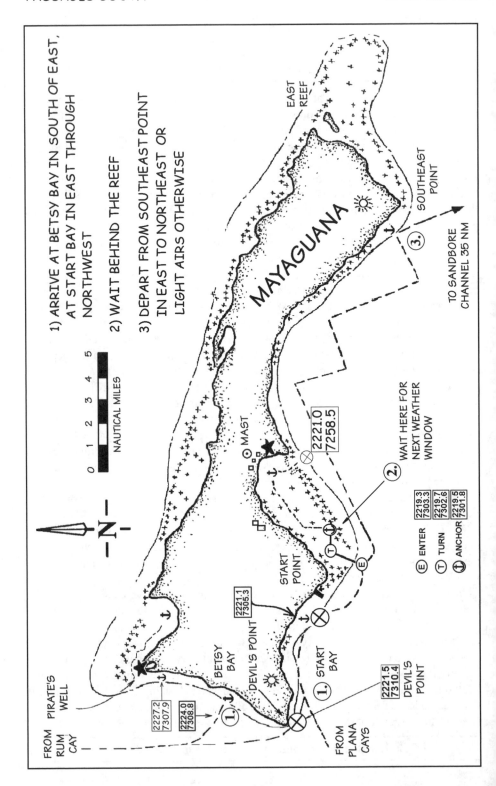

TRANSITING THE TURKS & CAICOS

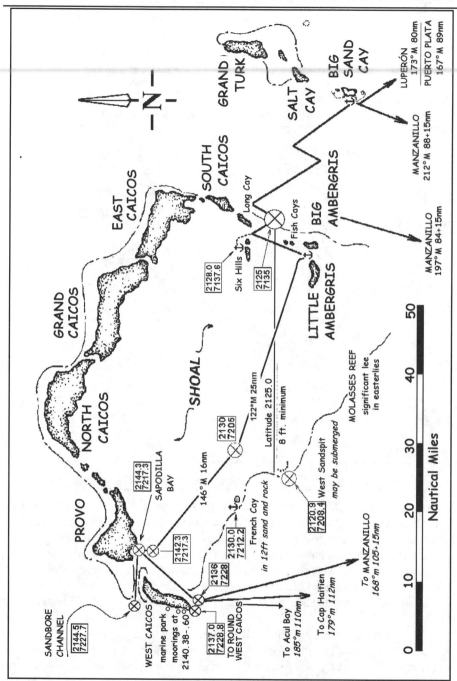

Coming from Mayaguana you should see low lying **Providenciales**, or **Provo**, shortly before you can pick out the reef marking the **Sandbore Channel**. Keep a sharp lookout, especially on days with poor visibility caused by high winds or upper level Saharan dust due to a northerly drift of the tradewinds. But you didn't go during high winds did you?

THE SANDBORE CHANNEL

Sail toward Provo in early morning light until you see the atoll-like reef with breaking seas dividing ocean blue from bright shoal green. You should already have spotted South Bluff (sometimes West Harbor Bluff), north of the Channel and some 6 miles east of the Channel's entrance. It shall appear quite grey and distant. Follow the reef south until you come to the half-mile broad ocean blue waters bordered by light green of the **Sandbore Channel** entrance. Can't miss it! Arrive early morning before the east wind begins to honk. It should have laid down overnight due to the intervening 60 miles of cooling banks.

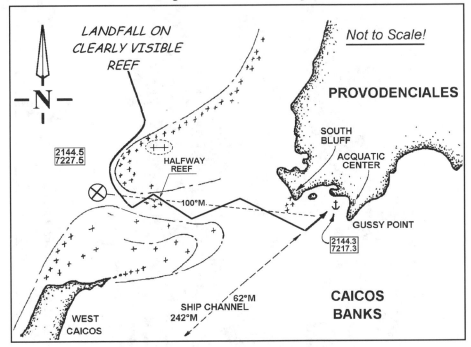

Sandbore Channel Entrance to Caicos Banks.

Motoring or sailing, tack the 8 or 10 miles to the ship channel and enter **Sapodilla Bay**. You will meet supposed *cognizenti,* locals and cruisers, who scoff at tacking the Sandbore in morning light, and motorboaters who say you should arrive around midday.

Look again at the chapter on *Playing the Island Lees: Bank Effects.* In **prevailing conditions**, the 60 mile wide shallow Caicos Banks comprise an extraordinarily large heat sink. It acts as light color land. If a sailboat doesn't get in before the wind rises, it may have to motor die straight into 20 knots and 3 foot chop in 8 to 10 feet of water for 3 hours at high revs.

So! Arrive in early morning calm. Halfway Reef ought to display itself quite well.

Why tack? If you sail east in a light early easterly, you either tack or get a sailboat not yet invented. If you motorsail or trawl, the sun glares dead ahead, but each narrow tack permits good up-light visibility either side of the sun as well as the advantage in boat speed. Once on the banks, you'll find few real heads, just shoals of veggies and a few rocks, most of which lie under 8 to 10 feet of water. Dodge them anyway for the sake of the odd rock which might stick up above the others in a trough. Tacking slightly while motorsailing, you can also keep a watch over your shoulder to know when you've passed

Halfway Reef and the shoals off **South Bluff**. Let the experts talk. I zigzag a morning up-light course over *any* shallows, any*where*. More fool you, if you don't, too. A beat up to the anchorage after the wind gets up could take several hours, so arrive early with a sailboat under sail. Never arrive after the wind strengthens with the rising sun.

Turtle Cove on the north shore of Provo

SAPODILLA BAY

Cruisers on a budget can pass up **Turtle Cove** on the north coast of **Provo** and anchor at **Sapodilla Bay**. You shall find Customs and Immigration at the government dock over the hill to the east or by dinghying around the point. Call HARBORMASTER on VHF Channel 16 for instructions.

Have your anchors well down. Although you'll find holding's fair to good, the occasional summer squall or winter front can have leading edges of up to fifty knots. Otherwise, you've got a good anchorage here.

If you didn't get enough **cash** in Georgetown try the banks here. And, believe it, you shall need cash if you stay long in Provo. However, if you plan to provision in the **Dominican Republic,** you can wait as the DR has become vastly more simple to provision and you can get **cash** with credit cards without fees from ubiquitous **ATMs.**

Remember that hours cut from the beginning of a passage really come off the end of the passage. If bound for **Cap Haïtien or Manzanillo** you might leave through the Provo ship channel and **stage** yourself off **West Caicos** for a passage shorter by several hours. West Caicos has buoys off the west coast for the dive boats that normally don't use them at night.

Plan to arrive about twenty miles offshore of *'Cap'* around 4 am. You will make up for any uncertainties of landfall by the loom of the city in the predawn hours. Refer to the directions for sailing from **Big Sand Cay** to Luperón or Manzanillo, and to the sections *Approaching Hispaniola, Manzanillo* and *Cap Haïtien* for detailed sailing directions.

Walk over the hill, past the hotel, and down to the customs house at the government dock, or .....

.....dinghy round the point to the beach just next to the government dock.

OVER THE BANKS

Bob Gascoine and Jane Minty (Wavy Line Publishing) make excellent charts of Caicos (as well as Great Exuma and Luperón). A caution for sailboats and *real* trawlers (i.e., *slow*): the banks routes shown basically apply to dive boats. Tidal set affects slower, large keel sailboats and real full displacement trawlers more than faster powerboats, and of course sailboats don't go to windward as well. Under prevailing winds, most sailing vessels should make better time on the route south of the center shoal area, both sailed and motorsailed. The **Six Hills** direct route works well for drafts under 5 feet. Stephen **Pavladis'** *Guide to the T&C* has great charts and tips for these routes.

From time to time you hear reports of the central shoal area having "gone away". Probably started by cruisers who got lucky in their trip through the maze. They then underrate the shoals. The slightly higher than the rest bulge in the middle of the northern half of the Banks, according to one theory, comes from a northeast-going space rock slamming into the ocean zillions of years ago, forming the Turks & Caicos. The geologist I talked with didn't think it would easily go away.

I devise my route for easy-to-remember coordinates, for safety of the vessel without GPS, for frail engines in severe cross tidal currents, and because I prefer the tried and true. Other routes may save you a half mile. You might do them safely a dozen times. Then again, maybe you'll hit the odd lump on the first try. Play it right. Play it safe.

Before Bob and Jane's charts and Stephen's guide of the Turks and Caicos, and before GPS, I took *Jalan Jalan*'s 6 and a half foot draft across the banks to **Six Hills** as an experiment, going *north* of the central shoals. I waited for calms and played the tides. It took two days of laborious backtracking in a sandbore maze. You reach **South Caicos** from Six Hills via Turks Passage. Pilot from Six Hills to **Turks Passage** only by eyeball and in good light.

Though you may not think so, the **Caicos Banks** lie on the Thornless Path. Why? You can *cross* the Banks easier than go around them. Believe me, I've tried all the ways. Leave **Sapodilla Bay** at dawn on a day when the wind blows light and *under 15 knots*. To clear out early you may have to pay overtime charges, even if you do the papers the day before during office hours. Pay it and go at daybreak. Don't delay departure. You don't want to get caught out on the banks at either low light or nighttime.

Leave Sapodilla Bay at *daybreak*. Cross the banks with a 7 foot draft from a position 2nm south of **Gussy Point**, proceeding along 146°M for 16 miles to a point 72°05'W, 21°30'N. Then motor lickety-damn in deeper water the 25 miles to **Ambergris** at 122°M.

Leave at dawn to arrive at **Ambergris** well before sundown. Reckon on a 1.2 knot northeast tide set at peak flood (northwest near the Ambergris islands) and use the **Rule of Twelfths** to interpolate your drift (see Glossary). Unless you have a GPS, keep a good **EP** (see Glossary). A **DR** alone won't do.

Even though the coral heads grow far and few between and deep, it doesn't pay to wax complacent on this run. Sailboats have grazed a coral head while in over twenty feet of water. So, with the Caicos Banks, as with the rice pudding in the school cafeteria, you would best avoid the dark spots.

If you have to anchor on the banks, do so at the risk of bending your anchor shanks, as I have done, while getting them up in a stiff chop the next morning. Perhaps you can chop your foot off with the chain which wildly snatches at the bow. Better you start out at *daybreak* or don't go at all. Never proceed within an hour of sundown. How can you, anyway? You've got to have your **SG&T** to stay on the Thornless Path.

Leave for points north from the Ambergris anchorage. Don't, as one fellow did, return to the approach waypoint first. That way you'll hit the elkhorn shoals shown on the chart to the north. For a lesson on GPS-guide-chart waypoints confusion, amply documented earlier in this book, look for the mast rising from Aeolus Reef on your starboard. Learn those lessons now, not while underway here. Review *GPS Cautions*, page 4. Now!

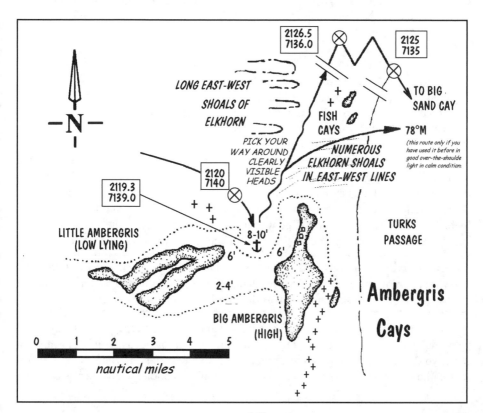

THE FRENCH CAY ROUTE

You can carry 8 feet to **French Cay** from **Sapodilla Bay**, exit the banks and re-enter between **French Cay** and **West Sand Spit**, proceeding along 21°25' in plenty of water to exit to the **Turks Passage** north of the **Fish Cays**.

To anchor at French Cay pick your way east as close to the island as you can. Anchor well in sand, and rest in security during prevailing easterlies.

AMBERGRIS CAYS ROUTE

The round the world cruise for a family of four nearly ended here scarcely before it began. They rammed a rock just at sundown trying to make the anchorage before dark. Start early and "arrive by 5" at **Ambergris** and anchor where shown, *not* near the land.

Anchor in 8 feet of water halfway between the islands, one mile east of **Little Ambergris** and one mile west of construction on **Big Ambergris**. This anchorage looks wide open, but in most conditions it provides good protection, good holding and a peaceful lie. I have stayed at this anchorage during quite heavy blows, passing **storm cells** and steady, strong **trades**, while it remained peaceful and serene with a light chop. Dive on your anchors. You might use two in case of wind shift from showers. Pick your way in.

One cruiser accosted me down islands with a harrowing tale of how he spent the night in 4 foot waves amidst hull-tearing elkhorn coral. He thought this guide irresponsible for recommending **Ambergris**. When asked if he stayed at the anchorage recommended above, he replied, "No, we couldn't find it because it was getting dark and we had to anchor".

This guide specifically warns, indeed rants, against anchoring on **Caicos Banks.** But my accuser had done exactly that. So, as the night followed Polonius' day, I asked:

"What time did you leave Sapodilla Bay?"

"About 8:30 or 9:00."

"What were the winds like?"

"Oh, southeast, 15 to 20."

"Couldn't you have left earlier, say, *daybreak*?"

"Well, we were with some other boats."

"Couldn't you wait for a better window, say, less than 15 knots?"

"We really needed to get going. We'd spent too much time in the Bahamas, and we needed to get to the Virgins to earn some money."

Four violations! He didn't leave at daybreak. He left in a southeast Force 5 on the nose. He didn't captain his own boat. And he sailed in a hurry ... The penalty almost came to fit the crime, but the perpetrator still saw himself as victim. And me as malefactor.

Large fields of elkhorn grow throughout this area and you need good afternoon light (before 5 p.m.) to identify them. The way into the anchorage from the Banks, however, has 10 feet and more except for obvious and only occasional heads showing quite blackly.

The first time you go south of the Fish Cays, go in good light only. You can find east and west running "streets" of 3 fathoms depth, but in poor light you may not recognize them. Do this channel in over the shoulder light until you know it.

Upon leaving the banks into the **Turks Passage** prepare for steep and short seas. Wind with tide, you have the Ocean trying to climb the wall onto Caicos Banks. Tide against wind, you've got cataracts underwater and overfalls above as the Banks empty themselves into the sea. In Turks Passage you'll have much smoother water. Purists can have a good sail north northeast to the shoals south of **Long Cay**, thence southeast between Long Cay and Fish Cays, long-tacking port to lee-bow the current down to a western approach into **Big Sand Cay**. Don't tack as far as dangerous **Endymion Rock**. If you short tack against the north going current, prepare for an all day sail to cover only 20 miles to Big Sand.

The current in the Turks Passage can really rip north, so *lee-bow* it.

TO GO AROUND THE BANKS

If you decide to go outside to avoid the banks, you can reduce the agony by nosing over to French Cay to anchor for the night. You then tightly follow the lee of the 60nm reef until the punishment of the **Equatorial Current** and full Trades start at its southeast end.

This route sucks under prevailing conditions. However, I have motored it quite comfortably in light southerly or variable winds caused by a strong front which suddenly wimps out and stalls just north of 22°. Do not expect to have a fun trip with northeasterlies, though. You might expect you can lay Luperón sailing southeast on a northeast wind, *but it never really gets fully northeast*, and the trade seas in the passage never really give up even in light northeasterlies. And, the surface current runs strongly west northwest there as well. All of which means: you can't lay Luperón from French Cay in wind south of 45° True, so follow the dictum: *go for comfort!* It almost always beats the rhumbline.

If you nonetheless *must* do it in **prevailing conditions**, break off before it gets rough and reach for the coast. Accept any easy entry harbors on the north shore of the Dominican Republic. *Don't* bash it. You'll break something. See *Approaching Hispaniola*.

BIG SAND CAY

Do **South Caicos** while cruising the **Turks and Caicos** but don't *stage* from there. Staging from South Caicos can add a day to the sail to Hispaniola due to the current in the **Turks Passage**. Stop at Big Sand Cay instead.

Big Sand Cay, though sometimes a bit rolly, has a large, deep sand anchorage. Thus the name. Waiting here puts you 20 miles farther to windward and up to a day's sail closer to **Hispaniola** than does any other route. Coming here also frees you from worry about **Endymion Rock**, 4 feet underwater and not always breaking, but now west of you.

Some DMA charts show **Endymion Rock** near Big Sand Cay and other charts don't even show it. Pavlidis' *Guide to the T&C* shows it correctly as does the *Bahamas Chart Kit*, about 7 miles bearing 215° True from Big Sand Cay light which stands at 21°11.7' and 71°15.5'W. Also note the clearly visible rocks, **South Rocks**, about a half mile south of Big Sand Cay. If sailing the windward coast of Big Sand on a route from **Salt Cay**, you can safely sail between South Rocks and Big Sand, swinging wide of the sandy shoals off the southwest tip of Big Sand.

Getting to Big Sand Cay can take a sailboat all day tacking due to the north setting current in the **Turks Passage**. But those hours shorten the sail to Hispaniola. Approach the island from the west on the light, and anchor in sixteen feet of deep sand about 150 yards southwest of the light. The light runs by solar cells and usually works. However, the switches often fail, leaving the light to work throughout the day, failing on dead batteries sometime around midnight. As with all lights south of Florida, assume they may not work.

If they work, assume their characteristics display wrongly because of poor power and poor maintenance. You shall find it all round best to flat distrust all markers in the Caribbean and the Bahamas. Navigate by pilotage. Transits of land features don't wear out.

The windward shore of this uninhabited jewel has the best beachcombing in the islands. Watch **whales** from here in the month of February where the humpbacks gather to mate from **Samaná Bay** to the **Silver Banks**. In their annual euphoria to get there the 40 and 50 footers will leap clear of the water, leaving echoes like cannon shots.

You can depart Big Sand Cay by starlight with safety. I've arrived there by starlight several times. Clear South Rocks well to your port, so as to arrive off the coast of Hispaniola just before daybreak. Schedule your departure time as early as 3 a.m. and as late as 4 p.m., depending on conditions and your boat. Knock 20% and ten degrees off what you think your boat can do, however, unless you face a dead calm motor trip.

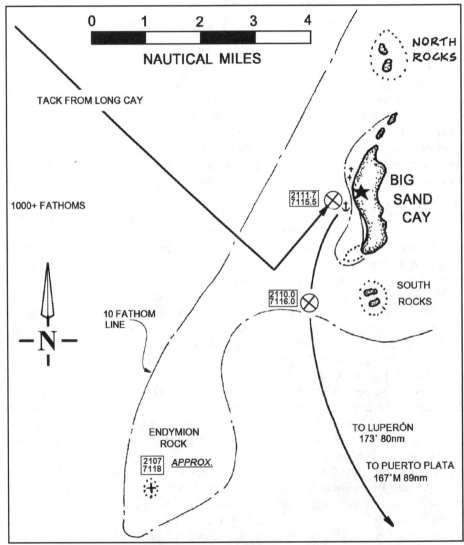

Big Sand Cay and Endymion Rock

As an alternate plan upon leaving the banks, sail to **Salt Cay** for an overnight on the mooring there before proceeding to Big Sand Cay. The visit shall pay off.

A mooring suitable for large freighters sits a third mile southwest of the small boat breakwater at the town. Other dive moorings exist from time to time. They sit in 40 feet atop a more than 300 foot wall. Scuba divers, don't miss it. Don't anchor off the town. The anchorage there has just a few inches of sand over rock. Same with the anchorage under the light. You'll bend your shanks in the chop or drag the anchor into a crevice from which it can't trip. Of course, use these anchorages only in settled weather and with an eye out for veering wind.

Salt Cay has super nice people. I used to do "cargo sail" for Ivy's grocery store here. Also, in the past the factotums at the Government House south of the dock have cleared me in and out when wheedled well.

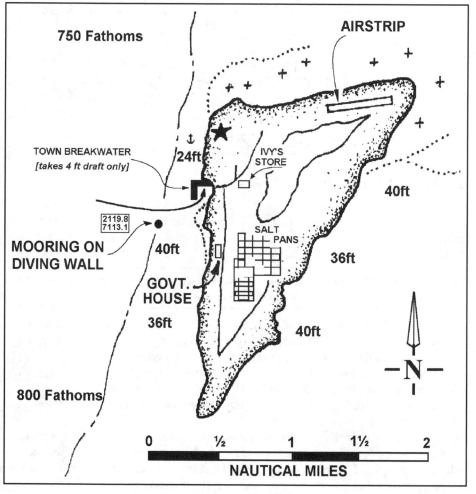

Salt Cay mooring.

APPROACHING HISPANIOLA

A mountainous island, **Hispaniola** has the highest and the lowest points in the Caribbean Basin, and they lie within a short distance of each other in the Dominican Republic. The north coast of the DR can offer the roughest passage for yachts island hopping to the Virgin Islands. But the oldest ploys in sailing, described in the next chapter, can make it quite pleasant. Landfall in Hispaniola requires radical departures in the southbound sailor's pilotage. In all of the more than 600 miles from north Florida, you only saw low sandy land and broad shallow banks. Now you only see towering mountains.

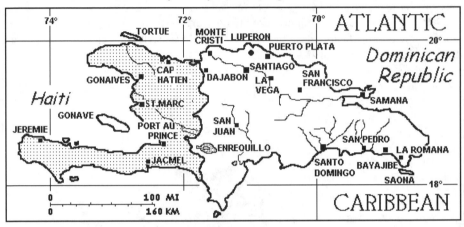

PICKING A WINDOW

Hispaniola draws a nighttime umbra of calm around itself which can reach as far as 30 miles offshore to the north and 20 to the east. Knowing how this works, you can do a much easier passage. At night, the huge land mass of Hispaniola gives up the heat it accumulated during the day, while the sea, which has a much longer memory for heat, does not.

Think of this as a "heat bubble" over the island which shimmers away from the direction of the gradient winds.

More north in the component of the **trades**, and the bubble shimmers south and west, shrinking the north shore's **night lee**. More southerly component to the trades, and the bubble shimmers further off the north shore, providing sailors a larger lee.

Additionally, the **katabatic** wind, the cooling mountain air that slides downhill after nightfall, lifts the easterly **trade wind** off the island's coast. The katabatic wind adds to a possible **land breeze**. The opposite of the day's **seabreeze**, the land, cooling faster than the sea, causes the night's land breeze.

All of these effects create the **nocturnal wind**, which blows lightly offshore. The island's heat loss and the nocturnal wind redirect the flow of the trade winds over and around the island like a stream flowing around a rock. The effect will start earlier (19:00) and last longer (12:00) on light wind days, and start later (00:00) and end earlier (07:00) on days with strong winds. Similarly, the effect will extend itself farther to sea on light wind days and stay inshore on hard wind days. The effect waxes greater after bright hot days and weaker after overcast days. Think of the shimmering bubble.

After hot, light southeasterly wind days you shall feel the warm breath of the land on your cheek, and you can smell the aroma of black earth, cows, and charcoal fires up to 30 miles at sea! You'll have an epiphany the first time you go through this.

Observing the backing and veering of the winds from day to day, the shrewd **Leisure Sailor** waiting at **Big Sand Cay** to lay a course for **Luperón,** or waiting at **French Cay** or **West Caicos** to jump off for **Cap Haïtien**, or **Manzanillo**, shall leave in less than 15 knots south of east so as to intersect this belt of flagging winds as far out to sea as possible. On the other hand, up to 15 knots north of east makes a fine sail despite a more narrow band of lee from the land. This calls for some iterative course planning to handle various assumptions of the **land effects**. After an overcast day of moderate trades, stay in port. But after a bright hot day of Force 4-5, consider giving it a shot.

The **Equatorial Current** can sometimes run as high as one and a half knots in the heart of the stream, but it usually does half to three quarters of a knot. It works for me to assume ½ knot WNW, anchors up to anchors down.

Trawlers shall want settled light southeasterlies from Caicos to **Luperón**. But Big Sand to **Manzanillo** can make a good trawler run as well in northeasterlies, and then harbor hop eastward up the coast in daybreak calms. A great trip!

BOUND FOR LUPERÓN

Normally one leaves for Luperón from Big Sand Cay in the Turks and Caicos. First sail or motorsail southeast, and eventually you may find yourself motoring flat out for Luperón in a slick, rolling calm. If at all uncomfortable, *don't beat into the seas*, but *reach* across them for the island and motor up the coast in an early morning Force 3 just off the starboard bow. The deep bar south of **Big Sand Cay** will give you a couple more feet of sea than you imagine. Get out 5 miles before making definitive judgment of conditions.

If already underway from Mayaguana in

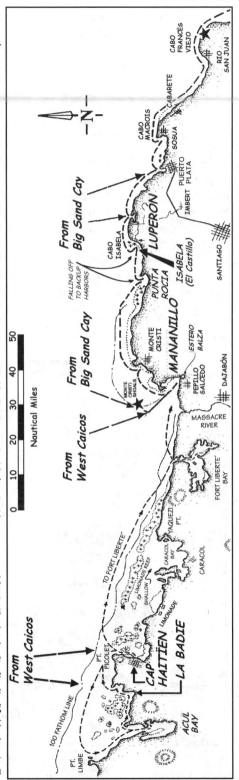

157

favorable conditions with a 36 hour outlook of the same (e.g., enroute in light southerlies), you can continue for Luperón from **West Caicos** or **French Cay**. This comes with rarity, so don't look for it. The first 20 miles you can get better easting in slighter seas by tracking **Molasses Reef** to your east as closely as you can. (Molasses Reef meaning the whole stretch of reef to south of Ambergris.)

If bucking into it, slack sheets and bear off for lee of land then coast up in a calm.
Also, both sail and power can turn for Manzanillo and quarter it.

FALL OFF FOR PETE'S SAKE!

If you had planned one tack to **Luperón**, but for *whatever* reason you can't make a daybreak landfall, for Pete's sake fall off and sail more directly for the island. Don't shy from changing your plan in midstream. Sail comfortably south, *across* the waves, for the shelter of the coast. *Don't* continue to buck into it. Then motorsail up the coast in a lee. The trip shall go faster and more comfortably than beating into seas. *Believe it!*

You may beat up the boat and the crew, all the while paralleling the edge of the retreating sanctuary of this massive island's **night lee**. Fall off, and look for that lee. Even if you don't find it, you'll make the wide and easy refuge of **Isabela** or **Punta Rocia**.

USE BACKUP LANDFALLS

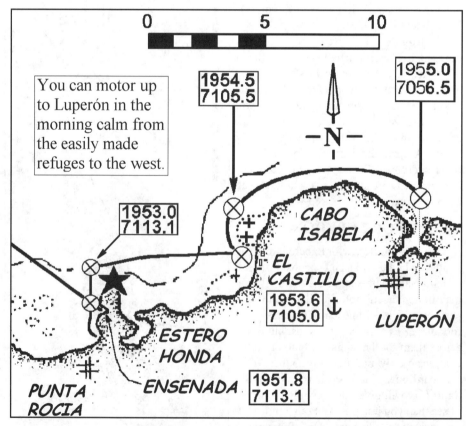

Fall off to El Castillo or Punta Rocia

I watch 3 out of 5 boats arriving in Luperón add a 3-6 hour nightmare onto the serene dream they already had: a pleasant 12-15 hour night passage. Some underestimate current or land effect. Most underestimate the importance of getting in before the coast-accelerated trades begin. If you do, don't try to cover your mistake by pounding into trade wind and seas. Fall off to backup landfalls and motor up in a dead calm real early next morning. Some see high dark land, and they think they've come too close. Then they heave to until dawn 5-10 miles out. Check out, then believe your depth sounders or your GPS.

Tuck under **Cabo Isabela** for the day if you get caught out when the trades start. **El Castillo** sits in a basin of 10-12 feet of sand a mile square. Enter as far downwind as you like from the small reef at the northern edge, then round up into the wind, anchor in a fine sandy lee, and visit the digs of the New World's first surviving settlement. If you get set even more, tuck into **Ensenada** behind **Punta Rocia**, both excellent anchorages. Motor up to Luperón the next morning. Leave so as to get anchored in Luperón before 8 a.m.

BOUND FOR MANZANILLO

For the safest passage sail for the western end of the **Montecristi Shoals**, then sail fifteen miles southeast to **Manzanillo**. If you wish, you can thread the shoals in daylight by sailing due south on **El Morro** behind **Punta Granja**, then following backwards the instructions given in the chapter, *Montecristi and The Shoals*. El Morro shows at night since it clearly interrupts the loom of Montecristi with its unmistakable mass.

BOUND FOR HAITI

As regards your approach to the big island, follow the same scheme as for **Luperón**. And *fall off for Pete's sake,* rather than beat into it. You shall make better time and enter the lee of this huge land before sunup catches you out in the trades.

Enter the port at Cap Haïtien after 8 am to ensure a non-defensive reception and proceed to the customs dock on the south side of the huge pier constructed by "Baby Doc" to receive the cruise ships which have, so far, not come. At Acul Bay anchor off **La Badie** and see American Norman Zarchin at his **Coco Beach** hotel for local guidance.

Always arrive off **Hispaniola** at dawn so as to square away your ground tackle by 8 a.m., before the trades renew. Leaving for **Cap Haïtien** from **West Caicos** or **French Cay** gives a beamier wind than from **Big Sand Cay**, and the first 20 miles you have some lee from **Molasses Reef** to the east. You can see the looms of **Montecristi** and Cap Haïtien up to 30 miles out (if the power hasn't failed). Don't confuse the two, as I did one year when I got into the Montecristi Shoals, thinking I lay 10 miles off **Cap**.

Recently, many yachts have chosen to sail directly to the cruise ship development at **Acul Bay**, west of Cap Haïtien. See the chapter on Acul Bay.

If in Sapodilla Bay, you might **stage** yourself the day before departure to either of: [1] the southwest end of **Southwest Reef** (approximately 2137.0-7226.5) just east of the Ship Channel entrance, [2] a mooring at the marine park west of West Caicos or [3] **French Cay**, depending on the wind and sea directions you expect to face during the crossing to Cap Haïtien. You may find it easiest to slip a dive mooring in the sea park west of West Caicos.

You can follow the **Provo ship channel** out through **Clear Sand Road** to get to Southwest Reef from **Sapodilla Bay**. The channel stretches 242° magnetic from **Gussy Point**. (See chartlet). When leaving Southwest Reef for Cap or Acul, clear the southeast spit of West Caicos, standing off the beach there about one half mile.

You can sail directly to French Cay from Sapodilla Bay in least water of 10 feet.

HAITI

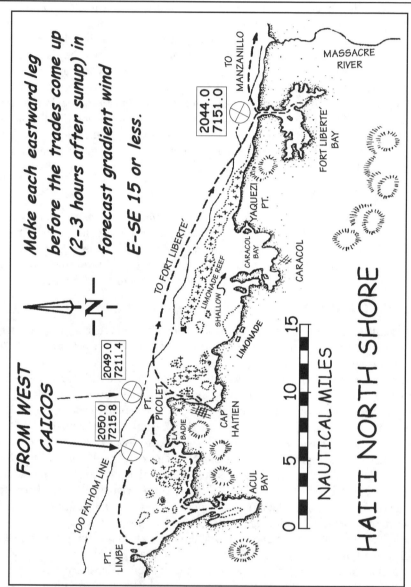

Haiti East from Acul Bay

Haiti, founded in bloody 1804 as the world's third republic since Rome, has a rich and dark history. Although the Spanish colonized the island in 1493, other New World colonies, not lying to windward, proved more profitable to the Spanish. Santo Domingo, as they called the entire colony, drifted into neglect. The French began to settle the western end of Hispaniola, and by 1697 the island consisted of French settlers on the western one third of the island and Spanish on the eastern two thirds. In 1795 the entire island came under French rule when Spain ceded the Spanish part to France against the will of its people. A slave uprising in 1804 saw all whites in the French part murdered.

Invest in a book on Haitian history. It shall enhance your visit ten fold. Start your history lesson with an excellent dinner at the *Hotel Roi Christoph,* owned and operated for many years by Henri-Paul and Joël Mourral amid cool gardens. Built to house the governor in 1724, the mansion has 2 foot thick walls and 15 foot high open rooms. Worm some invitations to some of the old residences in town. Go when the early evening cloaks the squalid streets and dingy facades in romantic luster. The interiors of the more maintained mansions shall certainly astound you with their elegance. Even those that lie half in ruin make historians weep.

In a lifetime of world travel I have met few people as sweet and pacific as the Haitian, when taken individually. Collectively, however, Haitians have a penchant for screwing up the world's third oldest republic (not counting that France has now its *sixth*). Unlike Latin Americans, Haitians cheerfully admit that they screw up without outside assistance. You won't find Haitians blaming you for their plight. You shall find them eager to share your resources, however, and squander them as they have their own. To prevent undue pressure on your purse, just practice what you do elsewhere, but industrial strength. Especially get all prices down firmly before accepting a service. It helps to speak French badly.

Haitians call their money the *gourde*. That's right, as in gourds, like Indians used to trade. They pronounce it "goo". The first time they give you change in a gooey ball of old one *gourde* notes you shall understand everything. Five Gourdes make a Haitian "dollar", a confusing name, like the American "nickel", whose ambiguity they gladly exploit. *Caveat emptor* rules in Haiti.

Don't think Haiti cheap, despite its poverty. Haitians have become accustomed to wringing every *sou* from the tourist. If you ask a price, prepare to hear astronomical sums quoted by people who haven't seen a penny in months. Not seeing it much, the ordinary Haitian hasn't got a grasp on reality when it comes to money.

Once, I hired a car for 6 hours to run over to the Dominican frontier. After a half hour of a-hemming and a-hawing the first driver finally quoted his *discounted* fee of US$150. Another gave us a quote of US$60, and finally Gabriel, a member of the national police, gave us a "reasonable" price of US$40. He offered the added security of having a cop as a driver, he noted, as he patted his monstrous 0.45 pistol!

Security

Those concerned about taking their boat into Haiti should not forego the opportunity of a visit while the boat lies safely at **Luperón** or **Manzanillo**. Many tour operations exist in the Dominican Republic.

You can also take public transport to **Dajabón** on the border, walk across the bridge at the **Massacre River**, and begin Haitian transport from the small town of **Oanamenthe**, sometime spelled Guanamenthe, but in any case a Créole corruption of *Juana Mendez.*

Until officials provide firm physical security measures for yachts at **Cap Haïtien**, a member of the crew should stay aboard while at anchor or at the dock. You should not expect any personal threat on the Haitian north coast, although pestering from beggars may exasperate you, and thievery at night can be expected if made too easy or too inviting.

CAP HAÏTIEN

Plan to arrive off Cap Haïtien at daybreak. Maneuvering at the docks may be difficult when the wind gets up by 9 a.m. The course from the **Ship Channel** windward of **West Caicos** lies 172° True for a distance of 112 miles. Add a half knot of west-northwest current, stir in some leeway, variation and deviation, and add a pinch of caution: several degrees to ensure you aren't set onto the **Montecristi Shoals**.

The lights of the port may not work but it has good buoyage. There are large red and green piles which follow the American "red right returning" (IALA 'B') rule. Make a daybreak landfall, sailing to within 500 yards east of the old lighthouse on **Picolet Point** on **Cap Haïtien** itself. Proceed down the well marked channel, turning right around the south end of the large pier. You shall find the Harbor Master's office midway down the long dock, between the freighters and the fishing boats. Hail the officials at the dock and tell them you shall tie up at the yacht dock. Or anchor out as you please, and tell them that you shall dinghy in shortly for clearance.

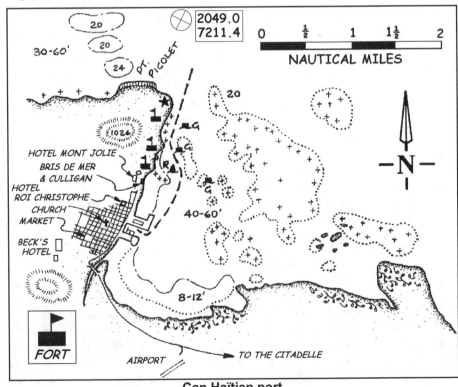

Cap Haïtien port

162

After clearing in at **Cap Haïtien**, visiting the **Citadelle** or whatever else you find to do there, clear out for **Acul Bay**.

Years ago, when the cruise ships came to **Cap Haïtien,** the officials there gave yachties short shrift . They had no facilities for yachts and you got ripped off for fuel and water and the labor to fetch it. Kids "seeking work" hassled you endlessly, but to them a paint brush presented a high tech tool. These harmless street urchins scammed quick bucks from ship's passengers, taking them to the market, shopping the *bric-a-brac* and art stalls and generally misguiding them around.

The marina built by dictator Jean-Claude Duvalier (Baby Doc) with sturdy steel pilings and bollards off a long dock has begun to rust and sag sadly.

Now fewer kids pull at you, you get fewer hassles and, with no cruise ships, officials have more time for yachts, not necessarily a good thing.

The marina facilities have sporadically functioned since they put them up in 1984. But they have had few yachts, no cruise ships and zero tourists. During all its recent troubles the north coast of **Haiti** has plodded along with its usual serenity. Problems have centered on the south and the west coast cities.

Boatboy at the Cap Marina

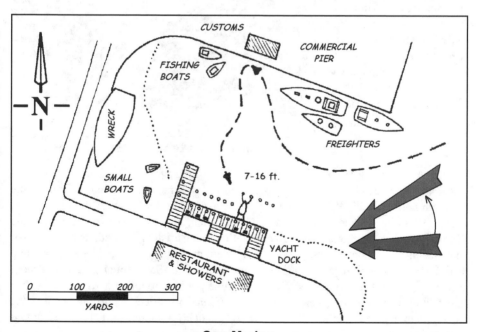

Cap Marina

Try to tie up to the yacht dock before the sea breeze comes up or after it dies. They unaccountably built the dock across the wind instead of into it. The docks lie on a former island. Since they filled the land to create the marina one can assume that they specifically designed the marina to lie across the wind. Welcome to **Haiti**, the land of the inexplicable.

The *Hotel Mont Joli* still has the loveliest deck on the island from which to enjoy your **SG&T**, but rooms run twice the price of the *Roi Christoph,* my hotel of choice. You'll find *Beck's,* the *Brise de Mer* and the *Hotel Universel,* downtown, all air conditioned and relatively cheap. Farther afield lies the *Hotel Imperial*, or you can go to the beach at *Cormier Plage.* Try the charcoal roasted cashews for the best buy in the iron market. Haitian art, usually cheap elsewhere, can prove quite expensive here. Since the devolution of "Baby Doc", artisans have emigrated to the Dominican Republic where they practice their trades in factories, as well as for the tourists. Do not expect bargains in Haiti. For instance, they haven't learned to make bottles, therefore the deposit alone on a bottle of beer may cost more than a full bottle in the DR. Never expect to find something like an engine part.

The Barbancourt 15 year rum still vies admirably with the best of the Dominican rums. Take care with the *clairin*, called *vingt deux* (22) by the locals. You may like to make your *p'ti' punch* from *clairin*, but watch it! You've come to Haiti, not Martinique.

CITADELLE AND SANS SOUCI

If you take a tour of the **Citadelle** and **Sans Souci**, you don't need to see the pyramids. Firstly because you have a comparable experience, and secondly because, unless quite careful, you may not have any money left. One would think that the con artists that take you there trained in Egypt. A new cost will arise every step of the way if you don't act to prevent it beforehand.

To go to Citadelle, get a firm, all inclusive, price due on completion of the tour, before you set out. A good and patient bargainer can do it for 15 to 20 beers a head (see chapter on *Beeronomy*) for 4 to 6 persons, half of which pays transportation to the second level.

Entrance to the brooding Sans Souci

The story of **King Henri Christoph** makes a Haitian parable. The Grenada born mulatto slave arrived in Haiti from a shipwreck. In a short time he named himself king of the northern half of Haiti. He managed 200,000 slaves to build a copy of the French Sun King's Versailles palace at **Milot,** near Cap Haïtien, and the great work above it, the **Citadelle**. When the work didn't proceed at the pace Christoph wanted, he used the Roman decimation technique, butchering every tenth man in a long line. The work sped up with 90% of the workforce. Under the grand staircase of **Sans Souci**'s grand ballroom Henri constructed an airtight room into which he popped troubling guests. They suffocated while he danced with their ladies. He disciplined his officers by drilling them on the 1000 foot high parapets of the Citadelle. He would delay a "column left" for a beat or two now and again just to keep his officers on their toes. Those who hadn't marched off into space, anyway.

Clear first in **Cap Haïtien** to cruise the bays west of there. Coasting east from **Acul Bay**, you must stop again at Cap Haïtien to pick up a clearance for **Fort Liberté**. In Fort Liberté, you need to pick one up for the **Dominican Republic**.

Not only have cruise ships continued here during Haiti's problems, but some Frenchmen have begun developments ashore to include an "eco-marina".

The miniature cruising ground of Acul Bay, a fine hurricane hole and only 5 miles west of Cap Haïtien, can easily absorb a week with a different anchorage every night.

Follow the **Limbe Channel** down the west side of the bay, rounding **Grand Boucan Point** a half-mile off, then steer for **Morro Rock**. This will bring you safely up into a good anchorage deep inside **Lombardo Cove**. Ashore you can find great avocados, grapefruit and coconut. You can get 20 of the world's best Haïtien grapefruits to a beer (see *Beeronomy*). You'll find a fine hurricane hole up between **Lunetta Point** and **Belie Point,** and another behind Lunetta Point.

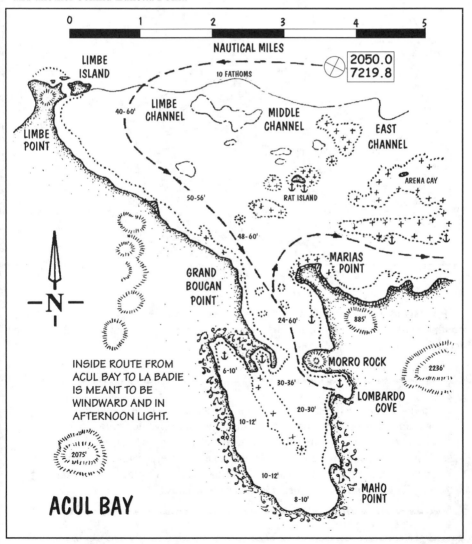

LA BADIE

Corsaires and **privateers,** and the **freebooters** and **buccaneers** they left in their wake (see Glossary), controlled this coast from **Ile de la Tortue** to **Puerto Plata** for more than 200 years. They used **La Badie** as a watering hole and bordello in those days. Today La Badie hosts cruise ships whose passengers sun themselves and picnic on the white sand beaches. While construction of expatriate villas tries to catch up with the development of cruise ship shore facilities, American Norman Zarchin finishes his third decade receiving cruisers at his **Coco Beach** hotel. You may find better security here than in Cap.

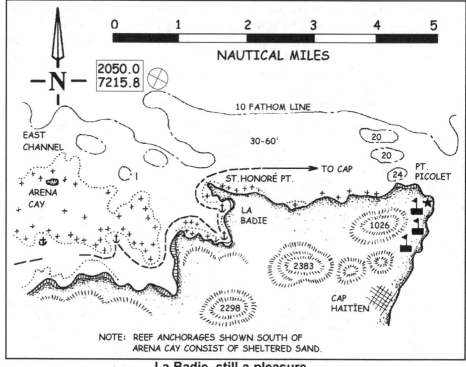

La Badie, still a pleasure

Rat Island, in the middle of the bay has good anchorages in clear water south and southwest of the island. You can snorkel and spearfish the reefs around the island which local fishermen use for an overnight camp.

La Badie and Coco Beach played an important role once as a free zone for buccaneers and freebooters, a place they could congregate without fear of rivalry or reprisal. The area now appears developing in the same mold with a 21st century tang: cruise ships, villas and hotels ashore, and a complement of snotty yachties and minimalists lying in the bay. As of press time no one appears to enforce government clearance procedures.

Fort Liberté makes an easy and safe port of entry as well as a fine hurricane hole.

Leave **Cap Haïtien** the same way you came in. You want, of course, to leave as early as possible to avoid the hassle of the trades. To minimize any hassles from the officials, talk with them the day before leaving. Show up at the harbor master's office at first light with the yacht moored as instructed when you called on them the previous day. Then press hard for a quick clearance.

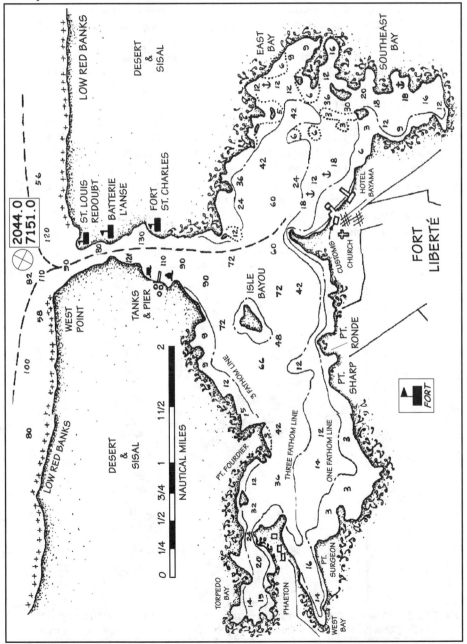

Leaving Cap Haïtien, turn on a course of 70° magnetic when close under the lighthouse at **Point Picolet,** proceed for one mile or more, then east for 3 miles. This should put you a mile or more north of **Limonade Reef,** where **Columbus** lost the **Santa Maria,** and well clear of danger. Now set a course of 115° magnetic for the entrance to **Fort Liberté,** only 18 miles distant.

You may have difficulty spotting the entrance to Fort Liberté from sea along this coast of desert and sisal plantations. Everything looks the same. For several miles east and west of the entrance, however, you can safely sail a quarter mile offshore. Go close in to not miss it. A narrow throat surrounded by low red cliffs, the entrance to the bay sounds nearly a 100 feet deep everywhere. Once inside the bay, like the approach outside, everything looks the same again, but, instead of brown rock you see mangrove green.

Mangroves line the entire bay in this great hurricane hole. Head for the *Hotel Bayaha,* run by M et Mme Nyll Calixte, a large stone building with a concrete dock on the east side of the town. The customs house lies by the old town pier a couple of hundred yards seaward of the hotel. *Le Capitain du Port* rules the roost here. He will organize the boarding party. Either dock has only a couple feet of water. You will have to anchor well off and ferry the boarding party from either dock. You'll find the hotel dock more convenient. The hotel has a verandah bar and restaurant overlooking the anchorage.

The water point near the customs house may not function. See Mme Calixte about jerry jugging water from a water point beside the hotel. Purchase fuel in gallon containers in the town. Practice your filtering and water separation techniques.

Leave for **Manzanillo,** 6 miles to the east, to arrive there around 8 a.m. while you still have dead calm conditions. Once again, do what you have to in order to get cleared and free of the harbor *early*. You don't want to crash eastward in full trades.

Part of a human chain of running Haitian women transporting provisions across the border from the Dominican Republic. In this case eggs.

THE DOMINICAN REPUBLIC

The **Dominican Republic (DR)** covers an area of 18,703 square miles. It occupies the eastern portion of **Hispaniola**, the second largest island of the Antilles. It shares the island with Haiti but the two neighbors have little in common.

HAITI vs. THE DR

Americans live closer to Hispaniola by both heritage and geography, but they normally get more confused than Europeans as to the differences between that island's two nations. The DR occupies two-thirds of the island with nearly 10 million people, 3 million of them in the capital, Santo Domingo, and 2 million more who live in the U.S. Haiti's third of the island has 9 million or more, 3 million of which live in its capital, Port au Prince, and another 3 million more live overseas. The two peoples differ startlingly and boldly.

The Dominicans talk Spanish. Haitians talk Créole, an extremely corrupted French. Dominicans kind of practice Roman Catholicism. Haitians practice forms of animism more than Catholicism. Dominicans run the gamut of skin color, averaging cinnamon. Haitians come satiny black, with a few mulattos who stay off-island as much as on. Historically the two countries have a bitter rivalry: Haiti invaded the DR to terrorize farmers. The Dominican army slaughtered Haitian immigrants.

A practically impenetrable natural border further distances the two peoples. It has only two crossing points. The 20 mile swath which alternates between desert in the north and the south, and *Haitises,* or jagged jungle hillocks, in the middle, creates the frontier that divides the two nations. The terrain either side of the frontier has gone unoccupied through the centuries due to its basic inhospitality to settlement. The inhabitants of Haiti have French and African cultural roots, and live in an overpopulated and deforested land. In contrast, the population of the DR has an Hispanic culture and live in lush and bountiful valleys among forested mountains.

While poor, the DR looks wealthy compared to Haiti, the poorest in the hemisphere. In Haiti you see Dominican businessmen, but in the DR you see only Haitian migrant workers who get dragged back and forth on retired American school buses. Army roadblocks in the western end of the DR search for Haitians smuggling themselves in. With the recent anarchy in Haiti, many thousands of Haitians (some with papers) live and work in the DR.

SHORT COURSE ON THE DR

I encourage the reader to buy a history book of the DR. It helps you to understand the people and the state the country finds itself in today. I recommend the university textbook, *Vision General de La Historia Dominicana,* by Peguero and de los Santos, and a book simply entitled *Trujillo.* Every boat that sails this coast should have Fuson's *Columbus Log* aboard. Exquemelin's *Buccaneers of America*, a diary written in 1678, reads as though he wrote it yesterday. Finally, good friend, and former German consul in Puerto Plata, Heinz Meder, wrote a lovely book, *Tales of a Caribbean Isle, By and For an Insider*, with scads of good skinny. All can be found at bookstores (*librerias*) and airports. Many small bookstores exist in the side streets of Santiago's or Santo Domingo's colonial zone. But you'd do best ordering English books from U.S. suppliers.

LAND AND CLIMATE

The DR has the most rugged and complicated terrain on any of the Caribbean islands. It has four major mountain chains enclosing three large and fruitful valleys running roughly east-west. The north coast, high and rugged, got formed by interaction of the Caribbean and Atlantic tectonic plates. The sailor arriving on the coast sees several ancient beaches carved in stone at 20, 40 and 80 meters height which document these abrupt rises of the land. The massive range of the **Cordillera Septentrional** backs up the northern coast. Only small coastal plains squeeze between these majestic mountains and the Atlantic Ocean.

The principal mountain system, the **Cordillera Central**, runs across the middle of the country from northern Haiti almost to Santo Domingo. It has more than 20 mountains with heights greater than 6,500 feet, including the highest peak in the Antilles, **Pico Duarte**, at 10,417 feet. The Cordillera Central has a maximum width of 50 miles, and makes up more than one third of the country. Two smaller mountain systems called **Sierra de Neiba** and **Sierra de Baoruco** lie in the southwest. Alluvial plains gently sloping from the southern cordilleras border the south coast. That area produces sugar cane and beef.

These four mountain systems enclose three lowlands. Between the Cordillera Septentrional and the Cordillera Central lies the **Cibao Valley**. It contains areas of flat, particularly fertile land to the east of the city of Santiago in a region called the Vega Real, where bananas, cacao (chocolate), premium tobacco, rice and canned fruits and vegetables produce export income. The **San Juan Valley** lies between the Cordillera Central and the Sierra de Neiba. This valley has excellent soil and, with irrigation, has become a major rice-growing region. Farther to the south, between the Sierra de Neiba and the Sierra de Baoruco, lies the Enriquillo Basin, which has deserts and contains the salt lake **Enriquillo** which lies 130 feet below sea level.

Although at tropical latitudes, the trade winds, the surrounding ocean and high elevations combine in some areas to produce a climate far from typical of the tropics. Ice commonly forms on the highest peaks of the Cordillera Central. In most areas, however, temperatures vary little from season to season. Rain normally falls the most on mountain slopes over which the easterly trade winds blow. Rainfall decreases on the downwind slopes and in the major valleys. The Cibao Valley counts among the world's most fertile.

Its wide variety of topographic and climatic conditions has given the DR the richest plant life in the Caribbean. Native species account for about one third of the nearly 6000 species. The Spanish had introduced the mongoose early on in their colonization to eliminate rats, but succeeded also in reducing populations of other native species.

PEOPLE

Dominicans, like most peoples, defy statistics. Even among amiable Latin Americans Dominicans command renown for their hospitality, graciousness and dignity. You may easily get to know them individually. Don't hesitate to. Statistically, however, the Dominicans have an 85% literacy rate and life expectancy at birth of over 70 years. Models of the American race, the population consists of almost one fifth white, three quarters mixed African-European-Indian and 11% black. Whites tend to dominate corporations, government and the teeming Dominican gliteratti. The state supported Roman Catholic Church claims the most adherents, but Evangelical and Protestant groups have grown exponentially in the last decades, while the Church's influence has diminished significantly.

Finally, Sammy Sosa, Felipe Alou and others come out of the 10% Dominican makeup of the Major League baseball players. Only California has higher representation.

ECONOMY

DR's income comes in roughly equal parts from industry, agriculture and tourism. Small farmers organically grow staples, especially bananas (plantains), yucas, beans, and sweet potatoes. Large exports come from sugar, tobacco and coffee. DR has most of the American sugar import quota (the Pujols of Miami). With 56 percent of the country used for crops or pasture, agriculture takes half of the workforce but makes up only one third of the country's earnings. Industry and tourism equally split the other two thirds of the economy, but take respectively a fifth and a third of the labor force.

Among the top ten gold producing countries of the world, the DR has the largest single gold mine in the Western Hemisphere. Industrial income comes largely from mining, especially silver, nickel, bauxite, and gold. However, **Zona Francas**, or duty free zones of light manufacturing such as of clothing, circuit assembly and jewelry exist in towns of any size. They now contribute to half of the industrial export income, and the government heavily promotes an electronics research and manufacturing zone near the Capital. Remittances from Dominicans working in the U.S. accounts for 13% of the Gross Domestic Product.

HISTORY AND GOVERNMENT

Christopher Columbus discovered Hispaniola on December 5, 1492. The native Indians had named the island Quisqueya but Columbus named it Hispaniola ("Little Spain"). The DR became the site of the first European settlements in the New World. Columbus' brother Bartholomew founded **Santo Domingo** in 1496. **El Castillo**, founded just a few miles from Luperón in 1493, later got evacuated to Santo Domingo for protection. Thus Santo Domingo has become the oldest permanently occupied town in the Americas. An estimated 300,000 Indians lived on the island in 1492, but by mid 16th century most pure blood natives had died of epidemics of European diseases, starvation, overwork in the gold mines, torture and suicide. The gold that their technology could mine gave out by 1530, and Spain lost interest in the colony after discoveries in Mexico and Peru. The Spaniards who remained on the island turned to cultivating sugar cane, using black slaves imported from Africa.

In 1697 Spain ceded the western third of Hispaniola to France. By the end of the 18th century, the new French possession known as St. Domingue (Haiti) became one of the world's richest colonies, producing vast quantities of sugar and cotton. The French colony had 524,000 inhabitants, 88 percent African slaves. Santo Domingo (the DR), with twice the territory of its neighbor, had barely one fifth that population by 1840.

France took control of the whole island in 1795, but slave uprisings in the west led to the creation of Haiti in 1804, the world's first black republic, and the third since Rome. In 1814 Spain, though disinterested, reluctantly retook control of the eastern two-thirds of the island. The Dominicans declared independence in 1821, beginning from a translation of the U.S. Constitution. Soon afterward the Haitians invaded the DR and reigned by terror for 22 years. Hatreds from that period still separate Dominicans from Haitians.

The Republic finally became a reality after General **Gregorio Luperón** mustered an army to expel the Haitians in 1844. During the rest of the 19th century, the Republic suffered more revolutions, more armed invasions from Haiti, and another period of Spanish domination from 1861 to 1865, while the U.S., despite its Monroe Doctrine, busied itself with its Civil War. Corrupt governments borrowed money recklessly, and by 1916 the country lay in political and economic chaos. Germany threatened to occupy the DR in order to make good their debts and, incidentally, use **Samaná Bay** for their **U-boats** to close off the Panama Canal route of resupply to England and France during World War I.

The United States preempted Germany and occupied the DR with the same excuse the Germans tried to use, but really to exclude the Germans and protect the approaches to the Panama Canal and assure the allies of their supplies. After the Armistice of 1918 the U.S. had difficulty withdrawing from its occupation for lack of an orderly government body to take the reins, and for lack of political will on both sides due to business interests. A government finally got cobbled together, and the Americans withdrew in 1924. Though opposition to U.S. occupation existed, the enforced political stability permitted major social and economic advances, and began a close U.S.-DR relationship with blood ties.

In 1930 another *coup d'etat* put the country into the hands of dictator Rafael Leonidas **Trujillo** Molina, a U.S. trained military strong man. Until his assassination in 1961, Trujillo headed a ruthless police state. At the cost of political freedom, the DR had another period of imposed stability that, combined with favorable sugar prices, stimulated impressive economic growth. Five years of political turmoil after Trujillo's death led in 1965 to another intervention by the U.S., concerned about the possibility of a Cuban-style Communist takeover. Not so outlandish an idea, since the DR has turned back invasions from Cuba twice since 1949. Reid Cabral, acting president at the time and one of only three men left in the government, recounts how he called Lyndon Johnson, while numerous factions skirmished in the Capital's suburbs. He *invited* a police action from the U.S. to pacify the city until the government reorganized. The DR has had relatively orderly and free elections since. Nonetheless, the Dominicans practice politics not unlike U.S. populations of comparable size such as Chicago or Boston. In other words, *rough* and *tumble*.

Austerity measures dictated by the International Monetary Fund, and executed by president Balaguer, pulled the nation out of its slump, leaving it with ruined water and power infrastructures. President Leonel Fernandez pushed through capital reforms in 1995 with attractive guarantees to foreign investors. This gave quite impressive gains. In the 4 years of 1996-1999, the DR had the hemisphere's highest Gross Domestic Product growth and, the most stable currency in the hemisphere. The electorate returned a populist government in 2000, as electorates often do, and once again the country got ruined — this time by bank frauds. Once again the DR plods the comeback trail with Lionel at the helm.

TOURISM

Whether touring or seeking parts for your boat, leave the boat at the yacht harbor at **Luperón** to go inland in the DR. If you fail to explore this wonderful country with its handsome and friendly people, you will have missed a major highlight of your cruise.

Tourists mainly come from the European and Canadian group travel market. Only 30% of foreign tourism comes from the United States.

Many American retirees live in the DR, some having come from Costa Rica and Mexico. Around 100,000 foreign residents and long term visitors travel the country routinely and with safety. Many live in the north coast retirement communities, others have built retreats and ranches throughout the island. Affluent visitors rent cars. Groups travel by bus. The more adventuresome, who want to meet the Dominican people and experience the country close up, simply wander the nation with backpacks, riding dirt bikes or by taking the ubiquitous local transport from mopeds to vans to metro liners.

TRANSPORTATION IN THE DR

Your choice of transport ranges from motorcycles, called *motoconchos* [moe-toe-CONE-choh], motorbikes upon which the passenger(s) ride on a pillion, to pickup trucks to *guaguas* [GWAH-GWAH, the sound busses made long ago with their ah-oogah horns].

These have a *cobrador* [cobra-DOOR], a boy who takes money and pushes passengers into place not unlike the pusher in Japanese trains. *Guaguas* travel fixed routes and don't leave the station until nearly full.

Japanese microbuses, mostly air-conditioned, run the interurban routes. For cross country trips you can choose the large air-conditioned buses showing two feature films, and sometimes a bar cart. Or you can take less luxurious but still commodious lines such as Transporte Cibao out of Luperón.

Passenger cars on fixed routes called *carros públicos*, or *carritos,* wait in ranks around the town squares, or at terminal facilities in cities, until enough passengers have signed up to nearly fill the car. If you wish to depart earlier or to travel in comfort, you may buy any unfilled seats. For best results, buy the 3 seats next to the driver. While públicos always gather and start from the same place, they usually deliver passengers to anywhere they wish to go, within reason, at the destination town. Puerto Rico has the same system.

Many cruisers who wish to do the hurricane season in the DR do what I do when visiting in the U.S. They buy a boater's special of a car, then sell it, sometimes at a profit when they leave. Cars usually come dear in island economies, and the DR does not make an exception. However, you can find genius mechanics under any shade tree, and they keep even the most disreputable old clunker running like a speedway champion.

PLACES OF INTEREST

The DR has great museums of American culture, the **Taino** museum at *Altos de Chavón*, in La Romana, the ***Museo del Hombre***, and the ***Natural History Museum*** in the Plaza de Cultura, **Santo Domingo**, and *Casa Real,* also in Santo Domingo in the colonial zone. Below I list some places of interest to tourists.

Boca Chica lies about a 30 minute drive east of Santo Domingo. This resort area has gleaming white beaches and a yacht club with a haulout facility. A few miles east lies **Juan Dolio**, a smaller but quieter beach crowded with hotels, restaurants, bars, casino and golf course. You can see Arawak Indian caves on a day trip from Boca Chica.

Casa de Campo, a rambling resort near **La Romana** on the southeast corner of the island, has 3 impressive golf courses designed by Pete Dye, reputed to be among the most challenging. The complex also offers polo, tennis, deep-sea fishing and beaching. Casa de Campo became the model for resorts that now stud the beachy coasts of the DR. Built by the American Gulf and Western company as a private club for their sugar plantations, Casa de Campo got used by Frank Sinatra's Rat Pack for their frolics. The resort expanded and opened to the public when it and the sugar lands, which reach across the country, got bought up by Florida's Cuban-American sugar magnates.

Altos de Chavón, a replica of a 16th-century Romany village, including a Roman amphitheater, subsists today as an artist center. Story has it the brother of Gulf and Western's CEO built Altos de Chavón to burn up the one dollar of profit their sugar concession had to leave in country for each dollar sent to the U.S. Regardless of origin, the Altos de Chavón Archaeological Museum has the most important collection of **Taino** artifacts found anywhere.

Saona Island interests the ecotourist for its historical and anthropological importance. A refuge for Indian holdouts, it has many unexcavated sites. Isla Saona has hiking trails.

Bayajibe beach has crystal clear, white sand-bottomed waters stretching to Isla Saona. Primarily used by ecotourists and beach enthusiasts, yachties like Bayajibe because it hosted Henry Morgan's immense pirate fleet of 36 ships and 2000 buccaneers in 1669. They staged for a year here for the infamous sacking of **Porto Bello** and the taking of Panamá in 1670. If you park your boat there, you might try sifting the sands beneath you.

La Vega, a coffee and cacao (chocolate) town in the center of the island, has fame for conducting the most artistic **Carnaval** in the country during February.

Jarabacoa, cool and mountainous, has a new golf course, but mostly known for its white water rafting and waterfall sites near to mountain lodges and forest resorts.

Constanza, also known for its forests, rivers and waterfalls, lies in a large valley high up in the Cordillera Central. There they export flowers and other agricultural products. The rough road to Constanza from Jarabacoa reminds many of Switzerland in the summertime. The highway up from the *Autopista* has spectacular switch backs and overlooks.

A sea encounter park, built by Al Meister, the same entrepeneur that built Nassau's *Swim witlh the Dolphins* park, nears completion at Cofresí, only 8nm east of Luperón. Meister calls it the largest such park in the world. He has sea lions, tigers and a tropical rain forest in addition to dolphin shows and dolphin encounters. A megayacht marina opens 2006.

National Parks in the DR number 14, and Reserves 7. At *Bermudez National Park* you can hike up and down **Pico Duarte**, the highest mountain in the Caribbean at 10,417 feet. It takes at least two days, but the trek has shelters provided. *Los Haitises National Park* on Samaná Bay, has incredible karst formations with caves full of Indian rock paintings. *National Park of the East*, north of Isla Saona, interests those who like beaches or want to explore caves, some of which have pre-Columbian petroglyphs.

The **Campo**, or the small towns in the DR, have become popular with European ecotourists who backpack about the country soaking up the hospitality of its good-natured people. Hiking, motorbiking or driving around the island, if you find yourself in any small town around dusk, you'll not do without friendly lodging, hotel or no.

TIPS FOR TRAVELING

All told, the DR offers astounding opportunities for tourism. You should expect to encounter vendors at tourist points. A polite "no thank you" and a firm attitude will put an end to any pestering. Many times a 10% service charge gets included in restaurant and hotel bills. You can give an additional tip if you feel you had quite exceptional service. Dominicans do not tip taxi drivers. A sales tax gets included in mainline tourist establishments. Traveling on *guaguas* and *carros públicos*, have the fare in exact change. If unable to make change right away, the *cobrador* or *chofer* may do so much later. You might think he stiffed you, but they rarely forget. I've had a *cobrador* return trifling change to me unasked several days after he forgot, and he had never seen me before the incident.

Don't wear beach attire in town. Dominicans have a great deal of pride and dignity. They consider cleanliness important. Standard yachtie attire of old floppy hat, sandals and spotted cutoff shorts, though clean, look dirty to townspeople. While traveling or in a city you'll do better wearing trousers or dress.

Ask for a discount when shopping, no matter how upscale the establishment appears, especially when paying with cash in hardware stores.

Don't expect a great sense of urgency from Dominicans. They tend to relax in all things.

Watch out for incompetent drivers of any conveyance whatsoever.

Learn to dance the merengue, and try staying in small remote towns.

A NOTE ABOUT BRIBES

Every season I hear the ridiculous chatter about *mordida* (Mexican for bribes: a "bite") in the DR ports. It usually starts with the age-old Dominican expression for people returning to the island from abroad: "Did you bring any presents for me?" When adults say it, the response usually goes something like, "Half of what you have for me!", and a great deal of laughter ensues. After a few $20 "presents" the surprised official becomes accustomed to the insolent response from the tourist. He goes with the flow, and **tips** become routine. If you "tip" egregiously in Latin America, don't cover your bonehead behavior with wild tales of "being forced to pay bribes". That could constitute a slander to your hosts and, under Napoleonic law, an arrestable offense. You won't get a bullet for not coughing up, but you will get respect. Just say a friendly "No", then share a beer or lunch with the official next day. If you feel you must "tip" officials, try it as a delayed favor, not a *quid pro quo*. Regardless what you've seen on old Viva Zapata movies, bribes offend. The Latino way does favors for friends. Also, if you do tip, have your tip ready, don't fish around for it. Ten pesos may get appreciated, but not off the top of a roll of hundreds.

The men of the *comandáncias* often get stationed far from their families, and travel money comes out of a pittance of a salary. Improvements to shore and harbor facilities largely go unfunded by their government. Upon checking out in the DR, offer a small recompense (e.g., a beer's worth) for the guy who types the *despacho*. Give it to him at the same time he hands you the paper. In other words, *before* he asks but *after* the service gets rendered. No fishing around, no haggling. He has already said thanks. In Manzanillo, they sent to town for the *technico* to do the typing, because the old Royal typewriter lacked the T key. I put myself forward as a typing machine expert, which greatly surprised the whole garrison. I got to type my own despacho. Then I asked for, but didn't get, a tip.

A WORD ABOUT HARBOR CONDITIONS

The usual North American cruiser encounters the DR ports as a first maritime experience in the Developing World. **Puerto Rico** and the **Virgins**, both deeply on the dole from their U.S. owner, show reasonable affluence. The tiny islands of the **Leewards** and **Windwards** have sufficient charter and hotel operations on their ports to disguise their campestral nature. Not the DR. But if you wanted it like home, you could have stayed there.

The 50nm long province of Puerto Plata which stretches from **Luperón** to **Cabarete** (of the Extreme Ocean Masters and Kite Boarding championships), has a huge tourist economy with more hotel rooms in this one province than all of Puerto Rico can boast, mostly east of **Cofresí** (name of a pirate who based himself there).

Cruisers in the DR contribute comparatively little to such an economy, therefore the situation in the DR harbors won't change soon. Enjoy your stay, but don't waste your time grousing about the conditions of harbors. Undeveloped ports grow rare for the cruiser. Enjoy the DR's while they last.

CONSULATES IN THE DR

Embassies and their consular functions are located in the capital, Santo Domingo. You can find their telephone numbers and addresses in the telephone catalog (*guía telefónica*), both white and yellow pages. Puerto Plata has **consular agencies** for:

Canada	689-0002
United Kingdom	567-9159
United States	541-2171

MEDICAL ATTENTION IN THE DR

Early on the DR established free medical training in exchange for years of service at clinics in country towns. After their service many choose to do further training and residency in the United Sates, where they hang out their shingle and serve the large Latin American population centers there. For decades now, many doctors with successful U.S. practice behind them semi-retire back to the DR, where they can have a better life and maintain a small practice. You commonly find specialists practicing in the DR but still on call at major centers in cities such as Houston, New York and Miami.

The outcome of all this? You find public health service clinics everywhere in the DR, and you can get excellent private care quite reasonably. I have preferred to have all my medical needs taken care of in the DR since 1984.

PUBLIC CLINICS

Public health facilities exist everywhere in the Dominican Republic. Use them. I returned to Luperón from Haiti once with a strong dose of paratyphoid which I couldn't shake off by myself. That tiny fishing village, with only 500 or so souls at that time, had a public clinic where one paid what one could — just like my widowed mom paid only what she could afford in the America of the 1940s. The doctor on duty told me which intravenous antibiotic to get at the pharmacy, along with a dozen syringes.

Three times a day, for four days, I reported to the clinic's emergency room where the nurses kept my antibiotics for me in their fridge. I embarrassed them by asking how much I owed, but they didn't know how to take payments. They wanted to prevent the spread of disease, not to make money. I contributed to the cash box they kept for incidentals.

One should never abuse public health clinics, especially in poor countries. They exist primarily, however to address just the kind of health problems most cruisers fear in foreign places: contagious diseases. The government wants it free, of course. That way it gets used early. You must not fear to use these clinics either.

MEDICAL TESTS

The DR, as in most countries except the U.S., permits its citizens to avail themselves of medical analysis services without the orders of a physician: blood analysis, all kinds of imaging, Holters, biopsies. You can get most blood tests in Luperón. **Puerto Plata** and **Santiago** have many more sophisticated labs (*Laboratorio de Análisis*). Medical labs in **Santo Domingo** cluster around the intersection of *Dr.Delgado* and *Independéncia*.

PREVENTION

In the DR they have an expression for gastrointestinal disorder: *la turista*. They call it that not because tourists get it, but because tourists *bring* it. Every winter season they step off their planes shedding billions of microbes and viruses from the common colds and epidemic flus of the northern cities. The little beasties ramp down onto the tarmac and gambol in the tropic heat. Then the whole island acts as a petri dish for the world's flu cultures. Dominicans, a touchy folk fond of embraces, kissing and handshakes, provide the germs a perfect medium with which to spread. Thus the winter plague: *la turista*.

How can you avoid *la turista* between the tropics? Easy. Do what your mother told you to do, and your Psychology 101 professor made you feel guilty about. Wash your hands and scrub under you nails at every opportunity. Don't poke fingers into any body orifice, including eyes, after shaking hands, handling money or a wet painter, until you've washed. And *always* eat any meat *well done*. Whatever you do, don't avoid kissing and hugging.

One would expect that the DR would have played large in Caribbean seafaring history after the 1500's. In truth, the country lay to windward of progress in the age of sail. By the age of motor vessels which could work against the tradewinds the DR lay well off the trade routes already established by sail. Its development languished. Today's sailors pick up a seafaring thread dropped 400 years ago. They can, if they wish, experience the DR as a seaman might have met Cuba in the 19th century. But with the rapid development in the DR, they also have access to 21st century convenience and shopping.

After many months in the isolation of the Bahamas, the metropolitan diversions offered by the DR may refresh your soul. If you choose to range wide on the economy for your shopping, you may also refresh your boat's stores quite reasonably.

As an island economy, some items may cost more in the DR than at home. On the other hand, this large island has a robust agricultural and industrial base as well as considerably shortened distribution chains when compared with continental nations. These character-istics often lead to much cheaper prices on even some imported items. Thus shopping in the DR requires you know *value* in order to compare prices. For good shopping tech-niques, review *Boat Stuff: Provisioning and Repairs*, and its section on *Beeronomy*.

GETTING IN AND OUT OF LUPERÓN

For touring the country, you can take many excellent organized tours, even to Caicos and Haiti. You can't beat these enjoyable and informative excursions for time and money well spent. Many tourists, however, especially the more adventurous yachties, prefer dis-covering things on their own, which takes lots of time but offers other rewards. If explor-ing appeals to you, you need to know first how to get out of Luperón and on the road.

For information on the town of Luperón itself, see (naturally) **the section,** *Luperón*

Transporte de Cibao buses leave **Luperón** daily at 1:30 p.m. (local time) for the capital with a stop at **Santiago** (see *Luperón*, #25 on the Luperón map, section *Luperón*). The same bus leaves **Santo Domingo** every day at 8:30 a.m. and returns to Luperón by 1:00 p.m. (See following section on Santo Domingo). No other direct service exists in Luperón. Unless you hire a taxi, rent a car or a motorbike, or have your own conveyance, all public transport out of Luperón gets you first to **Imbert**, the town 14 miles southeast at the intersection with the main DR highway, the *Autopista Duarte*.

To get to Imbert take a *guagua* from the *parquecito* (#35). These vans cost a beer (see *Beeronomy*). For max comfort, if you can't claim the front passenger door, sit at the window behind the driver. Also, all the way back and on the left may have a hard seat, but you won't have to get up every time someone boards or leaves. Have change ready. You had best at 6:30 a.m., for much later you hit the rush hour. After 8 a.m. school kids flood the system. After 9 a.m. traffic slows down and you have to wait to get a vehicle. Furthermore, if you don't leave early, you shall get to your destination close to siesta time. Family owned stores in Puerto Plata close from 12:00 to 2:00 or 2:30 p.m. Therefore, the 6:30 a.m. start gives you up to 4 hours more useful time in the city.

To return to Luperón from anywhere, take a bus to Imbert. A stack of *guaguas* waits at Imbert to fill up to go back to Luperón. They relay back and forth like a conveyor belt all day from 6:00 a.m. to 8:00 p.m. You'd best not try to make the 8:00 p.m. final *guagua* back from Imbert. It might have left at 7:30, and you must pay dearly for a taxi.

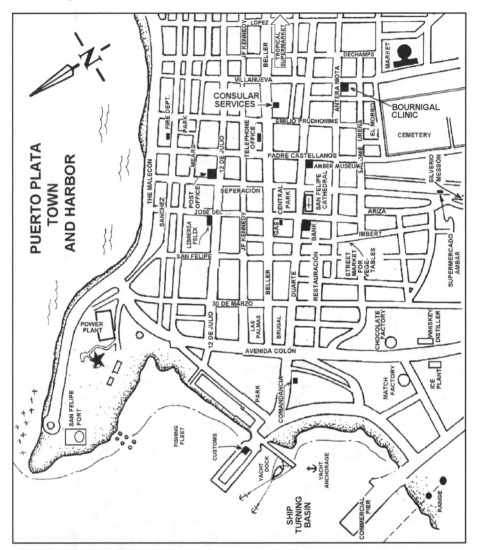

A TRIP TO PUERTO PLATA

To get to **Puerto Plata** from Imbert, cross the highway and get into an east bound *carro público* parked by the Texaco waiting to fill up with passengers, or minibuses from Santiago that stop nearby. Arriving by car to Puerto Plata, the driver will take you wherever you wish in town. On the bus, tell the driver you want off near *el Parque Central*.

Puerto Plata, the second oldest town in the New World, has had a massive tourism boom for three decades. They call this region, with the world's largest source of clear amber, the **Amber Coast**. Many pieces contain interesting examples of prehistoric plant and insect life. Moviegoers may recognize the area as the setting for Jurassic Park.

Just east of Puerto Plata lies the resort area of **Playa Dorada**, a seaside complex with 13 first-class resorts centered around a golf course designed by Robert Trent Jones. Several of the hotels have casinos and discos. Tourists from the surrounding resorts come to town for deep-sea fishing or shopping the gewgaw and bric-a-brac stores, but they enjoy walking tours of the town with its gingerbread architecture. Visit **Fort San Felipe**, the oldest European fort in the New World, with its moat and battlements, or ride the cable car to the top of **Isabel de Torres** mountain, where a massive sculpture of Christ looks out over the world. Spend some time at the new **Museum of Taino Art** and Aldo Costa's **Amber Museum**. Arrange excursions to Puerto Plata at the Luperón marina.

Annual events in Puerto Plata include the **Merengue Festival**, the second week in October, and the Cultural Festival, late January, or *carnaval*, February 27th.

Puerto Plata has a 500 year old tradition of independence from **Santo Domingo**. Despite its inherence to a Spanish colony, the town became the main trading center for the fleets of **corsaires** and **privateers** who harassed the Spanish for two centuries. For trading with the crown's enemies, Puerto Plata got burned to the ground and sacked by the Spanish themselves. Unlike the stone city of Santo Domingo, wooden Puerto Plata has few monuments of architecture that survived fire and rot. Its heritage as the second oldest town in the hemisphere resides in its fabulous people, not its buildings.

The handsome people on the north coast of the DR, the *Norteños*, or Northerners, rank among the most hospitable in the world. In genes and traditions they benefit from their pacific **Taino** ancestors, who would rather commit suicide than fight the Spanish. Recent research, the standard cant that all the Indians got annihilated notwithstanding, shows that more than 75% of the population have Indian DNA. It seems the Spanish did not count *mestizos* as Indians when they took a census. They also inherit from the freebooting **buccaneers** of the coast's past and from slaves brought in to cut the sugar. Finally, they reflect the **Hidalgos**, the mostly non-inheriting, and often drunken, scions of Spain's minor nobility sent to the boondocks to get shuck of them. Talk about a rich heritage! I have found the *Norteños* especially honest and trustworthy. Except for art shops where one negotiates value, everyone gets the same price without haggling. Violence just doesn't happen on the north coast, and armed robbery hardly ever. If you meet a cad it usually comes from a misunderstanding, or you have met a non-*Norteño*.

You can get **cash** for **credit cards** at ubiquitous Automatic Teller Machines or banks.

PROVISIONING IN PUERTO PLATA

In Puerto Plata you can get almost anything you need, otherwise go to **Santiago,** a city of a million or more, an hour away in the mountains. Take a *motoconcho* to either the *Supermercado Tropical* on 27 Febrero and Beller, or *Supermercado Silverio Messon* on Camino Real - Seperación, to look for good buys when you only need one or two of each item or when you wish to sample products before buying a case. These clean markets provide a good selection of local and U.S. products. Motoconchos cost a third of a beer for one way as far as you want.

Returning to **Imbert** from Puerto Plata, take a *motoconcho* to La Rotonda (lah roh-TONE-dah), the westbound terminal for minibuses, *guaguas* and *carros públicos*. Just say, "Luperón?" waving an upward turned palm back and forth, and you'll have representatives of each mode of transport eagerly showing you to the next vehicle scheduled to go. Have the proper change ready!

Puerto Plata's Glorieta, Parque Central

A TRIP TO SANTIAGO

The pleasant city of **Santiago**, the country's second-largest, has wide streets, museums, cathedrals and great modern hardware stores. Not a popular tourist destination, Santiago lies in the heart of the cigar producing region. The Monument to the Restoration Heroes dominates the city and has a spectacular view of the **Cibao Valley**.

Officially named Santiago de los Caballeros (Knights' St.James), the founders came here to create productive land holdings, and they certainly have. The Cibao stretches from sea to sea, Monte Cristi in the northwest to Sanchez on the Bay of Samaná, 120nm of farmland. Look for it as the bus comes over the mountains. Santiago has the prestigious Catholic university Madre y Maestra, the Folk Art Museum and the Tobacco Museum, and a theater with an enormous stage said to have perfect acoustics opened in 1995.

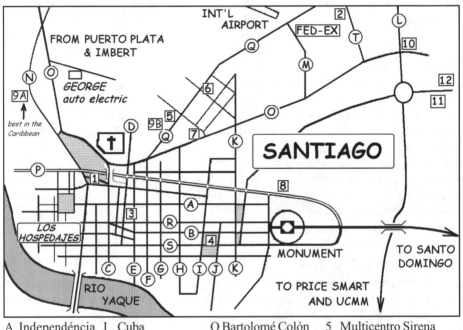

A Independéncia	I Cuba	Q Bartolomé Colón	5 Multicentro Sirena
B Beller	J Luperón	R Restauración	6 Bellón Hardware
C 30 de Marzo	K Sabana Larga	S Calle del Sol	7 Stainless & Pet shops
D España	L Estrella Sadhalá	T Av. Texas	8 Jade Express Rest.
E Duarte	M Metropolitana	1 Bus terminal	9 Ochoa (8A) Hardware
F San Luis	N Imbert	2 Dentist	10 Nacional Supermarket
G Mella	O 27 Febrero	3 Optica Central	11 Radio Shack
H Sanchez	P Carreras	4 Pez Dorado	12 Union Médica

To get to Santiago from **Imbert**, go to the ticket window in the kiosk on the west side of the Luperón road, north side of the main highway. Buy a ticket (1 beer) for the air conditioned express bus to Santiago. Like New York subways, don't take the local. The express comes every 15 minutes. For a real treat, sit in the front seat up by the driver. You should ask the driver to let you out nearest where you wish in the old town.

In **Santiago**, like in Santo Domingo, you use a "conveyor belt system" of cars marked "A", "B", "E", "G" and "M" which buzz all over town on fixed routes for one quarter of a beer. Taxis cost two beers.

PROVISIONING IN SANTIAGO

You can shop **Santiago** almost as conveniently as Puerto Plata. Santiago has fabulous supermarkets as good or better than the Publix, Winn-Dixie Marketplace or XTRA chains in Florida. The Imbert-to-Santiago bus terminal (#1) lies close to Supermercado Pola (#5). Supermercado Nacional (#10) at the corner of 27 Febrero (O) and Estrella Sadalah (L), and Price Smart out Estrella Sadalah toward the university shall also surprise you. Review the general guidance from *Provisioning and Repairs*.

Santiago has four large and modern hardware stores which sell everything from drill bits to drill presses, light bulbs to diesel motor-generators and Jacuzzis to outboard motors. Bellón (#6) and Ochoa (#9B), both a short walk from Multicentro Sirena (#5), and the big Ochoa (#9A), the best in the Caribbean, lie convenient to the buses for walkers. Ferreteria Haché lies on the corner of Estrella Sadalah and Bartolomé Colón on the *carrito M* route. You enter this hardware store through its swish multi-level coffee bodega.

Most boats with couples aboard have duties I call pink and blue. Arriving early in Santiago, send the Pink Watch up **Calle de Sol**, the principal shopping street, starting from Calle 30 Marzo toward the monument. Old time, multi-floor department stores such as La Sirena, El Encanto and Opera have replaced the insides of entire blocks here, but the façades still hold small businesses. You may find inexpensive name brand clothing. Boat shoes, for example? The next few blocks of Calle de Sol have their fame from their fabric and upholstery shops (Dumit, Opera). Then come Pizza Hut, McDonalds and so on.

While the Pinks shop Calle de Sol, the Blue Watch can do the mega-hardware store Ochoa on Avenida Imbert (#9A). While the Pink Watch chatted on the bus trip, the Blue Watch should have kept their eyes peeled for diesel labs (*laboratorios diesel*) or whatever other Blue stuff they want, so they can come back solo, injectors or fuel pump in hand, and hop off the bus at the right place. The industrialized agriculture of the Cibao means diesels, bearings, hoses and hydraulics for heavy equipment. It means stainless pipe, tube and sheet for food processing plants. All in Santiago. Watch for Ochoa hardware on your right as the bus approaches downtown. The Blue Watch can get off there.

Pink can treat Blue to lunch with their shopping savings by meeting at the Pez Dorado, on the park by the cathedral (#4). The *cafeterias* within the great supermarkets

Lastly, the Pink and Blue Watches can do Multicentro Sirena in the early afternoon for its heroic delicatessen with Sarrano hams, wheels of European and local cheeses, *chorizos*, and local and American products. It lies close to the buses. You only have to carry your purchases a few blocks to the air-conditioned bus back to Imbert.

Santiago has a section called ***Hospedajes***, similar to the old Les Halles section of Paris (now the Pompidou museum). Here you wander among piles of fresh fruits and vegetables and between 8 square city blocks of provisioners and wholesalers to compare caselot prices. Every building houses a wholesaler, usually specializing in categories of stuff. Go *early* to get products and prices. They start before daylight, and by noon, just like Les Halles, it becomes a garbage dump. Come back another day with a van to make your haul.

When I need new **glasses**, *Optica Cibao* (#3) gives me an eye test first thing in the morning. On my way home to Luperón that same afternoon they can have them ready. Ground on premises with European frames, usually for less than U.S. prices.

For those seeking gallon containers of **muriatic acid**, **stove alcohol** (anhydrous) or good **acetone** cheap, call in at *Agéncias Internacionales* between *Transportes Cibao*, the Santiago terminal of the bus line that leaves Luperón for the capital, and *Central de Hielo* at the first traffic light on 27 Febrero, immediately after the *La Rotonda* round-about on the autopista. The Blue Watch should look for it when you take the bus from Imbert.

A TRIP TO SANTO DOMINGO

The oldest city in the Americas, **Santo Domingo** can claim the Americas' oldest street, oldest cathedral and oldest university (the Santo Tomás de Aquino, built in 1538).

GETTING THERE

Take the Transporte de Cibao bus from Luperón at 1:30 p.m. direct to Santo Domingo, arriving at 5:30, more or less. You buy your ticket (about 4 beers) at the little house next to the restaurant (#25 on the Luperón map) around 1300. On a Monday when lots of week-enders return to the capital, I usually lunch in town so as to get a good seat on the bus.

Arriving in Santo Domingo, walk down Calle Duarte to Hostal Nader or the Palacio (see *Hotels...* below), or for hotels on or near Independéncia, turn off Duarte onto the El Conde pedestrian shopping street, where you shall walk left around the Parque Independéncia when you come to it, and thence along Avenida Independéncia (see map).

The streets between Conde-Independéncia and the Malecón have small grocery stores where the locals drag tables and chairs onto the pavement, drink beer and talk on summer evenings. These pleasant neighborhoods have small hotels of good quality sprinkled through-out. By taking these detours I meet the most interesting people, drink a lot of beer and arrive late to my hotel -- if I don't find a new one. Another rule I follow that you might like: never pass up an ice cream shop, especially if it has an Italian owner.

Once you've done the Capital, you'll realize how simply you can do it again.

USING PÚBLICOS IN SANTO DOMINGO

Like most huge Latin American cities, Santo Domingo comes dirty, noisy and confus-ing. But you can get anything you want there if you know where to go. Look in the Yellow Pages (*paginas amarillas*) to find what you want. Yes, they work the same as the Yellow Pages do at home, and no, you don't need to talk Spanish. Get a map and go to it.

In Santo Domingo the *carros públicos*, either step-on buses or little cars, run like con-veyor belts at right angles to each other all over the city. If you know the *X* and the *Y* streets where you want to go, simply ride one *guagua X* blocks one way, then ride another *Y* blocks on the perpendicular, and — *mira!* — you got there. Refer to the city sketch. *Carritos* in Santo Domingo run west the length of *Bolívar, Mella* and *San Martín*, and east on *Independéncia*, and both east and west on *John F. Kennedy* and *27 Febrero*. They run both north and south on *Máximo Gómez, Lope de Vega, Avraham Lincoln* and on *Winston Churchill;* north on *30 de Marzo*. Thus, you can hop two of these conveyances and in just minutes get to within a block of your destination for less than the cost of a local phone call most places. This grid covers the whole city, and more routes exist than I have shown.

Taxis cost from 2 small beers to 2 big beers. Always establish a price before stepping in. Note of caution for cruisers who insist on traveling in groups: you'll never find a *carrito* with 4 to 6 seats empty. So learn to forage alone and meet for lunch, or else ride taxis.

ATTRACTIONS

Annual events in Santo Domingo include *Carnaval*, held in conjunction with Indepen-dence Day on February 27, and the Merengue Festival, held the last week in July and the first week in August when the **Malecón**, the seaside boulevard named for George Wash-ington, gets cleared of cars and set up with 2 miles of merengue bands and dancefloors.

Walk the old town and do the museums. Attractions you can walk to in Santo Domingo include the Casa Real Museum, the Alcazar (Columbus' son Diego's palace) and a walk along the defense parapets. For a longer walk, or a *carro público* ride, do the Museum of Man with its Taino Indian displays, the Museum of History and the Museum of Fine Arts.

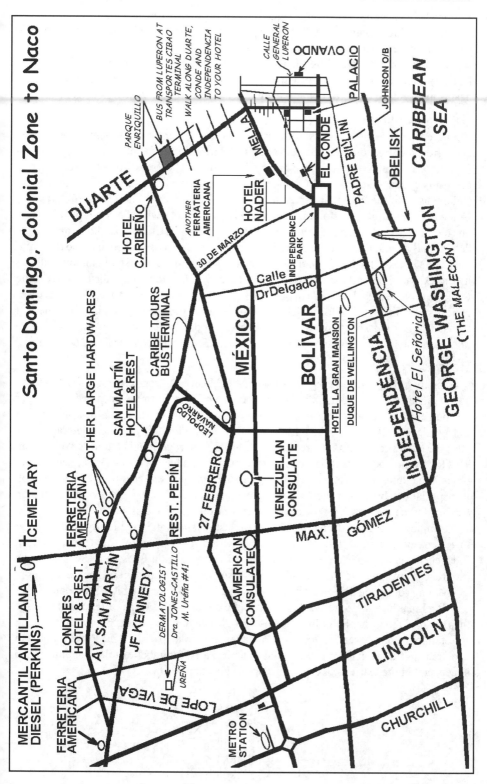

Santo Domingo, Colonial Zone to Naco

For a half a beer bus ride from Parque Enriquillo you can see the fabulous luminescent underground Indian lagoons at **Tres Ojos** park, next to the Columbus Lighthouse (*Faro á Colón*). President Balaguer built this last with cement which could have seen better use in schools and clinics. A big, cross shaped concrete slab, it houses exhibits of the country's history and holds the remains of Christopher Columbus. The monument projects laser beams in the shape of a cross onto the night sky -- sometimes. Visit *Tres Ojos* instead.

HUNTING COLUMBUS

Interesting for Anglophones, the misnomer Christopher **Columbus** probably comes about from an early equivocation between **Cristóbal Colón** and a fellow named Cristoforo Colombo, a Mediterranean cargo captain of the period. The Press created history even in the 14th century it seems, and Crown and Church worked mightily to obscure the real Columbus with the cant that serves as popular history today. The real hero, Cristóbal Colón, with his brother Bartolomé, operated his own vessels, when he couldn't gull someone else, like a Portuguese widow, out of theirs. Cargo on a Colón boat didn't always get delivered if he and Bart spied a more interesting horizon. He swashed and buckled from the Cape Verdes to the Faroes and even to Iceland. A bit of a bounder, but undoubtedly an heroic explorer, he parlayed himself into a royal grant of the vice kingship of half the world. Of course they threw him in prison when he tried to claim the prize. Colón deserves honest study, the sources for which grow quite rare. Hunt Santo Domingo for the real Chris, history's most brilliant navigator. (See Morison's *Admiral of the Ocean Sea, A Life of Christopher Columbus*, and Taviani's *Christopher Columbus, the Grand Design*).

RESTAURANTS

I highly recommend a twilight walk along the Malecón (Avenida George Washington), and a dinner of Riki Takis and beer or coconut milk from the pushcarts (2 beers per person). I greatly commend to you the Argentinian steakhouse, *Asadero Argentino*, on Independéncia between Avraham Lincoln and Winston Churchill (15 beers without wine). Also the *Villars* restaurant left around the corner as you leave Hotel Duque de Wellington. This lovely old house has rooms of elegant dining from a haute cuisine Dominican menu -- yes, such things really exist. Try the *crema de habichuelas negras* (black bean bisque). For special celebrations try the world renowned *Vesuvio* for excellent northern Italian cuisine. Of the two Vesuvios, celebrate in the one on the Malecón.

Mornings I like to read a paper while breakfasting and watching the city come alive, 7 to 8 a.m., on the street terrace at *Villars Reposteria y Cafeteria,* just to your left on Independéncia as you leave the Wellington. I lived 5 years in Paris, and I fail to see the difference between Café Villars and the brasserie near my apartment on Rue Madame.

Evenings doing the Blue Watch, I like to dine at *Pepín*, about which, more later.

After breakfast, the Blue Watch can go to the diesel dealer, **Mercantil Antillanas** (see map), and talk to owner Felix Juan Barros (U. of Michigan), or wander San Martín looking for stainless bolts (even *keel bolts*), Yamahas and solar panels. The Pink Watch can backtrack to Calle Duarte, up Mella and as far as Paris, for unbelievable shopping on the streets and in the warrens. Keep your flap pockets buttoned.

HOTELS IN SANTO DOMINGO

To get current rates, call from Luperón, and reserve early in high season.

First timers will find it most convenient, and most pleasant, to stay the first night at one of the old palaces in the *zona colonial*. I like the smaller **Hostal Nader** (tel. 687-6674) at the corner of *Luperón* and *Duarte*, a short walk from where the **Luperón** bus stops. Built in 1514 for General Alvarado, the Spanish military commander, the Nader served as headquarters for the expeditons of **Cortéz**, **Ponce de León** and **Pizzaro**. The government operates, and poorly maintains, the larger **Nicolas Ovando**, at the corner of *Luperón* and *Damas*, the palace of the first governor after Columbus. Near the Nader you'll find another privately operated **parador**, the **Palacio** (tel. 682-8340), at *Duarte* and *Salomé Ureña*, luxuriously redecorated. The **Señorial** (tel. 687-4367), Swiss family owned with pleasant verandah, lies just up from the obelisk on the Malecón (sea side avenue) and facing the Boy Scout park. They include a super breakfast. Just round the corner you'll find the **Duque de Wellington** at *Independéncia* 304.

Big tourist Sheraton and Hilton type hotels line *George Washington*, also called the *Malecón* (meaning dyke, or seawall). But I think you will find the paradors more comfortable, plus they lie in the heart of the old colonial city where you find the shopping and night life, *and*, of interest to cruisers, they cost a quarter as much.

While in **Santo Domingo** to see my dermatologist, I also do some shopping, stock up the medicine chest, and so on. It often takes two nights. The first night I usually stay at the the Señorial or the Duque de Wellington for both convenience and luxury. On the second night I might move to a smaller, more out of the way place.

Not for prudes: If I stay a third night to round up hardware and diesel stuff, I may take a cheaper and less commodious room at one of the neighborhood hotels near the industrial areas. These may cost a tenth of what the *paradors* cost, but they accommodate the less priggish cruiser.

All over the world Chinese restaurants, like French cafés, often rent rooms upstairs for the economical traveler. The standard may vary. Mostly they have full bath and a noisy air conditioner and cost just a few dollars. The DR has the same game. You may find large beds, European baths *and* mirrors on the ceiling, in the type of room which mostly gets used for brief periods in the daytime. After 8 p.m. they go empty, and they sure get cheap.

One with a not so firm mattress sits over a Chinese cafeteria, the *San Martín,* near the best *Gallego* restaurant this side of Gallicia: the *Pepín* on Avenida San Martín.

You even have a great ice cream store and an international newspaper and magazine vendor across the street from *Pepín's* 24 hour super cafeteria. I run my errands all day, then go to *Pepín's* back room, air conditioned dining room to read my paper over a drink, followed by a great leisurely *comida gallega* accompanied by the Movie Channel. Around 9 p.m., I check into the hotel San Martín, scrub off the city dirt and crash onto a king-size bed for the night. I try not to look up. With the superb security of this class of hotel, no traveling commercial man ever had it better. You can get a higher standard at the *Londres* Chinese restaurant down the street for only one beer more.

GETTING BACK

You don't need to stay over just to catch the 8:30 a.m. bus direct to Luperón. You can take the Metro (7, 8 and 11 a.m.) line to Puerto Plata, or the Caribe Tours line (6 a.m. to 6 p.m. every hour) to Imbert. That way you get another 4-6 hours in the city as profit from your last overnight stay. These super buses cost only five beers. See map for the terminal locations.

NORTH COAST SAILING DIRECTIONS

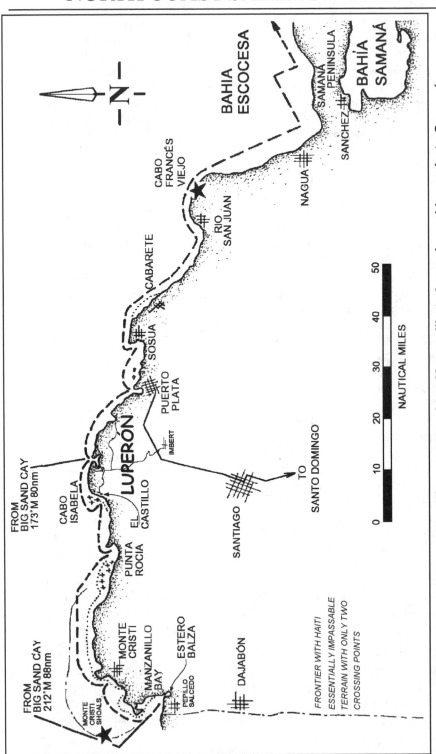

-N-

BAHIA
ESCOCESA

SAMANÁ
PENINSULA

BAHÍA
SAMANÁ

SANCHEZ

CABO
FRANCÉS
VIEJO

NAGUA

RIO
SAN JUAN

CABARETE

SOSUA

PUERTO
PLATA

IMBERT

LUPERÓN

CABO
ISABELA

EL
CASTILLO

SANTIAGO

TO
SANTO DOMINGO

FROM
BIG SAND CAY
173°M 80nm

PUNTA
ROCIA

FROM
BIG SAND CAY
212°M 88nm

MONTE
CRISTI

MANZANILLO
BAY

ESTERO
BALZA

MONTE
CRISTI
SHOALS

PEPILLO
SALCEDO

DAJABÓN

FRONTIER WITH HAITI
ESSENTIALLY IMPASSABLE
TERRAIN WITH ONLY TWO
CROSSING POINTS

0		10		20		30		40		50

NAUTICAL MILES

Divided into two legs with different strategies; Manzanillo to Luperón and Luperón to Samaná

TECHNIQUES

You definitely should have Fuson's book, *Columbus Log*, when sailing this coast. Each harbor gets detailed by the admiral himself along with their adventures. In the book, you will learn that little or no remains of the *Santa María* exist, all the hoopla over efforts to find it notwithstanding. **Columbus'** journal reveals that they scavenged the ship down to her keelson before leaving her detritus to wave and rock. He had to do even as you would do if you landed on Mars and the largest of your three transports crashed, while the next biggest got stolen. You would have left some of your people on Mars to make do there with whatever scrap they could salvage. Since **Martín Pinzón** had stolen the **Pinta** and run off to the Raggeds, Columbus had to carry on with the **Niña**, no bigger than some couples' cruising yachts today. The Niña's size forced him to leave more than half his crew ashore. *Santa María*'s bones went into construction of shelters there at the lost settlement of **Navidad** (Christmas). Colombus left his troublemakers, of course. The fact that no one survived at Navidad cannot be blamed on the Admiral of the Ocean Seas. Based on later behavior of the Spanish crews in Hispaniola, you can make a safe bet that they stirred up the Indians some and suffered due retribution, probably the last of their breed to do so.

If you know how even Colombus navigated, not *sailed*, this coast, and how he lost the *Santa María*, you shall understand what you must also do, and not unduly afflict yourself with feelings of inadequacy as a sailor.

AN OLD PLOY

For almost 500 years the few sailing vessels that have navigated the north coast of **Hispaniola**, against its trade winds and seas, have done so by hiding behind its headlands and capes during the day and proceeding close to shore at night where the more moderate conditions of the **night lee** permit a sure progress against the trades.

Sailboats coasting against the wind have used this tactic all over the world for longer than recorded history. Traders with the Caribbean from Brazil and Surinam still caravan this way when returning along the South American coast.

Columbus had to sometimes tow his ships at night with longboats under oars. The *Santa María,* Columbus' flagship, got lost on the **Limonade Reef** off **Caracol Bay**, east of **Cap Haïtien,** while being hauled in this fashion. After the ship touched they could not float her off, and the swell over the coral ground her slowly to bits. Lucky you have an auxiliary. When the mate carps at pulling the sweeps, don't cavil at starting it up.

GO WITH THE FLOW

The authorities on the north coast will seldom give yachts clearance to any port other than the official ports of entry: **Pepillo Salcedo** in **Manzanillo, Luperón, Puerto Plata, Samaná** and **Punta Cana**. A small, poor country like the DR cannot afford to place a customs house in every pokey little village for the odd cruising yacht to visit twice a year. Even the U.S., which can but doesn't, has the same policy. However, it doesn't mean they don't welcome you, given the right circumstances. I know many cruisers, including myself, who have stayed as long as they wished in these *puertos no habilitado*, or unequipped ports, going ashore with kids and pets as they pleased. But you won't want to tarry at most of these ports, as they don't offer much protection. Why do some cruisers have no problem with the local *gendarmes*? My guess? They go with the flow...

Don't emulate my old Swiss friend Josef, who tried to cruise the United States. Being a good Germanic Swiss, he insisted everywhere on proper papers which followed the letter of the law. None of the American officials were quite certain of the rules relative to Swiss yachts since they have no coastline and no maritime industry, but Josef insisted that they research it and give him the proper skinny. Coming from a cruise across the top of the world and down the east coast, he got as far as Washington, where he fled directly to the Bahamas under the weight of harbor fees and the welter of regulations whose lines he felt he had to toe. Though a dear and close friend of this American, he dislikes most Americans and America to this day. He had no trouble in France, England, Iceland, Greenland, Canada. He had less trouble with the DR officials. In fact, he settled in the DR. He just couldn't get the hang of the American flow, and therefore he couldn't go with it.

One man, an American HAMster, chased DR bureaucrats for weeks looking for a temporary license before using his radio in their territorial waters. He finally received assurances that the usual treaty between the two countries provided the usual 30 day grace period in which a visiting ship could use its radio. Armed with at least this verbal approval he counted the days he had stayed in the country. They amounted to 31. He never did use his radio in the DR. The Children's Hour and the Breakfast Shows went on without him.

I *do not* recommend having improper papers. I *do not* recommend violating laws of your host countries. But, if you want to have pleasure out of your pleasure yacht, I *do* recommend you ease off on the expectations you place on officialdom and *go with the flow*. For instance, if you ask to be cleared into ports other than the official ports of entry in the DR you shall most certainly be told that you cannot do that. If you declare your plans to "stop at" **Sosua**, for instance, you will be told that they cannot clear you for Sosua. True enough. A more careful communication would have you "pausing off" Sosua while the wind and seas around **Cabo Macoris** subside. On the other hand, why mention it at all? I have usually met understanding officials along the way. But life calls for some understanding of the officials by cruisers as well. Re-read the section on culture shock.

From **Manzanillo** you only need a simple *despacho* (clearance paper or dispatch) to **Luperón**. From Luperón I clear to **Samaná** regardless of how many stops I shall make, or even if I continue to Puerto Rico without a stop at Samaná. Once I actually got cleared "with intermediate ports" (*con puertos intermedios*) without problems. I just waived the paper at each new *comandante*. But don't bet on it, and don't waste your time grousing about it like Josef did in the U.S. You can't lightly go offshore here as he did there.

CRUISING IN COMPANY

Remote anchorages offer problems for border and drug enforcement in the DR. Years ago they would stake out an 18 year old soldier with a rusty rifle as the only authority in a small village. He had never seen a foreigner. His consternation at a great fleet of boats showing up on his beach came close to that of the Nazis in Normandy on the morning of D-Day. Things have changed since then. The 18 year old now wants a tee shirt.

No jilling about, yoo-hooing and mooning each other. If anchoring to rest and wait for the daytime conditions to abate, then ghost up to anchor unobtrusively, well beyond casual reach from shore and slip below for, guess what? A rest and a wait.

Respect the Coast Guard's situation, and if cruising in company, do so modestly. If the poor kid's superiors tool up in a jeep and see you careering around naked like you've established a commune in a *puerto no habilitado*, he has had it. And for that reason alone, so shall you have. One couple I know got asked to leave harbor during the height of a trade blow when the brass found their yeomen with rifles stuck in the sand giggling at the buck naked cruisers cavorting in front of the family living there.

Dominicans prize modesty and dignity. Yachts got short shrift at **Punta Macao** for quite a while after that. And don't look for the family's house. Hurricane Georges took it away — along with the old *comandáncia*.

DEPARTURE TIMING

Coasting the north coast of the DR and the south coast of Puerto Rico you must take small hops making the best use of the **night lee** available, ensuring good light early landfalls before the trades make up.

I subdivide the sailing directions into sections *Manzanillo to Luperón*, *Luperón to Samaná* and *Crossing the Mona Passage*. I discuss the characteristics of **weather windows** with which to leave port under the heading of *Picking Windows* within the chapter for each of these three main harbors. Basically, however, you should look for three day windows of settled weather between these ports.

Sailors might find opportunity to do some sailing if they wait and plan well. Everyone shall have lots of opportunity to motor. But if you do a really good job of picking windows, and of coasting, you shall motor flat out as though on a smooth blacktop road.

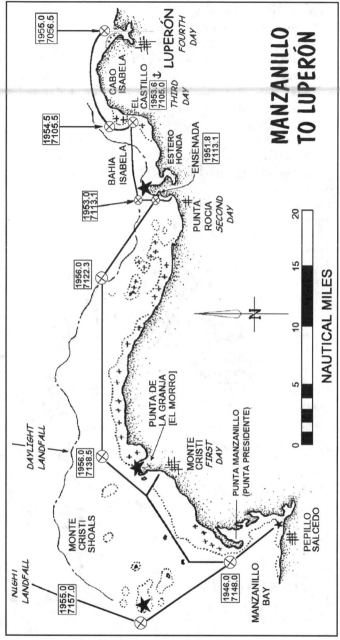

MANZANILLO TO LUPERÓN

Shelter under the capes at **El Morro**, the table-like mountain on **Punta Granja, Montecristi**, then at **Punta Rocia** (or Punta Rusia) with its Bahamas like water and diving, and finally at **Cabo Isabela**, where you can visit **El Castillo**. Make **Manzanillo** to Montecristi a morning 17 mile motor trip. Don't try farther. Make Montecristi to Punta Rocia a 28 mile motorsail in a flat calm before dawn. You can leave Montecristi easily and safely at night. Offshore dangers on that leg lie more than a mile to starboard at any point in the trip.

MANZANILLO BAY

Try to be inside **Manzanillo Bay** in the early morning when you have a calm bay, and proceed directly to the Estero anchorage. The high, creosoted pier presents a danger to a small boat in the high chop and surge usual by midday. If you cannot arrive early, anchor off the *comandáncia* to the west of the pier and ask to clear the next morning if you wish.

Estero Balza, the estuary three quarters of a mile east of the large pier on the south shore has a fine hurricane hole. The bar at high tide accommodates a 7 foot draft, 5 feet at low. If you draw less than 5 feet, or if you have fair wind and tide, enter the Estero (*ace-STAIR-oh*, or estuary) before the wind gets up, and clear from there by walking to the *comandáncia* at the foot of the pier (if they don't arrive first).

Occasionally you'll find a range of mangrove stakes at the entrance to the estuary, but don't expect it. You may ask for a guide to enter the Estero if you draw more than 6 feet. The channel can change slightly, and you may find it best to have a pilot aboard.

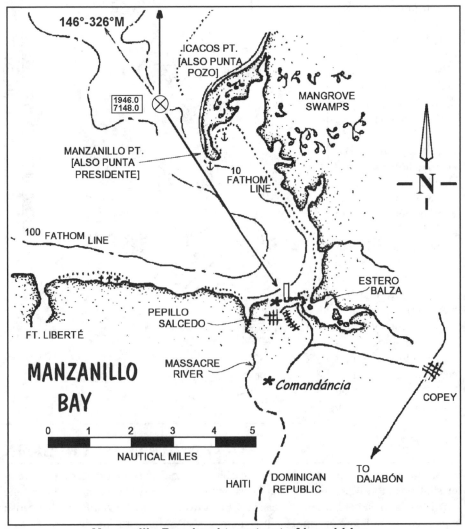

Manzanillo Bay, hard to get out of by midday

PEPILLO SALCEDO

Pepillo Salcedo [*pay-PEE-yo sal-SAY-doe*], a Grenada Company town built under the Trujillo regime in 1947 by United Fruit, took 3 years to build the town and facilities before exporting one banana. During the political vacuum of 1965, the Company gave up and pulled out, leaving factories, equipment, houses and the physical infrastructure of a sizable American town. A government patronage project to rehabilitate the enterprise barely survives, and the town languishes with a few bananas being exported and fish being sent inland. Don't either wait for the resort complex long hoped for by land poor residents.

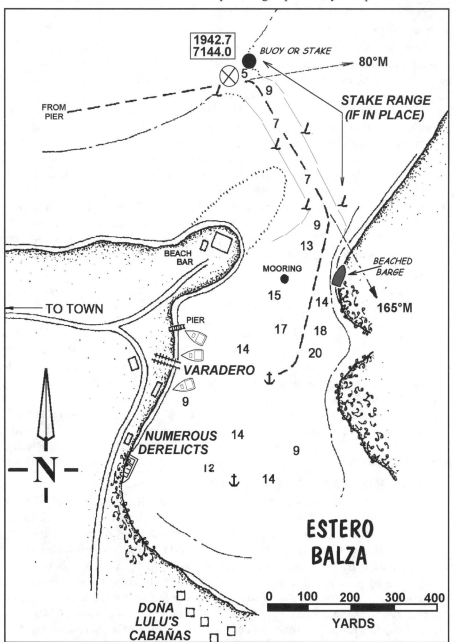

The stone houses lining the wide curbed and sidewalked streets shelter hospitable but poor Dominicans. For a huge and interesting Hatian market go to **Dajabón**, [*dah-hah-BONE*] a 20 minute drive away in the foothills by the Haitian border. But keep your valuables in your boots. For super modern hypermarkets, supermarkets and hardware stores or medical facilities, go to **Santiago**. For transportation to Santiago take the Caribe Tours bus at 07:00 and 14:30. They return from Santiago at 10:00 and 17:00.

For a real friend and help, see Fianchy [*fee-AHN-chee*], a former immigration officer. He speaks good American. He now exports tropical fish, runs a café and runs for mayor. Occasional salvage and diving operations take place for galleons on the reefs outside.

ESTERO BALZA

An excellent hurricane hole and long term anchorage with several deep bayous.

While at **Estero Balza**, see Fianchi for the latest on fuel, water, repairs or secure storage of the boat. He can set you straight on most anything. If not at his restaurant/bar on the central park, or at his tropical fish acquaria, then call him at home at 579-9536. You'll find the best provisions at Luis' clean and well stocked supermarket next to the school.

You'll see a beach bar and restaurant, with the inevitable *Merengue* dance floor, at the entrance to the Estero Balza. At the southern end of the estuary Doña Lulu runs an apartment hotel from her row of cabañas. For bilge keels and multihulls of modest draft, the *varadero* (var-a-DAIR-oh) beaching operation can, with patience, serve your haulout needs, provided you can squeeze in among the derelicts.

The seabreeze rises from the northwest around **Manzanillo Point** — **Punta Presidente** in some charts — about 10 a.m., veers throughout the day and dies in the east toward 6 p.m. to make room for the gnats, or *gegenas* [*hey-HEN-na*s]. The bugs are usually gone by 8 p.m., but, nonetheless, have your screens in or plenty of repellent handy.

LEAVING MANZANILLO

Leave the bay in early morning calm or get penned in for a hard beat!

Even trawlers may have difficulty punching out of the bay after 9 a.m.when the trades, augmented by the seabreeze, wrap around the points and blow in your face. If you draw more than 5 feet and don't have a fair tide in the early morning, move the boat over to the anchorage off the *comandáncia* on the west side of the pier the day before leaving and clear out the afternoon before leaving.

Get underway first thing in the morning, crossing the bay before the wind gets up, as it shall accelerate around Icacos Point and it will *pen you into the bay* for many hours. Motor across the flat *early* morning calm of **Manzanillo Bay**, north toward the island of **Tororu**. Sailboats then can often *sail* to **Montecristi**, tacking in the light morning air.

MONTECRISTI AND THE SHOALS

If you leave Manzanillo at sunup and sail some too, you'll suck on a cold beer in the beach hotel at Montecristi for lunch. Masochists can leave later than advised and slog against the **Equatorial Current** in Force 6 conditions due to cape effects along and in the midst of the **Montecristi Shoals**. Motorists *can* leave **Manzanillo** for **Montecristi** even later, but put the pedal to the metal, Gretel, if you want to get there before dark.

Stay on a longitude through **Tororu** to avoid the shoals off **Icacos Point** — also known as **Punta Pozo** — and **Yuna Point** -also known as **Punta Luna**. When a half mile south of Tororu tack northeast within the angle projected from the island of **Monte Chico** to the north and **Punta Granja** to the east. When one half mile west of **Cabra Island** steer 150°

Magnetic onto the large yellow hotel with the seawall, anchoring 300 yards off the marina in a sand patch in 10 feet. You may easily and safely leave in the dark here. See DMA chart 26141 or 26142 if you don't believe my chartlets, But don't necessarily believe the latitudes: edition 11 of DMA25801 corrected 1976 shows lattitude off by a full *mile*.

Founded in 1533 by 60 families shanghied by the Spanish from the Canary Islands, the sizable town of Montecristi has a budding ecotourism industry due to its mangrove rivers

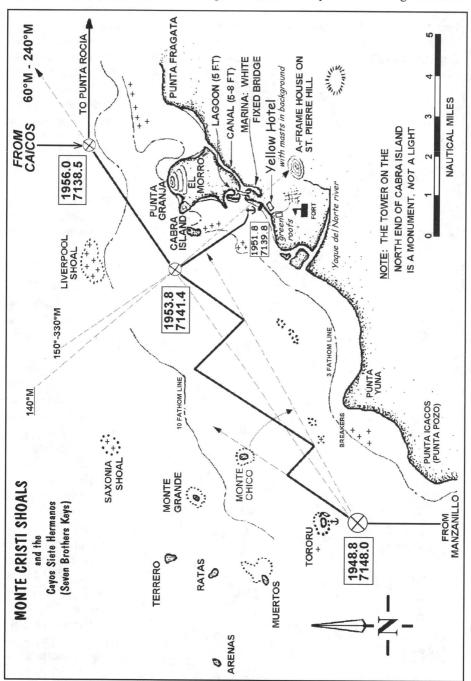

and lagoons. Extensive salt pans, about the only industry, still work between the town and the sea. The canal accessing the marina (*El Caño*) has had a haulout facility (*varadero*) for drafts under 5 feet reported in the works for many years. You can access El Caño from the west side of El Morro.

Fine in most conditions, the wide open conch grass harbor at Montecristi can expect occasional weather from the northwest in the winter months as fronts come down.

Leave Montecristi for **Punta Rocia** after midnight with plenty of night lee left, during a forecast period of less than 15 knots south of east **gradient wind**. Follow a course of 330° Magnetic from the anchorage, passing close under **Cabra Island**, until **Punta Granja** clears to the east. Steer 62° Magnetic for 4 miles to a point 3 miles north of **Punta Fragata**.

Then steer true east (following latitude 19°56') for 14 miles to the 100 fathom line, thence 126°M for **Ensenada** harbor at Punta Rocia. With a latitude corrected DMA 25801, GPS, fathometer , and a radar, you may run even closer inshore, well clear of all dangers.

PUNTA ROCIA

Punta Rocia, a remote Dominican vacation village with beautiful white sand beaches and extensive Bahamas-like coral reef snorkeling and fishing. An Austrian dive operation, a delapidated hotel and several cantinas dot the shore among the vacation homes.

Upon meeting the 100 fathom line on the eastward motor trip from Montecristi, turn east southeast for the 9 mile run to **Punta Rocia**, arriving shortly after first light. Be careful not to go too close to the point itself which, surrounded by a shelving coral bottom only 10 to 30 feet deep, has choppy seas. Proceed True south, or 190° Magnetic, from a point one half mile west of the point's shoreline to a red zinc roof on the beach. Or, turn onto 120° Magnetic after one third of a mile to enter the anchorage at **Ensenada**.

To get to the town anchorage proceed south on the red zinc roof for 1.6 miles from the point, then steer to the blue building to its east until in 2 fathoms of sand about 200 yards from shore. The blue building and the thatch roofed building next to it made part of a beautiful hotel complex which attracted foreign tourists seeking a more simple scene than at the great resort complexes farther east. It changed to Dominican ownership and it went out of business — not an uncommon thing. The Coast Guard will visit and inspect your papers. They may prefer you to anchor off the town, especially if you look like you do drugs.

It pays to get friendly with the coastguardsmen here. In settled easterly weather one can stop here for many days of diving. If a weekend, look for a fishfry on the beach, and join in.

The last Bahamas- like water before Puerto Rico's **Margarita Reef** lies behind these reefs. Park behind **Cayo Are-**

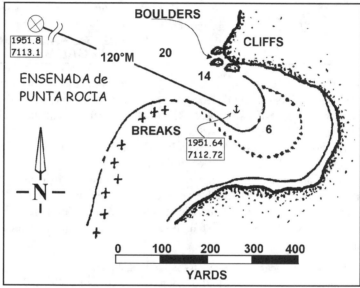

nas (called Paradise Key by tourist operations) for superb fishing.

Exit at sunup to make the short 7 mile leg over to **Cabo Isabela** for another day's pleasure and a tour of the New World's first successful European settlement.

If you missed Punta Rocia by sea, rent a motorcycle or car in Luperón and do it by land.

ENSENADA

An easily recognized landfall when you've got caught out too late in the morning while approaching Hispaniola from the north, and you need to give it up to continue on in the next morning's calm. Entering the **Ensenada** anchorage, you must go exactly between the coral awash on the south side of the entrance and the boulders on the shore at the north side. When inside, pick a sandy patch between grass and coral patches, and get your anchors well down.

You can exit Ensenada in poor morning light, or moonlight. Simply motor slowly a half mile on 300°M, turn north for 1 mile and then head east.

CABO ISABELA

When coming from **Punta Rocia**, duck inside **Isabela Bay** to get the most of the morning calm. Do *not* continue to **Luperón** if you chance getting in any later than 0830. Approach the Isabela beach anchorage due east to avoid the reef a half mile north of it. You landfall

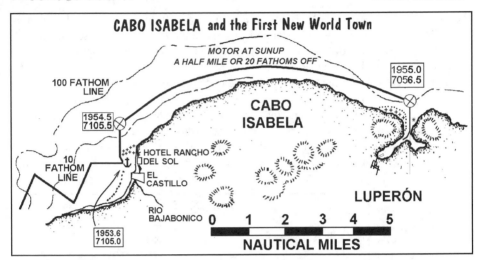

CABO ISABELA and the First New World Town

at Columbus' **El Castillo**, just north of the mouth of the **Bajabonico River** (also known as the Isabela River), a low red rock promontory which stands out as the only variation in miles and miles of dark sand beach. Sailing from the north, sail due south and one mile off. Turn up wind and motor east to anchor in calm conditions.

Anchor directly in front of Hotel Rancho del Sol in 2 fathoms and await the arrival of the Coast Guard, nice young men, full of smiles, stuck in a lonely outpost with no opportunity for advancement. A Belgian-Dominican couple, Herman and Sonja, own and operate the Rancho del Sol which has an excellent restaurant. Herman's Prout catamaran, *Baracuda*, stays in the anchorage in all but hurricanes. Close to shore the bottom runs to shallow rock. Shoreward of 2 fathoms lie a few rocky heads for which you must *go slow*.

EL CASTILLO

El Castillo, near the town of **La Isabela**, holds the ruins of the first settlement of Europeans in the New World. Founded by Columbus in 1493 and named for Queen Isabela, the town held nearly 5000 people before Spain moved it to the new capital of Santo Domingo in 1502. The modern Temple of the Americas, consecrated in 1994, commemorates the first mass in the New World celebrated by the priest who accompanied Columbus. As you can see, the site selected for the first colony presented free fields of fire on all sides, including over the rocky palisades to seaward. This snug redoubt fronts a mile square sand bottom harbor, which in those days made it easy for a square rigged ships to enter and leave in all conditions.

Don José María Cruxent, a Venezuelan archeologist ran the digs at El Castillo while the University of Florida used computers to make sense of the findings. They used computerized archeology because in the 1950's, the dictator Trujillo ordered a crew to clean up the site in preparation for a visit by Spanish archeologists. They did what you might do if a dictator orders you to clean up a ruin. They bulldozed the remarkably intact ruins to a cleared depth of 80 centimeters. Nonetheless much got restored, and the site makes for a very interesting afternoon's visit. No one knows what happend to the 'dozer driver.

A terrific fresh seafood restaurant sits under the seagrapes on the beach to the NNW.

A calm and tranquil anchorage in prevailing conditions, you can leave here at sunup for the 10 miles to Luperón, swinging wide of the rocks and reef projecting north of the anchorage. Motor in calm to Luperón at first light, not later or the 10 miles may seem 100.

LUPERÓN

These mile deep bays provide the best harbor on the island of Hispaniola. In November 1492 **Martín Pinzón** anchored the stolen **Pinta** off the low cliff face that projects from the east side of the entrance channel to trade with the Indians for gold. **Columbus'** guys found him when their longboat rounded Cape Isabela from El Castillo looking for the **Niña**'s next anchorage. "Surprise! Why, there's old Marty!" You will enter on this historical cliff face.

TO ENTER LUPERÓN

Turn of your chartplotter and *pilot* your boat by eye. Nor should you use the untrust-worthy buoys or stakes. The following foolproof, old-fashioned method beats any advice you may get from fellow cruisers, the likes of which I've heard to date can wreck you.

The westernmost edge of the east side of the entrance makes the best transit with which to enter, headed due south — 180° True. At the waypoint, put cliff face on the east side of the channel true south on your bow. Then make a **range** (see glossary) with the cliff face and any feature on the ridge in the background (see chartlet and photo). If you keep your feature over the cliff face, you shall eliminate all drift and slide true south into the harbor. You can also go by a good GPS by holding to the waypoint longitude of 7056.500.

Leave the red buoy, if there, *well to starboard*. When just past the "swimming hole" (see chartlet) start a wide sweeping turn to the southwest, avoiding the sandy shoal on the south of the *Playita*. When the channel through the mangroves opens up keep to the middle of it to avoid rocky shoals on its south shore. *Pilot* using the line on the chartlet.

Always enter in the early morning. Always set your anchor to the eastern trades.

ANCHORING IN BAHÍA LUPERÓN

Do *not* trust the stakes or buoys. Go slow. Use your depth sounder. To avoid shoals, trust the approach lines and the 1 fathom (6 foot) shore line shown on my chartlet.

Anchor where you will. Except for shoals shown on the chartlet, the harbor has depths of from 12 to 22 feet everywhere, and it often runs deep along the mangroves. Luperón has the best holding anywhere: soft mud over hard mud over caliche (old ocean bottom). When wet, caliche acts like marl; deeper down it gets like clay; eventually, calciferous rock.

In early morning calm, the yachts will lie to the flow of the creek at the southwest of the bay. Most will lie to a bight of chain and actually sit over their anchors. Set your anchor considering where you and they will lie when the trades come up from the *east*.

Set the anchor for east winds, knowing that 20 knots over the ocean can get to 30 in the bay. Set with a scope ten times the water depth plus the height of your bow over the water.

a) lay the anchor gently on the bottom while making *very slow* sternway (e.g., ½ knot), this will insure that the anchor lies flat on the bottom with its shank pointing west

b) lay out a scope of 10:1 (120 feet or more) due west along the bottom— don't put one ounce of tension on the anchor (e.g., do *not* let the anchor pull rode from the locker)

c) when stopped, back down on the anchor gently to get any snakes out of the chain, then do so with successively stronger pulls until you get up to half your horsepower

d) come back up to 5:1 scope for all chain, 7:1 for fiber rode to give others room

Do not anchor in the channel running between the west bay's entrance and the govern-ment dock. Mosquitoes and no-see-ums only come out an hour each at dawn and sunset. Do not listen to advice to "let the anchor cook". I have hundreds of anchor trials here, and this method *always* works and prevents dragging in strong winds with most anchor types.

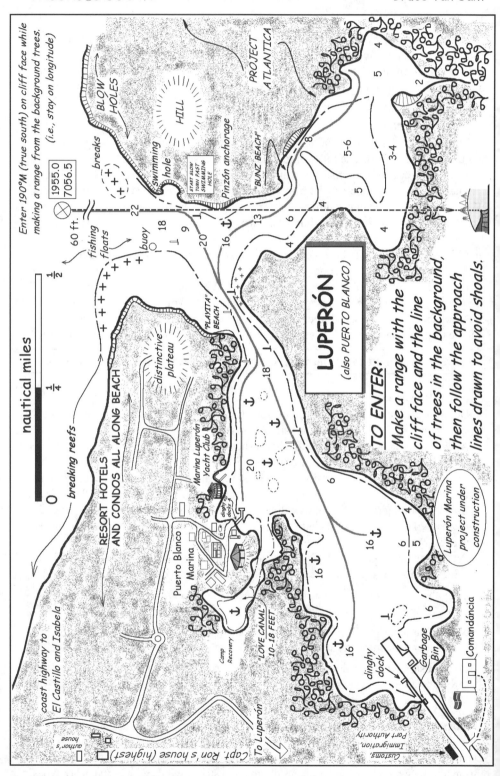

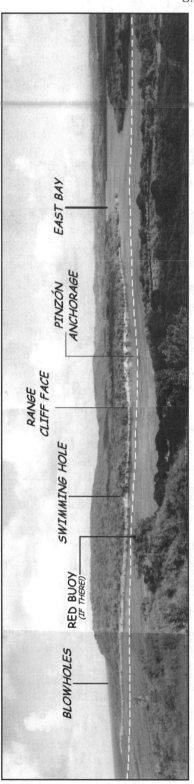

BLOWHOLES

RED BUOY
(IF THERE)

SWIMMING HOLE

RANGE
CLIFF FACE

PINZÓN
ANCHORAGE

EAST BAY

Enter Luperón with a range on the eastern side of the entrance

BLACK
BUOY
(IF THERE)

RANGE
180°T

ANY TREE

(ALWAYS
THERE!)

EASTERN
CLIFF FACE

RED
BUOY
(IF THERE)

You have entered a new time zone. Set your watch to AST (EST + 1 hour, UTC-4 hours).

Eye the place well on the way in, you may want to come out in the dark without a moon. Not to worry, it goes dead calm at night. Motor *slowly* and if you nose into a mud bank, you can slide right off into deep water. If you get stuck, you'll just have to prolong your stay in this lovely bay that looks more like a Swiss lake than a bay of the sea.

Clearance In

Anchor where you want and await the arrival of the Port Captain. If he doesn't arrive, or you missed him while you slept, or you get antsy and want to go to town, dinghy in to the *Comandáncia* (see chart) with your papers. After processing by the Port Captain see Customs, Immigration, Ports Authority, Agriculture and who-all-else in the blue steel building at the foot of the government dock.

THE TOWN OF LUPERÓN

You shall find local business people cheerful and friendly, willing to help you with anything. Congeniality counts with Dominicans. In the DR, *smile*, that's the style.

After resting and provisioning Luperón shall likely capture you awhile anyway. Luperón, though a small rural town, boasts markets and hardware stores, discos, hospital, police, a dentist, and all the other amenities a civilized place needs including ice cream. Don't mistake lack of sophistication for lack of civilization. You may feel restricted in what you can find in Luperón, but it will surprise you what a little persistence can produce. Otherwise, you have to travel to **Puerto Plata** or **Santiago**, an hour's time to either city.

DR has the most tourist traffic in the Caribbean. The large hotel complex on the beach runs on the Club Med type of all-inclusive plan. Cruisers can participate for a daily fee.

DR has the broadest industrial and agricultural bases in the Caribbean. You should provisions long term and get a full set of spares aboard. The rules for provisioning: buy *singles* of everything you might like, then *cases* of what you find you really do like.

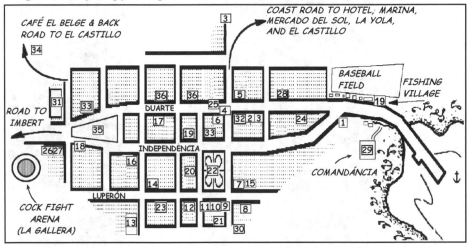

1 WELDING SHOP	10 FIRE DEPARTMENT	19 MARKET	28 CAPT. STEVE'S
2 GINA'S REST.	11 FUTURE THEATER	20 GENERAL STORE	29 COMANDANCIA
3 CHICKEN SHACK	12 CHURCH	21 COURTHOUSE	30 BAKERY
4 MOTOCONCHOS	13 HOSPITAL	22 CENTRAL PARK	31 PRIMARY SCHL.5
RESTAURANT	14 STATIONER'S	23 AUTOMOTIVE	32 **PHONE CO.**
6 BEVERAGES	15 HARDWARE	24 WELDING	33 PHARMACY
7 REST./DISCO	16 DENTIST	25 BUS TO Sto. Domingo	34 CAFÉ EL BELGE
8 NAT'L GUARD	17 LUCAS RESTAURANT	26 HIGH SCHOOL	35 GUAGUA PARK
9 POST OFFICE	18 HOTEL	27 POLICE STATION	36 SUPER MARKET

Local markets stock most everything *if you ask*, but a trip to buy samples in Puerto Plata or Santiago and to case the hardware and repair shops there will set you up for a quick provision run later, at prices often much better than in remote Luperón.

You may find old time stuff hard to get in the U.S. but readily available in the DR. You can find real sail canvas and real blue denim for instance. Stainless fasteners, stainless stock, diesel parts, exotic woods, fabrics, upholsterers, machines shops, etc., etc.

More than you can eat of rice, beans salad and either steak, chicken or pork cost less than two beers. Try the "Chicken Shack" with the blue doors near the phone company, for *La Bandera* (the Dominican Flag, or staple meal of beans, rice, salad and a choice of meat).

COMMUNICATIONS

Altagrácia and Nati run the phone company (#32 on the map) with a high speed **internet** operation. They exchange cash and traveler's checks and operate a **travel agency**. The best and friendliest business women (or men) in town, they have made it the cruiser crossroads. Find the telephone company 2 blocks up Duarte on the left. The harbor stands by nonstop on VHF Ch.68. Cruiser Nets on VHF Ch. 72 at 08:00 Sundays and Wednesdays.

CASH AND MONEY EXCHANGE

The phone company and most tourist shops accept dollars. You'll find an ATM cash machine further on across the street from the police station. While shopping in Santiago you'll find ubiquitous ATMs.

TRANSPORTAION AND TOURING

You'll find the town dinghy landing on the north side of the government dock and a garbage depot further down the dock toward town. You'll find buses, taxis, and motoconchos all on Duarte, the main street; rental cars and motorbikes on the road to El Castillo (see map) and in the marinas.

Call **TINGAL** on VHF 68 for **tours** anywhere, especially to the best waterfall chutes in the Caribbean, and for all ages. Anybody can do it, and for ladies of any age and size, they have young Dominican hunks to see you effortlessly and pleasantly through the hurdles.

When you go to the waterfalls, or *cascadas* (cas-CAH-das), you must go early to see it like the Indians saw it and avoid the crowds of resort tourists. Get there first, and the water will sparkle clear as gin. Wear old shorts, shirt and sneakers. Take a change and a towel. Arrange a tour with Rosa soon on your arrival. It will get you out of Luperón and into the country, so that you won't feel awkward about going out on your own later.

MARINAS

Puerto Blanco Marina lies north of "Love Canal" (see chartlet) in the NW corner of the harbor. Marina Luperón and Yacht Club lies on the hill to the east of it. **Tropical Marina** has begun construction on the south shore. The mega-marina **Ocean World** lies 8 n.m. to the east. The English speaking Non-Denominational Evangelical church, to starboard as you enter "Love Canal", has four slips with water and 30 amp. electricity for 5½ foot drafts.

Marina Puerto Blanco has a cruiser's dinner/dance every Friday night with live music. They organize fuel or water or propane delivery. Call "Handy Andy" for all services.

Los Bomberos

The Luperón Firehouse

CHECKLIST FOR GOING EAST FROM LUPERÓN

Tips from well over 100 dispatches to always tranquil sails of the DR coast, more than 50 serene Mona crossings and 27 years watching others get hammered easting from here.

AFTER SPENDING A HURRICANE SEASON IN LUPERÓN
(or if you haven't done these in awhile)

1. CHANGE oil, oil filters and fuel filters, add coolant and biocide (Biobor)

2. INSPECT your rigging truck to keelson: sand and examine your swedges, tangs & chainplates. Check spreader angles, mast foot, deck tensioners, keel bolts, raw water pumps, impellers, stainless clamps and hoses. Hoses have dried out over the summer; they may have cracked or loosened.

3. PREVENT OVERHEATING, clean your thru-hulls and raw water strainers. Restricted intakes cause overheating at the worst times: like when you *need* sustained high RPMs. Run acid through your heat exchangers. Just before leaving, scrub your bottom and *sand* the propeller to a shine. Dirty props not only lose you speed, but they usually cause engine overheating only after *extended* use. That means you don't know you've got a problem until you've got beyond the point of no return.

4. SEA TRIAL: untangle the rig, and stir up the fuel tank on a downwind sail to Punta Rocia. Sharpen up your night coasting skills on the pre-dawn return. Then fix up and go.

NAVIGATION

1. **Wx:** NWS+Chris+Herb+George+Arthur+Maurice+*YOU* minus (~~VHF buddies~~). Interpolate SWNA and EC Offshore Reports to get **gradient**, *then* apply island effects.

2. **Don't get caught** dead on a tradewind coast in the daytime. You'll hug the shore in the night lee until the Virgin Islands. The night lee *settles in* between 1900 and midnight, the more forecast wind, the *later*. The night lee *dissipates* between 0700 and noon, the more forecast wind, the *earlier*. Only go on a forecast gradient wind less than 15 Kts: <15 KTS S OF E doesn't blow strong enough to overcome the night lee, and -------- <15 KTS S OF E from *behind* the island reduces the effects of coastal acceleration.

3. USE OVERSIZE WINDOWS. 2 days more than required: 1 for seas to go down, 1 for safety.

4. LEAVE ONLY AFTER THE WIND ceases in harbor. It will blow much stronger outside. Sunny days of S'ly wind or west-going moist air masses can create **Island Lows** which cause strong easterly circulation late on the north coast. Otherwise, by 10 p.m. to midnight, *night lee* flattens the sea and gives you 6-8 knots landbreeze just forward of the beam.

5. NAVIGATE *by fathometer* in 80 to 120 feet. Glue your eyes to the depth sounder, not the compass. Stop during the daytime, update your weather picture and plan the next step. Turn off the chartplotter, clear any offsets on your GPS, and *never, ever* pull GPS waypoints from Caribbean charts, nor mix waypoints between charts and guides. My true waypoints have 18 years of use by many thousands of boats without incident.

6. AVOID THE "GARBAGE LINE": high seas flotsam along a line 1-2 miles off the capes and 3-5 miles off bays; and within 2 miles west-northwest of rivers on outgoing tides.

7. KEEP DEADLINES: Pass Puerto Plata after 10pm. Pass Cabo Francés Viejo by 8am. Make Punta Macao by sunup. Stop at Escondido to evaluate: Should you go on to Samaná? Punta Macao? Punta Cana? Mona Island? Set out from Escondido for points east of Samaná by sailing for Cabo Rafael, then follow that coast's night lee to Cabo Engaño.

LUPERÓN TO SAMANÁ

> Most cruisers, especially Pacific sailors, underestimate the Atlantic trades. Great variations of depths exist around the Greater Antilles through which pour voluminous, though not always rapid, currents. The tumbling of these large flows across uneven bottom found on the edge of the Caribbean tectonic plate cause steep seas or spurious currents not warranted by gradient conditions. You shall see an example of this while going from Luperón to **Punta Patilla**.

Sailing or motoring to windward on this coast during so-called *moderate trades* (20-25 knots, 6-8 foot seas) rates as flat out suicidal. New to the tradewind belt, southbound yachties can't shuck themselves of the idea that the wind will eventually back or haul around to get them where they want to go. Well it won't, of course, that's why they call them tradewinds. When they hear a forecast of **gradient winds** with a *northerly component* some shout "Huzzah!" and charge out to sail east on it. They find it 5-10 knots harder than forecast due to coastal acceleration, and actually blowing *east by south* as it follows the coast. To get off the coast to where gradient conditions prevail, it would take you a full day tacking 30 miles out and back, while drifting westerly. If you truly get clear of land, you would then bear the brunt of the Equatorial Current trying to get east.

The Super Maramus and the young delivery skippers apart, cruisers can't make a knot eastward from Luperón on a real northeast wind given the seas, the current and the northerly swell that develops to make most north coast ports untenable. And of course, like me when I've sat in port too long, they've got sludge in their tanks, ropes in their props, thumbs up their bums, and the rough conditions make it needful to call in someplace.

In short, in any wind north of east most have to turn back. What about westerlies? Well, if you ever have a westerly on this coast, you have a moving front coming in, or a depression north of you moving west. You know the answer to the first, or should: *Never try to ride a moving front on this dangerous lee shore*. If a west moving depression, the seas it stirred up probably won't let you out of the harbor. At least for your sake, I hope they don't let you out, for you may get murdered. You chose to come through the islands. If you want to use open sea strategies, go back to San Salvador and take "I65" (65°W).

So what have you got left? **Prevailing conditions** when they have moderated. You should study carefully the effects documented in the sections: *Island Strategies* and *Playing the Island Lees,* as well as the specific sailing directions given for each leg along this coast. Get yourself in a position to *know* when the moderations will come.

In the islands one must use island strategies. The snug harbor of Luperón and the **land effects** on this coast shall blind you to the conditions offshore. For signs from Luperón, see: *Island Weather: Weather Windows: Harbor Telltales.* By making the *nogo* tables and figures shown, and by listening to the **Offshore Report** each day, you can attune yourself to the music of the trades. You shall have no question your window has arrived. Remember to wait for the seas to subside, and don't count on the last day. It may melt away on you.

You can get a jump on a window by using the small night lees available in the wee hours of its beginning if you stage to the **Pinzón anchorage** for a night exit (~11 p.m.) to **Rio San Juan**, after the rugged seas west of Punta Patilla have gone down. You can do the same using 6-8 hour mini-windows on consecutive days by leaving pre-dawn (~4 a.m.) from Pinzón for the 5 hour run to **Sosua**, then on to Rio San Juan the next morning (~3 a.m.), another 5 hour run..

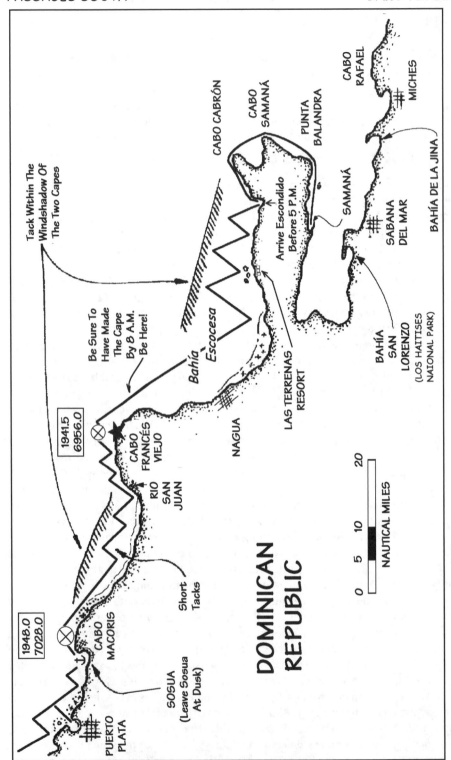

North Coast of the DR: Puerto Plata to Samaná

PICKING WINDOWS

WIND If the offshore **gradient wind** has blown less than 15 knots from south of east during the day, you usually shall have a flat calm motorsail in deep water close inshore before dawn. Hide behind the capes in the daytime and transit them at night, taking the wind that comes on a down-tick of a trade cycle. Go only when the forecast gradient wind blows less than 15 knots from behind the island (i.e., south of east), less than 12 knots if blowing dead east (along the coast), and less than 10 knots if the wind has any northerly component (onshore). These winds lack the strength and direction to overcome the **night lee**. If you want to coast in daylight reduce these wind strengths by 5 knots or more due to seabreeze. The section of the coast from **Luperón** to **Punta Patilla** runs high and rugged with the 100 fathom line less than 2 miles offshore.

The night lee will establish itself between 1900 and midnight, the more the forecast gradient wind, the later. The night lee will melt down between 0700 and 1200, the more the forecast gradient wind, the earlier. To get the forecast gradient wind for your passage you must interpolate, or as they say in billiards, you must apply *English* to the numbers by weight averaging all reports. For example, consider the following two reports.

Eastern Caribbean: N OF 16N WIND SE 10 TO 15 KTS.
Southwest North Atlantic: S OF 26N WIND E TO SE 15 TO 20 KTS.

Out at 20° N by 68°W, just north of the Mona Passage, expect a forecast gradient wind strength of 13 kts. Why? Because 26°N to 16°N gives a spread of 10°, split 6° in the Atlantic report (E to SE 15 to 20) and 4° in the Caribbean report (SE 10 to 20). With the wind strength climbing a half a knot per degree of latitude, you would expect by pure interpolation that the forecast wind at 20N 68W would get up to 4 degrees times one half knots, or a rise from the 10-15 range to 12-16, average 14. But favor the much closer Caribbean report with some *English* and say 13. By the same logic expect a forecast gradient wind at 20N 68W coming from southeast-by-east.

If I received these reports at Luperón I would interpolate a forecast gradient wind at Luperón of E 15 knots or more, by using an 80/20 apportionment of the two Offshore reports. I give 20% to the Caribbean report evaluated at my latitude as above, and 80% from the Atlantic report. And with E 15 knots or more I would have a clear *Nogo*.

If I received the above reports while pausing at Escondido, near the Mona and on the edge of both report zones, I would apply a 20/80 rule and expect ESE 14 knots, making it, if the outlook showed improvement, a *Go* from there to Puerto Rico.

SWELL Finally, you must accept no northerly swell. Zilch. During the winter months this means you must stay aware of the lows and gales to the north. It may take them 3 days to shed swell in your area if they just came off the U.S. coast, but one on its way to England may already sound in the Luperón blowholes at night like Napoleon's canon at the battle of Borodino. Ask the headboat skippers to report swell. Caicos, Turks, Muchoir, Silver and Navidad Banks reduce the swell reported by the forecasters. They also act like a diffraction grid and change and confuse swell direction.

WEATHER FEATURES In mid-October through mid-December, and the spring months May through June, look for stationary **troughs** which stretch from the southwest Caribbean to north of Hispaniola. They can run from the Andes to Newfoundland. Year round, the approach of weakening cold **fronts** can turn into stationary troughs as well. This phenomenon, shown in the figure below, opens a window for going east along the coast, because a wedge of relative calm gets created between the coast and some distance out toward the trough. Stationary gale systems may imbed in the troughs, and they can produce ferocious swells that, of course, say *nogo*.

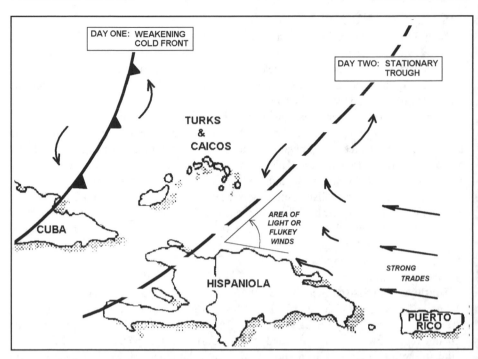

Stationary fronts or troughs developing north of Hispaniola can give protection from the trades for going east.

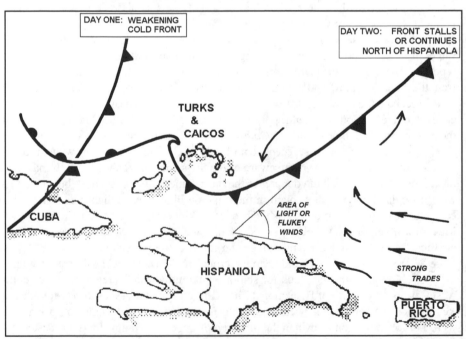

Occluding fronts also may provide a window as the belly of the otherwise strong front slides on by to the north.

PREPARATION Do the following in all mangrove harbors. The north coast harbors leave your ground tackle a mud and growth encrusted mess. You shall have a cleanup job on the ground tackle that will leave you exhausted and in an ill mood for a bad start to sea. You'll need a night's sleep after your labors. The day before leaving, get anchors unfouled and clean the rodes. Lay to a single fresh hook, make ready for sea. Hire a service, or use the Pinzón anchorage to scrub prop and bottom for the motoring ahead.

Get your *despacho* for Samaná, even if you think you may go on to Puerto Rico. From **Luperón** you need a 3 day window for **Samaná**, or a 6 day window for **Puerto Rico**, in order to proceed without daring midday coastal winds. You should consciously plan to call at Samaná even if you want to proceed to Puerto Rico if the weather holds. U.S. Puerto Rican Customs won't mind, and you won't have to pay another clearance fee in Samaná if you wind up there — which you almost certainly will anyway. When you stop at Escondido you can review your weather window, and if it hasn't extended, you can cut to Samaná. If you need to leave after dark, stage to the Pinzón anchorage, and don't leave before the wind has died. Sometimes an **Island Low** will keep some circulation going quite late.

TIMING Customize your departure from Luperón to the weather window available. No fixed rule can calculate a fixed departure time for every window possible, but in many years of departing Luperón, I have made all my departures at dawn, dusk or near midnight. Use the night lee by motorsailing at night close along the capes. If you don't stop at **Rio San Juan**, you must turn the corner and hoist sail well east of **Cabo Francés Viejo**, free of land by 8 a.m. when the next day's easterly flow shall hit.

ITINERARIES FROM LUPERÓN ACROSS THE MONA TO PUERTO RICO

I selected the following itineraries from my sailboat's logs of motorsailing in Offshore Reports of ESE gradient wind less than 15 knots and no northerly swell. Departure and arrival times reflect appropriate use of night lees and exit/entrance constraints. Average knots reflect 4.5 directly into light seas or 5.5 in full lee. My trawler does about the same.

				Depart	Arrive
Luperón	Sosua			4 am	9 am
	Sosua	Rio San Juan		1 am	7 am
		Rio San Juan	Escondido	9 pm	8 am
Luperón		Rio San Juan		8 pm	7 am
		Rio San Juan	Escondido	9 pm	8 am
Luperón			Escondido	6 pm	12 noon
Luperón	*[sailing Escocesa]*		Escondido	6 pm	3 pm
Escondido	Samaná			4 am	8 am
	Samaná	Pta Macao		6 pm	6 am
		Pta Macao	*[motoring]* Boquerón	6 pm	12 noon
		Pta Macao	*[sailing]* Boquerón	6 am	10 am
Escondido		Pta Macao		7 pm	7 am
		Pta Macao	Pta Cana	4 am	8 am
			Pta Cana	Mona Is.	6 am	1 pm
		Pta Macao		Mona Is.	7 pm	6 am
				Mona Is. Boquerón	10 pm	7 am
				Mona Is. Ponce	5 pm	7 am
Escondido			Pta Cana	5 pm	8 am
Escondido				Mona Is..	3 pm	12 noon
Escondido				Boquerón	8 pm	12 noon

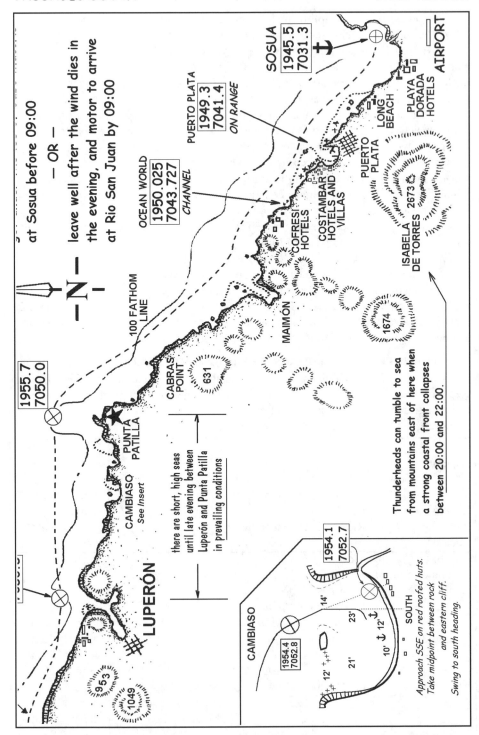

at Sosua before 09:00

– OR –

leave well after the wind dies in the evening, and motor to arrive at Rio San Juan by 09:00

SOSUA
1945.5
7031.3

AIRPORT

PUERTO PLATA
1949.3
7041.4
ON RANGE

PLAYA DORADA HOTELS

LONG BEACH

PUERTO PLATA

OCEAN WORLD
1950.025
7043.727
CHANNEL

COFRESI HOTELS

COSTAMBAR HOTELS AND VILLAS

ISABELA DE TORRES 2673

100 FATHOM LINE

MAIMÓN

1674

CABRAS POINT

631

1955.7
7050.0

PUNTA PATILLA

CAMBIASO
See Insert

there are short, high seas until late evening between Luperón and Punta Patilla in prevailing conditions

Thunderheads can tumble to sea from mountains east of here when a strong coastal front collapses between 20:00 and 22:00.

LUPERÓN

953

1049

CAMBIASO

1954.1
7052.7

1954.4
7052.8

14'

23'

21'

12'

12'

10'

12'

SOUTH

Approach SSE on red roofed huts.
Take midpoint between rock and eastern cliff.
Swing to south heading.

North Coast of the DR: Luperón to Sosua including Cambiaso

NORTHBOUND FROM LUPERÓN

Westbound boats can simply reverse my sailing directions. Boats anxious to make time yet sail thornlessly, should take the following route, cautious always to have good weather windows, downwind or not: look for easterlies 15 knots, no northerly swell. Leave Luperón in the evening on a broad reach to the southeastern point of the Caicos reefs (2100.0, 7150.0). Leave so as to arrive at the reef shortly *after daybreak*. Not to worry, the southeast end of the reef runs deep, and you shall go on soundings well before seeing it. Follow the lee of the reef in 10 fathoms up to **French Cay**. You must not overshoot the reef on its southern end, or you might follow it *inside* rather than *outside*. I did that once. Following the reef closely shall cut the seas by up to 3 feet. I've proved this route cuts a couple of hours off the Luperón-to-French Cay direct rhumbline. First you quarter-sail up to the reef, broad reaching more than running free, then you run free along the reef in a *lee sea* with no corkscrewing, faster and more comfortably than on the downwind, open ocean rhumbline.

Arrive at French Cay for a late lunch and some hook fishing. Don't go ashore on this bird sanctuary. Next day, sail from French Cay to Sapodilla Bay directly. To skip Caicos, stay around for more fishing and a *mariscos* lunch, then jib sail the 20 miles to diveboat moorings in the lee of **West Caicos**. Arrive around 1600 when most diveboats have gone. Drop the mooring in early morning dark for a high, over-the-shoulder light morning entrance to **Mayaguana**. Take all reef entrances thereafter in high, over-the-shoulder light.

Clear in at Mayaguana. Then fish every day underway and anchor every night. The route I take almost never varies (see the Chartlets for Turks & Caicos and the Bahamas):

Luperón	⟹ Molasses Reef	⟹ French Cay	⟹ West Caicos
	⟹ Mayaguana	⟹ West Plana	⟹ Attwood Harbor
	⟹ Landrail Point	⟹ Clarence Town	⟹ Rum Cay
	⟹ Conception	⟹ Calabash Bay	⟹ Georgetown

COFRESÍ

The state-of-the art Ocean World Marina lies adjacent to the Ocean World Adventure Park, the largest marine park in the Caribbean which features wildlife interactive programs with dolphins sea lions, stingrays, sharks and rainforest birds. You can also feed Bengal tigers through a feeding hole in a glass window. They have a private beach, showers, restaurants, laundry, weather service, photo lab and video services, Customs & Immigration, casino entertainment, clubhouse dining with pool, dive shop with air fills, dive charters, liquor store and shops.

The marina features 104 slips on concrete docks with cable TV, R/O potable water, electricity, internet access, 24 hour security and telephone, as well as finger piers for up to 230 foot LOA vessels. Enter a buoyed dogleg channel with a controlling depth of 12 feet initially going southwest.

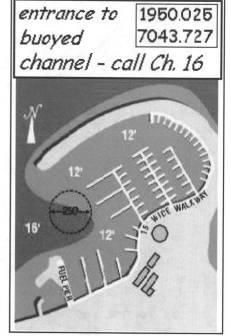

entrance to 1950.025
buoyed 7043.727
channel - call Ch. 16

PUERTO PLATA

With **Luperón**, the preferred port of entry for yachts, and only a bus ride away, you have no reason to take your boat into Puerto Plata except in an emergency. In daytime you can see the range as two white pylons with orange tops. Keep a sharp lookout when picking up the range, and stay well off until you do.

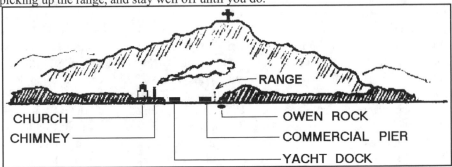

CHURCH
CHIMNEY
RANGE
OWEN ROCK
COMMERCIAL PIER
YACHT DOCK

Approaching Puerto Plata: Isabel de Torres mountain seen south 3 miles

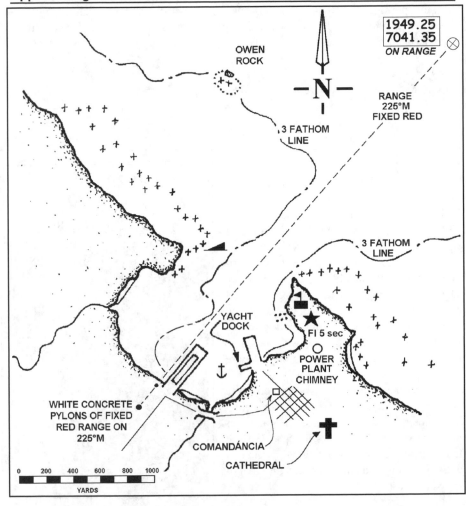

OWEN ROCK

1949.25
7041.35
ON RANGE

RANGE
225°M
FIXED RED

3 FATHOM LINE

3 FATHOM LINE

YACHT DOCK

Fl 5 sec

POWER PLANT CHIMNEY

WHITE CONCRETE
PYLONS OF FIXED
RED RANGE ON
225°M

COMANDÁNCIA

CATHEDRAL

0   200   400   600   800   1000

YARDS

SOSUA

Cleared from **Luperón** for **Samaná**, take a **leisure sail** over to **Sosua** [soh-SOO-ah], standing well off the reefs along the shore. Leave Luperón at first light or a few hours earlier, anchoring overnight in the entrance, if necessary. As you tack toward the airport near Sosua, you shall feel the **Cape Effect** of **Cabo Macoris**. Get closer inshore at this point to get cover from the stronger winds produced. You can easily see the reefs here.

Anchor outside the public swimming area, not going ashore. Forego your **SG&T** toward a safer voyage. Take a nap and prepare a thermos or two and a pressure cooker full of hot *burgoo* (see Glossary). If bound for Escondido, raise anchor toward sunset and sail around Cabo Macoris, usually an exciting sail in the ebb of the day, until the fun goes for lack of wind. Any white horses shall soon disappear, assuming, of course, you picked a proper window. Going to **Rio San Juan,** you will depart Sosua after midnight.

Don't anchor close enough for swimmers to come out and hang onto your boat, thereby making a scene of yourself and looking like a drug trader. If, despite your intentional low profile, a representative of the Puerto Plata *comandante* wakes you up, simply explain to him that you shelter under the headland until evening, and shall leave when seas permit.

German Jewish refugees from the Nazis founded this touristy town, popular for its lovely beaches, dive sites and dives. Dictator Rafael Trujillo gained favor with the U.S. by letting them in at a time when the U.S. did not permit their entrance. The immigrants started sausage and dairy production, and established a yogurt tradition on the island. Today the town has lively nightlife, an arts community, and has many immigrants from Germany and Quebec. Among the world's top wind-surfing and kite-surfing spots, **Cabarete**, lies just around **Cabo Macoris**. East of Cabarete's beaches you shall see no more shoal shores.

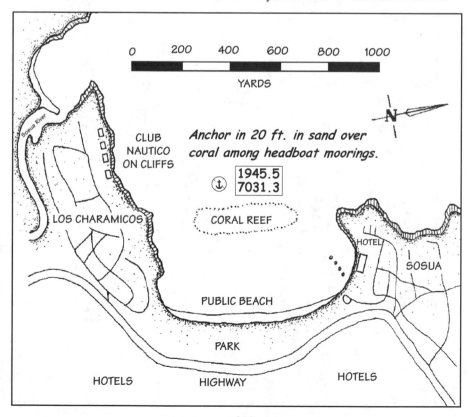

0   200   400   600   800   1000

YARDS

CLUB NAUTICO ON CLIFFS

Anchor in 20 ft. in sand over coral among headboat moorings.

1945.5
7031.3

Sosua River

LOS CHARAMICOS

CORAL REEF

HOTEL

SOSUA

PUBLIC BEACH

PARK

HOTELS   HIGHWAY   HOTELS

RIO SAN JUAN

Whether bound east or west, I usually call at the little fishing harbor of **Rio San Juan**. This port offers a good lee in **prevailing conditions**: i.e., easterly wind with no northerly swell, no threatening weather features approaching. I anchor at the mouth of the entrance to the fishing harbor or in the harbor itself if for a longer term stay, or when swell comes.

Put this harbor on your itinerary from Luperón. It lets you jump up a day or two on an 'iffy' window by using the scraps of lee available midnight to dawn before the window opens wide. I arrive here at 08:00 after a 50nm run from Luperón or a 25nm run from Sosua.

Continuing east, wait for the night lee to set in solidly before rounding **Cabo Francés Viejo**. You also don't want to round the cape before the lightning from the day's coastal front drifts over the cape and sparks on out to sea. Escondido lies 55 miles to the east.

I stop here westbound, sometimes just for a few hours, to ensure an early arrival at **Luperón** before the breeze gets up and makes it difficult to anchor there. Setting anchor properly in mangrove mud gets difficult as the midday winds set up. Instead, I take a calm night sail from Rio San Juan, listening to the late night classical Spanish ballad stations.

I then cap it off by entering Luperón sipping coffee, drifting lazily between the bird calling hills topped with morning sun. I set my anchor in the morning calm without a peanut gallery of cruisers shouting helpful hints. I get the boat better prepared to withstand the day's eastern trades in the absence of officials and dock boys ploughing wakes around me with earnest, but unintelligible, entreaties. *I arrive while they all still sleep.*

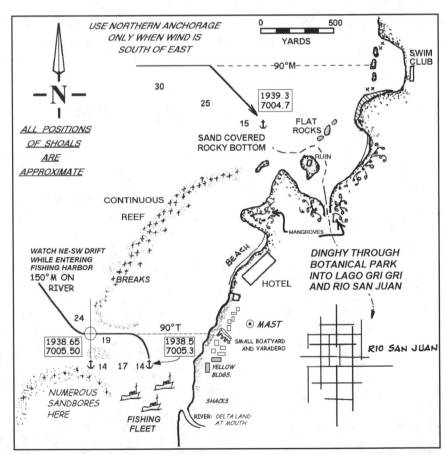

CABO FRANCÉS VIEJO

It seems to take forever to get around **Cabo Francés Viejo**. Tightly hugging the shore makes it easier. If you think yourself a latter day Lt. Maury, no doubt you will use your GPS to discover all sorts of eddies and counter currents. Don't make a fool of yourself reporting them to your buddies back in Luperón. When they get there it may go counter-counter. I've had apparent lifts of up to six knots here sustained for as much as 15 minutes. Curse or praise your private luck, but in no case go public with your discovery of the *Lost Current*. Like the Mona, the bottom conditions coupled with the **Equatorial Current** cause hydro-thermodynamic chaos, the prediction of which makes a fool's game. Refer also to the section on *Playing the Island Lees: Cape Effects*.

The Cabo Francés Viejo light lies about 1.5 miles south of the waypoint shown on my coastal sketch. As with many marks in the Caribbean, it may not work.

BAHÍA ESCOCESA

Time your passage around **Cabo Francés Viejo** to arrive well into the **Bahía Escocesa** before 8 a.m. It may prove near impossible to make the Cape later in the day, and you need lots of sea room off **Nagua** to begin an inshore tack in the rising tradewind. One friend who failed to do so lost a beautiful Baltic Trader there.

One or two tacks south-southeast across Bahía Escocesa should carry you to the high offshore rocks east of Nagua and west of **Escondido**, at **Las Terrenas**, a mostly French eco-resort area which you should visit while ashore. From this point east you can hug the

shore closely and tack up to Escondido within a band of smooth sea. Motorsailers or trawlers leaving Rio San Juan at midnight can set anchors in Escondido by mid-morning, if not before.

Difficult to spot from sea the first time, you will recognize the mouth of the Escondido fjord by the two rocks lying off the northwest arm of the bay.

Someone interestingly named the bay "The Scots Woman" while they named the two headlands surrounding her "The Old Frenchman" and "The Cuckold". Furthermore, a woman supposedly haunts the bay. On different occasions I've talked with sober and mature merchant seamen who told me they have heard the crying of a woman while crossing the bay at night. During my first trip across the bay we logged a peculiar melancholy that night, attributed at the time to the sorrow over leaving the Caribbean islands behind us. Only years later did I learn of the supposed haunting.

ESCONDIDO

Surveys by the USS Eagle in 1905-1906 named the port at El Valle **Escondido** (HO2648). DMA25723 shows it as **Puerto El Valle** and shows little Puerto Escondido about where it lies several miles east, but much scaled up. I choose to follow tradition and call the large anchorage at El Valle **Puerto Escondido**. I don't recommend you look for the other. You shall not find it easily, nor shall you easily fit in.

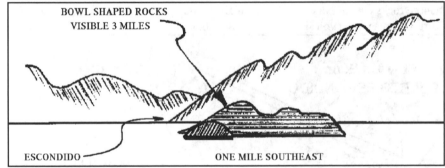

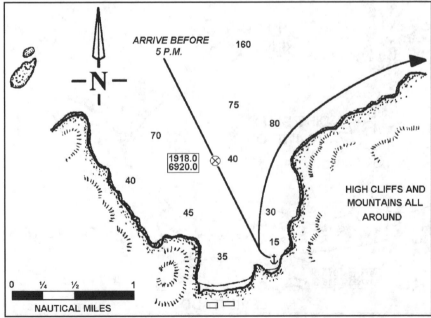

This deep Norwejian-like fjord makes a peaceful anchorage in light easterlies. Do not enter Escondido with northly swells running. Instead, sail around **Cabo Samaná** about 2 miles off shore (a half mile off in daylight) and enter **Samaná Bay**, heaving-to inside the bay a mile south of the **Balandra Head** light. Put a lantern out and go to sleep.

In **Escondido** the local Coast Guard shall visit in a dugout canoe rowed by fishermen he must hire but can't pay. They shall ask for handouts because that's the way they get paid. Welcome aboard only officials with identification, not the fishermen. Treat all with dignity and friendliness, but the fishermen have no business aboard your yacht. If you've got your **SG&T** when they come, ask them to join you, perhaps by a small bottle of rum which they can share at home, since you won't have a mood for staying guests after your journey. Of course you purchased a case of small rum bottles while in **Luperón** just for this purpose, didn't you? While you finish your SG&T the locals may give an exhibition of community net fishing either from the beach or from their canoes.

Next morning leave **Escondido** between midnight and 4 am, following the towering east wall 200 yards off. If you haven't a moon, you can even use starlight. Motor tight against the cliffs in the flat calm, while scrambling eggs in the galley, up to **Cabo Cabrón**, cutting its cliffs as close as a boat length if you dare. One German reader's English caused him to interpret this literally. Coming out onto the dark deck, his wife screamed at the weight of looming rock and nearly frightened him overboard. Not to worry. I wouldn't have used the allusion had I not actually tried it myself beforehand.

Be sure to round **Cabo Samaná** well off, a half mile minimum, and sail south by 9 a.m., before trades make it difficult to round the capes, and set sail. I always sail into **Samaná** harbor shortly after daybreak in order to anchor unplagued by the wind, and before the dock has a pestilence of teeming idlers to hoot for your attention.

Take an early **SG&T** that afternoon, and toast all the slicker clad yachties huffing and puffing into Samaná from their offshore trials.

Sit in a Samaná bar and listen to their tales of the ultimate wave. One year I met 5 crews exactly in this way. We had all left **Puerto Plata** together. They motorsailed while I mostly sailed. The only single-hander in their fleet, I had a comfortable, upright and dry trip. Their decks, strewn with drying slickers and cushions, showed the kind of passage they had. Hard to believe? Every season a fleet of hardnose cruisers carries on too far offshore instead of hugging the coast with the **night lee**.

TIDAK APA

The trawlerized Schucker 440 motorsailer *TIDAK APA*

(Malayu for "it doesn't matter anymore....")

SAMANÁ

The remoteness of **Samaná** [sah-mah-NAH], the Appalachia of the Dominican Republic, both curses and charms it. The city stands out as a cultural oddity in a country dominated by the Spanish. American former slaves settled the area in the 19th century. More ex-slaves joined them from Philadelphia at the turn of the century.

The dictator **Trujillo** built a road into Samaná in 1949. He then burned down the town to force the population to heel, making them speak Spanish. With that background it should not surprise you that a visit to **Samaná** won't give you an in-depth look at the Dominican Republic, its people, nor its culture. It enjoys a certain uniqueness. For instance, you shall find many remnants of African cultural practices in Samaná as in Haiti.

Many natural splendors of karst geology surround Samaná. In the caves to the east the **Taino**s made their Masada-like last stand against the *conquistadores*. Many tourists come here to watch humpback whales December through March. Check out **Las Terrenas** and **El Portillo** on the north side of the peninsula for a handful of hotels in idyllic palm-fringed sandy beach settings, and for more "eco", **Las Galeras** at the tip of Cabo Samaná.

SECURITY

In the last years Samaná has become notorious for dinghy and motor theft, even occasional boardings by someone looking for a motor. The **Mona Passage** compares to Samaná as the Rio Grande does to Tijuana: a focal point for smuggling to the U.S. A market exists for big outboards. A secondary market exists for little outboards on which a clever man could parlay himself to a big outboard (in horsepower: 2+2=5, 5+5=10 and 10+10=25). Many Americans assume the *yola* traffic between here and Puerto Rico takes innocent and hungry Dominican refugees desperate to flee their poor country. Universally proud of their country, and having a better diet than Puerto Ricans, Dominicans don't fit that picture. The desperation on the *yolas* comes from the desperados aboard them. Young Dominican adventurers and law-dodgers may pay $500 to cross the Mona in an open boat. Chinese may pay $3000, Cubans $2000. Police interrogators from former Latin American dictatorships of either the left or right might pay $25,000! Once in Puerto Rico, American soil, constitutional guarantees prevent easy discovery of the illegals. They can establish a new life as Americans free to travel from Puerto Rico to Samoa. A terminus for smuggling illegals, you should not leave the boat in Samaná and tour the island. Use **Luperón**, located centrally on the island, secure and nearer to airports and important cities for shopping. Therefore, *as you would certainly lock your car in Tijuana, lock your dinghy in Samaná.* Put the motor aboard if you can't secure it well. See *Crew Stuff: Dinghy Security.*

COMMUNICATIONS

Mail and telephone work here, but add a few days or even a week to Puerto Plata mail times. Nonetheless, the service works surprisingly well with friendly personnel. For comfortable transportation within Samaná flag down a *motoconcho*. In Samaná they use a motorized rickshaw carrying 6 passengers, with a canvas roof to keep you dry.

WHAT TO SEE

Samaná has some of the best scenery in the DR. You can tour waterfall sites almost as good as the one near Luperón. Take swimsuits to each. Try the cascades east of the town, with water chutes which drop to successive baths from a lovely tree shaded river which runs along the ridge above. Take a *motoconcho* to the falls 8 kilometers west of town where a 150 foot wide falls slides into a treed gorge down a 100 foot high cliff warmed by the sun. You can bathe in the cool lagoon below and shower under the hot waterfall. Before taking the path up to the falls, buy your lunch of cheese, salami, bread and ice cold Presidente beer from the *colmado* [coal-MAH-doh] on the highway.

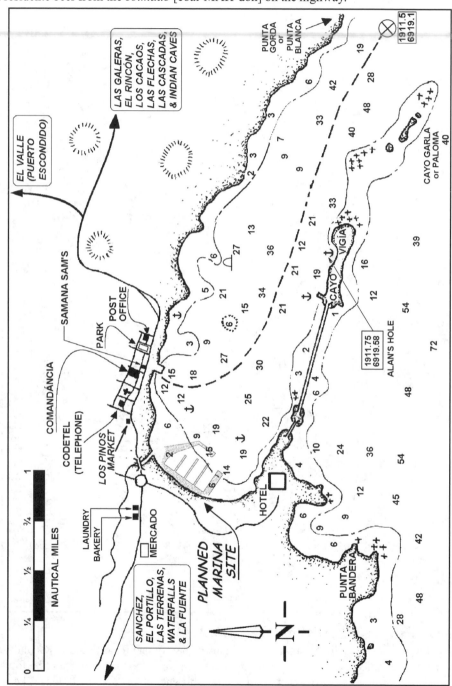

Harbor of Santa Bárbara de Samaná

LOS HAITISES

You can also sail to the grottos across the bay in the **Bahía de San Lorenzo** at **Los Haitises**. Samaná, the closest you can come to Bora Bora while still in the Caribbean, seems painfully remote, and likely to remain so despite all claims to the contrary. This spectacular national park proves the point. Don't miss it!

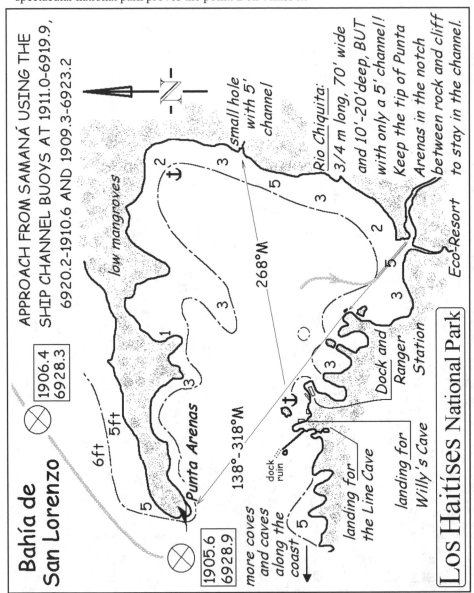

BOATS WESTBOUND FROM SAMANÁ

Downwind sailing from **Samaná**, anchor at any harbor on the north shore. **Escondido** can get untenable in swell from the north, a common winter phenomenon, but I've found the fishing boat harbor at **Rio San Juan** comfortable enough in those conditions. Choose a window from **Samaná** that permits anchoring at each spot, and time your landfall at

Luperón for 07:30. Rounding **Cabo Cabrón**, if you don't stop at **Escondido**, *don't* set a course directly for **Cabo Francés Viejo**. Instead, follow the coast into **Bahía Escocesa**, toward **Las Terrenas** (see chartlet *Luperón to Samaná*) for a faster downwind sail. Follow the 10 fathom line in smoother water protected by the point. Near the rocks of Las Terrenas the wind angle permits a broad reach up to **Cabo Francés Viejo**. Sailboats shall save at least an hour on the passage this way, sometimes much more.

BOATS EASTBOUND FROM SAMANÁ

Leave the way you came in. The peninsula funnels wind into the harbor on that route, causing a heavy chop for your exit. You leave at night after it lays down. You can **stage** to Cayo Leventado. See *Crossing the Mona Passage* for details on picking windows from here, and my recommendations for here in *Stage Your Departure, Don't Fear the Dark*.

By following the **National Weather Service**'s *Eastern Caribbean Report* you can predict when the **trades** shall lighten up and favor your tack. While you wait for weather in **Samaná** you may receive the Puerto Rico VHF Wx channels. *Use only the data for the subzone out to 68°!* You shall cross open ocean, not coast the west coast of Puerto Rico.

Do not rely on data received by radio from friends in Puerto Rico, less able to gauge the weather from their lee harbors than you can in Samaná. And you can't gauge it well from Samaná which sits in the bottom of a wind funnel. You shall hear reports of strong winds in **Ponce**, calms in **Boquerón** — even westerly winds, actually common enough as a southeast Force 5-6 wraps around **Cabo Rojo** and backwinds Boquerón bay. These coastal effects in Puerto Rico don't affect you. Don't listen to them. Construct a decision table like the one below and update it after listening to the **Tropical Prediction Center's Offshore Report**s for the *Eastern Caribbean* and the *Southwest North Atlantic* on **NMN**, or with **NAVTEX**, each morning. Unless you spend some time in **Samaná**, you must start collecting this data already in **Luperón**, even **Caicos** for those boats moving fast through the islands. You can't establish a trend without sufficient collection of data.

DAY	WIND DIRECTION	WIND SPEED IN KNOTS	SEA CONDITION IN FEET	QUALITATIVE CHANGE IN OFFSHORE RPT.	GO/ NOGO
1	E	10 to 15	4 to 6		
2	E	10 to 15	<5	better	go
3	SE to E	10 to 15	4 to 6	worse	nogo
4	SE to E	15 to 20	4 to 7	worse	nogo
5	E to SE	15 to 25	5 to 7	worse	nogo
6	E to SE	20	5 to 8	same	nogo
7	E to SE	15 to 20	4 to 7	better	nogo
8	E to SE	15	4 to 6	better	go
9	E	10 to 15	4 to 5	better	**gone**

Example of a Go-Nogo Decision Table

CROSSING THE MONA PASSAGE

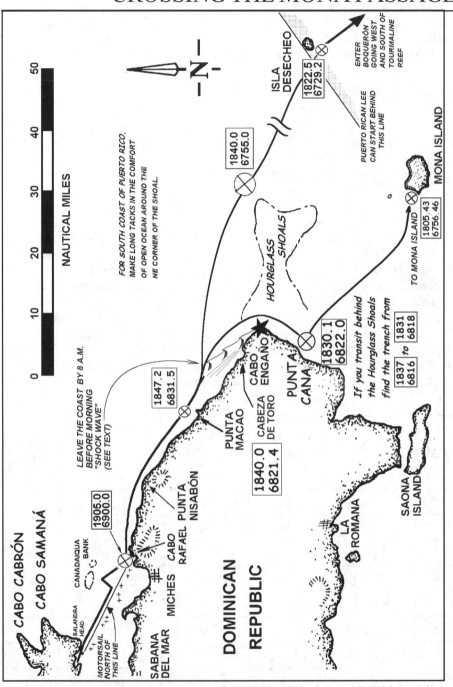

The **Mona Passage**'s reputation comes from stories dished out with relish by delivery skippers motoring dock to dock with someone else's property, or first time cruisers who crash a straight rhumb line in easterlies right through the shoals, and by still others who collect their guidance over the bar (or on the SSB Breakfast Show) from anyone who made the trip enough times to think they can hand out advice — usually only once or twice, and usually done the hard way. I have 4-5 dozens of Mona crossings, all in comfort and safety, using the following methods.

Review the description of this passage in *Island Stratagies: Don't Fear the Dark*.

I can't call the strategies for hugging the coast in the **night lee** of a mountainous shore, nor of making little harbor hops at dawn on the shores of an alluvial plain, *my* strategies. As the *only* methods that work *all the time* against **prevailing conditions**, they belong to Mother Nature. But to *sail* the Mona you can choose a strategy which I *do* call mine. Non-motorsailers will find it near necessary, but any sailboat can use it with multiple benefits.

The **Mona Passage** has unpredictable currents everywhere and rough shoals east of **Cabo Engaño** and **Balandra Head**. Thunderstorms, often severe, get set adrift from Puerto Rico's **coastal front** by the cooling of the night. The deep shoals fool newcomers to this area. One doesn't expect rough water. The newcomer doesn't expect ranks and files of thunderstorms after receiving a fine weather forecast. Sailboats can avoid both the shoal areas and the storm cells by the strategy below which calls for coasting, then sailing.

PICKING WINDOWS

The ever cyclic **tradewinds** switch back and forth like a cat's tail. Record them until you get a handle on each cycle, always remembering to weight average the **Offshore Reports** for both the eastern Caribbean and the southwest North Atlantic. Then take the first down-tick in the cycle that has sensible wind (see *Harbor Tells*).

Motorsailers and trawlers make the run in less than 24 hours in calm conditions. Accept the gift and do it. But, to find a window *under prevailing conditions*, I strongly recommend using the **night lee** on both sides of the channel. Refer now to the Mona crossing illustrations at the end of the chapter *Playing the Island Lees: Integrating Effects*.

You'll find the Mona itself a great sail in a northeasterly if you wait long enough for it. *But the actual Mona makes up only half of a 150 mile package.* Unless a calm comes along, I advise sailboats take a window of Force 3-4 easterly, usually ESE, with no unusual swell, taking 2 nights and a day to cross: two nights of lee sailing and one day of smooth, open ocean sailing. Trawlers can take the same window with appropriate stops. Again, see the illustrations in *Playing the Island Lees: Integrating Effects.*

Should you leave **Samaná** in the morning, trying to reach Puerto Rico in one day, you shall have no margin for error or problems enroute, and you probably shall have the stuffing kicked out of you during the daytime on both sides of the passage. Deservingly.

SHOALS: Many cruisers don't recognize the shoals on the charts because they run several hundred feet deep and more, and that does not, in their experience, mean shoal. However, the water these shoals are trying to contain comes from the **Equatorial Current**. That means a lot of water and a lot of energy for the shoals to dissipate, and you don't want to take part in it. Stay clear of any area much more shallow than another if it lies west of sharp bottom gradients, and they abound! Recall the **Puerto Rican Trench**, second deepest hole in the oceans, lies not far away. The first shoal, the **Canandaiqua Bank**, lies south and east of the **Samaná** peninsula. The second area I call what my long gone friend, Tony Joos, named the **Hourglass Shoal**, because it has the shape of an hourglass lying on its side. It lies east of **Cabo Engaño,** directly on the motoring rhumb line from Samaná to **Boquerón,** a sure hit for most delivery crews, one of which got dismasted twice there. The *thornless* transit of the Mona Passage counts for comfort and safety on tacking away from or passing behind these areas. Behind **Hourglass Shoal**, you'll find dead calm in the early morning under prevailing conditions. And you get to visit Mona Island!

STORMS: A line of thunderstorms drifting west-northwest gets released from Puerto Rico's heat by the setting of the sun. Sometimes they dissipate to squalls or showers or nothing at all within 30 miles of the coast. Sometimes they grow more wicked and charge like bulls. The fiercest storm cells I've seen in my life came from their ranks. And I include the North Sea and the Med. If you have satellite pictures or long range radar, you may find alleys between them, if any exist. Mom and Pop and me make a *veronica*-like tacking maneuver around the charging bulls as shown below. Power boats and strong motorsailers can outflank them to the south.

These views of Mona storms belong to a true story told in two halves: **first in** *Weather Windows: Flying Windows,* **and below under** *Picking Windows: Timing.*

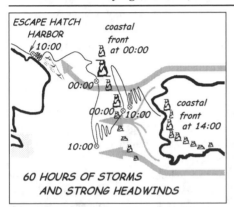

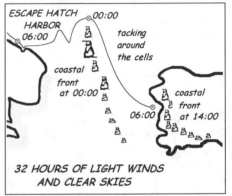

The daytime Puerto Rican coastal front moves into the Mona and frustrates boats who haven't got their timing down. Trawler and motorsailer routes (described at right) avoid this trap with timing.

The Puerto Rican coastal front drifts south of you when you use the sailing route described below. Delivery skippers in a hurry famously sail the obstacle course on the left, damaging their charges.

CURRENTS: United States Navy Lieutenant Matthew Fontaine Maury, the hydrographer who initiated the idea of sea lanes in his *Sailing Directions* in 1859, created a repository of data on world currents and winds which today you see in the American Pilot Charts and the British Routing Charts. This data, confirmed and refined for a century and a half, doesn't preclude Captain John Courageous of the *S/V Chicken Little* from differencing his GPS from his speed log and announcing to the world the discovery of a new current. One year a whole fleet out of Georgetown put me on the spot. They radioed me with insistent requests that I sponsor a notification to the U.S. Navy and NOAA that the **Equatorial Current** had reversed itself and flowed *east*. I put it all down to giddiness of overnighters approaching Hispaniola for the first time. They urged I act, feeling they had uncovered an incipient Atlantic *El Niño*, and that the world must have warning. To no avail I listed the extensive variety of phenomena at play: logs, GPS, microcode algorithms, standing hull waves playing on the impeller, tide, upwellings, eddies, hydraulic curlicues and hallucination. To end the embarrassment I asked they mail me data logs from each ship with exact times and instrument readings. I committed to forwarding the data to a disinterested Navy (ornithologists brought the original *El Niño* to their attention). Of course I heard no more.

My point? For course planning: ***If it ain't on the Pilot Charts, it don't exist!*** Plan no currents in the Mona, *because* you can't predict them. They'll average themselves out.

LANDFALL: If you have more favorable conditions than you had expected, or if you get edgy and motor hell-for-leather, you may make landfall in the dark. If you planned on *sailing* the Mona, motor less and sail more to ensure a morning arrival. **Mayagüez**, the official port of entry, has a well marked, well lighted entrance with an open roadstead.

MOTOR: Small trawlers or motor sailers, unless they find a calm, should take the Mona Island route. Sailboats who want to motor the Mona may have to wait a month of Sundays to get a calm sufficiently long for them. If you can motorsail in easy conditions, do it, but in **prevailing conditions**, the way across for Mom and Pop comes within a window of 36 to 48 hours of easterly under 15 knots. It mostly comes in summer and mostly from southeast — remember? *Veering* winds get lighter? In the winter, a mild, or stalled front or trough, or a gale system passing to the north, might provide the same window, even occasional light northeasterlies!

TIMING: When the guy a day ahead of you radios back about a strong northerly current he just named *Chicken Little Gullywash*, don't alter your plan for crossing the Mona. I see it done every year and every year I see people lose their timing crossing the Mona. They either get off the coast too late in the morning and get pinned by the trades, or they get run down by the drifting storm cells, or, with no GPS, they just get lost. The timing of sailing tacks, even of a flat out motor passage, must take into account:

(1) the **night lee**s on both sides of the passage,

(2) the drifting **coastal front** from Puerto Rico (see illustration), and

(3) the vigor of even light Atlantic trades undiminished by wind shadow or **night lee**.

Here you have an example of what can happen. The first half of this story appears in the chapter on *Weather Windows*. The pair of yachts that followed me out of **Samaná** to shoot a flying window against my urging spent *60 hours* getting hammered in the Mona while I drifted dreamily in the Puerto Rican night lee at the end of a 32 hour easy sail. Why?

I heard them on the VHF. They woke me up, discussing the lovely sail they had tacking down the nighttime DR coast. They didn't play the night lee, they played *in* the night lee. Meanwhile, I had a serious look at my progress. To control passage timing, and to make my deadline for a decision at Punta Macao, I needed to step it up a bit. First I took shallower tacks by running the engine at a little over idle. When I decided I had a *Go*, I furled the jib and escalated to a motorsail to ensure I made **Cabo Engaño** at dawn.

You must reach the end of land and tack off the coast by daylight because the cape effect (see *Cape Effect*) on **Cabo Engaño** can murder you. It didn't look like they'd make it. I called them and told them this. They said they understood, yet they still didn't budget their time. They got nowhere near **Punta Macao** by daybreak, when according to their VHF chatter, every time they tacked out, a wedge of swift and raging water rounded the cape to assault them, and they turned back into "smoother water". If you liken tacking in a sailboat to making *zigzag stitches* on the ocean, these guys did a narrowing *button hole stitch* inside the **Cape Effect**, getting nowhere fast. I lost them on the VHF because I was *basting a hem stitch* toward the northeast in 12-14 knots of wind just forward of the beam in 4 foot long seas. Their saga continued that night when **storm cells** from the collapsed Puerto Rican **coastal front** hit them. That kept them busy and pushed them back a fair bit. I saw the tops of the storms at sunset off my quarter, where my northeast tack had flanked them. Exhaustion began to worsen their case. Next they got served the roar of the trades around Rincón during the daytime. Then came ... Never mind. See the sketch above.

Get off the coast before the trades begin, and don't go to windward in 15 or over!

SAILING THE MONA PASSAGE

The following discussion requires the chartlets in *Playing the Island Lees: Integrating Effects*. Use nighttime lees on both sides of the passage. This took my ketch 32 to 40 hours depending on her draw of wind and wave. Count on leaving in less than 15 knots easterly and do not go over the windward part of the **Hourglass Shoal**. In 10 to 15 knots wind, follow the method below and you can do the **Mona Passage** in as little as 2 tacks with little or no roar of the motor *and* comfortable conditions.

1. Leave Samaná on a day when the gradient winds (weighted average of the Eastern Caribbean and the Southwest North Atlantic **Offshore Reports**) blow easterly under 15 knots, no unusual swell running. Leave **Samaná** in the evening to take best advantage of whatever **night lee** the island extends eastward. Have your rode cleaned and on short scope and the boat squared away for sea. Up anchor about dusk with enough good light left to clear **Cayo Leventado**. You may get heavy chop here in the late afternoon which you can avoid by **staging** yourself to the anchorage west of Leventado and leaving later. Halfway between Cayo Leventado and the mainland take up a 120° Magnetic course for 19°05'N, 69°00'W (see chartlet *Crossing the Mona Passage*).

2. Leave the land behind and long tack southeast and short tack northeast to **Cabo Rafael**, well east of the shoals off **Miches** on the south shore of Bahía Samaná in the **Bahía de la Finca**. Miches at night, and **Sabana de la Mar** across the bay from Samaná, have easily confused looms. To avoid the reefs off Miches make the southern limit of tack lie on a line bearing 120°Magnetic from Cayo Leventado to a point 19°05'N, 69°00'W. In a head wind you may have to take a short tack or two off the coast to stay clear.

3. Close with Cabo Rafael 2 miles off, then sail or motorsail the coast on the 15 fathom line (often a mile or less off) to **Punta Macao**. With luck your first offshore tack can come near **Cabo Engaño** itself as the lee you have used all night begins to waiver. Rather than hurry on, pause at Punta Macao should your conditions permit.

4. Plan to tack off the coast before 8 a.m. The acceleration of wind around Cabo Engaño shall form a "shock wave" of heavy conditions offshore of you if you remain inshore too long in daylight. You may get hemmed in by it.

5. Carry on northeast until you can lay a southeast tack to a safety waypoint, 18°40'N and 67°55'W, well off the northeast corner of the **Hourglass Shoals**. That should give you smooth sailing in open ocean. Storm cells from the decay of the Puerto Rican **coastal front** should sweep westward well to your south.

6. Carry your last southerly tack under starry skies past a line from the northwest corner of Puerto Rico through **Isla Desecheo**. Conditions moderate southeast of that line and you can lay **Mayagüez** or **Boquerón** for morning arrival by using the Puerto Rican **night lee**. You can pass Isla Desecheo on either side, but if you head for Boquerón instead of Mayagüez, be sure to pass west of **Tourmaline Reef**. From **Desecheo** onward you usually motor or motorsail in calms with Puerto Rico lit up like a city seen from an airplane at night.

Buoys and lights in Puerto Rico usually work, and they follow U.S. standard.

TRAWLERING OR MOTORSAILING THE MONA PASSAGE

The following discussion requires the chartlets in *Playing the Island Lees: Integrating Effects.* A thornless option takes 3 legs in night lees when forecast gradient wind blows east to southeast less than 15 knots, no northerly swell. This makes a good run for small trawlers. You can also use this option to sail up to the west coast of Puerto Rico. A careful watch on satellite pictures before and after sundown helps. If any dangerous storm cells drift off Puerto Rico, the sun over the horizon shall light up their high tops on the visible light satpics.

1. Follow points 1, 2 and 3 described in the last section, hugging the coast from Cabo Rafael to arrive at any of **Punta Macao**, **Cabeza de Toro** or even **Punta Cana** so as to have yourself safely moored by 08:30 at the latest.

2. If at Punta Macao leave at dawn or before for the 25 miles to Punta Cana in order to arrive there by 08:30, or leave sometime after midnight to do the 55 miles to **Mona Island.** Proceed around **Cabo Engaño**, then pass west of the **Hourglass Shoal** while the **night lee** still holds sway. (Use the trench shown on the chartlet.)

    If bound for **Isla Mona**, you must reach the lee of that island before the trades pipe up. If at Punta Cana, leave there at early dawn to make the 30 miles needed to fetch Mona Island's lee before the trades scatter the night lee of Hispaniola.

3. Leave Mona Island late evening, timed to outflank any storm cells drifting west from Puerto Rico and to arrive at your south coast destination before 08:30. You can choose to arrive at Boquerón, Cabo Rojo, Parguera, Guánica or Ponce).

WESTWARD BOUND FROM PUERTO RICO

Don't succumb to the temptation to skip the Dominican Republic thinking to sail a direct long passage to the Bahamas. First of all, one should always *wear* (tacking downwind, sail or power) while going directly downwind in trade seas, and the only course possible carries your boat past **Cabo Samaná** on the northeast point of the DR. Secondly, one has not *done* the Caribbean without visiting Americas' cultural cradle, that great, high island of Hispaniola. Try the following easy steps:

Boquerón - Mona Island - Punta Cana - Punta Macao - Samaná or **Escondido**.

Of course, time your departures for good landfalls. If bound directly for Samaná or the north coast, stay behind the line from the northwest corner of Puerto Rico and **Isla Desecheo** as long as you can, and pass well outside the **Hourglass Shoal**.

Americans on American vessels do not need to clear out from Puerto Rico.

EASTERN HARBORS OF THE DR

All these harbors have a Coast Guard station, and officials will visit to look at your *despacho*. Both Cabeza de Toro and Punta Macao get used by the agencies of the Dominican Republic and the United States in the so-called war on drugs, as well as in the battle against illegal migration in the Mona Passage. Have respect for the official point of view, and you shall get respect in return for your right to seek shelter. If I find my window has a possibility of closing early, I use **Punta Macao** or **Cabeza de Toro** as long as I've got *settled easterlies with no northerly swell*. From either harbor I can make a predawn or daybreak dash down the coast and west of the Hourglass Shoal to **Punta Cana**, arriving before Hispaniola loses its night lee — or even continue on to Isla Mona.

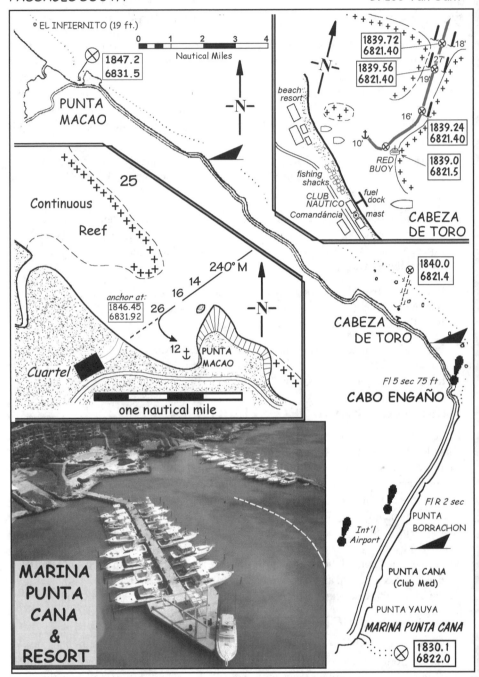

PUNTA MACAO

Enter **Punta Macao** with a rock awash close on your port hand. Anchor in 12 feet of deep sand less than 100 yards from the eastern cliffs. You shall not have seen a prettier cove than this little basin since the Bahamas. You may easily leave Punta Macao in the dark, since even starlight will illuminate that "rock awash" that you came in on. The boys at the Coast Guard station might pay you a call.

CABEZA DE TORO

Cabeza de Toro has a fuel dock. Nearby **Bávaro Beach** has many large resorts as does this whole coast with a more than 25 nm stretch of white sand beaches lined with coconut palms. Isolated and sparsely populated, the area has an international airport, golf, beaching, casinos, and home sites for wealthy Dominicans and foreign expatriates.

**The trench to leeward of Hourglass Shoal runs 1837N-6816W to 1831N-6818W.
See *Playing the Island Lees: Trench Effect.***

PUNTA CANA

Across the **Mona Passage** from Mona Island, on the eastern tip of the DR, the **Punta Cana** resort complexes include golf, villa projects, hotels, a Club Med and a modern marina. The full service marina includes a restaurant, fuel and, unless they have a billfish tournament going on which takes participants from the whole Caribbean basin, it shall have many slips open for you. Slips include cable TV, telephone, electricity and water for about one fourth of a beer per foot per day for transients (*see Beeronomy*). Follow the friendly advice of the dockmaster. He really knows where you'll lie most tranquilly.

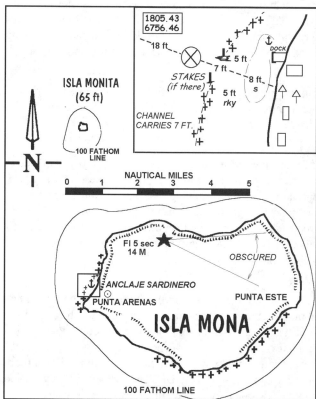

MONA ISLAND

Mona Island, a Puerto Rican national park and wildlife refuge with resident rangers, has a beautiful reef anchorage used by Puerto Rican fishermen and vacationers. It also serves as a base for the oceanology branch of the University of Puerto Rico located at La Parguera.

Enter in daylight on a range of two triangular day boards which stay lit all night. The ranged channel carries 7 feet to a sand anchorage with 8 feet along the beach. Either side of the channel has spots of only five feet on rocky ground. Fly a Q flag.

I haven't found a decent shallow anchorage outside **Sardinero**. With *Jalan Jalan*'s 6 and a half foot draft I left the anchorage in good tide and good light, and if necessary, hove to in the shadow of the island until departure time. Lesser drafts will have no problem here. Plan your departure time to *avoid evening storms* and to *control your time of landfall*. You leave at night by going slow and using the range behind you.

PUERTO RICO

Columbus discovered the main island on his second voyage to the New World in 1493. He named the island, called Borinquen by the **Tainos**, San Juan Bautista to honor Prince Juan, the son of Ferdinand and Isabela. Ponce de León, who explored the southeast United States, founded Puerto Rico's first settlement and became its first governor. The European powers alternately ignored or disputed many of the smaller islands during the four centuries in which Spain colonized the main island of Puerto Rico. Spain ceded all the islands to the United States in the 1898 Treaty of Paris. The Commonwealth of Puerto Rico comes under the United States' territories acts. The most affluent population in Latin America, Puerto Ricans have U.S. citizenship and about half can speak English. More than half the population receives financial assistance from the U.S. Government. A significant amount of the illegal drugs entering the U.S. do so through Puerto Rico. For that reason you may expect inspections by the U.S. Coast Guard and boardings by local marine police.

REGULATIONS

BOAT AND DINGHY REGISTRATION

Vessels remaining in Puerto Rican waters more than 60 days must register in Puerto Rico. Fees run similar to Florida, e.g., a couple of hundred dollars for a 35 foot boat, plus separate registration for a dinghy with motor. However, like the Florida "gotcha" of charging sales tax upon registering a boat, PR wants 6.6% of the boat's value in import taxes.

FIREARMS

Puerto Rico requires Puerto Rican registration for all firearms within their territorial limits, even at sea. They further require any arm aboard to have a *carry license assigned to a Puerto Rican resident aboard the vessel with the firearm.*

TOURING BY RENTAL CAR

Like in North America, one must have access to a car in Puerto Rico. If you decide to rent a car to tour the country, get a road atlas and follow the purple lines, the *Ruta Panoramica*, through the mountains and small towns, staying at designated **paradors**, usually historic or otherwise noteworthy inns. A good rule to use while driving: stop at every *lechón* (roasting pig) at the roadside, buy a beer and rip off a piece of the *lechón*. It's delicious, you'll meet many good Puerto Ricans, and in this manner you'll only make about 20 miles a day on weekends and holidays.

TOURING BY *PÚBLICO*

You can still backpack in Puerto Rico like you can in the Dominican Republic. They don't have, however, the elaborate public transportation system found in the DR. Like North America, nearly everyone has access to a car, and for those that don't, Puerto Rico still has a *público* system, though it wanes as island affluence waxes.

In Puerto Rico the *públicos* use large, honky old American cars with not much more interior space than the little Japanese ones used in the DR. The *públicos* in Puerto Rico cost much more than they do in the DR, but they only cram in 6 passengers instead of 7.

Públicos hang around the town square, or at terminal facilities in cities, until enough passengers show up to fill the car. If you wish to depart earlier than the driver wants to, or you wish to travel in spacious comfort, you may buy any unfilled seats. For best results, buy the 2 seats next to the driver. While *públicos* always gather and start from the same place, they deliver passengers to wherever, within reason, they wish at the destination.

FIESTAS PATRONALES
Whoever schedules the *Fiestas* sequences them to permit the traveling entertainers, rides and food concessions to appear at every one. Yet each *Fiesta* has its own atmosphere as the town turns on for a full week. The *Fiestas* in the smaller towns will bring back the July Fourths of 50 years ago for older cruisers from Main Street, U.S.A. The larger towns and county seats, such as Fajardo, often have fiestas which ring the central plaza for 3 and 4 blocks deep. Each port in Puerto Rico lies either at or within a *público* ride from at least three *Fiestas*. Some world class entertainment may come to these festivals. You may find yourself face to face with José Feliciano or Ricky Martin.

USEFUL TELEPHONE NUMBERS IN THE CRUISING AREA

US Coast Guard	Search & Rescue San Juan	722-2943
NOAA Weather Service	San Juan Airport	253-4588
Customs	*See chapter on Customs and Clearances*	742-3531
Charters	Sun Sail, Puerto del Rey	860-6100
	Club Nautico Powerboats, Pto. del Rey	860-2400
Engine/Generator Repair	Marine Energy Svc., Puerto del Rey	863-6965
	Re-Power Marine Svc., Fajardo	863-9786
Services & Repairs	Captain Ron, Puerto del Rey	381-9146
	El Español, Puerto del Rey	863-6965
	Island Marine, Isleta	382-3051
Marinas and Haulouts	Villa Pesquera, Puerto Real	851-5690
	Ponce Yacht Club	842-9003
	Palmas del Mar	850-2065
	Puerto del Rey	860-1000
	Isleta Marina	384-9032
	Villa Marina	863-5131
	Varadero de Fajardo (Las Croabas)	863-4193
Chandlers	Larry's Playa Marine, Salinas	824-5337
	Basic Marine, Puerto del Rey	860-5151
	El Pescador, Villa Marina	863-0350
	Skipper Shop, Villa Marina	863-2455
Chain, Anchors, etc.	Astro Industrial Supply (wholesale)	721-4021
Sailmakers / Canvas	Atlantic Canvas & Sails, Pto. del Rey	860-1433
	Isleta Canvas, Isleta Marina	376-9324
	Tradewinds Sail & Canvas, Salinas	824-1611
	Fajardo Canvas & Sails, Villa Marina	863-3761
Inflatables	Caribbean Inflatables	792-6002

SAILING DIRECTIONS, WEST COAST

Coming from the west one can choose to approach Mayagüez from either side of **Desecheo** (dess-aye-CHAYE-oh, the discarded one), a barren rock island 10 miles west of **Punta Higüero**. A completely rockbound anchorage on the south coast has room for a single boat to moor. North of Punta Higüero, in the bight of Aguadilla, you can use an open roadstead anchorage subject to a good deal of surge, or a roadstead anchorage south of the point at **Rincón**. **Puerto Real** and **Boquerón** constitute the only good harbors on this coast for cruising sailboats, unless a plan for a marina at **Aguadilla** goes through.

MAYAGÜEZ

The harbor at **Mayagüez** gets used by large ships. The pier may cause damage to your yacht, and they charge for laying alongside. Anchor between red buoys numbers 8 and 10 on the spoil bank in poor holding, but the dredged deep areas have even worse holding.

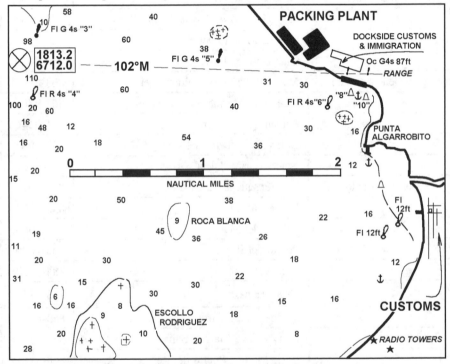

You'll find Sears, K-Mart, Western Auto, WalMart, Burger King, Kentucky Fried Chicken and Pizza Hut two *público* rides away at **Mayagüez**. However, Ponce has more and better malls.Leave for **Boquerón** or **Puerto Real** before the wind comes up. It can get gustily onshore in this wide open bay. Arrive before 8 a.m. to do Customs when they open in order to get under way and out of there by 10 a.m.

MAYAGÜEZ TO BOQUERÓN

Leave Mayagüez by 10:00 a.m. before the wind is up. This open harbor gets williwaws from the hills, especially when the coastal front builds up with large thunderheads in summer afternoons. The route to either **Boquerón** or **Puerto Real** goes inside **Tourmaline Reef** leaving red nun buoys numbers 6 and 4 on the port hand. South of Joyuda you'll pass the *Club Deportiva*, a private marina for shallow draft motorboats.

230

PUERTO REAL

Follow the 2 fathom line paralleling the coast south of the harbor entrance. Enter on an east northeast heading passing about 200 yards off the southern side of the entrance. Crossing the bar just seaward of the harbor mouth, you may not see less than 10 feet, but a 6 foot spot exists at extreme low tide.

A small fishing village with facilities for haulout and repairs, Puerto Real hosts tourists from around the island during the weekends because of its seafood restaurants. Pescaderia Rosas has extended their dock for loading ice and unloading catches. Besides watering and fueling, yachts can berth there for making repairs. Nearby, the **Villa Pesquera** boat yard can haul boats to 5 foot draft with their 35-ton Travelift and fix anything that needs fixing. The haul out facility, though reasonably priced, has little room ashore, and layday rates escalate. Working boats take preference at this fisherman's cooperative.

BOQUERÓN

Approach **Boquerón** [boh-kaye-ROAN] along a line of 155° Magnetic on **Punta Aguila**, by **Cabo Rojo**, turning onto 128° Magnetic on **Punta Guaniquilla**, the northern point of the bay. Round the point one quarter mile off, and enter the bay, keeping a quarter mile off up to the anchorage off the town dock. With the shore close at hand as a guide, this makes a clearer entrance than the one through the reef in the middle of the bay.

If you haven't already done so, check in by phone in the little park (read carefully the chapter on clearing under *Boat Stuff: Customs and Immigrations: Puerto Rico*).

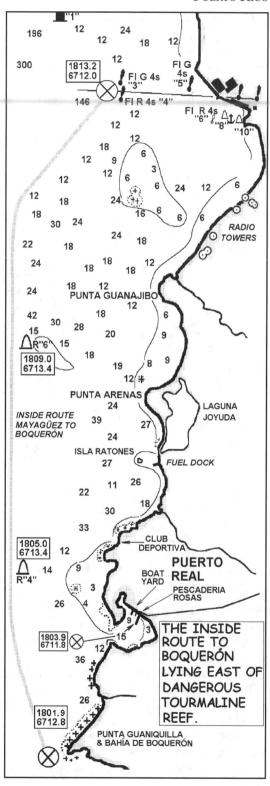

231

If you need transportation to Mayagüez for Customs or shopping, call Raul Santiago on hiscell phone (787-519-3177) or by his VHF handle "Rolling Thunder".

In **Boquerón**, a beach-and-beer getaway for university students and bohemians, weekends can get wild, but the police force usually understands. You'll find bars and restaurants everywhere, and you can buy oysters and clams and tacos on the street. Try the conch salad at the *Shamar* beach bar. Conch is called *carrucho* [car-ROO-choh].

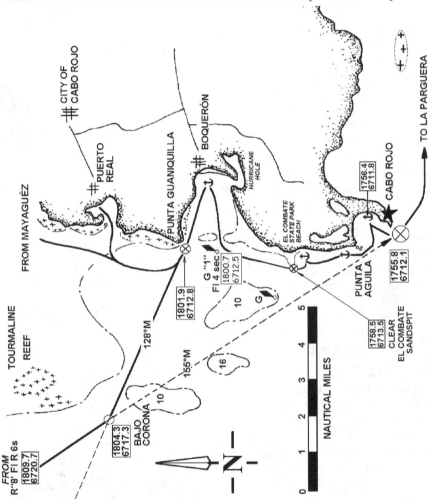

If you never did a sophomore year in college, or you did, and you miss it, you'll love Boquerón. Because you've spent so much time in the boonies in the Bahamas and the straighter society of the Dominican Republic for the last months, you will love this Latin version of Key West or Fire Island.

A hardware store, LusCar, lies on highway 100 outside town.

But don't confuse this convenient and amusing landfall with the refit and reprovision point you need. Use all those 800 numbers to have stuff shipped in, but as far as provisioning, or local parts procurement or mechanical work, wait until **Ponce** if you can. Caselot stores, big malls, mechanics and parts in Ponce lie handier to the anchorage at the **Ponce Yacht Club** than Mayagüez lies to **Boquerón**.

Then too, **Salinas** makes a more tranquil and convenient harbor in which to decommis-

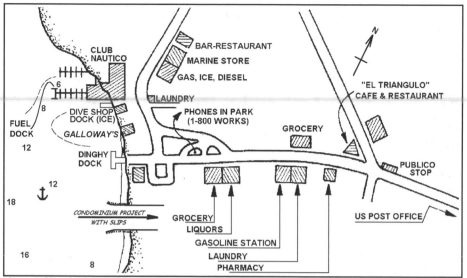

sion stuff and take on fixit projects. And the Marina de Salinas dinghy dock makes a better shipping address for parts.

Wind yourself down in Boquerón, but address any serious projects in Salinas/Ponce.

Boquerón's big but shallow hurricane hole has long narrow channels which boats of any draft can plug up just when you want to use it. Also, on a serious storm threat the Club Nautico may empty its power boats into this hole as well. Compare this hole with the extensive mangrove rivers by Salinas.

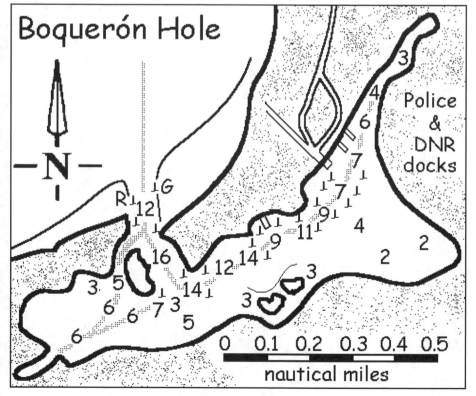

233

SAILING DIRECTIONS, SOUTH COAST

Detailed DMA or HO **charts** of this coast come expensive, if you can get them. The **Imray-Iolaire** charts provide detail here for the small keys around **La Parguera** and **Jobos**. I use the excellent **Waterproof Charts** of Puerto Rico available in most marine stores.

An Australian couple on a circumnavigation told me the south coast of Puerto Rico gave them the roughest sail. After reading this book in Salinas, they understood why, and the thorns got taken out of the leg from Salinas east.

I have made the south coast of PR the easiest sail on the chain by stopping at most harbors. I prefer 2 to 4 hour pleasant motorsails at dawn to dancing the "Caribbean Two Step" one minute. I begin my coasting by staging from the bay of **Boquerón** in the midmorning, after shopping, over to a beach anchorage at **El Combate** or **Cabo Rojo**. Short moonlit and dawn sails, with lots of time to explore the small villages during the day, shall highlight your Caribbean cruise. Some anchorages could capture you, so plan a slow cruise here.

Take advantage of the night lees on this coast as you did in the DR. Unlike the high coast of the DR, the south coast of Puerto Rico has wide coastal plains which further mitigate the minor calming effects of this smaller island.

East, and in winter northeast, winds may come from the shore at night as the central *cordilleras* [core-dee-YAIR-ahs] divide the wind. With the **katabatic** effects added to it, the wind slides downhill and offshore. Real offshore night winds come rarely, however.

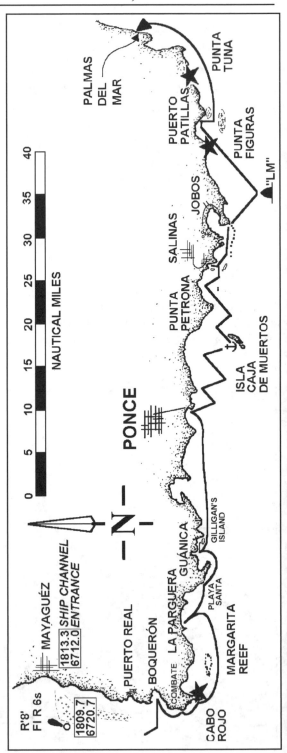

Therefore, don't look for much of a **night lee** from this tiny island. You must stay close inshore to get any effect at all. Often you only can get the effect of a shifting of the gradient winds to slightly north of east, which anyway hits you on the nose. You will need the extremely rare light offshore wind and a full moon if you want to do the coast in one run

Stay close inshore (10 fathoms or under) to avoid the **garbage line** with junk from the Atlantic trades, the Equatorial Current and the South American Rivers (Orinoco). Think semi-submerged containers or trees here. See my experiences in *Playing the Island Lees: The Garbage Line*. Stay inside it.

Don't get fooled by the apparent closeness of each objective. You shall have your first encounter with the *Caribbean Two Step* here: two steps forward, one step back. The Caribbean swell comes usually from the southeast and 4 to 8 feet high. More like a chop than a swell, you will swear it throws 3 at you within the length of your boat! With a clipper bow the *Caribbean Two Step* becomes more like two back and two to the side. Unless you get that rare offshore breeze, prepare to motorsail close inshore after dawn with full main and no jib, while tacking.

If clever, you shall leave each little harbor at dawn, or before, and arrive before 9 a.m., before the trades come back. Row ashore to a *café* and have breakfast, reading a daily (English) newspaper. then go back to the boat for a late morning nap. If you must carry on, lay up a thermos of coffee and a pot of hot *burgoo* before retiring in the evening. You can breakfast underway just after daybreak.

Coasting Puerto Rico, look for an *Eastern Caribbean Forecast* on NMN of easterly 10 to15 knots. In summer, late afternoon storm cells spawned by the **coastal front** may intimidate. Local winds, especially the seabreezes, or beach winds, may blow stronger than expected off the sea as a result of circulation around these towering cumulo nimbuses. Review the graphic in *Playing the Island Lees: The Reed Switch Effect*.

If you have a good **Offshore Report** don't let these effects inhibit you. They shall all dissipate after dusk when the **gradient wind**, as reported in the forecast, reasserts itself.

If you listen to the **VHF Wx Channels** and AM broadcast coastal reports, ignore the south coast inshore section, and use the Offshore Report's data.

CABO ROJO

When hopping from Boquerón to **La Parguera** you would best shorten the passage into 2 or 3 smaller legs by moving out of Boquerón in the daytime to one of several anchorages along the public beaches off **El Combate** or **Punta Aguila,** or in the snug little mangrove anchorage immediately under **Cabo Rojo** lighthouse. There you can pick your way to within a couple of hundred yards of the beach with a high sun, farther out if you draw over 6 feet. Do a bottom scrub in the clear water there.

I prefer the mangrove anchorage under the Cabo Rojo lighthouse, and I find this site ideal for watching the weather. The night wind over the point comes from the open sea, showing you what to expect on rounding the cape.

The state park beaches at El Combate have many tourists on weekends. After scrubbing the bottom I mingle with the crowds, buying beer and *empanadillas* for a late lunch and watching the monkeys which inhabit the place. They escaped from a research center and breed like rabbits (or monkeys, I suppose). Watch it, they bite!

Jump off from **Cabo Rojo** for La Parguera by daybreak or earlier. Never later! Leave your anchorage in the predawn hours by hoisting anchor and drifting back due west, over the same ground you covered on the way in. Go south of **Margarita Reef** in 12 fathoms. Most of the fish traps on the south coast lie here in 10 fathoms or less.

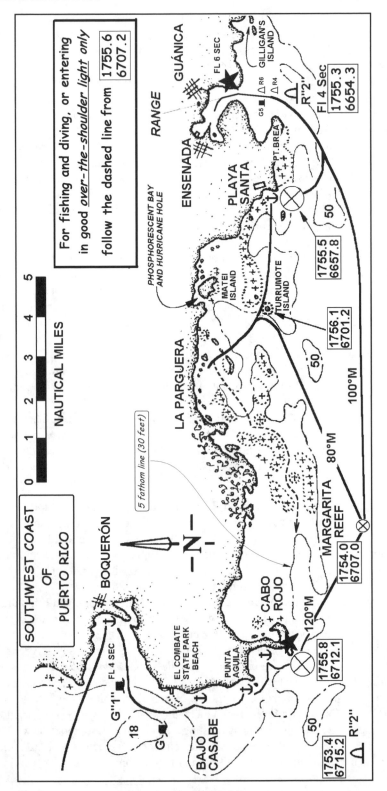

LA PARGUERA

La Parguera [par-GAIR-ah] shows adequately on International Sailing Supply's **Waterproof Charts** and on the **Imray-Iolaire charts**. The Waterproof charts not only have waterproof paper, but they print charts on both sides, making them less expensive.

Enter between **Caracoles Cay** and **Enrique Cay** following the buoys. Drafts under 5 feet can anchor in the clear sand lagoon behind Enrique Cay.

To reach the anchorages near town, proceed toward a small boats dock on the southwest corner of **Maygueyes Island** until you see the larger dock of the University of Puerto Rico's oceanographic research station on the island's northwest corner. Continue toward town until abreast of the University's dock, then swing west into the 12-15 foot deep channel south of a row of mangrove keys. Drafts under 6 feet can continue northwest, rounding between the second and third little cay, to arrive in a small anchorage in front of the town.

You'll find an excellent **hurricane hole** 2 miles to the east, northwest of **Matei Island**. In the right conditions this becomes a highly phosphorescent bay.

To leave **La Parguera** by night, sail that afternoon to **Playa Santa** (Galeta Salinas on the charts). Wait there for the **night lee**. Anchor off the public beach with condos north of **Punta Jorobado** and 5 and a half miles east of La Parguera. Anchor in 8-10 feet of sand and leave while still dark for **Guánica** or **Ponce** by sailing south midway between Punta Jorobado and the small cay three quarters of a mile to its west.

A few years ago the town closed its borders to the bottle throwing students and the dykes on bikes crowd. These went to Boquerón. Adults came back to La Parguera where freedom loving houseboaters regularly flout the government, turning miles of mangrove rivers into a Caribbean Venice. Reef diving, beach excursions, seafood restaurants, *sangria* bars and live *salsa* and *marengue* bands bring many Puerto Ricans here on weekends.

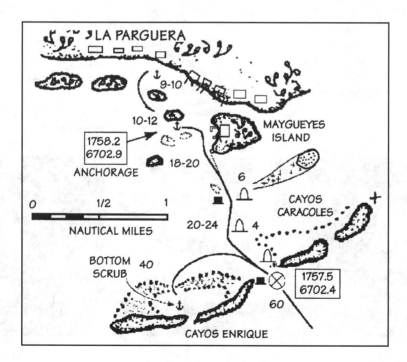

You'll have excellent snorkeling and fishing on the reefs offshore. Nearby El Pináculo (the pinnacle) on **Margarita Reef** has coral formations which rise out of 10 fathoms to less than 15 feet beneath the surface. Mushroom corals grow like 20 foot wide shade trees with interconnecting branches protecting the myriad species of sea creatures beneath.

GUÁNICA AND ENSENADA

Don't use the anchorage off the town of Guánica [GWAH-knee-kah], north of the entrance. It suffers from heavy afternoon gusts directly through the gap at the entrance to the bay, especially in the summertime. Anytime the wind blows south of east, it will combine with the onshore beach wind in the afternoon and roar through the cliffs at the entrance directly onto your anchorage. In addition, this anchorage has a foul bottom with construction material randomly placed, but surely under your tackle. Finally, the old dock there actually gets used occasionally. When it does, it off-loads *fertilizer*, just about the time the wind picks up. Not to worry. An excellent anchorage lies off the pleasant little town of **Ensenada**. The anchorage to the southwest can be used much closer to shore than shown in most charts and the one to the northwest makes a good **hurricane hole**. *Ensenada,* meaning small bay, or cove, in Spanish, began life as an old sugar mill town

which became a near ghost town when sugar lost its majesty. It looks early 20th century American, even down to oak tree planted swales and slate sidewalks.

You may easily exit at night if you looked around on the way in. Leave Guánica at 3 a.m. to arrive in **Ponce** before 8 a.m. (see the section on Ponce for why). Follow the light buoyed, wide and deep ship channel out. However, real cruisers, not *Globetrotters*, leave in daylight to spend a few days at **Gilligan's Island** nearby.

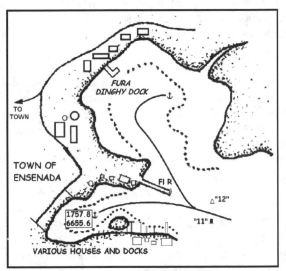

GILLIGAN'S ISLAND

Enter from the west by the **Guánica** ship channel. Turn east at the green can marker No.5. Follow the coast 400 yards off, staying in 3-4 fathoms. With a high sun and mild conditions you can enter from the east through the broad channel between the outer reef and the **Caña Gorda** reef, taking care to avoid the shoal inside and west of the channel.

Find the best anchorage west of Punta Ballena where the water stays flat and the wind funnels through the last narrow channel, or *caño*, between the mangroves. Anchor out of the ferry wakes on weekends (see chartlet). Moored off the docks of the restaurant San Jacinto and the hotel Copamarina you have access to either *criollo tipico* or fine dining. There may be a slight roll there.

Gilligan's Island, the first in a chain of keys east of **Guánica**, earlier got called **Cayo Aurora** after an extraordinary woman who, at the age of 40, escaped misery and mistreatment in the workers' barracks of the nearby La Ballena farm, and swam to the island. There she made a Robinson Crusoe home and lived off the sea until quite ancient.

Locals who used the island for pig roasts began calling it Gilligan's Island after a 1970's American television show of that name. The island looked like the one on TV, and one of the fishermen looked like the lead actor, Bob Denver. The keys have appeared recently on charts as the **Cayos Caña Gorda**. Chart makers don't bother to ask locals about the small stuff. By 2050 it shall no doubt have another name, but I prefer Aurora.

Now a state park manned by rangers, Gilligan's Island gets quite crowded on weekends. Midweek any but the summer months you can have its blue lagoons and white sand *caños* all to yourself. Dive Copamarina (787-821-6009) can orient you for snorkeling or wall diving adventures. On weekends you may want to talk to Sr.Fundador Ortiz Matos who sells his stories and local histories outside the San Jacinto restaurant.

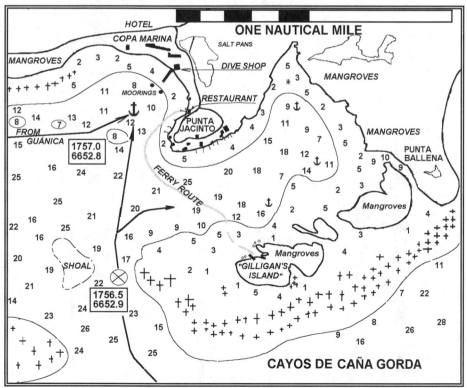

CAYOS DE CAÑA GORDA

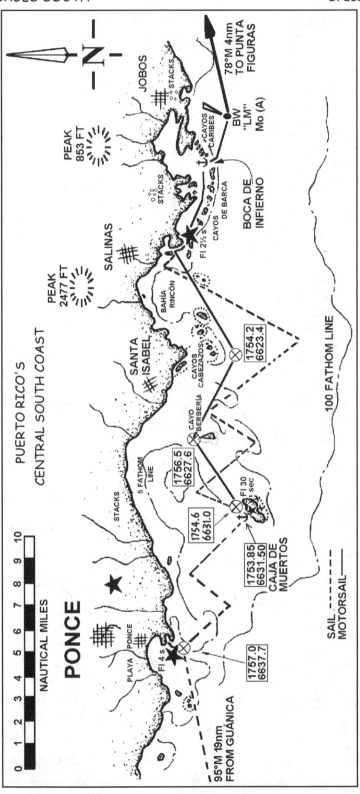

PUERTO RICO'S
CENTRAL SOUTH COAST

PONCE

Anchor in the deep but relatively small Yacht Club anchorage. The Club has a 70 ton Travelift and a convenient yard. For many years **Ponce Yacht Club**, along with **Crown Bay** in St. Thomas, has met my fuel and reprovisioning needs. The dock makes a single hander's dream before 8 a.m. The light land breeze at that time shoves me gently onto the fuel dock. By the time I've tanked up on the clean and inexpensive fuel the Club's members insist upon, the wind has come up from sea to blow me gently off the dock.

Ponce [PONE-say], an industrial center with a renovated Caribbean Victorian downtown merits a walking tour. Hypermarket XTRA and the luxurious Plaza del Caribe Mall lie on the way to town from the yacht club. A Sam's membership warehouse lies west of town on Route 2 near Big KMart and Walmart. You can get just about anything done here in Puerto Rico's second city, a real working town. Ponce has an excellent fine arts museum. If you haven't done it, nor toured the town, you haven't done Ponce. The beautiful colonial US Customs house, built in 1842 as Spanish military headquarters, and used from 1898 by the US military, sits on the waterfront opposite the old Coast Guard station.

Ferries to **Caja de Muertos** had caused loud weekend gatherings in the fields called La Guancha across from the Yacht Club. Taxpayers built parks and an old fashioned boardwalk to bring order to the pandemonium, and they succeeded in institutionalizing the party. Join the throng and dine from the vendors' *pinchos* [PEEN-chose], Latin *shish-kabobs,* fried chicken and *empanadillas*. But unless you're deaf, you won't stay long here.

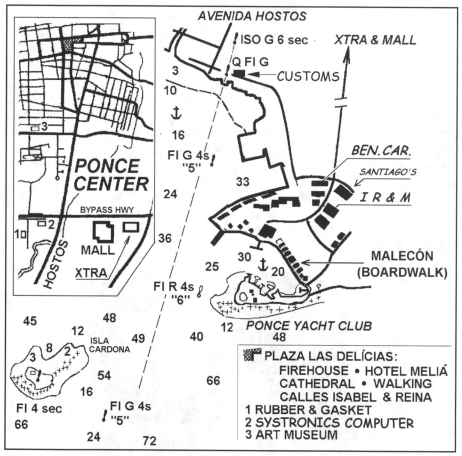

If you tour the island, do it from **Salinas**!

Sail to the island of **Caja de Muertos** for a Bahamas-like breather. And missing Muertos can mean a much rougher trip.

Ponce has the most amazing warehouse a yachtie can ever visit: Rubber and Gasket of Puerto Rico (843-8450). They have sheet rubber, **Teflon, Lexan**, and any kind of **hose** you want, including *stainless flex*. You can find everything in Ponce. For **stainless** fabrication visit Accurate Tooling (AT Metal, 788-4090) on Avenida Hostos in Playa Ponce. Owner Luis Ojeda, whose steel yacht *Casi Casi* berths at the PYC, doubles as a commodore of the Club, and he will bend over backward to help yachties. On the Ponce Bypass Highway you'll find a shop called Tornicentro del Sur (Southern Screw Center, 259-4419), with a world class collection of stainless **fasteners**. Nearby you'll also find the Casa de Tornillos (House of Screws) and the TechniCraft **upholstery fabric** center -- all near Wendy's, Baskin Robbins, KFC and McDonalds.

To reprovision, tie the dinghy up at the fisherman's cooperative dock, politely asking them first, of course. Walk to **Santiago's Cash and Carry**, in the nearby industrial park (see map). There you can grab a cart and heave on cases of canned goods, sausage, cheese and booze at discount prices. Out on the loading dock with a full cart, call 840-9126 or 9127 for a taxi back to your dinghy at the fisherman's cooperative in the harbor.

In the second godown on the northeastern quarter of the industrial park find Industrial Rubber and Mechanics (see map), where they make up any belts, fuel and **hydraulic hoses** you want and have all the brass and copper fittings you could hope for. In the lot across to the west, the northernmost godown has a store taken from the dreams of the mechanically adept skipper: Benitez Carrillo (see map) has **vee belts**, **bearings**, gears, seals, motor controls and every ball bearing known to man, even your roller furling's. If they don't, they'll deliver it next day.

The magnificent Plaza del Caribe Mall lies a short ride (or a long walk) from the Yacht Club. It has Sears, J C Penny, Radio Shack, cinemas, foodmall and whatnot, just like suburbs of the USA. A sort of fire sale discount store called Capri, in the basement floor of the mall, often has great deals for cruisers in anything from mosquito netting to cocktail snacks. Across the mall's parking lot you'll find the supermarket XTRA, exactly like the ones you used in Florida. You'll also find Big K, Walmart and SAM'S a short taxi ride from the Yacht Club.

With a fast vessel one could motor direct from Ponce, proceeding east from the **Isla de Cardona** light to a point one mile north of **Cayo Berberia** and thence 126° True to round the **Cayos Cabezazos** off **Punta Petrona**. If you do this, leave Ponce at oh-dark thirty. I, on the other hand, choose to *never* miss Caja de Muertos.

242

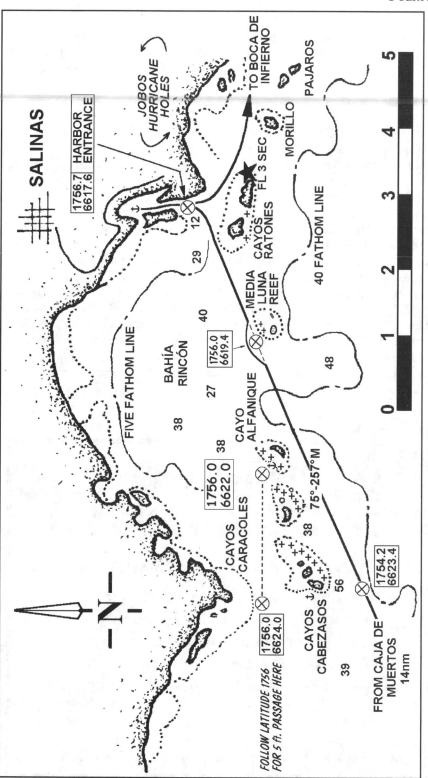

SALINAS

TO BOCA DE INFIERNO

PAJAROS

JOBOS HURRICANE HOLES

1756.7
6617.6 HARBOR ENTRANCE

MORILLO

CAYOS RATONES   FL 3 SEC

12

29

40 FATHOM LINE

FIVE FATHOM LINE

BAHÍA RINCÓN

40

27   1756.0
6619.4

MEDIA LUNA REEF

38

48

CAYO ALFANIQUE

38

1756.0
6622.0

75°-257°M

CAYOS CARACOLES

38

N

56

1754.2
6623.4

1756.0
6624.0

CAYOS CABEZASOS

39

FOLLOW LATITUDE 1756
FOR 5 ft. PASSAGE HERE

FROM CAJA DE MUERTOS
14nm

0   1   2   3   4   5

Do not use the VHF Wx Channel Coastal Report for passaging on this coast. Use the Offshore Report.

243

CAJA DE MUERTOS

After a quick fuel up, and after quickly loading 6 months of provisions on deck from Santiago's, I take a late morning sail out to **Caja de Muertos,** a state park which has 4 guys in Smoky the Bear hats that live over the beach. The Park Service has installed sand screw moorings, sufficient for most yachts in most weather, to protect the seabed from anchor depredations. The moorings usually stand empty on Monday through Thursday. Inspect them. Local power boats can wipe them out nearly as fast as they put them in.

Caja de Muertos, or Coffin Island, looks in the golden light of sundown more like a shrouded and vigiled body than a "corpse's box": toes up, cross-armed chest and backward lain head. The lighthouse, built 20 years prior to the Yankees walking ashore at **Guánica** to take possession of Puerto Rico, offers a perfect example of 19th century Spanish public works architecture.

Paths wind from the anchorages and mooring fields on the west side to the lighthouse on the summit, and from the snorkeling park on the east coast to the *balneario* (beach and bath houses) near the rangers' complex in the southwest. Hike up to the old light house, visit the Park Rangers for information on the rookery, and visit the spooky caves here.

Ponce lies in a deep bay. You may get the collywobbles kicked out of you east of Muertos even though the wind doesn't honk. **Stage** to the lee of the island of Muertos which sits offshore, astride the true sea conditions, and depart for Salinas around 3-4 a.m.

Wait for a 3-4 a.m. departure from Muertos to **Salinas**, a motorsail against easterlies. The chartlet shows both motoring and sailing routes from Muertos to Salinas. I prefer to sail from Muertos by tacking southeast between it and Berberia in the light northerly of the predawn hours, then northeast into **Bahía Rincón** in a spectacular sunrise blended with Puerto Rican mountain expresso.

SALINAS

Coming from **Caja de Muertos**, enter **Bahía Rincón** on a northeast course splitting the difference between **Cayos Cabezazos** and **Media Luna reef** further east. Leave **Cayo Alfenique** one mile to port. Head east in the sheltered bay, rounding **Cayo Mata** into Salinas harbor. For drafts over 6 feet favor the channel behind Cayo Mata slightly left of center until midway down the island, then favor the channel slightly right of center (intersecting perpendiculars from the shores). Anchor in 10 feet of mud and sand (mostly sand) near the **Marina de Salinas**. You cannot easily read the mangrove murky water.

Salinas, a well protected hurricane hole, makes the best spot to leave the boat while touring. The many reefs and keys 5 miles east or west of Salinas provide good weekend diving destinations. With a car you have a better commute to the shops and sights at **Ponce** or **San Juan** from safe moorings here than from any other harbor in Puerto Rico.

Público trips to Ponce from Salinas go faster by taking two rides: Salinas to Santa Isabel and Santa Isabel to Ponce. **Guayama**, to the east, has a *público* terminal for all destinations north and east. The Guayama mall has Sears, KMart, Walmart, etc. See Sarah at the marina for reasonable limo service to anywhere on the island.

Salinas makes a great harbor for refit. Restaurants abound here, both around the harbor and on the bay shore. The village of **Playa Salinas** outside the gates of the marina has two hardware stores, a pharmacy, a sail loft, a boatwright and the best marine store in Puerto Rico. For metal repair and fabrication, call H.R. Machine Shop at 824-1098. Downtown Salinas has two alternator shops. For a mechanic, use Mike Swanson at 824-4565.

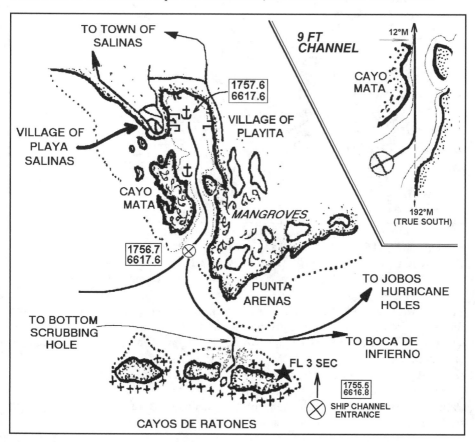

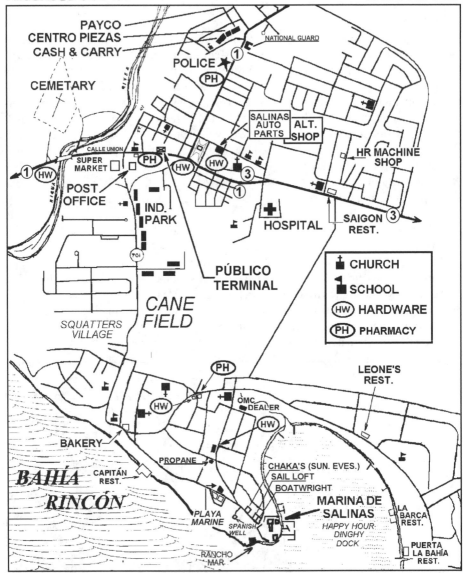

From Salinas you can finally get English weather reports on standard broadcast from San Juan and St.Thomas (AM 1030 and 1000 respectively). Use the *Eastern Caribbean Offshore Report* for the south coast, and use the VHF Wx channel for the east coast.

Visit **Caño Matías** [CAHN-yo ma-TEE-us] which has pleasant bathing behind the reef and between the **Cayos Ratones**. Between the two keys lies a third with a channel on either side. The western shore of either channel has deep water. You can bring in the bigger boat for a scrub. I scrubbed here with my 6 and one half foot draft. Keep the small middle islet a bit open with the eastern key until the western key opens. Then keep both keys equally open until you've got deep water. Moorings in the shallows on the eastern side of the *caño* really work, because the current always flows north and the wind always blows east.

If you get good north in the wind, and you sail nonstop east, leave at dusk to arrive at **Palmas del Mar** next morning, careful not to wander far offshore as current and confused swell make a northeast tack across **Point Tuna** difficult. In daytime it will blow hard east.

246

SALINAS HURRICANE HOLES

Just across Salinas harbor, on the east side of the eastern shore's mangroves, lies the only wetlands national park outside the continental U.S. These bayous and creeks have small niches and boat sized coves appended to deep creeks with 8-10 feet of water. More room exists to tie into these mangroves for hurricane threats than they have demand to fill them, simply because Salinas lies unstrategically far from the boating centers of Fajardo and the U.S. Virgin Islands. Not close enough to run to with every threat, and no one wants to get caught out at sea within the Hurricane Watch period.

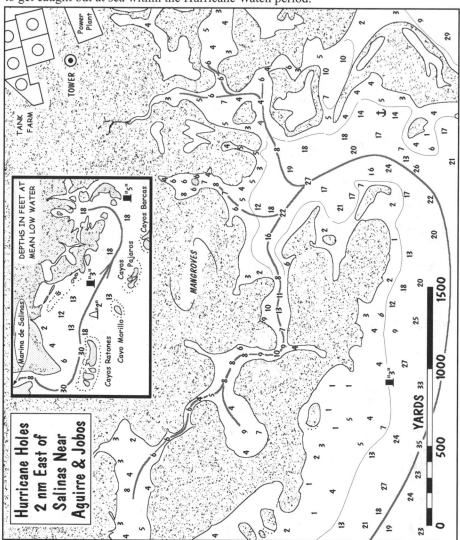

To continue this coast thornlessly, you must stop at least twice more before Palmas del Mar: **Boca de Infierno,** where you **stage** and watch the actual outside conditions from a snug mangrove anchorage, and **Puerto Patillas**. See details in my recommendations for here in the examples given in *Island Strategies: Stage Your Departure*. Leave **Boca de Infierno** at sunup through the 12 foot deep cut if conditions remain settled with the wind easterly under 15 knots. You may stop over at the little port of **Arroyo**.

BOCA DE INFIERNO

The final long leg east can get awful. For a shorter, easier leg go *inside* to **stage** at **Boca de Infierno** [BOH-kah day een-fee-AIR-noh]. When approaching the anchorage take bearings in good light of the Central Aguirre pier, distinguished by two old fashioned brick chimneys almost in line. Note also the breaking of the reef and the sea conditions outside.

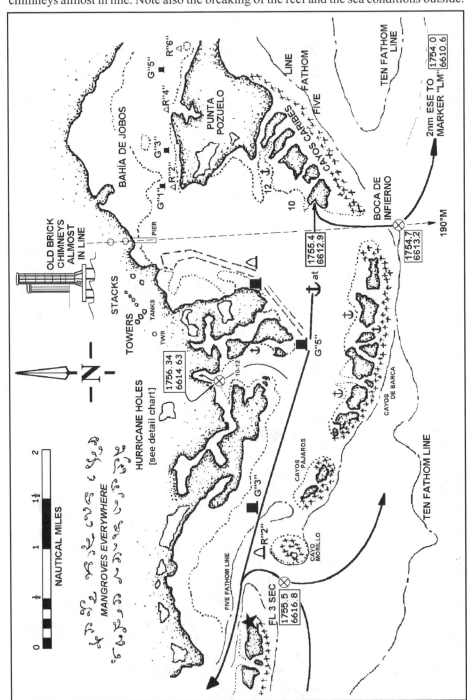

You must motor through this pass in *early morning* light conditions. Ground swells on either side can become quite heavy in daytime conditions. As with the anchorage at Caja de Muertos, you benefit from waiting at **Boca de Infierno** in that you can see for yourself how the sea runs on the morning of your departure. Depart through Boca de Infierno at first light, keeping the *Central Aguirre* pier at a 10° Magnetic bearing. When a half mile clear of the pass, head for the 'Lima Mike' sea buoy 2 miles east southeast before taking up your course for **Punta Figuras** in order to enter **Puerto Patillas**. I feel one *must* stop at Patillas, but if you don't, keep well clear of **Guayama Reef** between Punta Figuras and Punta Viento. I prefer to inside Guayama Reef to better avoid offshore garbage.

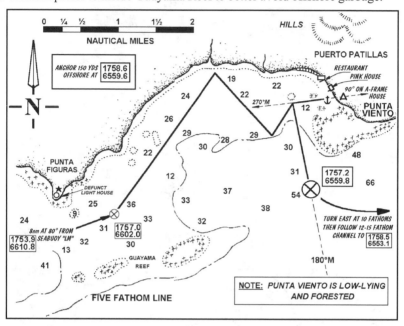

PUERTO PATILLAS

Puerto Patillas [PWAIR-toh pah-TEE-yahs], once a small boat fishing village supported by **Guayama Reef** 2 miles offshore, lies northwest of **Punta Viento**, a low-lying treed point 3 miles east of the **Punta Figuras** light (FL 6 seconds).

Rocky shoals extend southward from the town to beyond the point giving good protection to the anchorage in anything but south to west. Approach for 11 miles on 80°M from the sea buoy [Mo(A) BW "LM"], leaving Punta Figuras one half mile to port. Continue until high cliffs backed by hills come on your north and an A-frame house, just south of a power boat dock, shows to your east. This puts you in 12 feet of water. Continue east toward the A-frame and anchor in 7-8 feet of sand and mud, 150 yards offshore between the A-frame and a pink walled house to its north. Go slow because of old moorings in the area. Dinghy in to enjoy the park beaches along the point and the harbor's restaurants.

Leave Patillas in dark to take advantage of the **night lee**. Stay south of the shoals by heading due west for 3 quarters of a mile before turning south. Turn east in 10 fathoms for either **Vieques**, or **Palmas del Mar**. Stay in the 12-15 fathom, 6 miles long, one half mile wide, **trench** between Patillas and **Point Tuna**. The 7 fathom ridge to seaward trips the seas, and the landward shoaling makes groundswells. The trench, like deep waters in a brook, runs still. You not only make better time, but you shall avoid trash as well.

SAILING DIRECTIONS, EAST COAST

The east coast of Puerto Rico, the western boundary to the **Spanish Virgin Islands**, hosts six major marinas and five haulout yards. It also has a wealth of cruise-worthy islands off its shore, a diver's paradise in the setting sun's shadow of **El Yunque**, Puerto Rico's highest peak and America's only tropical rain forest.

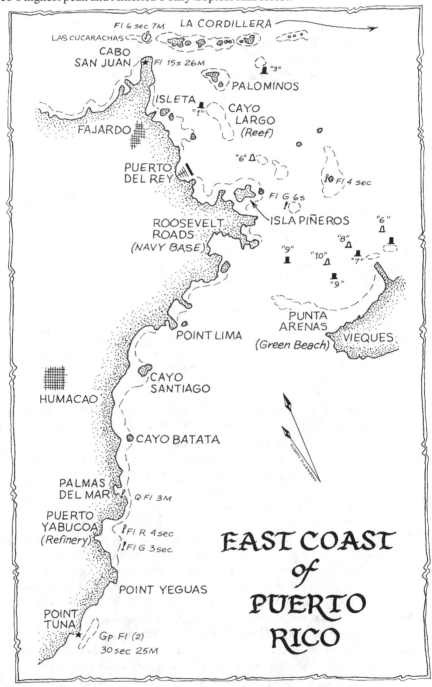

PALMAS DEL MAR

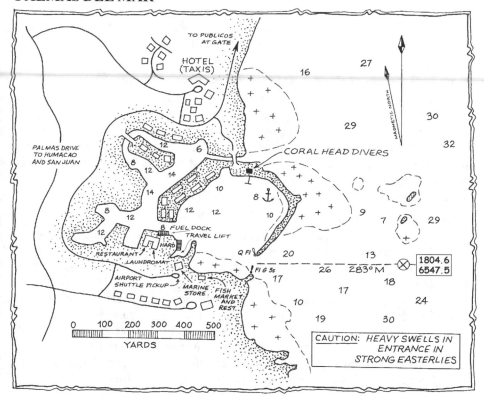

Enter in good water directly from the east. You can use the anchorage temporarily, rumor notwithstanding. You'll have good holding in 10-12 feet everywhere except the northeast corner which has silted to a depth of 5-6 feet near the seawall, but there you'll avoid rolling in swell which can sometimes penetrate the harbor.

The **Palmas del Mar** resort and condominium project looks along the lines of Mediterranean seaside resort communities. It has golf, tennis, scuba, sport fishing and sail charters available to owners or guests of the hotel, marina or shipyard. At a condo slip, in the marina, or laid

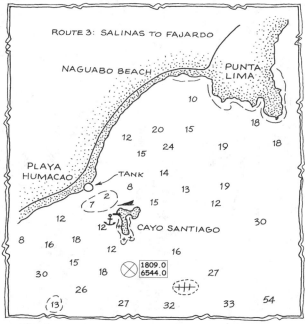

up ashore at the yard, this harbor affords reasonable hurricane protection. Boats fared well here as Hurricane Hugo passed close by. If you lay up ashore, ensure for yourself that

251

the jackstands lash securely together with nylon warp, and use Spanish windlasses to maintain tension. During Hugo, boats on the hard blew over due to inadequate lashings.

Try Chez Daniel, an excellent authentic French restaurant. A great fisherman's restaurant and seafood store lies in the southeast corner of the anchoring basin.

CAYO SANTIAGO

Enter from the south and east. A surge may come in southeasterlies.

Also called "Monkey Island", **Cayo Santiago** has a free range for the Caribbean Primate Research Center. Inhabited by well over 1000 monkeys, whose crazy antics include biting persistent tourists. Do not molest nor feed the monkeys. You may not go ashore.

However, you can enjoy the cerulean water and the abundant snorkeling around the island. Day charterers and snorklers from Palmas del Mar may join you, but this anchorage normally empties late afternoons and nights.

Rumors persist that Punta Lima has a marina planned.

ROOSEVELT ROADS NAVAL STATION

Long an emergency refuge for all but retired career military and their guests, **Roosevelt Roads** had a small marina in its R&R area (see chartlet).

Since the Navy abandoned its firing ranges on the island of Vieques, the mission of this base has become obscure. Veterans have long touted the base as the U.S. Navy's largest base -- not in population nor in ship arrivals and departures, but in *land area*! We have yet to see final disposition of the land. Why not call in and see for yourself?

If you leave the boat here in hurricane season, have someone to react to severe threats in time to get to the holes near Salinas or the closer **Ensenada Honda** in Vieques. Note: the latter could get crowded by boats from Fajardo and the USVIs. They find it too far to trek to the fine holes at Salinas where the smart cruiser here at "Rosie Roads" will go.

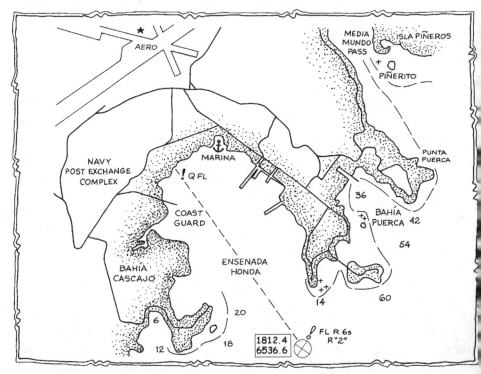

ISLA PIÑEROS

A well protected anchorage quite secluded during the week, yet only 3 miles south of the largest marina in the Caribbean. The Navy does not allow going ashore on this island which belongs to the **Roosevelt Roads** Navy Base. Nonetheless one can normally anchor overnight for excellent swimming and snorkeling when not in use by the Navy. Call Puerto del Rey's harbormaster at 860-1000, or on VHF Channel 71 for information regarding Navy maneuvers. The cove in the northern reef makes a nice lunch anchorage in summer months with wind south of east. Enter **Pasaje Medio Mundo** from the north with the rocks west of the pass clearly visible. The less visible shoal on the island's southwest corner extends quite far. Don't pass between **Isla Piñeros** and **Cabeza de Perro**.

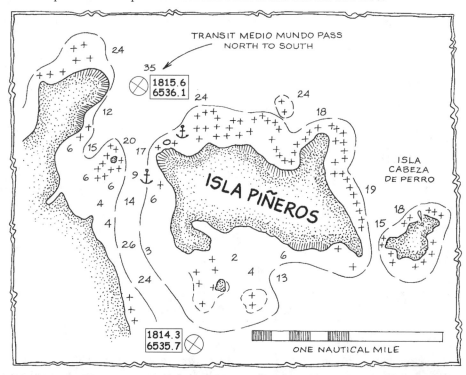

The MARINA DE SALINAS

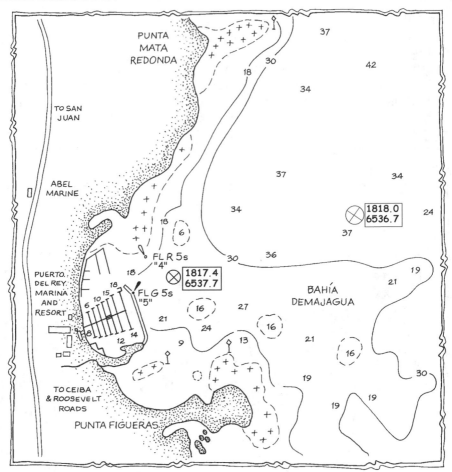

Puerto del Rey Marina and Resort

PUERTO DEL REY

The largest and most modern marina in the Caribbean with over 1000 slips, a well equipped yard and long term land storage, you'll find any yacht service desired here, including a sailmaker. Puerto del Rey's has Travelifts of 35, 77 and 170 tons and a 60 ton Brownell trailer. Call the harbormaster on VHF channel 71 for a slip or a transient dock.

A large Amigo supermarket stands less than a mile from the marina. The marina has rental cars, restaurants, delicatessen and a marine store on site. Puerto del Rey makes the best sense for an east coast base from which to tour the country. Otherwise use centrally located and cruiser friendly **Salinas**, on the superhighway, linking Ponce and San Juan.

East coast marinas such as **Isleta**, with its ferries and curfews, might make a good xenophobe hangout, but it can create major inconveniences for the cruising skipper who needs to get in and out to hunt stuff down.

You have reasonable hurricane protection here if laid up ashore. As with any yard, ensure jackstands get securely tensioned to the boat with Spanish windlasses of nylon 3-strand line. Also see the yacht gets laid up in a spot unlikely to require moving around in your absence, thus canceling your good work on the jackstands.

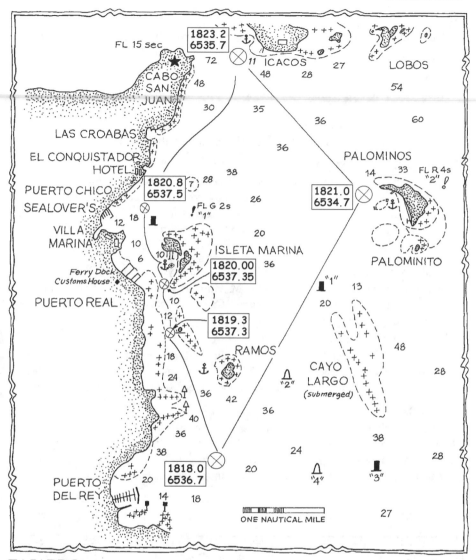

FAJARDO

Use a careful eyeball method to approach ports on the mainland via the ship channel or via the "inside route", behind the keys and the reefs. If taking the inside route, watch for a cross set at the GPS waypoint shown on the chartlet just south of Isleta.

When approaching downwind from the east, be careful to avoid **Cayo Largo**. You may not see the backs of the ground swells to windward of this dangerous reef.

The district of **Fajardo**, catering to yachting enthusiasts from around the world, hosts the Heineken International Cup, the CORT regattas and the Round Puerto Rico Race. Excepting Chez Daniel in Palmas del Mar and Rosa's seafood restaurant in **Puerto Real**, sailors ashore seeking fine dining need a car.

Fajardo lies at the foot of the only tropical rain forest in US jurisdiction, the 28,000 acre El Yunque national forest, where annually 100 billion gallons of rain nurture 240 species of trees. You can see the forest's 3,532 foot peak, El Toro, throughout the Spanish Virgins.

RAMOS

A private island, has floats off the beach with which the owner has marked his territory. You may not go ashore. You may anchor outside the string of buoys.

ISLETA

Anchor off **Isleta Marina** (265 slips) west of the marked shoal in the bight of the two islands. Close to the marina you shall suffer from the ferry wakes. They have two ferry services to **Puerto Real**, one for residents of the condominium and marina, another, at a cost, for visitors. They run from 06:30 to 21:30, quarter after and quarter of the hour.

PUERTO REAL, FAJARDO

Shoals surround **Puerto Real** except for dredged ferry channels, and it lies to windward. You'd best approach by dinghy or by the ferries from **Isleta Marina**. Ferries run here to and from Culebra and Vieques. Dine at Rosa's for seafood, a short walk inland. Find Customs and the Post Office across from the ferry terminal.

VILLA MARINA

With 250 slips and a 60-ton Travelift, caters mostly to power craft. Marine stores Skipper Shop and El Pescador behind **Villa Marina** have the most extensive marine stock in the area. On the same street find Fajardo Canvas and Sails, and Re-Power Marine Services for engine, prop and machine shop needs.

PUERTO CHICO and SEA LOVERS

Immediately northeast of **Villa Marina** lie the marinas of **Sea Lovers**, near the beach, and Puerto Chico, the larger marina which lies to the east behind the seawall. **Puerto Chico** has a fuel dock and handles drafts to seven feet. Sea Lovers suits smaller craft.

LAS CROABAS

An inexpensive and fun place to haul with lots of nearby *tipico* restaurants and cantinas. The yard, **Varadero de Fajardo**, does not permit dry grinding or paint spraying. No hardware stores lie nearby, so take everything with you. I made one of my most memorable hauls here, thanks to the many musical cantinas across the street.

Puerto del Rey Marina, Fajardo

THE SPANISH VIRGIN ISLANDS

The **Spanish Virgin Islands** embrace 400 square miles to the west of the U.S. Virgin Islands. Unlike the USVI, Puerto Rico has an extensively developed industrial and agricultural infrastructure. Yet like the USVI, the Spanish Virgins depend entirely on tourism. But they stand many years behind in the development of tourist infrastructure. Not good for the typical resort tourist, but *great* for the getaway cruiser and diving enthusiast. It means unaffected townspeople, undisturbed anchorages, pristine beaches and productive fishing (with a year-round lobster season). Ashore, the Spanish Virgins offer immersion in the Spanish Caribbean with the escape clause of bilingualism and the convenience of U.S. institutions. You have four cruising areas in the Spanish Virgins:

Puerto Rico's East Coast • La Cordillera • Culebra • Vieques

Be sure to schedule ample time to enjoy each of these very special areas.

December through March, distant northern gales often create swell in exposed northern anchorages, and some day anchorages might become untenable. Fortunately, the lovely harbors of the south coast of Vieques and the reef anchorages of Culebra, **Icacos** and **Palominos** don't feel northerly swell. Cold fronts that make it this far south often stall or have dissipated into troughs which persist for several days. While not good for the avid sailor, these conditions make for fluky winds which create diving and snorkeling opportunities across **La Cordillera**, in **Culebra**'s outlying keys, and on **Vieques**' north coast.

From late July to early September you may find some "bloom" in the water which can restrict visibility for divers. You'll have great sailing in the cooling summer trades which make these islands cooler and less humid than most of North America at this time of the year. Long hauls to windward become pleasurable, and you find anchorages often empty.

Like a **front** in the winter, **tropical waves** during the summer create breaks in the tradewinds, and otherwise exposed diving sites become open to exploration.

By April to June, strong fronts usually have petered out, while well organized tropical waves have yet to begin. Conversely, the waves peter out and the fronts haven't started by October and November. In these 'tweener months trade winds moderate and days dawn clear and sunny. Late afternoons see the accumulated daytime heat producing cooling rain. Northerly swells run infrequently in these months and Vieques Sound has minimum chop. Diving sites and day anchorages have their highest availability during these months.

WOSO San Juan, 1030 KHz Am standard broadcast band, gives local meteorological and marine reports hourly after the news. WVWI broadcasts a brief "Sailor's Report" on 1000 KHz AM, at 6:30 a.m. Monday through Friday. This includes the short range NOAA coastal report and the next 12 hours of the National Weather Service's Offshore Report. NOAA broadcasts continuously on VHF Wx2 from San Juan. VI Radio, however, broadcasts a continuous summary of the meteorological, coastal and **Offshore Report** on VHF Wx3, as well as the **Tropical Weather Outlook** and **Tropical Weather Discussion** during hurricane season. You can receive this in eastern Puerto Rico.

While the coastal reports work for most islands and anchorages, out on the open Sound in the daytime, or anywhere east or south of Vieques, you must listen to the Offshore Forecast for the Eastern Caribbean on WVWI's Sailor's Report, or on VHF Wx3 Channel. No other report will do but the Offshore Report.

NOTE: *Do not navigate these reefed islands within one hour of sunup or sunset.*

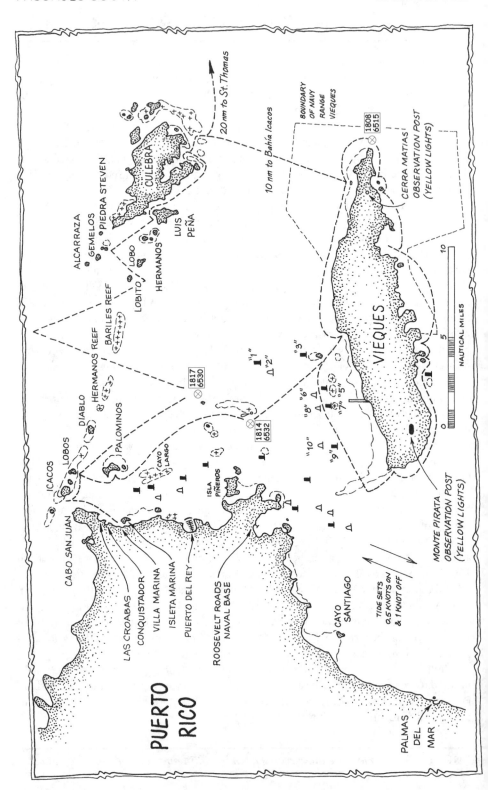

SAILING DIRECTIONS, VIEQUES SOUND

From **Vieques Sound** (vee-AYE-case) until the end of all the Virgins, you shall always see the next island. Nonetheless, you should not try to cross this stretch in one bound.

For many years I have experimented with sailing to windward across Vieques Sound. I find that I save a couple of hours by tacking in the area south of **La Cordillera**, where the current and chop runs less adverse, tacking into the lee of **Culebra**. However, a strong motorsailer can barrel down the middle in heavy chop and contrary current with more stress in less time. The south coast of **Vieques** makes for tough going to windward in onshore easterlies and against the equatorial current. Best you sail the south coast of Vieques *downwind* and with several stops at its beautiful beaches and anchorages. In short, if you circumnavigate the **Spanish Virgins**, *do so clockwise*.

Cross the shoaly Sound with pleasantly short and easy trips. Notice from the chart that to avoid a visit to **Isla Palominos**, one would have to go out of one's way and bash 9 to 12 hours to windward across Vieques Sound. From Palominos you use the lee of Culebra and the keys west of it to pleasantly sneak-tack one's way to **Dewey** in only 6 to 8 hours.

CURRENTS AND TIDES

Cruisers in the Spanish Virgins should take special note of set in **Vieques Sound**. Yachties from the Virgins on their first trek to Puerto Rico and back get surprised by it. It sometimes takes twice the time to sail east as it took to sail west, something to bear in mind when setting out late in the day from Fajardo. You don't want to be caught out among the reefs in bad light! The **Equatorial Current** flows west northwest in this area at a clip of 0.4 to 0.7 knots. When it mounts the shallow plateau of the Sound, sheering forces increase its velocity in chaotic ways. The tide floods west and ebbs east, but on the Sound's north and south borders tidal flow runs more north-south as it pours onto or spills off the Sound's shallow plateau. These currents approach 1 knot on flood, a half-knot on ebb. While these effects seem relatively small, when taken together, they can lead to unpredictable landfalls and arrival times. To arrive at reef entrances in favorable light, you must use conservative course planning.

The shallow Sound can whip up a vicious chop in a forecast gradient wind of 15 knots or above. Whether motoring, sailing or motorsailing, tack the chop for comfort.

STAGING

Start at Punta Arenas and take whatever route you wish to get to **Culebra**, just not direct. Stop first at Roosevelt Roads for retired militaries, the Fajardo marinas and boat yards, or **Palominos** for those wanting to scrub their bottoms and enjoy a Bahamas-like respite before going eastward over the Sound.

If bound for the USVIs, make several stops at Culebra before pressing on to the hurly burly of the commercial U.S. ports. Anchor at the little beach behind **Luis Peña**. Carry on to **Dewey** or **Ensenada Honda** next day. You can also wait out summer storms in Culebra. Some cruisers make a pattern of summer in Culebra, winter in the Virgins, never moving their yachts more than a few miles in an east or west direction all year. They put down a mooring in a select spot before the rush, summering there in relative security, watching the fire drills of the Virgins exodus with each hurricane warning.

Await favorable conditions in **Dakity Harbor** or **Bahía de Almodóvar** before moving on to St. Thomas or back to Puerto Rico. If bound for a circumnavigation of Vieques, set sail from Dakity or Almodóvar.

PUNTA ARENAS

Punta Arenas, on the northwestern tip of Vieques, makes a good stopover either entering or leaving Vieques Sound. A good anchorage lies 40 yards off a flat crescent beach, which the Navy calls **Green Beach**, one half mile south of Punta Arenas itself. Another lies just south of a ruined dock backed by a couple of large, rusty and ruined storage tanks. Head east on the tanks and turn to the anchorage when in 30 feet of water. Pick a grassy sand spot to avoid the patches of sand colored coral ledges here. An isolated anchorage on weekdays, Green Beach has clear water that often goes mirror calm at night. Great for bottom scrubbing and skinny dipping. You can get conch and an occasional lobster on the rocky shores to the south. They call an area of extensive sandbores and rock, which stretches north northwest from Punta Arenas, the **Escollo de Arenas**. It has only 6-10 feet of water covering it. A warning: *escollo* means trouble. This permanent rocky ridge collects storm detritus for the entire Sound. You may cross it without incident. Each season some foolish yachtie brags to me that he blindly crossed the Escollo in a high chop and never saw less than 10 feet. Let him try it ten times in a row! Don't let the one time experts fool you. Play it safe. Debris on the bottom can combine with 3 foot troughs to give you a nasty bump on some old wreck or steel tank. Except in a calm, I mostly take a 2 fathom bridge across the Escollo on a pleasant, reaching sail rather than motor across it.

ISLA PALOMINOS

The Department of Natural Resources (DNR) has placed a number of free moorings here. If none available, anchor between the harbor's central shoal and the beach, or close in under **Palominitos**, to avoid the wash of ferries to Palominos from **El Conquistador** resort on the mainland.

Whether running west from the USVIs, or beating eastward on the start of a cruise, Palominos makes either a fine farewell or introduction to the Spanish Virgins. Going west, you've got a jewel of a tropical island from which to watch the sunset over El Yunque's rain forest on a last night's return to Fajardo.

If headed east, you must stop at Palominos to break up what otherwise could turn out a bear of a windward close-hauled leg. If on your way to Vieques, having overnighted in **Palominos**, take a morning sail down to **Isabel Segunda** for lunch and a look at the fort. If bound to **Culebra**, tack up to **Diablo** from behind Palominos, and continue tacking east along the Cordillera, making successively shorter tacks as you gain lee from Culebra. Let anchors-down at **Luis Peña** for the evening. See the chartlet for Vieques Sound.

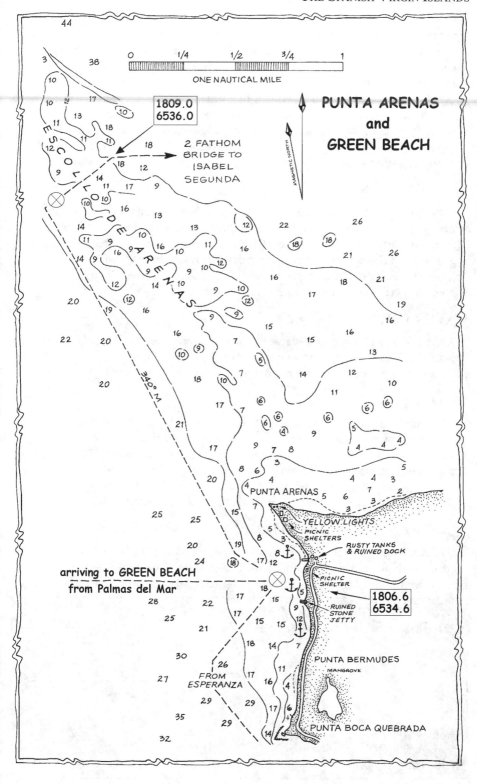

ONE NAUTICAL MILE

1809.0
6536.0

2 FATHOM
BRIDGE TO
ISABEL
SEGUNDA

PUNTA ARENAS
and
GREEN BEACH

MAGNETIC NORTH

ESCOLLO DE ARENAS

340° M

PUNTA ARENAS

YELLOW LIGHTS

PICNIC
SHELTERS

RUSTY TANKS
& RUINED DOCK

PICNIC
SHELTER

1806.6
6534.6

arriving to GREEN BEACH
from Palmas del Mar

RUINED
STONE
JETTY

PUNTA BERMUDES

MANGROVE

FROM
ESPERANZA

PUNTA BOCA QUEBRADA

261

LA CORDILLERA

Puerto Rico's East Coast Marine Reserve, known as **La Cordillera**, or *the mountain range*, consists of 12 miles of islets and reefs. The larger keys can be used to day anchor the mother boat in lee from the easterly trades and in shelter from northerly swell in the winter. Diving expeditions can then run by dingy to the surrounding reefs and walls. Wind and swell in the winter months constrain diving opportunities on the Cordillera. Northerly swell rarely occurs in the summer months when mild easterlies prevail. In general, look for minimum swell days with a favorable wind of less than 15 knots before choosing your day anchorage and dive sites.

CAYO ICACOS

Arrive at the waypoint shown on the chart and then proceed into the cove of deeper water by eyeball, snugging up to the white sand beach in seven feet of glass clear water. The Department of Natural Resources (DNR) has placed a number of free moorings here. A good night anchorage under prevailing trades, **Isla Icacos** provides endless diving, snorkeling and shelling on the surrounding reefs and secluded beaches. It might roll a bit in winter, however, when gales have passed off to the north.

CAYO LOBOS

Cayo Lobos, a privately owned resort island, has a protected harbor marked by red and green floats. Make a day anchorage just inside or outside the buoys and well off the channel, respecting the access and privacy of the owners on the beach and in the channel.

CAYO DIABLO

Shoal draft vessels can work close in to the beach, while deeper drafts must avoid the coral formations and anchor in three-to-four fathoms of clear sand farther out.

Dive the rocks and islets with a reliable motorized tender downwind. Pay out enough anchor rode, including enough chain for bottom chafe. Use **Cayo Diablo** as a day anchorage only, and only in settled conditions of less than 15 knots east.

The east shore has a diveboat mooring which doesn't get continuous use.

LOS HERMANOS AND BARRILES

The two long reefs called **Los Hermanos** and **Barriles**, east of Cayo Diablo, provide productive diving during calm conditions. Experienced divers shall greatly enjoy these reefs, as well as the many islets strung out to the east, which belong to the Culebra group.

The "Puerto Rican Navy" at
GREEN BEACH on a weekend

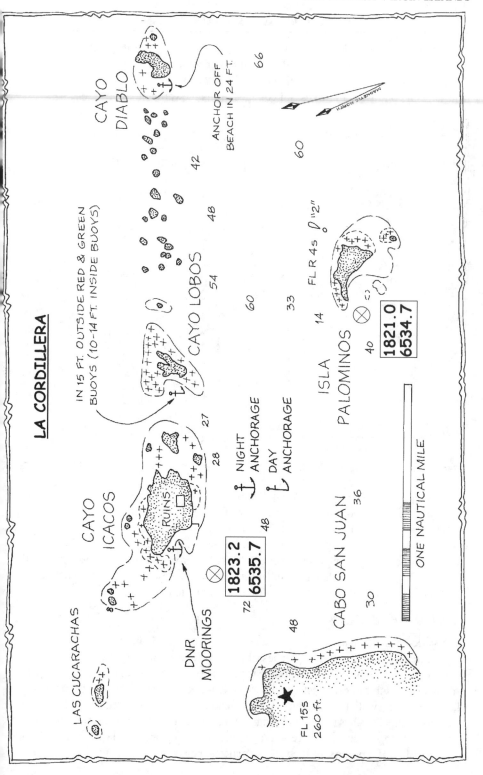

LA CORDILLERA

CULEBRA AND ITS OUT ISLANDS

Unspoiled **Isla de Culebra** attracts most people by its seclusion, its spectacular beaches and the quaint and insular town of **Dewey**. It has become a winter retreat for some and a permanent expatriate refuge for others. Secluded mansions begin to dot the windward landscape in contrast to the weekend cottages of the leeward and town side.

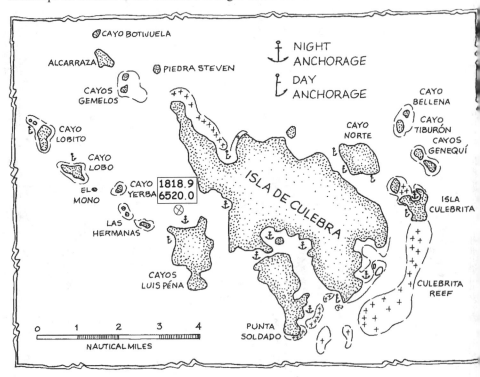

Unexploited diving opportunities abound in the rocks, islets and keys centered on Culebra. Dive any number of day anchorages, though swell can affect them in the winter months. Culebra and its outlying islands can absorb the serious cruiser or diver for weeks. Arriving from Puerto Rico, make your landfall at **Luis Peña**. Arriving from the Virgin Islands or foreign ports enter at **Ensenada Honda** for clearance at the airport in Dewey. Anchor that night in **Dakity Harbor** behind the reef for a most tranquil evening, and to lie near the Club Seabourne for happy hour.

CAYO LUIS PEÑA

In settled easterlies, the beach on the north shore of **Luis Peña** provides anchoring in clear white sand roads between patches of coral rock. Stay in one to two fathoms, since the water shoals quickly. The anchorage inside the reef accommodates drafts of five feet and less. In winter the northwestern point of Culebra shields the anchorage from the worst of any northeast swell, but the southeastern anchorage might do better. A wildlife refuge, 2 mile long Luis Peña has hiking paths and secluded beaches. Except weekends, you might enjoy the island's solitude, where you toast the sun going spectacularly over the rocky skerries of **Las Hermanas**, backed by the majestic peaks of the El Yunque rain forest.

264

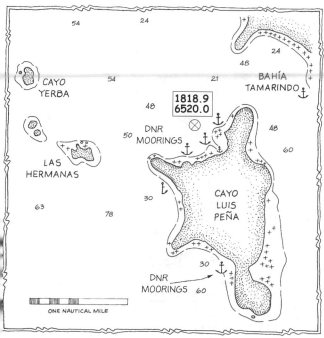

In light conditions, use Luis Peña as a base from which to launch diving expeditions in gofast dinghies. Dive the reefs under Culebra's **Northeast Point** and the offshore keys of **Alcarraza**, **Los Gemelos** and **Piedra Steven**. Las Hermanas and **Cayo Yerba** lie closer to the west.

Culebra National Wildlife Refuge

This sea park protects large seabird colonies and sea turtles. It consists of 23 keys as well as four large tracts of land on Culebra itself. You may explore the islands of Luis Peña and Culebrita only during the hours from sunrise to sunset.

CAYOS LOBO AND LOBITO

Unless you have a large launch, these keys lie too far downwind to safely visit by dinghy from **Luis Peña**. However, under settled east southeasterlies with no northern swell, you may use day anchorages at either key. You'll find both reefs and walls to satisfy snorkelers and scuba buffs. As with most day anchorages, the skipper might want to post an anchor watch aboard while the diving party goes out. Always dive up wind and current of the dinghy, and anchor the dinghy securely.

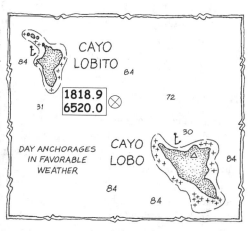

FLAMENCO BEACH

A spectacularly beautiful beach whose anchorage becomes untenable in northerly wind or swell, which often occurs in the winter months. Under favorable conditions Flamenco makes a great sand anchorage until ebb tide when you might find it starts to roll. Plan your trip to go in for lunch on a morning's rise of tide and exit on the ebb in the afternoon. If a northerly swell runs, you can visit by road with your camera. Walk out of town to the airport, then proceed over the hill. You won't regret a stop at **Flamenco Beach**.

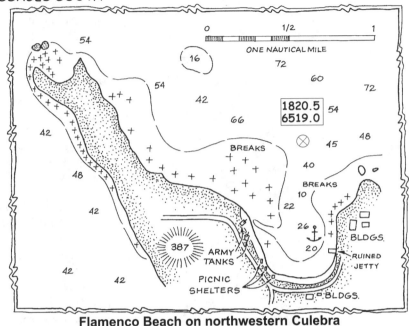

Flamenco Beach on northwestern Culebra

Turtle Watch Program

Playa Resaca and **Playa Brava** on the north coast of Culebra, east of **Flamenco Beach** consist of turtle nesting reserves. The Culebra Leatherback Project conducts nightly beach surveys from April 1 to August 30th. Interested cruisers may participate by previous arrangement with project management.

To participate, call 787-742-0115.

BAHÍA SARDINAS

You can enter **Dewey** at night by **Bahía Sardinas**. Don't sail around these reefy islands in the dark, but sometimes stuff happens. More likely, the skipper failed to read the *Sailing Directions, Vieques Sound*, and missed a sensible departure time. In any case, you got caught out. Now you need a nighttime landfall.

Position yourself one half mile south of the flashing seven second light marking the reefs west and north of the harbor entrance. From there take up a heading of 87° Magnetic on the brightly lit old ferry dock on the south edge of town. Anchor in 12 feet of clear water over white sand to the northwest of the new ferry dock. The ferries stop running after 6 p.m., after which you shall not take their wakes. Conveniently, however, the 7 a.m. ferry shall come by to wake you, should you oversleep. Remember, the above advice notwithstanding, you should never sail these waters at night.

CUSTOMS AND IMMIGRATION

Clear Customs and Immigration from anchorage on the Ensenada Honda side. You'll find them at the airport, a five minute walk from the El Batey restaurant's dinghy dock, a long ell pier west of Cayo Pirata, which lies just north of the stadium that you can see from the water. See the chartlet of Ensenada Honda. Returning from Customs, lunch at El Batey where Digna and Tomás serve the island's best sandwiches with the coldest beer.

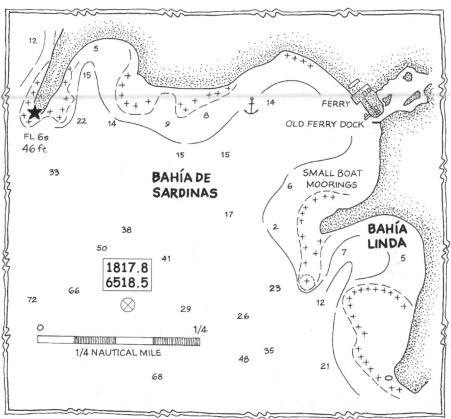

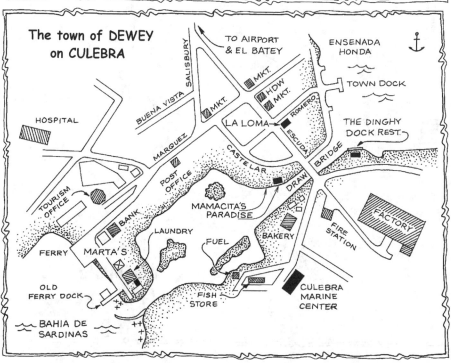

DEWEY

The town offers a variety of restaurants, bars and boutiques with conveniently staggered, if not randomly chosen, opening hours.

Ferries to Fajardo run frequently from **Dewey**, if you want to revisit Fajardo without sailing back. Fresh fruits and vegetables come by truck from the mainland twice a week. The truck parks in front of the Post Office. Otherwise shop at the small grocers.

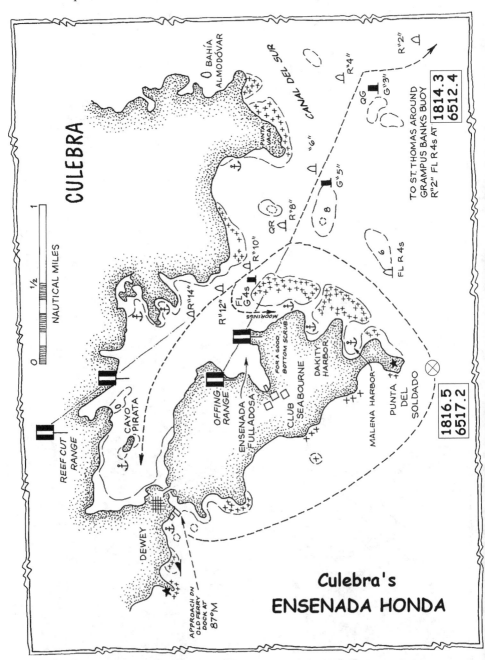

Culebra's
ENSENADA HONDA

ENSENADA HONDA

Green can No. 9 and red buoy No. 10 clearly mark the narrow reef entrance to **Ensenada Honda**. To moor near town and out of traffic, anchor in 16 feet on a bottom of sand and mud west of **Cayo Pirata**.

The finest anchorage within the bay lies behind the reef at **Dakity Harbor** in 2-3 fathoms of clear water over white sand. The DNR has set moorings out for you here. **Malena Harbor**, southwest of there can get tricky. Best leave it to local powerboats. Dinghy around the corner to the happy hour at the **Club Seabourne** pool at the foot of **Fulladosa Bay**. Then stoke some sleep for tomorrow's assault on Culebrita.

WESTBOUND BOATS

Spend your last night anchored in **Dakity Harbor**, perhaps dinghying around to happy hour beside the Club Seabourne pool. Next morning slip your mooring and broad reach down to **Bahía Icacos** on the north shore of Vieques. Only 11 miles, you can time your arrival on this leg to enter Icacos in calm water before the trades start. Or enjoy the day at Dakity and enter Icacos with over-the-shoulder light as usual. But don't miss Vieques.

Proceed to the beautiful anchorages of **Culebrita** and **Almodóvar** via the **Canal del Sur**. The diving from the keys northeast of Culebrita, through Cayo Norte and along **Culebrita Reef** to **Grampus Banks** can absorb active divers for an entire season. Just snorkeling the area and soaking in the Jacuzzi's of Culebrita make a few days' visit well worthwhile.

BAHÍA DE ALMODÓVAR

Round Culebra at **Punta Vaca** into **Canal del Sur**. Enter **Puerto Manglar** heading 325°M on a large wedding cake of a house overlooking the bay. Pass between small red and green markers in three fathoms. Round the double mangrove islet of **Pelaita** through a 10 foot deep channel and between another set of markers. You now sit in **Bahía de Almodóvar**'s deep, still waters. Anchor west of the reef in 2-4 fathoms of white sand and gin clear water. The cooling trades blow over the reef out of a clear horizon, where the lights of St.Thomas come on at night. Locally they call this harbor **La Pelá** or just Manglar. Bahía de Almodóvar and **Dakity Harbor** make the most tranquil anchorages of Culebra.

ISLA CULEBRITA

Within the northern arms of **Culebrita** lies a 400 yard diameter basin with 7 to 25 feet of clear water bordered by white beaches. If you missed Flamenco, don't miss Culebrita. Hike to the seaward pools known locally as "the Jacuzzis". Snorkel the nearby reefs and ledges, or dive the Cayos **Ballena**, **Tiburón** and **Geniquí** a mile to the north. In 20 knots of wind or more heavy seas can set up between Geniquí and Culebrita. Once inside the basin, easterly seas disappear, but occasional heavy northerly swell may penetrate the bay in winter. Overnight here only in settled weather with no northerly swell forecast. DNR has free moorings available. *Inspect the riser for propeller chops before trusting them.*

If conditions don't permit a visit to the northern anchorage, stop on the southwest coast of Culebra. Visit the northern beach afoot by mounting the hill to the old lighthouse. Take a camera. Anchor by the small piers north of **Punta Arenisca** in 16 feet of sand just east of a 72 foot drop-off and surrounded by 4 to 6 foot coral heads. **Culebrita Reef** stretches almost two miles from here to the south southwest. For serious fishing expeditions, shoot out to **Grampus Banks**.

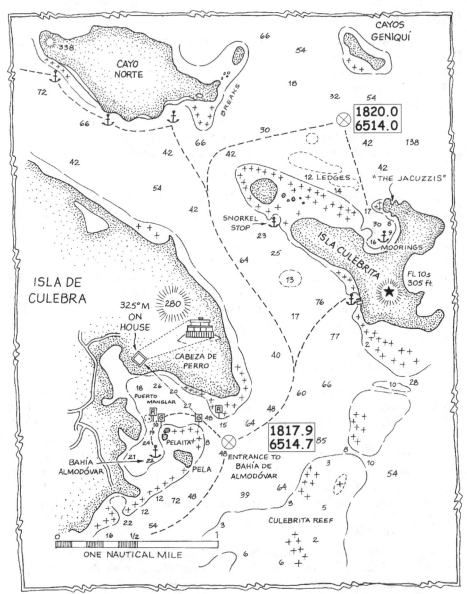

The Canal del Sur, Bahía de Almodóvar and Culebrita

CAYO NORTE

Depending on swell, you can take 2 day anchorages on the southwest shore of **Cayo Norte** for diving expeditions by gofast dinghy.

Anchor on the shelf in 25 feet of sand off rocky ledges with a 72 foot wall to their west. In settled light easterlies, such as one gets in the summer months, you can anchor overnight on the east end of the southern shore of the key in 18 feet of sand, west southwest of the red fisherman's cottage. You shall get sheltered by the breaking reef to the east. The passage between Culebrita and the islet to its northwest makes a great snorkel stop when sailing to or from Cayo Norte, or to stay overnight in **prevailing conditions**.

VIEQUES, FORMER NAVAL RANGE

Many consider these bays, coves and beaches the best of all Virgin Island anchorages. Untouched by developers, they have stayed off limits most of the last hundred years, and they have had little use as anchorages before that.

US and NATO navies have used the east end of Vieques for land, air and sea based war games. The Navy often allows yachts to use the anchorages and beaches when they don't need the test range, or when they haven't got political problems. Both Puerto Rico and the U.S. Government have advanced various plans to close the Range in the not too distant future. Discussions likely shall go forward with some energy as land-grabbing opportunists poke around in the politically charged issues. Don't let the day to day politics deter you from using these lovely and pristine harbors. Especially if Puerto Rican protestors have occupied the range. They know how to party! The following procedures, developed by the Navy in normal times, will no doubt govern its use in the uncertain future.

You may normally visit these anchorages weekends. However, you may go at any time with Navy permission, which you may easily obtain by calling **VIEQUES RANGE CONTROL** on VHF channel 16 and inquire if they have a *hot range*. If no response after repeated tries within VHF range of the observation

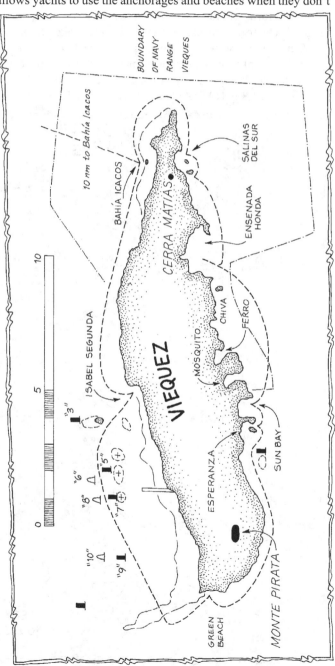

posts on **Cerro Matías** (see chartlet for **Salinas del Sur**), or **Monte Pirata** on the island's west end, consider the range available for your use. If, after diligent but fruitless attempts to contact the Navy, you wander into a closed zone, not to worry, the Navy will graciously let you know in good time. Keep VHF channel 16 on. I think it unrealistic to depend on constant harmony between the Navy's use of its test range, your cruising schedule or your draw of wind and wave on that coast - especially during a Terror War. A good plan would launch a cruise of Vieques from **Culebra**. While enjoying superb *Culebrense* cruising, you can watch for a window of favorable weather and no operations in the Vieques Navy ranges. When that happens, which it shall, you'll take off for a memorable cruise.

When visiting the beaches, do not go inshore. Do not molest any devices found on the beach — certainly not shells made by man! As a service to the yachting community, Puerto del Rey Marina in Fajardo will provide the Navy's weekly Vieques *hot* exercise schedule. Call Puerto del Rey HARBORMASTER on VHF 71, or dial 860-1000 by land line. You

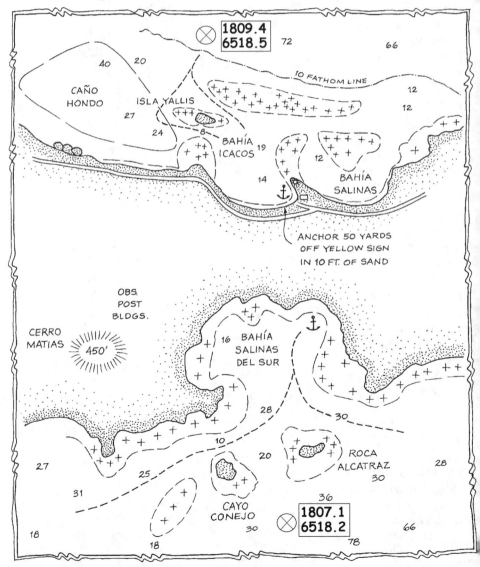

may also call the **Vieques Range Control**'s Fisherman's Notice line, 865-5216.

Recent political moves in Puerto Rico make it probable the Navy shall soon stop its hot fire activities on Vieques, if not remove themselves entirely. After munitions cleanup, perhaps years, you can look forward to rampant development to spoil these beautiful coves more than bombs could.

BAHÍA ICACOS

Ranks of reefs surround the beautifully protected azure bay of **Bahía Icacos**, giving excellent protection for anchoring and snorkeling. Approach from the west with high afternoon light over your shoulder. The narrow gap between the mainland shoals and **Isla Yallis** shelters from swell an eight foot channel on its south side. No clear sand road exists in this channel, however, and you might find it uncomfortable for anything but a shallow draft. The north side of **Yallis** has a 17 foot minimum depth channel between it and the breakers on the seaward reef. **Bahía Salinas**, to the east, hides a lovely secluded beach, but it stands exposed to northerly swells through a gap in the reef. Leave the bay the same route you entered it in the afternoon, but with morning light over your shoulder.

When you circumnavigate Vieques, whether coming from Dakity on Culebra or a lunch stop in **Isabel Segunda**, make your first evening's anchorage in this lovely bay. Then stay the next day to play on the reefs.

SALINAS DEL SUR

Under east to north winds **Bahía Salinas del Sur** protects a calm, beach lined anchorage. Tuck up into the northeast corner behind the reef and select a patch of bare sand in 10 feet of water in which to anchor.

This beach has had more than its share of amphibious assaults, strafings and bombings, but it shall show the most spectacular of all when replanted. If you use the beach, don't go further inland nor pick up man made objects.

ENSENADA HONDA, VIEQUES

Enter **Ensenada Honda**, a wonderfully tranquil and secluded mangrove anchorage, going northwest by north on the first point of land inside the bay. Make your first turn to the northeast at three fathoms toward a baby mangrove off the tip of the third point of land inside the bay. When north of a group of rocks called **Los Galafatos** ("The Thieves"), make your second turn east southeast for the anchorage. See the chartlet for the turns.

Nominally an excellent hurricane hole, you should think twice before relying upon Ensenada Honda. Firstly, a hurricane must cooperate and not blow from the west or southwest. No anchor mooring in the open can withstand SE through W wind from a Category 3 hurricane. However, you might get well up the river at the eastern end of the bay.

If your hurricane cooperates, or if it looks as though you can get deep into the river, you have a second concern. Ensenada Honda lies convenient to the Virgin Islands with its thousands of boats and commercial fleets. It also lies handy to a couple of thousand boats in Fajardo, and more in Palmas del Mar and Roosevelt Roads. You must claim a spot in the river early. So early, in fact, that simple arithmetic shows that for successive threats, you might as well stay there all summer.

The river takes 6 feet, but you must reckon on plowing through mud or winding around some mounds to wiggle well in. Get well round a bend, if you can, to avoid the crush of loose boats in a south blow — so get there first!

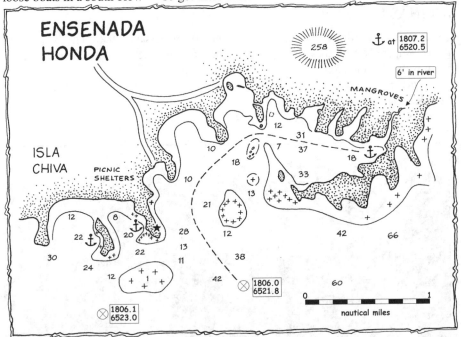

ISLA CHIVA

Isla Chiva, a Navy Rest & Recreation beach with picnic shelters, remains quiet and private at night. Find good holding in fern and fan covered sand. The calmest anchorage lies in 10 feet of water in front of the southernmost picnic shelter, close to the beach, protected by the reef west of the point. On the west side of **Isla Chiva** you have a fine anchorage tight up against its northern end, or, for a lunch or snorkel stop, off the rock crevice at the island's midpoint.

BIOLUMINESCENT BAYS OF VIEQUES

Both Puerto Ferro and Puerto Mosquito are strongly phosphorescent. If you don't overnight at them, you can visit by dinghy from **Sun Bay** or **Esperanza**. You can take night tours from Esperanza arranged through several local dive and tour operators.

PUERTO FERRO

Puerto Ferro, a mangrove anchorage with a narrow entrance has a seven foot controlling depth on the bar. Use a day anchorage outside the bar when the wind blows north of east or less than 15 knots south of east.

PUERTO MOSQUITO

Puerto Mosquito accommodates drafts under five feet, or slightly more at high tide (with infinite patience). Under settled conditions use the day anchorage shown for snorkel trips to the rocks and caves about the harbor's mouth.

To the west of the entrance lies perhaps the loveliest palm lined, white sand, azure water swimming beach in the Caribbean. Nature has already begun to restore it following its ruination by Hurricane Georges.

275

FORMER CIVIL VIEQUES

Initially a redoubt of **Tainos** and Carib Indians from which they could maraud the Spaniards, Vieques became a refuge for all stripes, from army deserters and runaway slaves to the renegade *Portugee*, as they called whites on their own in the Caribbean regardless of nationality. Today the island hosts a fiercely independent and proud population dotted by sometimes dotty expatriates.

SUN BAY

This southern anchorage lies outside the Navy zone and next to the fishing village of **Esperanza**. Enter the middle of the bay headed north, steering clear of the shoal off its southeast arm. Anchor in grassy sand tight against the east southeast shore to avoid roll in strong wind blowing east or south of east. **Sun Bay** public beach stretches more than a mile in length. A bath house sits in the northwest corner of the bay.

ESPERANZA AND PUERTO REAL

Blue Caribe Dive Center maintains moorings at the north end of the anchorage. Pay the fee to use them, if you wish to use this anchorage long. As always, dive moorings to inspect their risers. The bottom has Teflon coated grass in fluffy sand. **Puerto Real, Vieques**, the anchorage northwest of **Cayo Real**, can get rolly, but once dug in, you've got fair holding in sand and coral. Local boats have moorings. Lunch ashore after you visit the small archeological museum west of town. For fresh seafood, see the fishermen when they bring in their catches in the morning, or when they gather at the town pier to pack them off on the ferries later on.

Seas can build up in strong easterlies west of Esperanza on a two fathom shoal. Official charts notwithstanding, only green can No. 1, marks it on its eastern edge.

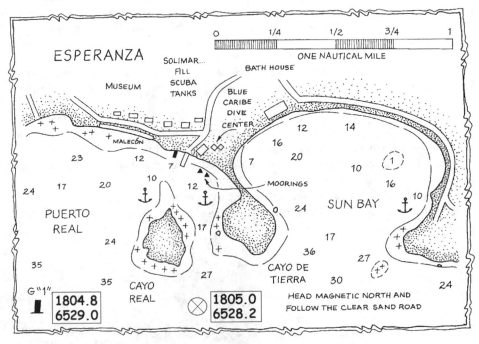

ISABEL SEGUNDA

Arrive at **Isabel Segunda** in the morning in time for a walk up the hill and a visit to the museum and gallery in **El Fortín**. The **Conde de Mirasol** fort protecting the harbor became the last fort constructed by Spain in the New World. Puerto Plata's Forteleza San Felipe has honors as first.

This anchorage can roll viciously. After a seafood lunch in a harborside restaurant, up anchor in time to make your night's anchorage: Bahía Icacos to the east, Punta Arenas or Palominos to the west, all calm anchorages in prevailing winds and easy to make while the sun still rides high and westing. Best to get in with time to spare for fishing, though.

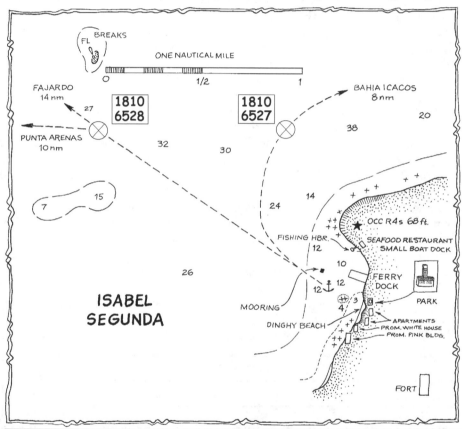

DIVING IN THE SPANISH VIRGINS

One doesn't have to go to the South Pacific to explore extensive coral reefs such as the mile-long formations southeast of **Culebrita**. The Spanish Virgins appear in a submarine photographer's dream.

These lovely keys and islands provide cruising and diving opportunities as good as or better than their Anglophone cousins to the east, but they have the added spice of "going foreign". American tourism has grown recently in this area of Puerto Rico. The islands of **Culebra** and **Vieques** have particularly blossomed as getaways.

Still virgin territory as a diving destination, the Puerto Rico Tourism Company estimates that dive operators have exploited less than 20 per cent of the snorkeling and scuba opportunities in Puerto Rico. A Mecca for the sportfishing enthusiasts for decades, Puerto Rico tourist dive boat operations have developed relatively recently. Significant charter sail operations have only begun.

Narrow shelves of white sand beaches edge the islands by rocky cliffs over coral outcroppings, where snorklers wander and wonder. For the scuba divers, precipitous dropoffs of 12 to 14 fathoms surround most keys, where morning sun brilliantly lights up the windward walls in the morning, and the afternoon sun gilds those of the leeward anchorages.

Lobster season in Puerto Rico, thanks to the crustacean's continuous mating season, runs year round. You must restrict your catches to male adults, or females without eggs, and which have a carapace (antennae base to beginning of tail) of 3.5 inches or more.

The more adventurous divers should focus on **La Cordillera**, the 12 mile long string of islets, keys, reefs and sea mounts which stretch from **Cayo Icacos**, near Cabo San Juan on the mainland, to **Arecife Barriles** west of Culebra. You should use some spectacular snorkeling and diving sites in the Cordillera, as elsewhere in the Spanish Virgins, from day anchorages only. On days too inclement for La Cordillera, consider basing in **Almodóvar** to dive the sites along the Culebrita Channel, from **Cayo Norte** to Culebrita reef itself.

When planning each day's activity, cast a cautious eye at the strengths and directions of wind, wave and swell. At many of the recommended day anchorages, and depending on conditions, you should keep an anchor watch aboard while the diving party goes out. Of course, always snorkel or dive upwind and upcurrent of the dinghy in exposed areas.

DIVE OPERATORS IN PUERTO RICO		
OPERATOR	LOCATION	TELEPHONE
Puerto Rico Diver Supply	Fajardo, Villa Marina	863-4300
Coral Reef Divers	Villa Marina Center	860-REEF
Sea Ventures	Puerto del Rey Marina	863-DIVE
Coral Head Divers	Palmas del Mar	850-7208
Culebra Marine Center	Dewey, canal southside	742-3371
Dive Isla de Culebra	Gene Thomas, Dewey	742-3555
Blue Caribe Dive Center	Esperanza	741-2522
Solimar (tank service)		741-8600
ReefLink Divers	The Dinghy Dock, Dewey	742-0581

SOUTH FROM THE VIRGINS

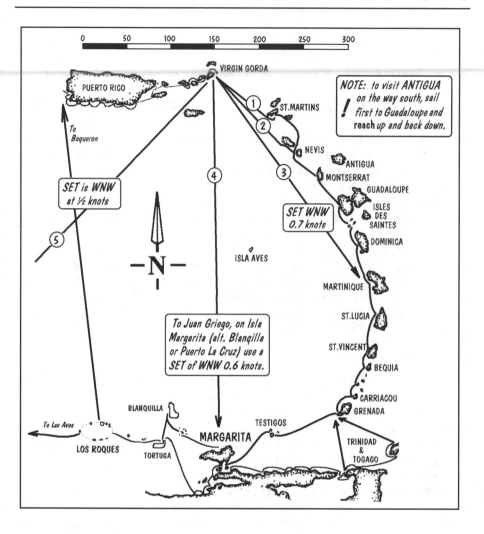

Crossings to South America

[1] hard motorsail to St. Martin from Virgin Gorda   80 nm. minimum
[2] beating to St. Kitts from   Virgin Gorda   120 nm.   "
[3] long tack to Martinique from   Virgin Gorda   300 nm.   "
[4] close reach to Venezuela from   Virgin Gorda   450 nm.   "
[5] broad reach to Bonaire from   Fajardo or St.Thomas   420 nm.   "

When crossing the **Caribbean Sea** from Virgin Gorda south to the **Windward Islands** use 3 quarters of a knot of west northwest going current and reckon on leeway equaling, in degrees, the Force Beaufort encountered.

WHY THE CLOCKWISE ROUTE?

The counterclockwise route takes you to **Tucacas**, Venezuela after a 400 mile jump to **Bonaire**. Clockwise or counterclockwise you have the same amount of windward sailing. You just put it off until northing through the **Windwards** rather than take it up front while southing the **Leewards**. Disadvantages of the counterclockwise route? First, the 400 mile rolly passage relatively early in your cruise, and second, if you decide to continue on to the western Caribbean you must retrace any cruising you do in the Antilles and Venezuela.

In order to get a comfortable, nearly quartering lay on Bonaire, Puerto Rico should lie downwind of you. In that case, you already have the major links of the chain behind you, and the piffling daysails through the **Virgins** lie ahead. Why stop now when the islands you must hop lie only spitting distances apart? Except the jump to **St. Martin**, which you should take in a proper window. Even then you'll never have to leave sight of land since Saba stands out brightly on clear days.

On arriving at the end of the chain, I prefer summer in the Venezuelan gulfs and off-shore islands and coastal summer vacation resorts, then turn to **Trinidad** for winter. After Carnival in Trinidad you may return home via the island chain. Or you may cruise farther afield by heading back to Margarita to stock up, and proceeding from **Puerto La Cruz** to the Dutch Islands via **Los Roques** and **Las Aves**, thence to **Cartegena** and on to Central America, while you do the San Blas Islands and the Honduran Bay Islands, before going up the Rio Dulce in Guatemala for the next hurricane season. Then you continue north behind the world's second longest barrier reef in Belize, along Mexico's Quintana Roo coast, Isla Mujeres and home, whether via the Gulf or the Florida Keys.

STRATEGIES

Easting from the **Mona Passage** to **Bitter End, Virgin Gorda** comes so easy *(if you follow this guide)* that you have no reason to jump off into the Caribbean any earlier. I often meet cruisers in Puerto Rico who, having what they think the devilish part of the trip behind them, have grown hell bent to make South America on a beat across the sea to **Margarita**. They usually fetch Puerto Cabello instead. Take a few more days to get further east, and you shall have a much more comfortable trip south.

Each **Virgin Island** lies only a few hours of lee sailing from another. Even though you shall still beat to windward until you get to **Martinique**, the passages run in long, open-ocean swells instead of the Caribbean's *two step* chop and coastal hazards.

The farther north one makes landfall in the **Leewards**, or the **Windwards**, the better. The best route, even during hurricane season, crosses to St. Martin. You wait in the BVIs until you can make St.Martin in two long tacks or a motor in calms with a long low swell. This give you additional islands to visit with your windward advantage at St.Martin. From there south you island hop again with each new high island appearing over the horizon just as the last one sinks behind. **Saba Rock** in **Virgin Gorda Sound, British Virgin Islands** makes the best jumpoff point for St. Martin.

If I have **St. Kitts** as my windward objective, or **Martinique**, or farther off to **Grenada**, I still jumpoff from **Saba Rock** for the windward advantage. **Spanish Town**, on Virgin Gorda, has a Barclays Bank where one can get one's bankroll with little or no fees before going. The marina at Spanish Town has an easy and friendly checkout crew as well as an easily made fuel dock. You *don't* have all these elsewhere. Virgin Gorda Sound itself makes a pleasant miniature cruising area. Watch the sea in the afternoon from the bar at **Biras Creek**. It reminds me of Scandinavia where I sailed many years.

ENCORE STAGING

Better enjoy the passage through each of the **Leeward Islands** and the **Windward Islands** by *staging* properly. Whether headed north or south, whether you fly your Q flag and just anchor through, or whether you stay weeks at each island, when you want to shove on, *stage* yourself the night before at the last safe anchorage next to the ocean pass you must cross. Next morning you shall have a swift, safe sail and sway to your anchor before the lunchtime squalls and williwaws get you.

CROSSINGS

I have given you detailed sailing directions as far as the **Virgin Islands**. Thereafter I recommend you use the guides *Cruising Guide to the Virgin Islands by* Nancy and Simon Scott, and *all of Chris Doyle's Cruising Guides* for the **Leeward Islands**, the **Windward Islands, Trinidad, Tobago and Barbados** and **Venezuela and Bonaire.** Nonetheless, for your *thornlessness* here as well, I offer you my notes from many personal passages.

After many trials, I've found **Virgin Gorda Sound** the best departure point going east or south, by motoring through the reef to clear the island south of Anegada's Horseshoe Reef. Leave **Bitter End** at 3 p.m. when the sun rides high enough to guide you through the clear cut in the reef which bears 64° Magnetic from **Saba Rock**.

When selecting a route to **Venezuela** don't make the mistake of many I've met who have crossed the Caribbean Sea from Hispaniola or western Puerto Rico. Coasting back east in the night lee along Venezuela does not present a problem, but making a comfortable crossing does. If you don't plan to coast Venezuela, you should know that the **Equatorial Current** offshore runs up to 3 knots against you while its maximum up north runs less than half that. If you *do* end up in **Puerto Cabello** because you tried to sail to Venezuela from a point too far west, then treat the route eastward as though coasting **Puerto Rico**'s south coast. Get some charts and do predawn harbor hops of about 20 miles each from one little harbor to another. That can make a good trip, but you should have planned it that way.

For the entire Eastern Caribbean you need nothing but the **Caribbean Yachting Charts** series verified by Chris Doyle, and his cruising guides for harbor chartlets. The Leeward and Windward Island groups overflow with celebrating charter boats and fly-in tourists. Because of the year-round charter businesses and the transatlantic traffic in the winter months, you have a wealth of good information available on the routes down to Grenada. Select your crossing from **Virgin Gorda** to **St. Martin**, **Margarita** or **Puerto La Cruz**. But when you get to the continental coasts and coastal islands on the other side, always proceed by island and harbor hop.

St. Martin

A straight forward motorsail. Leave Saba Rock at 3 p.m. with good over-the-shoulder light and sail next morning up into **Phillipsburg**. Or, stop at **Pelican Point** in **Simsons Bay**. The **Lagoon** acts as the summer stop of many hard core cruisers, though the number of boats mitigates hurricane security. Condos and marinas thrive in the lagoon. **St. Martin** provides shopping and touring as well as a miniature cruising area of its own. Chandleries line the lagoon, while in Simsons Bay you can dinghy through the lagoon to the French side at **Marigot** for lunch and shopping. Phillipsburg, though fun and relatively cheap to visit, can roll a bit, and it can become a *deathtrap* in southerly winds.

St.Kitts

A pleasant close hauled sail in light easterlies or winds north of east in winter. You haven't got the "Caribbean Two Step" here. You sail into longer Atlantic swells in ocean sailing at its best, assuming you go on light wind days. Wait for weather in **Virgin Gorda Sound**, and leave from **Saba Rock** for a better point of sail. The anchorage at **Basseterre** on **St. Kitts** rolls and has lots of small freighter and ferry traffic. You can also make a stop enroute at little **St. Eustatius** (Statia). After a good night's sleep carry on to **Nevis**, anchoring off the beaches north of Charlestown in sand.

Martinique

For a better point of sail, leave **Virgin Gorda Sound** via **Saba Rock**. The only trouble with this passage, you miss **Guadeloupe** and my favorite anchorages of **Des Haies** and the **Iles desSaîntes**. I like to make landfall at **St. Pierre** in **Martinique** and watch the villagers work their fish nets while I have coffee on deck early in the morning.

Venezuela

Crossing the Caribbean from Virgin Gorda to Puerto La Cruz, use a west northwest set of a half knot door to door. In the summer make sure you have a clear 4 day forecast with no tropical waves or disturbances on the way over from Africa.

Puerto La Cruz makes an easier destination with a rapid close reach under summer conditions. You can try to make **Porlamar** on **Isla Margarita,** but go for **Juan Griego**, on the northwest coast. You can clear in there with a little more trouble than if you went to Porlamar and had Vemasco's help.

ISLAND HOPPING TO SOUTH AMERICA

You'll use Chris Doyle's guides here, of course, but I'll clue you in on my fast path if you need it. I've taken these easy hops many times for rapid transits down island, stopping only at these islands, flying a yellow flag. This route makes a fast but pleasant passage if you don't wish to see more of the islands on the way down. I certainly hope you would go slower on the way back, however.

Stage to the overnight anchorage closest to the pass you wish to hop: the southernmost on the way south, the northernmost on the way north. While hopping the ocean passes of the **Leewards** or the **Windwards**, get underway at daybreak to avoid any midday summer squalls on arrival at your new anchorage. Take an hour or two motoring in calm behind the island, making breakfast on the way. The boat shall stand upright as in a protected anchorage, and breakfasting underway shall give you a couple of more hours to enjoy your next harbor in the afternoon. See *Playing the Island Lees: Channel Effect.*

Take every anchorage and you'll never sail more than a few hours each day. Try to get in by lunchtime or prepare to turn up into the lunchtime squalls coming down the mountains or through the passes as, for example, between **Guadeloupe** and **Iles desSaîntes**.

Gustavia, St. Barts

You'll find it difficult to get a spot in the inner harbor. Temporarily anchor in the deeper water but good holding sand bottom of the outer harbor. **Customs** and **Immigration** may behave quite laid back and relaxed. Look for them but don't strain yourself.

NEVIS

Anchor off the beaches north of **Charlestown**. Dinghy into the beach club there for a drink. If you move on the next day, fly a yellow flag and don't go ashore. If you do go ashore for a drink at Crappy's beach bar, inquire after **Customs** and **Immigration** at the bar (after you order).

MONTSERRAT

Use Chris Parker's Wx net to find out the status of the volcano before going. Pass to windward if ash vents. If no crisis pends, anchor under the hills of the northwest coast, and weep for the ruined beauty of the former gem of the English isles. Fly the "Q" flag and move on at daybreak.

DES HAIES, GUADELOUPE

Des Haies [day HEY], my favorite anchorage in the Leeward Islands. The people and the town delight you in the daytime, and at night you would swear that the scene of the town, as seen from the black mirror calm of your anchorage, got set up by a Broadway stage designer. Fly your "Q" flag and don't expect **Customs** and **Immigration** to fall all over you. In general in the French islands, the officials act courteously and agreeably. They realize they have a tourist economy. They do their best to make your touring pleasant. They usually see you before you see them. Make a modest effort to find them and clear in, but don't pound their tables. If you force them to shuffle your papers, they may insist in the correctness and order of your papers. You must have national documentation in the French islands. You must check in, of course, but better go with the flow. Let them know you've arrived, but don't press them. If you decide to stay awhile and you haven't found the officials in a day or two, go up to the office *during office hours* and have a chat. They've seen you and shall expect your visit.

ANTIGUA

Not my favorite place because of repeated ugly behavior from officials and locals over the years. If you go here from the west, do so by first following the route above to Guadeloupe, then close reach *back up* to **Antigua** [anne-TEE-gah]. Trying to get here in a straight line can murder you, even from Montserrat. Besides, you get to see Guadeloupe twice that way, since you must come back to continue south.

ILES DESSAÎNTES, GUADELOUPE

At **Iles desSaîntes** [eel day SANT] anchor on the north shore of the island one mile west of **Bourg**, sheltered on the east by a large round rock. The **Customs**, or *Le Douane*, often plays hard to find. Dinghy in for a farewell to French cuisine here. Say hello to the *Gendarmes*, but don't get disturbed if they don't care you've come in for one overnight.

ROSEAU, DOMINICA

Landfall in **Dominica** [doh-mee-KNEE-kah] at **Prince Rupert's Bay.** Anchor off the old Coconuts hotel site on the south shore, *not* off Portsmouth on the north shore. Next morning truck on down to the hotel south of **Roseau** [roo-SOH], the capital. You may tie stern-to at the Hotel pier, but you don't have to. You can anchor a boat's length from the shore as the nights go dead calm, and more than a boat's length away it drops off to China. I've found Dominicans [accent on the "ni", pronounced "knee"] among the nicest people in the Leewards or Windwards and the island offers much to see. Leave from **Soufriere**.

St. Pierre, Martinique

See *Virgin Gorda to Martinique*. As you proceed down the island, you shall see lava flows that look like blacktop roads climbing inland from the sea. You sail near the site of **Mt. Pelée** which erupted in 1902, killing between 30 and 40 thousand people and wiping out a bay full of ships along with the capital of the Lesser Antilles. Only one survived. A drunk in the jail. Visit the museum to see the finds from the digs. You clear in here at the bakery.

Fort de France, Martinique

Good, but expensive, yacht chandlers and French cuisine will keep even a hell bent for leather passage maker in the area awhile. **Martinique**, just about the only cruise worthy island between **St. Martin** and **Venezuela** as far as using your boat, has little bays with their little villages and great restaurants. Great diving on the east coast. Try the seafood restaurants at *Bourg du Robert*. Martinique also offers the best girl watching between the Dominican Republic and Trinidad. Hard core cruisers hang out at **Anse Mitan** [aunt's me-TONG], or **Anse des Cocotiers** [aunt's day co-co-tee-AIRH] on the charts. *Stage* to St. Lucia at Grand Anse or **Cul de Sac Marin** (cull-duh-SACK-mah-RAN).

Rodney Bay, St. Lucia

A fabulous marina. Tie up or anchor out, You base here to tour the island.

Marigot Bay, St. Lucia

Stop at this historic and scenic bay for lunch and press on to the **Pitons** well before dark. You can't count on room to anchor overnight here. Although a hurricane hole of sorts, the crush of charter boats and docks in this petite harbor shall sink you in a real storm. Marigot Bay became one of Lord Nelson's hidey holes. The man had a genius for finding harbors where enemies literally at the entrance didn't know they stood before a mess of ships (e.g., Mahón, in Minorca, English Harbor, in Antigua).

Pitons, St. Lucia

A tricky spot in a blow. If you have all chain, you may find yourself with 2 hundred feet of it hanging straight down after casting off next day. The beach boys used to behave quite ugly here, but they seem to have mellowed out and entered an establishmentarian phase of their Rastafarian lives. They expect tips and they do provide a useful service. Bareboat charterers on vacation have determined the size of the tip for us broke cruisers.

Chateau Belaire, St. Vincent

An unspoiled jewel of the island. Anchor forty yards from shore in 20 feet of sand just north of a little river at the north end of the bay, at the end of the line of beach. The kids will give you good service. Send them out for fresh fruits and veggies, but anchor your own boat. Use 2 anchors because of the nighttime swing. Another good anchorage lies under the cliffs with coconut trees just north of the bay.

Bequia, St. Vincent, Grenadines

At Bequia [BECK-wee] all the good shallow spots get taken. Resolve to anchor in forty feet and forget about it. Go for Christmas fun here where you'll find cruisers from Mom and Pop to the maxis returning from the Mediterranean. One party after another.

THE GRENADINES

In the **Grenadines**, one initially has a certain temerity about bearing full sail, given the strength of the **trade wind**. The wind's rock hard steadiness, however, and the fine lees available from the seas, let you carry a full rig. Your boat shall perform as never before. Sailing the passes exhilarates. No need to drop sail in a squall, just turn head to wind and let it rattle awhile, then continue. If you don't head up, however, you could get knocked down between Union and Kick'em Jenny, since squalls can have 50 knot leading edges.

TYRELL BAY, CARRIACOU

While not a great harbor and a little out of the way for passage makers, **Hillsboro** has Customs. The hurricane hole at **Tyrell Bay**, while the best available since you left Puerto Rico, has no room to match the demand on it. You'll find this a pleasant community with a rough boatyard and gringos living ashore and opening and closing restaurants.

ST. GEORGES, GRENADA

Visit the neat little bookstore below the Nutmeg restaurant, across the harbor. Rumor has it that this store hosted a U.S. Army lieutenant while he used their phone to call the Pentagon to patch him into the Navy offshore to tell them to stop shelling him. So much for combined strike force technology. The Navy of course ignored yachties in the harbor when they volunteered use of their shortwave radios because they "weren't secure". By the way, English Grenadians pronounce their country's name greh-NAYE-da.

GRENADA TO THE TESTIGOS

Depart **Grenada** from **St. Georges** or **Prickly Bay** at dusk to make the **Testigos** [test-TEE-gohs] for breakfast. Don't risk a night arrival there. Anchor north of **Isla Langoleta** to the west of **Isla Testigo Grande**. This makes a good spot for a bottom scrub.

On the crossing allow for 1.3 knots of current setting 300° True door to door. Have a full rig up since you shall encounter calms to Force 3 on this passage. You might encounter a belt of squalls 20 miles or so northeast of the Testigos, however. The **Equatorial Current** really rips around here, and this miniature weather system seems to always hang around in the early morning. You'll doubtless have a smooth and uneventful trip.

Columbus named the Testigos (*witnesses*) because they testified to the existence of the Equatorial Current on his fourth voyage. The great navigator, having no knowledge of the Caribbean Sea, proceeded to make his new colony of Santo Domingo in one single tack from there. At the anchorage on Testigo Grande you'll see the houses of five fishing families. Five sons from that island married five of the six daughters born on the island west across. These families make up the only inhabitants of the Testigos. See Benjamín in the first house for information on the Testigos, and for fishing tips.

TESTIGOS TO MARGARITA

Motor from **Testigos** at first light to **Porlamar** [pour-lah-MAR]. Even if you have a fast boat, get going early so you can make your **SG&T** at your destination. Approaching **Isla Margarita** in the dark or in late afternoon, when squalls often strike with restricted visibility, could be a problem due to all the fishing activity around the island. Best you sail overnight and arrive in the morning with good margin and good visibility. Dinghy into the beach bar at Porlamar and let **VEMASCO** clear you in while you suck a cold beer.

TRINIDAD

After several nighttime motorsails along the **Paria** peninsula of Venezuela, don't continue directly into **Port of Spain** harbor. Checking in and out of **Trinidad** may require time and patience. *Stage* yourself down into Trinidad by anchoring in the beautiful little cove of **La Tinta** in **Boca Grande** on the island of **Chacachacare**. Columbus called all the channels which enter into the **Gulf of Paria** *bocas* (*mouths*) because, certain he approached the Japanese offshore islands, and knowing Orientals liked dragons, he thought of them as the several "Mouths of the Dragon".

Next day, the boat all clean and sparkling, the crew all rested, bright eyed and bushy tailed, you can motor over to **Chaguaramas** to clear in.

After the exit hassles, *stage* yourself *out* of Port of Spain by going over to **Scotland Bay** and anchoring on a shelf of sand all the way up the bay.

The way to *do* Trinidad, you must arrive in November just to ensure a slip at the yacht club, or a mooring at the Yachting Association in **Carenage Bay**. The original of the steel band carnivals, Trinidad's **Carnaval** gets going already in December with each band's preparation a strong cause to party. You must understand the jargon of Carnival in order to know how to best enjoy it, and just doing that shall take a month. Trinidadians come from an eclectic melange of races: African, black Hindu from southern India, Chinese and white European. The mix of customs, cuisines and beautiful people provides a tourist smorgasbord. By the time Carnival actually goes live in February, although a huge event, you can sneak off. You've already seen it all -- backstage.

CROSSING BACK

If you insist on crossing the **Caribbean,** do so from **Los Roques** to the **Mona Passage**, or from **Margarita** to the **Spanish Virgins**. Don't pinch the wind to make St.Thomas directly. A fast, comfortable trip to Culebra will leave you only a lee day sail across the sound to St. Thomas.

Use a west northwest average set of one half knot door to door. Crossing over to **Grenada**, you have to motor the coast almost to **Trinidad** so you might as well call in at **Port of Spain** and take the way back through the islands from there.

If you scurried down islands in a rush to get out of the hurricane belt, the trip back up islands gives you a chance visit them properly. Some great flotilla parties come in the holiday season which include all the returnees from the Mediterranean. Try **Bequia** for Christmas and **Petit St.Vincent** for New Year's. If you can't make the New Year's party at Foxy's on **Jost Van Dyke**, that is.

Leave Trinidad from Scotland Bay for an easy sail to **Grenada** in settled trades south of east. Alternatively, beat back up to **Martinique**. In either case, bear in mind the dictum you learned upon approaching Hispaniola (you did learn it, didn't you?) to ease sheets and run across the wind if the seas and wind begin to bite. *Do not* try to beat directly into it. So you arrive a few miles to leeward of Grenada. So what? Tack back up to the big island in its great lee. But don't blow out your sails and risk your hide doing a dumb rhumb just because you programmed it into your GPS!

SPANGLISH FOR CRUISERS

The following method to achieve rapid pidgin Spanish, or *Span-glish* as some call it, means to guide you, *not*, God forbid, provide you with instruction in **Spanish**. It proposes to permit you, if you know nothing about the language, to get things done ashore by employing a pidgin Spanish which you can learn in minutes.

I give you a list of nouns with which you can join necessary modifiers and a verb to form a sentence which you then can phonetically read aloud in American English to a listener who shall understand it as Spanish. Got that?

Cruisers should worry more about pronunciation than spelling or grammar, since many of the people they talk to ashore might barely read or write anyway. Showing written statements may get you a donation faster than comprehension. You need to talk.

You can successfully talk in nouns only, using your hands for verbs, and pointing around to find descriptors of size, location, color and so on.

All the correct grammar in the world doesn't help the perennial yachtie who goes all over town looking for the hardware store (*ferreteria*) by asking for the furry-TARRY-uh instead of the FAIR-ray-tah-REE-ah. After a few days this type usually goes and sulks on his boat, sails out of the country, and tells tales on the SSB how you can't get anything there but unfriendly people.

To accurately name the thing you want you must string together several items from the list of *nouns*. For instance: "motor head bolt". I know most head bolts come as studs, not bolts, but keep it simple. Nothing transliterates.

Talk like an Indian in an old movie: "Ugh! Me need'em motor head bolt". In Latin lingos you put nouns that modify each other in backward sequence with a *de* [day] (meaning "of") between them. A head bolt then: bolt of a head. A motor head: a head of a motor. Thus, your movie Indian might say "Ugh! Me need'em bolt of head of motor." So this becomes: "*Oye! Mi necessita tornillo de cabeza de motor*", [mee nay-say-SEE-tah tore-KNEE-yo day kah-BAY-tsah day moh-TOR]. Look it up in the following pages.

This example has the wrong pronoun and the third person verb, but no matter, they shall clearly understand you when you quickly read the phonetics aloud.

Verbs and modifiers are given later for the intermediate student. Those aspiring to black belts can dabble in pronouns and prepositions after that, ensuring massive miscommunication. For now, let's go in search of a bolt for your motor's head. Remember, you won't learn the King's Spanish, but you shall learn to communicate in need.

NOUNS

The words given below often don't reflect the most "correct" Spanish but you can use them throughout the Latin Caribbean. I show common American usage as opposed to European usage, not surprisingly. American English, after all, differs significantly from British English. For example, the word *mani* [mah-KNEE] for *peanuts* instead of the Castillano *cacahuete* [kah-kah-WAY-taye]. Both have Indian origins but American Latins never heard *cacahuete* in their lives, and it sounds like something nasty.

Other words, like *suiche* [SWEET-chaye] for *switch*, appear because, all other factors equal, the English speaking boater can remember it easier than other nouns for switches. After all, *suiche,* the most commonly used form, reflects real Spanglish.

I spell the words below with "phony-netics". Rather than have the reader learn the Spanish pronunciation or the international semanticist symbology, I mimic the Spanish with written American English as commonly spoken.

A speaker of General American gives a good imitation of American Spanish when just reading aloud the phonetic words below with *strong emphasis* on the capitalized syllables. I use English words when the American pronunciation best simulates the Spanish (e.g., *ace* and *day*). Roll your R's if you can but don't sweat it: some Latins don't either.

I spell the American "A" sound "aye". And "I" I spell "eye". Just read what you see. Spanish speakers usually aspirate their vowels. That means they use lots of breath. In Spanish, "O" is pronounced "Oh!", "A" is pronounced "Ah!" (as in "father"), "I" always sounds like "Eeee...", "E" like "Aye" (as in "say"), and "U" makes an "Oooo..." sound. Thus you will read below *-ah, -aye, -ee, -oh,* and *-oo.* Just say them breathily in English.

When listening to Spanish, take care with "V" and "B". Both sound the same, and each pronounces somewhere between the two. In American Spanish, anyway, versus the Spanish spoken in Europe. The American hispanics will also drop their "S" sounds. The fewer "S" sounds, the less educated the speaker, normally. Kind of like "dese" and "dose" in U.S. immigrant dialects, but it can really buffalo a foreigner when words whose principal sounds need esses and they get spoken entirely free of the esses.

For instance, when the street urchins ask you if you "peek a panich?", they don't want you to peek at a dirty post card, but they want to know if you "(s)peak (S)panish".

Almost all Spanish speakers add a vowel in front of any initial "S" sounds when speaking English, because Spanish does that. And when the waiter adds an "E" and drops the "S", *espagueti* (spaghetti) can come out "up a Getty!" Don't take offense, Mr. Getty.

'Y' when all alone (the word for "and") sounds like "ee" and they call it "*y griega*", or greek wye. Otherwise it becomes a 'J', sounding like Jewel; 'J' (*jota*) pronounces like the 'H' in Hotel; 'G' (*ge*) comes out a guttural 'H', like a throaty "Hey!" with lots of mucus, and 'LL' makes an English 'Y' sound, like in "Yeah!". If your Mom named you Judy Yeltsin, they'll spell it 'Yudy Lleltsin'. Having said all that, try saying these nouns:

acetone	*acetona*	ah-say-TONE-ah
adapter	*adaptador*	ah-DOPT-ah-DOOR
air filter	*filtro de aire*	FEEL-tro day EYE-ray
air vent	*ventil de aire*	vent-EEL day EYE-ray
alternator	*alternador*	all-tern-ah-DOOR
aluminium	*aluminio*	ah-loo-ME-knee-um
amperes	*amperes*	am-PAY-rees
anchor	*ancla*	AN-klah
anchorage	*anclaje*	an-KLAH-hey
avocado	*aguacate*	ah-gwah-KAH-taye
awning	*toldo*	TOLD-oh
back	*posterior*	post-tier-ee-OR
bananas	*guineo*	ee-NAY-oh
band-aid	*curita*	koo-REE-tah
batten	*listón de vela*	lee-STONE day VAYE-lah
battery	*bateria*	bah-taye-REE-ah
beam, boat's	*manga*	MAHN-gah
bearing	*bearing*	BEAR-ring
bilge	*sentina*	sen-TEEN-ah

block	*bloque*	BLOW-kay
block (pulley)	*polea, motón*	poe-LAY-ah, moh-TONE
block & tackle	*tecle*	TAYE-clay
boat	*bote*	BOAT-aye
boathook	*botavara*	BOAT-ah-VAH-rah
bollard	*hierro*	E-AIR-roe
bolt	*tornillo*	tore-KNEE-yoh
boom	*botalón*	BOAT-ah-LONE
bottom paint	*pintura de fondo*	peen-TOO-rah day FONE-dough
bow, boat's	*proa*	PRO-ah
brass	*latón*	lah-TONE
bread	*pan*	PAHN
breakwater	*rompeolas*	rome-pay-OH-las
bronze	*bronce*	BRONE-tsay
bulb	*bombilla*	bom-BEE-yah
buoy	*boya*	BOH-jah
bushing	*bushing*	BOO-shing
butter	*mantequilla*	mahn-taye-KEY-ya
can	*lata*	LAH-tah
case	*caja*	KAH-hah
catalyst	*activador*	act-tee-vah-DOOR
caulking	*calafate*	cal-ah-FAH-taye
caulking putty	*masilla*	mass-SEE-yah
celery	*ápio*	AH-pee-oh
certificate	*certificado*	sair-tee-fee-KAH-dough
chain	*cadena*	kah-DAY-nah
chain plate	*cadenote*	kah-day-NOH-taye
charger	*cargador*	car-gah-DOOR
chart	*carta*	CAR-tah
cheese	*queso*	KAYE-so
circuit	*circuito*	seer-QUEE-toh
clamp	*abrazadera*	ah-bra-sah-DAY-rah
clearance	*despacho*	day-SPAH-cho
cleat	*tojino*	toe-HEE-noh
clutch	*cloche*	KLOH-chaye
come-along	*gato*	GAH-toh
compass	*brújula*	BRU-hu-lah
conch (DR)	*lambí*	lahm-BEE
conch (PR)	*carrucho*	car-ROO-choo
conch (Ven)	*concha*	CONE-cha
connector	*conector*	coh-neck-TOR
copper	*cobre*	KOH-bray
cotter pin	*pasador abierto*	pass-ah-DOOR ah-bee-AIR-toh
coupling	*copling*	KOH-pling
cove	*enseñada*	ain-sane-NAH-dah
crab (DR,Ven)	*cangrejo*	khan-GREY-ho
crab (PR)	*jueyes*	HWAY-jace
crew	*tripulante*	tree-pew-LAHN-tay

cushions	*cojines*	co-HEE-nays
customs	*aduana*	ah-DWAH-nah
damage	*daño*	DAHN-yos
depth	*profundidad*	pro-foon-dee-DAHD
diesel	*gasoil*	gas-OIL
dinghy	*lanchita*	lan-CHEE-tah
dinghy dock	*muellecito*	mwaye-yea-SEE-toh
dock	*muelle*	MWAYE-yea
documentation	*documentación*	dock-oo-main-tah-see-OWN
dolphin fish	*dorado*	doh-RAH-dough
draft	*calado*	kah-LAH-dough
eggs	*huevos*	WAY-vos
electric	*electrico*	aye-LAKE-tree-ko
electrician	*electricista*	aye-lake-tree-SEE-stah
engine	*motor*	mo-TORE
exhaust	*escape*	ace-KAH-pay
eye	*ojo*	OH-ho
eyebolt	*tornillo de ojo*	tor-KNEE-yo day OH-ho
fathometer	*sonda*	SOHN-dah
fees	*derechos*	day-ray-chose
fender	*defensa*	day-FAIN-sah
fiberglass	*fibra de vídrio*	FEE-bra day VEE-dree-oh
fins, swim-	*chapuletas*	chap-oo-LATE-ahs
flag	*bandera*	bahn-DAY-rah
flashlight	*linterna*	leen-TAIR-nah
floor	*suelo*	SWAY-low
fresh water	*agua dulce*	AH-gwah DOOL-say
front	*frente*	FRAIN-taye
funnel	*embudo*	aim-BOO-dough
fuse	*fusible*	foo-SEE-blaye
garbage	*basura*	bah-SOO-rah
gas, natural	*butano*	boo-TAH-no
gasket	*junta*	HOON-tah
gasoline	*gasolina*	gas-oh-LEE-nah
gauge	*medidor*	may-dee-DOOR
generator	*generador*	hey-nay-rah-DOOR
glue	*pegamento*	pay-gah-MAIN-toh
grapefruit	*toronjas*	tore-OWN-hahs
grease	*grasa*	GRAH-sah
grouper	*mero*	MAY-roh
guns	*armas*	ARM-ahs
hammer	*martillo*	mar-TEE-yo
harbor	*puerto*	PWAIR-to
harbormaster	*capitán de puerto*	kah-pee-TAHN day PWAIR-to
hardware store	*ferreteria*	fair-ray-tah-REE-ah
head (motor)	*cabeza*	kah-BAY-tsah
head (toilet)	*inodoro*	een-oh-DOOR-oh
heat	*calor*	kah-LORE

heat exchanger	*enfriador*	ain-free-ah-DOOR
hill	*loma*	LOH-mah
hose	*mangera*	mahn-GAIR-ah
hull	*casco*	KAH-skoh
hurricane	*ciclón,*	see-CLONE,
also....	*hurracán*	oor-roo-KAHN
ice	*hielo*	ee-AYE-loh
impeller	*impeledor*	eem-pay-lay-DOOR
injectors	*inyectores*	een-jake-TORE-ace
insurance	*seguros*	say-GOO-ros
iron	*hierro*	ee-AIR-roh
jack	*gato*	GAH-toh
juice	*jugo*	HOO-goh
kerosene	*kerosina,*	kay-roh-SEE-nah,
also....	*kerosena*	kay-roh-SAY-nah
knot	*nudo*	NOO-dough
l.o.a.	*eslora*	ace-LORE-ah
laundry-place	*lavanderia*	la-VAHN-dah-REE-ah
laundry-clothes	*ropas sucias*	ROPE-ahs SOOj-see-ahs
left	*izquierda*	ees-key-AIR-dah
license	*licéncia*	lee-SANE-see-ah
liferaft/vest	*salvavida*	sal-vah-VEE-dah
lighthouse	*faro*	FAH-roh
light	*luz*	LOOSE
limes	*limónes*	lee-MOAN-ace
line	*linea*	LEE-nay-ah
list	*lista*	LEASE-tah
lockwasher	*arandela de muelle*	ah-rahn-DAY-lah day MWAYE-yea
margarine	*margarina*	mar-har-EE-nah
marmelade	*mermelada*	MAIR-may-LAH-dah
mask, swim-	*alcafondra*	ahl-kah-FOND-rah
mast	*palo, mastil*	PAH-loh, mah-STEEL
mayonnaise	*mayonesa*	my-oh-NAY-sah
meal	*comida*	comb-EE-dah
mechanic	*mecánico*	may-KAHN-ee-Koh
metric	*metrico*	MAY-tree-koh
miles	*millas*	ME-yahs
milk	*leche*	LAYE-chaye
mineral spirits	*thinner*	TEEN-air
mountain	*montaña*	moan-TAHN-yah
mountain range	*cordillera*	core-dee-YAIR-ah
nail	*clavo*	CLAH-voh
nut (hex)	*tuerca*	TWER-kah
oars	*remos*	RAY-mos
oil	*aceite*	ah-say-EE-taye
oranges	*naranjas*	nar-AHN-hahs
outboard	*fuera bordo*	FWAYE-rah BOOR-doh
packing	*empaque*	aim-PAH-kaye

paint	*pintura*	peen-TOO-rah
paintbrush	*brocha*	BROH-chah
parts (spare)	*repuestos*	ray-PWAYE-stohs
peanuts	*maní*	mah-KNEE
pear	*pera*	PAY-rah
pineapple	*piña*	PEE-nyah
pipe	*tubo*	TOO-boh
pistons	*pistones*	pee-STONE-ace
plantains	*plátanos*	PLAH-tah-nos
pliers	*alicates*	ah-lee-KAH-tace
porpoise	*delfín*	dale-FEEN
portside	*babor*	bah-BORE
pressure	*presión*	pray-see-OWN
propane	*propano*	pro-PAH-no
propeller	*hélice*	AYE-lee-say
pump	*bomba*	BOHM-bah
registration	*matriculación*	mah-TREE-koo-Lah-see-OWN
repair	*reparación*	RAYE-pah-RAH-see-OWN
resin	*resina*	ray-SEE-nah
regulator	*reguladór*	ray-goo-lah-DOOR
rigging	*járcia*	HAR-see-ah
right	*derecha*	day-RAY-chah
rings	*aníllos*	ah-KNEE-yos
rope	*soga*	SO-gah
rubber	*goma*	GO-mah
rudder	*oja de timón*	OH-ha day tee-MOAN
rust	*óxido*	OAK-see-dough
sail	*vela*	VAYE-lah
sailboat	*velero*	vaye-LAIR-oh
salt water	*agua salada*	AH-gwah sah-LAH-dah
sailcloth	*tela de vela*	TAYE-lah day VAYE-lah
sandpaper	*papel lija*	pah-PAIL LEE-hah
sauce	*salsa*	SAHL-sah
saw	*serrucho*	say-ROO-cho
screw (bolt)	*perno*	PAIR-noh
screw (machine)	*tornillo máquina*	tore-KNEE-yo MAH-key-nah
screw (wood)	*tornillo madera*	tore-KNEE-yo mah-DAY-rah
screwdriver	*destorneador*	day-STORE-nay- ah-DOOR
scrubbrush	*cepillo*	say-PEE-yo
seacock	llave de toma	YAH-vaye day TOH-mah
seal	*sello*	SAY-yoh
seas	*oleaje*	oh-lay-AH-hey
seasick	*mareado*	mah-ray-AH-dough
shackle	*grillete*	gree-YAYE-taye
shaft	*eje*	AYE-hey
shell	*caracol, concha*	car-ah-COAL, CONE-cha
ship	*barco*	BAR-coh
shower	*ducha*	DOO-chah

showers	*aguaceros*	AH-gwah-SAY-ros
shrimp	*camarones*	kah-mah-ROAN-ace
side	*lado*	LAH-dough
smoke	*humo*	OO-moh
snapper	*chillo*	CHEE-yo
soup	*sopa*	SO-pah
sparkplug	*bujía*	boo-HEE-ah
spring	*espring*	ace-SPRING
stainless	*inoxidable*	een-ox-ee-DAH-blaye
stainless (PR)	*estainles*	ace-STAIN-lace
starboard	*estribor*	ace-tree-BOOR
starter motor	*motor* de arranque	mo-TORE day ah-RAHN-kaye
stay	*soporte de mastil*	so-PORE-taye day mah-STEEL
steel	*acero*	ah-SAY-roh
stern	*popa*	POPE-ah
storm	*tormenta*	tore-MAIN-tah
straight	*derecho*	day-RAY-choh
strainer	*colador*	coal-ah-DOOR
street	*calle*	KAH-yaye
stuffing box	*estopa, prense*	ace-STOW-pah, PRAIN-say
swells	*oleadas*	oh-lay-AH-dahs
switch	*suiche*	SWEET-chaye
swivel	*eslabón*	ace-la-BONE
tank	*tanque*	TANG-kaye
tape	*tape*	TAYE-pee
tax	*impuesto*	eem-PWAYE-stow
telephone call	*llamada*	yah-MAH-dah
temperature	*temperatura*	taim-pair-ah-TOOR-ah
thermostat	*termostato*	tair-moh-STAH-toh
thread (string)	*hilo*	EEL-oh
threads (screw)	*roscas*	ROH-skahs
through-hull	*valvula de casco*	VALVE-you-lah day KAH-skoh
tiller	*timón*	tee-MOAN
time	*tiempo*	tee-AIM-poh
tip	*propina*	pro-PEE-nah
tomato	*tomate*	toh-MAH-taye
tools	*herramientas*	air-rah-mee-AIN-tos
top	*parte arriba*	PART-taye ah-REE-bah
transducer	*cebolla*	say-BOY-yah
transmission	*transmisión*	trahns-me-see-OWN
tropical	*tropical*	troh-Pay-KAHL
tropical storm	*tormenta tropical*	tore-MAIN-tah
tropical wave	*onda tropical*	OWN-dah troh-pay-KAHL
turnbuckle	*torniquete*	tore-knee-KAY-taye
two-stroke oil	*aceite dos tiempo*	ah-say-EE-taye dose tee-AIM-poh
valve	*valvula*	VALVE-you-lah
vanilla	*vanilla*	vah-KNEE-yah
varnish	*barníz*	barn-EES

Vee-belt	*faja, correa*	FAH-hah, core-RAY-ah
vegetables	*vegetales*	vaye-hay-TAHL-ace
volts	*vóltios*	VOLT-ee-os
washer	*arandela*	ah-rahn-DAY-lah
water	*agua*	AH-gwah
watts	*vátios*	VAHT-ee-os
waves	*olas*	OH-las
welding	*soldadura*	sold-ah-DOOR-ah
wheel	*rueda*	roo-AYE-dah
wing nut	*tuerca mariposa*	TWER-kah mar-ee-POSE-ah
wire	*alambre*	ahl-AHM-braye
wood	*madera*	mah-DAY-rah
work	*trabajo*	trah-BAH-ho
wrench	*llave*	YAH-vaye
yacht	*yate*	YAH-taye
zinc	*zinc*	TSINK
zinc annodes	*ánodos*	AH-no-dose

VERBS

To talk movie-Indian Spanish, forget the finer distinctions. Use "need" for both "need" and "want". Use "go" for all of the go's, such as come, walk, ride, fly and so forth. The only pronoun you really need? The English "Me". For everyone else you point a finger. I don't include "being" verbs, an art form in Spanish. Better just to not use them. Or just say *es* [ACE], anywhere you want to have "is", "was", "will be", "were". Use ACE, Ace.

Below find a list of the verbs a *gringo* [GREEN-goh] needing help can use. To use a verb, piece together the words above, in backwards order with lots of *de*'s [DAYs] thrown in, and stick a (3rd person singular) verb on the front. Thus: "BOO-skah tore-KNEE-yo day kah-BAY-tsah day moh-TOR" means, "me look-um for motor head bolt". It works. If you want to talk better Spanish then learn their 24 (mostly irregular) verb forms. The guy behind the counter has become so used to the dumb tricks of *gringos* that he won't blink an eye, but he *will* hand you the bolt. Here are some verbs for the intermediate student:

buy	*compra*	COMB-prah
do, make	*hace*	AH-say
eat	*come*	COMB-aye
find	*consigue*	cone-SEE-gay
go	*va*	VAH
have	*tiene*	tee-AYE-nay
leave	*sale*	SAHL-aye
listen	*oye*	OH-jay
look	*mira*	MEE-rah
look for	*busca*	BOO-skah
need	*necesita*	nay-say-SEE-tah
rent	*renta*	RAIN-tah
repair	*repara*	ray-PAR-ah
sell	*vende*	VAIN-day
sleep	*duerme*	DWAIR-may
talk	*habla*	AH-blah
work	*trabaja*	tra-BAH-hah

NUMBERS

Unlike adjectives, Spanish puts numbers in front of the word they numberfy to make it easy for *gringos*. One *gringo*: *uno gringo*. Two *gringos*: *dos gringos*. And so it goes. Now count to a Zillion *gringos*.

zero	*cero*	SAIR-oh
one	*uno*	OO-noh
two	*dos*	DOSE
three	*tres*	TRACE
four	*cuatro*	QUAH-troh
five	*cinco*	SINK-oh
six	*seís*	SAY-ees
seven	*siete*	see-AYE-taye
eight	*ocho*	OH-cho
nine	*nueve*	NWAYE-vaye
ten	*diéz*	dee-ACE
eleven	*once*	OWN-say
twelve	*doce*	DOSE-say
thirteen	*trece*	TRAY-say
fourteen	*catorce*	kah-TORE-say
fifteen	*quince*	KEEN-say
sixteen	*diéz y seís*	dee-ACE ee SAY-ees
seventeen	*diéz y siete*	dee-ACE ee see-AYE-taye
eighteen	*diéz y ocho*	dee-ACE ee OH-cho
nineteen	*diéz y nueve*	dee-ACE ee NWAYE-vaye
twenty	*veinte*	VAIN-taye
twenty-one	*veinte uno*	VAIN-taye OO-noh etc.
thirty	*treinta*	TRAIN-tah
forty	*cuarenta*	quar-AIN-tah
fifty	*cincuenta*	seen-QUAINT-ah
sixty	*sesenta*	say-SANE-tah
seventy	*setenta*	say-TAIN-tah
eighty	*ochenta*	oh-CHAIN-tah
ninety	*noventa*	no-VAIN-tah
one hundred	*ciénto*	see-AIN
two hundred	*dos cientos*	DOSE see-AIN-tos
thousand	*mil*	MEAL
million	*millón*	me-YONE

For example, 2989: *dos mil novecientos ochenta y nueve*.

You can now say you're looking for two motor headbolts: BOO-skah DOSE tore-KNEE-yo day kah-BAY-tsah day moh-TOR" — and you don't have to go shopping twice to get them!

Linguists always come up to me to complain that I corrupt readers with my pidgin Spanish. If you want to learn Spanish, go to it for real. But if you want to kick start in emergencies, just put together a sentence from these tables, write the phony-netics, and go read it to someone. Hey! You just spoke Spanish without knowing it!

MODIFIERS

If you must modify a noun, do so by putting the modifiers in backwards order but without all the *de* [DAY] stuff you put between the nouns when you strung them together. Thus "two big black motor head bolts" makes "two bolts of head of motor black big" or,

BOO-skah DOSE tore-KNEE-yo day kah-BAY-tsah
day moh-TOR GRAHN-day NAYE-grow.

And just like in English, let everyone guess if it's the motor or the bolts which the adjectives "big and black" apply to, or do you mean some combination of both?

COLORS

black	*negro*	NAYE-grow
blue	*azul*	ah-TSOOL
brown	*marron*	mar-ROAN
green	*verde*	VAIR-day
grey	*gris*	GREASE
orange	*naranjo*	nah-RAHN-hoh
pink	*rosado*	rosa-AH-dough
red	*rojo*	ROH-hoh
white	*blanco*	BLANK-oh
yellow	*amarillo*	ah-mah-REE-yo

ADJECTIVES AND ADVERBS

big	*grande*	GRAHN-day
broken	*roto*	ROH-toh
cheap (thing)	*barato*	bah-RAH-toh
clean	*limpio*	LEEM-pee-oh
closed	*cerrado*	say-RAH-dough
cold	*frio*	FREE-oh
deep	*hondo*	OWN-dough
different	*diferente*	dee-faye-RAIN-taye
dirty	*sucio*	SOO-see-oh
down	*abajo*	ah-BAH-ho
dry	*seco*	SAY-koh
electrical	*eléctrico*	aye-LAKE-tree-ko
expensive	*caro*	CAR-roh
fast	*rápido*	RAH-pee-dough
fine	*fino*	FEE-noh
fixed-repaired	*reparado*	ray-pah-RAH-dough
fixed-unmoving	*fijo*	FEE-hoh
galvanized	*galvanizado*	gal-van-ee-SAH-dough
heated	*calentado*	kah-lain-TAH-dough
heavy	*pesado*	pay-SAH-dough
high	*alto*	AHL-toh
hot	*caliente*	kah-lee-AIN-taye
less	*menos*	MAY-nose

light	*ligero*	lee-HAIR-oh
little	*no mucho*	NO MOO-cho
long	*largo*	LAHR-go
loose	*flojo*	FLOW-ho
low	*bajo*	BAH-ho
more	*mas*	MAS
open	*abierto*	ah-bee-AIR-toh
portside	*babor*	bah-BOOR
same	*mismo*	MEESE-moh
self-tapping	*autorroscante*	ow-toe-ros-KAHN-taye
shallow	*bajita*	bah-HEE-tah
slow	*despacio*	day-SPAH-see-oh
small	*pequeño*	pay-CAIN-yo
thick	*grueso*	grew-ACE-oh
thin	*delgado*	dell-GAH-dough
tight	*apretado*	ah-pray-TAH-dough
up	*arriba*	ah-REE-bah
wet	*mojado*	moh-HAH-dough
wide	*hancho*	AHN-cho

PAST AND FUTURE

Movie Indians conjugate their verbs by modifying them with a word like "yesterday". Thus "Me need'um head bolt yesterday. Today need'um band-aid". So, say anything you want in present tense and add from the following list:

today	*hoy*	OY
tomorrow	*mañana*	mah-NYAH-nah
yesterday	*ayer*	ah-JAIR
last night	*anoche*	ah-NO-chaye
day before yesterday	*ante* ayer	auntie ah-JAIR
...days ago	*hace.....dias*	AH-say.....DEE-ahs
...weeks ago	*hace.....semanas*	" ...say-MAH-nahs
...months ago	*hace.....meses*	" ...MACE-ace
...years ago	*hace....años*	" ...AHN-yos
next week	*próxima semana*	PROHKS-ee-mah say-MAH-nah
next month	*próximo més*	PROHKS-ee-moh MACE
next year	*próximo año*	PROHKS-ee-moh AHN-yo

PREPOSITIONS

The condiments the advanced students will sprinkle onto their crude sentences in order to throw the hearer off the track. Proper use requires years of practice.

after	*después* de	days-PWACE day
before	*antes* de	AHNT-ace day
between	*entre*	AIN-tray
by	*por*	PORE
to	*á*	AH

for	*para*	PAH-rah
from	*de*	DAY
in	*en*	AIN
inside	*dentro de*	DAIN-troh day
of	*de*	DAY
on	*en*	AIN
under	*abajo de*	ah-BAH-ho day
with	*con*	CONE
without	*sin*	SEEN

PRONOUNS

Finally, for the black belters, peppering a fancy construction with pronouns will ensure confusion but impress the dickens out of fellow yachties. Advanced students use pronouns as tools with which to make clear that which they had best leave vague. When instead of a big, black head bolt for your motor, the guy behind the counter hands you two tickets to the cock fights, as a real black belt student you say, *grácias*, and thread your way through the throng of thunderstruck fellow boaters with a satisfied grin and just the hint of a swagger. You can get the headbolts tomorrow; today go to the cockfights.

Once again, this short list of pronouns only enables you to rapidly employ a pidgin tongue by reading gibberish that comes out Spanish, *not* to speak properly.

Now you can say "ME look'um for 2 big black motor head bolts FROM THEM TOMORROW". Or,

> ME BOO-skah DOSE tore-KNEE-yo day kah-BAY-tsah day moh-TOR
> GRAHN-day NAYE-grow DAY AYE-yos mah-NYAH-nah.

I	*yo*	yoh
you	*tu*	TOO
he	*él*	AYEL
she	*ella*	AYE-ya
it	*lo*	LOW
we	*nosotros*	no-SO-tros
you all	*ustedes*	oo-STAID-ace
they, them	*ellos*	AYE-yos
this	*esto*	ACE-to
that	*eso*	ACE-oh
each	*cada*	KAH-dah
which	*cual*	QUAL
something	*algo*	AHL-go
nothing	*nada*	NAH-dah
other, another	*otro*	OH-troh
any, -thing, -body	*cualquier*	qual-key-AIR
all, everybody -thing, -one	*todo*	TOE-dough
none, nobody, no one	*ninguno*	neen-GOO-noh
some, -body, -one	*alguién*	ahl-kee-AIN

QUESTIONS

Questions best get asked as statements with lots of body language, helpless expressions and the voice turned up in pitch toward the end, even panicky, as in
DOAN-day me BOAT-aye?!

for "Where's my boat?!" A very important question if you can't find it.

You can also make up a declarative sentence as shown above and slap any one of the following words on the front to have a neat question to go to town with:

how	cómo	KO-moh
how much	cuánto	QUAN-toh
when	cuándo	QUAN-dough
where	dónde	DOAN-day
who	quién	key-AIN
why	porqué	pore-KAY

But beware of asking why or how. You may get a torrent of rapid Spanish. Also, beware to phrase your questions bluntly in movie-Indian talk. For instance, "I wonder if you could tell me where I might find oil pressure transducers for sale?" becomes "Where sell oil pressure transducers?" or:
DOAN-day VAIN-day say-BOY-yah day pray-see-OWN day ah-say-EE-taye?

— accompanied by a lot of shrugs and wiggling of the eyebrows. Other questions are:

What is that?	Que es eso?	KAY ACE ACE-oh
What's it/he/she called?	Como se llama?	KO-moh say YAH-mah?
What time is it?	Que hora es?	KAY OR-ah ACE?
At what time?	A que hora?	AH KAY OR-ah?
How far?	Qué lejos?	KAY LAY-hos?
Where is it/he/she?	Dónde está?	DOAN-day ace-TAH?
What's it cost?	Cuánto cuesta?	QUAN-toh KWAYE-stah?
How do I get to ...?	Cómo llegaré a ...?	KO-moh yaye-gar-RAY ah ...?
Can you help me?	Puede ayudarme?	PWAY-day ah-you-DAHR-may?
How do you say...?	Cómo se dice..?	KO-moh say DEE-say...?
What do you mean?	Qué quiere decir?	KAY key-AIR-aye day-SEER?
What does it mean?	Qué quiere decir?	KAY key-AIR-aye day-SEER?

Now try it out! Paste together a sentence to take to town, and try it out. Tomorrow hazard a question. The next day an answer. See? Only 3 days and you can converse.

NEAT STUFF

WHEN YOU CAN'T GET FORECASTS

STORM STRENGTH AND DIRECTION

If caught out without radio reception, or you just plain want to check on the old **NWS**, you may consider playing with the following rules to guess at the bearing, strength, direction and arrival time of a storm or hurricane.

Appearance of a long swell, mean period of 2 to 5 per minute
(normal is 10-15 per minute)
With a clockwise change in swell direction, the storm shall pass you from left to right
With an anti-clockwise change in swell direction, it shall pass you right to left
Swells travel from 2 to 3 times faster than the storm travels
To find the velocity of the swell in knots, take 60% of the ratio of the crest-to-crest length of the swell, in feet, to the swell's period expressed in seconds

$$\frac{0.6 \times \text{Length}}{\text{Period}}$$

Swell height reduces by one third for every **L** miles traveled, where **L** stands for the crest to crest length of the swell in feet, or:
Observed Height = 67% of the Height **L** miles away.

To find the center of the storm add 115° to the present wind direction.

Didn't I tell you? **Neat Stuff**, *right*? Now what do you do if you believed the drunks at the bar and actually went to sea to ride out a hurricane? Besides slit your throat, I mean. Well, you should handle direction changes in the sustained wind as follows:

If the wind *veers* you stand in the dangerous semicircle:
you should *put the wind on the starboard bow*
If the wind *backs* you stand in the navigable semicircle:
you should *put the wind on the starboard quarter*
If a steady but *increasing* wind, you stand in the path:
you should *put the wind aft of the starboard quarter* and pass out prayer books.

STORM PATH

It is possible to make a fairly accurate guess as to storm path knowing its present bearing, its bearing at the time it created the observed swell and the velocity of the swell.

For example, at 1200 you observe a swell from the south and you estimate the swell as 200 yards long at 4 per minute. (200 yards = 600 feet.) This means swell velocity of 0.6x600/15=24 knots. Therefore, the storm moves about 10 knots, or one half to one third as fast as the swell. If you also observe an east wind while the swell came from the south, then you know the storm lies along a bearing of 90°+115°, or 205° from your position.

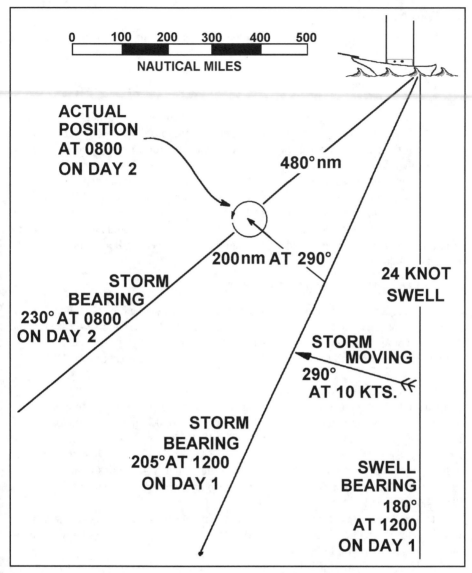

0 100 200 300 400 500

NAUTICAL MILES

ACTUAL
POSITION
AT 0800
ON DAY 2

480° nm

200 nm AT 290°

STORM
BEARING
230° AT 0800
ON DAY 2

24 KNOT
SWELL

STORM
MOVING
290°
AT 10 KTS.

STORM
BEARING
205° AT 1200
ON DAY 1

SWELL
BEARING
180°
AT 1200
ON DAY 1

Storm Location, Track and Severity

Refer to the figure for the following discussion. Lay off a swell vector of 24 knots with its head on your present position. Lay off the storm's bearing of 205°. Make a storm track vector of 10 knots with its head on a line of the storm's bearing. "Slide" the storm track vector's head on the storm's bearing until you can connect the tail with the tail of the swell vector. Adjust vector and bearing until you get a fit. You now have a guess at the current heading of the storm, and you have an idea as to its bearing and velocity at 1200. In the example, the swell is moving 360° at 24 knots. Therefore, the storm, which moves at 10 knots, must move in a direction of 290°.

STORM SEVERITY

What can you guess about the storm's intensity? Let's say the swell you observe has a mean height of about 10 feet. Since the swell has a 600 foot length, you know that 600 nautical miles down the swell's bearing the swell had reached to 15 feet, or half again higher than now, having lost one third of its height enroute. If, indeed, the swell traveled that far.

The force of the storm can be estimated by projecting the swell height back to its incidence. You interpolate the original swell height at various distances off for the storm, then look at the **Beaufort Windscale** to arrive at various storm forces for each assumed distance off.

For instance, if you assume the tails of the swell and storm vectors connect at a point 400 miles away then the original size of the swells, roughly speaking, would have to have been higher than they are now by 4/6ths of the 600 mile loss of 5 feet.

Or, 10+(15-10)x(400/600)=13.3 feet. You will see the storm would have to have had a sustained strength of Force 7, and that would have happened 17 hours ago (400 miles divided by 24 knots).

LOCATING THE STORM CENTER

Reckon the actual location of the storm through combining the results of two observations. Let's say that next day at 0800, 20 hours after the first observation, you see that the swell now comes from somewhere between 200° and 210° and the wind has veered two points (22.5°) to between 110° and 115°. This makes the storm's present bearing 115°+115°, or 230°.

Since you think the storm travelled 290° at 10 knots you also know it covered 200 nautical miles during those 20 hours (Distance = Velocity x Time). Only one spot on your chart exists where your dividers, spaced on the scale to 200 miles and set along a 290 degree line, will rest their points on the 205 and 230 degree lines radiating from your position. One point where the storm lies now, at 230°, and the other at where the storm lay 20 hours ago, at 205°. You now know the storm lies roughly 480 miles to the southwest traveling at 10 knots toward the west northwest and blowing Force 7 because it produces 10+5x480/600, or 14 foot waves.

Whatever **Force Beaufort** you estimate, remember that gusts in a severe storm can blow 30% to 50% higher than the sustained winds. That means that even a baby 'cane (64 knots) can have gusts up to 96 knots.

If all the above discussion ruins your complacency, good! You shouldn't have any!

WHAT TO WATCH FOR

Squall lines and cumulonimbus may sweep your area. These and their high altitude cirrocumulus forerunners called feeder bands, sometimes run hundreds of miles in length, spiraling into the storm's center. If you lie directly in the storm's path, you won't mistake its approach. The *bar* heralds the onslaught of the center of a major storm, or hurricane. It shows as a long, low, intensely black area topped by dark and chaotic cumulonimbus and with torn patches of black stratocumulus scudding in front. Prepare for the wind to gradually double in strength. If in the calm of the eye, prepare for the winds to strike from the opposite direction with sudden maximum force within a half hour. The eye "wall" shows up frighteningly apparent in its approach.

You can buy from a plethora of pamphlets, books, fish identi-kits and even dowsing tools at any gas dock or bait and tackle shop. You'll find useful and serious information in a good marine bookstore such as *Bluewater Books & Charts* in Fort Lauderdale (1-800-942-2583). In keeping with the rest of *Passages South*, I will only give you here information which strikes me unique to the hard core cruiser and generally unavailable elsewhere.

My good friend and fishing mentor, Bob Cockerham of *Moon Lady*, now *Jazmyn*, has long experience fishing in the southern Bahamas. Some of his rules:

First you have to decide if you shall fish for fun or to feed yourself — hunger catches more fish than diversion.

You can't catch fish without a hook in the water. "Hook time" catches more fish than fancy lures or luck ever did.

Don't listen to the crybabies who complain someone has fished out the whole world — the fish swim where you find them.

SKIN DIVING

You should view fishing underwater as primarily a hunting expedition. To hunt, you have to take time. You have to watch the fish and learn their habits. You have to let them get used to your presence. If you missed a shot and spooked the fish, give them time to get unspooked. All that adds up to time with you in the water just like hook fishing requires lots of time with the hook in the water. Wear a wet suit, even in the summer.

Some fish have extremely tough skins, hard to penetrate with a spear. Before starting out make sure your spear tips get freshly sharpened. Coral rock shall dull even your stainless points. Use a sharpening stone to shape a triangular point. Always the same triangle.

Sharpening Spear Points

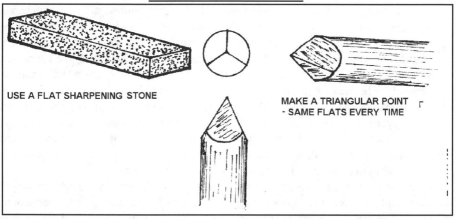

USE A FLAT SHARPENING STONE

MAKE A TRIANGULAR POINT
- SAME FLATS EVERY TIME

Good tasting fish like grouper and snapper usually hide under something. Sometimes you can spear them through a hole above, like a skylight to their living room. More often than not you have to get them through a side door down near the bottom. If they run into one door expect them to leave from another. If they go around a rock, creep over the top and be prepared to shoot down on them. With time in the water you shall observe and learn their habits, and you can anticipate their responses to your shots.

Only with many shots can you become good at it, so shoot lots. If you can't get that fat grouper you've been chasing and you feel close to hypothermia, shoot a couple of small grunts or a trusting trigger fish. You should always come home with bait at least. If you just began spear fishing it shall surprise you to learn that you need to get quite close to the fish to hit it. The tip of your spear should generally get no farther than two feet from your prey. Even closer for a pole spear or a Hawaiian Sling.

For coral fungus that won't heal, try monosodium glutamate (MSG).

As a boy I ran away to Cuba. When I slunk back I could only show a sore foot as my reward. I'd scraped the top of it on some coral. Working through highschool as a bellhop, I could never go barefoot to dry it out. For 3 years I paid dermotologists and slept with bags of gentian violet and other muck on my foot. And the wound leaked sticky, smelly lymph for 3 years. Surprising I didn't grow up a serial killer. My mom's boyfriend, a professional diver, suggested MSG. I sprinkled some on, and 5 days later I had a new foot. And a lifetime of healthy distrust of medical doctors began.

For lobster, conch and whelk, swim low along the undercut shore ledges at the time of day when the sunlight slants in under the ledge and lights it all up. For lobster around rocks and coral heads, swim around the pile with your cheek on the sand, looking into every crevice and hole. Wear gloves to protect yourself against skin reactions to various corals when you pull yourself along by grasping rocks.

The good eating, such as grouper, snapper and lobster, doesn't always swim around coral heads, rocks and ledges. Often enough you can see sizable grouper playing 'possum in the branches of a bush while lobster are hidden in the roots. When all the jocks go roaring off in their Zodiac Grand Raids to dive the forty feet on the windward side because the harbor got "all fished out", leisurely peruse your own anchorage and get ready for surprises. No one fishes the anchorages, and yet they seem just the places where fish thrive due to the edible debris falling from the boats above. This assumes a clean anchorage with good flow, of course.

Take a catch immediately to the surface. Hold the thrashing animal still with both hands, or hold it above the surface of the water, until it safely lies in the dinghy which you always keep nearby. Shark and barracuda get unjustly blamed for mythical mayhem to swimmers. Yet you cannot hold them responsible for instinctual behavior. Especially the barracuda. The barracuda in the Bahamas and on the reefs of the Caribbean acts as a territorial garbage collector. He owns the reef and when something dies and goes through the vibrations of extremis, the barracuda has the task of darting in and cleaning it up. You can get away with letting your dying catch slide down the spear and rest against your fist and never have an incident. But with low luck your catch shall someday meet with a set of flying teeth which may, wholly unintended, carry away a few knuckles. Let the fish trail away from you until it's clear of the water. And, of course, wear no shiny objects.

A pleasant way to fish a reef and ensure that you have the dinghy always handy, just have the dinghy painter in hand or tow it around with the anchor and chain looped around one arm. When you see something interesting plant the anchor noiselessly and pursue your pleasure.To fish the seaward reefs this way as, for example, at Rum Cay, wait for slack low tide plus one hour. Then ride the tide back into harbor with dinghy in hand. The reef community shall all come to meet the incoming nutrients from Mother Ocean with their mouths agape, and won't they get surprised by you and your spear instead.

For cracked lips, try Preparation-H . . . but keep two separate tubes on hand!

TROLLING

When you have fed all your expensive lures to the lure monster, try making your own for free. The corner of a plastic garbage bag with appropriate slits can make an excellent squid, or skirt. So do small translucent tubes of shampoo or whatever. Do you remember how to make those little yarn dolls that you hung on the Christmas tree as a kid? Make one out of the yarns from an old piece of nylon 3-strand rope. Wind the head of the doll around a 3 ounce oval lead and leave off the arms. Let the hook just shimmer below the skirt.

You don't need fancy equipment. The Cuban reels (plastic doughnuts, or yo-yos) work great. Instead of a drag to alarm you to a bite, or more likely, seaweed, put a bight of the line through a clothespin spring and then around the clothespin. Then clamp the clothespin to a lifeline with a couple of yards of slack line behind it.

Use stainless clamps to fix an old reel to the pushpit. Surprisingly, I have got 10 years of maintenance-free operation out of an old reel exposed continuously to salt and sun.

Use 80 to 100 or more pounds test line. Have lots of large swivels and use lots of heavy stainless leader and big hooks. Run a line on each side of the boat. Four, if you like. Two short and skipping, two long and deep. Don't make sharp turns with the boat, though.

Now tend those lines. Keep them free of seaweed — a frustrating and monotonous task. People who complain they never catch any fish usually wait until they sail in open sea before they put out a single puny line. Then they tow seaweed around and reel it in when they first sight their landfall. Keep your hooks sharp and rust free.

Have your lines (plural) out while going through cuts or entering and leaving harbors. If you get a strike while going through a cut, ignore it, of course, and tend to your boat first. When you do reel in your catch it may have drowned, saving you the trouble of dispatching it. Tending lines first and boat second caused the death of a Newporter Ketch in **Conch Cay Cut** at **Georgetown** one year.

FISHING THE SHOALS AND HEADS

Many places you can dip your lure right into fish living rooms. For example, between **Black Rocks** and **Forbes Hill,** trail a line for grouper and wigwag your way around the shoals, dipping the lure onto them. To dip your lures onto heads and shoals have about eighty yards of line out. Maneuver the boat, or use the wind, to get the lure over your target. Now put slack in the line by turning upwind or, for sailboats, by putting the helm hard over in both directions several times to lose way. When the line drops almost to the bottom, fill sail or thrust throttle and run away with the lure.

Crossing the banks from Georgetown to Salt Pond, the blue trench along the sandy bar east of White Cay has good trolling. Also, traveling the bar keeps you clear of the sand bores to the north. When you leave the banks headed north and you come into blue water making for **Calabash Bay**, trail and dip your lures over the deep heads a mile southwest of Calabash before turning through the reef for the night.

BOTTOM FISHING

Save the carcass for bait after cleaning your fish. Save the heads for making soup. Swap your lure leader for a leader with bare hook and bury it in a fist size, or larger, hunk of bait. Before your second **SG&T**, walk to the bow with the baited line. Using large coils, hold a good boat length of line in one hand and, with the other, swing the baited hook in wide circles. Let go of the whole mess and the wind should bring it back to a boat length off your beam where the bait shall rest on the bottom.

Sometime between your second SG&T and four in the morning your drag will go off like a siren. Nocturnal types, like grouper and snapper come out at this time to graze the anchorage. Sometimes you'll get a shark, but more often a good eating bottom fish.

A GOOD FINISH

I lost many fish trying to board them until I began to stun the fish with rum. Now I use my aftershave lotion, a squirt bottle of **alcohol**. If you still use the perfumed kind of aftershave, you can invest in a water pistol filled with alcohol. You shall need lots, so buy lots when the drugstores have sales. Squirt a goodly shot into the gills. This shall immediately stun the fish. Hit the other gill while he's out to ensure he stays out. Now board the fish without drama.

For a humane and healthy way to sacrifice the fish, perhaps even a kosher way, you must dump all its blood, a vehicle for toxins, at one gush at the same time you sever its spinal column. If you don't use an axe, you'll have to have a sharp, large Bowie type knife. Insert the knife downward in the soft spot behind the dorsal edge of the gill, cutting edge up, and give it a good hard karate chop. Do the other side. The spinal cord shall part and the blood dump, all while the animal lies out cold and still. Decapitate, slice from anus to throat, scoop out the guts, chop off the tail and fillet with a good boning knife. The head on bull dolphins has much meat, as do the jaws on a grouper. Keep the cat busy with the scraps, and bag remnants for bottom fishing bait.

I once had a girlfriend from Florida, a class fisherman, too (fisher-woman?). Anyway, she threw bonito away, called it a garbage fish, as I've since heard others do. Nonsense. Bonito can serve up like the finest albacore. All tuna and bonito, or other oily fish, should get poached, or par-boiled, in water until the flesh turns white and the oils come out. It also makes the meat a little firmer for you to more easily sauté or fry it. Lots tastier, too. And if you catch too much tuna, make a vinegary tuna salad. It keeps forever.

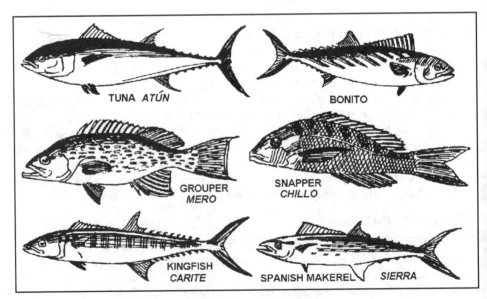

Good Eating Fish

WHAT TO DO WITH PLANTAINS

Anything you would do with a potato. But plantains don't taste for those of us not raised on them. Here's how to make them taste.

For the simplest method just wait until they turn yellow. They then taste slightly banana flavored. Let them get black spots and they taste like bananas. Let them turn black entirely and they *become* bananas, but not rotten. Think of it this way: bananas mature (or rot) from the inside out while plantains mature from the outside in.

To make excellent French fries, use a yellow plantain. If slicing disks instead of match sticks, slice thinner for more taste. Douse with good old salt and ketchup.

To make *tostones* [toast-TONE-ace] slice up a plantain, or *platanos* [PLAH-tah-nose] in Spanish. Spread the slices into real hot grease, seasoned with garlic, salt and hot pepper if you like. Turn them over and squash them with a spoon when they get half done. Blot on paper and serve hot or cold with a dip or doused in ketchup, but always with ice cold beer.

Again, use more mature plantains for more sweetness and slice them thinner for more taste. Foreigners living in the Dominican Republic learn to like their plantains, and therefore they call them "plantainized", or *platanisado* [plah-tah-knee-SAH-doh].

NEAT RECIPES

LECHOSA BATIDA [PAPAYA MILKSHAKE]

Put in a blender:

2 cups cubed fruit	[16 oz]
2 tablespoons sugar	[1 oz]
quarter cup evaporated milk	[2 oz]
1 teaspoon vanilla	

and blend until smooth.

Dump in 2 cups chopped ice and blend *twice as long* as you think necessary to make it thick, smooth and ice-free.

You may use any other fruit or melon. Zapote, the brown football shaped melon, tastes just like strawberry. Pineapple (*piña*) or banana (*guineo*) also taste delicious.

You may substitute condensed milk for both the evaporated milk and sugar, or you may substitute milk powder for the evaporated milk. You can leave out the sugar.

You may think a fruit *batida* thicker and better tasting than any ice cream milkshake.

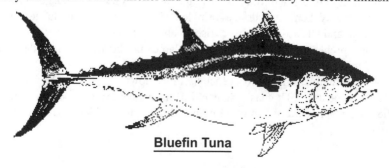

Bluefin Tuna

Black Bean Soup

For 12 ounces of dried black beans, or "turtle beans", use
   4 ounces ham bone,
   quarter cup olive oil,
   half cup wine vinegar,
   half a large onion,
   2 green peppers,
   1 crushed pod of garlic,
   1 bay leaf,
   1 quart of water,
   1/2 tablespoon salt.

Clean the beans and soak them overnight. Add all the ingredients but oil and vinegar
   and simmer covered for 3 hours, stirring occasionally. Add the oil and vinegar and
   simmer covered for one more hour.
Keep up the water level while boiling so you have a rich black soup. Ideally, the beans
   should be mostly disintegrating. But this comes from restocking a pot which you
   keep going all week, not easy to do on a boat.
Serve over rice with side garnishes of finely chopped onion and green pepper.
For a quick method, stick everything all at once into a pressure cooker and cook for
   75 minutes. For an even faster method, buy cans of black beans (Goya brand).
In Spanish say, *habichuelas negras* [ah-bitch-WAY-lahs NAY-grahs]. In Venezuela,
   caraotas [car-ah-OH-tas]. Don't ask why.
Buen provecho! [bwayne pro-VAYE-choh] *Bon Appétit!*

English Muffins

For simple stove top English Muffins which keep without refrigeration, try the following recipe. It shall make 10 two and a half inch muffins.
   1 cup warm water
   1 tablespoon dry yeast
   1 teaspoon sugar (and honey if desired)
   2 teaspoons salt (or less)
   quarter cup liquid shortening
   3 cups flour (up to 1 cup may be whole wheat)

Sprinkle the yeast over the water in a large bowl and let sit a few minutes. Thoroughly
   combine the dry ingredients. Mix them gradually into the bowl with the water.
Roll out the dough to one third of an inch thickness. Cut it into 2 and a half inch
   circles and lay them on a surface sprinkled with cornmeal. Sprinkle the tops with
   cornmeal and allow the muffins to rise — about double in 2 hours.
"Bake" on a preheated griddle with medium flame until brown on both sides — about
   5 to 7 minutes each side. Put away until ready to serve.
To serve, split with a fork and toast each half face down on a buttered griddle. These
   taste as good as the Thomas' English Muffins made in America. Englishmen, by
   the way, never heard of Thomas' English Muffins, which like pizza, comes from
   America.

BEER BREAD

For a tasty sourdough type of bread with no kneading necessary, try mixing:
1 can of warm beer with
3 cups of flour,
2 tablespoons baking powder and
3 tablespoons sugar (for the beer to eat)
Allow the dough to set up in a greased pan for 1 hour and bake until it looks done.
Add raisins, citrus, bananas and so on, to make it complex.

THORNTON'S GROUPER *AU VIN BLANC*

2 pounds fresh grouper fillet (must be fresh)
2 tablespoons olive oil
1/2 fresh garlic clove
8 oz mushroom slices
1/4 cup dry vermouth
1/4 cup evaporated milk
1 teaspoon dill weed

Sauté the mushrooms and paper thin garlic slices in one tablespoon olive oil. Lightly fry the fish fillets, covered, in one tablespoon olive oil mixed with dill until white all the way through. Turn the fillets several times.

Turn off the heat, add the vermouth and cover the fish.

Pour off the water from the mushrooms into water for rice.

When ready to serve, pour the wine and juices from the fish into the mushrooms and continue to *sauté*, agitating briskly with a fork while dripping in milk. Continue *sautéing* until you have sauce as thick as desired. *Never* thicken artificially.

Serve the fish with rice and the sauce on the side.

MAUNY'S EASY BAKED FISH

This shall amaze you the first time you do it. Just cover the bottom of a fish-sized Pyrex baking dish with olive oil. Now cover the oil (just) with raw rice. Lay in the whole cleaned fish. Place whatever spices or garnish you wish on top of the fish. Bake about 350° for 35 to 45 minutes, or until the rice begins to brown on the bottom.

The water released from the fish shall cook the rice. The whole blamed thing works like simplicity itself, yet you have a gourmet meal ready to present at a gourmand's table.

MAUNY'S ROACH COOKIES

Use these cookies for killing roaches, not for human consumption.

3 tbspns Boric Acid powder
1 tbspn flour
1 tbspn sugar

Mix to a paste with milk, form into **cockroach**-sized cookies, and sun dry on paper. Feeds thousands when placed out of sight. Health nuts can use whole wheat flour.

GLOSSARY

Air Pressure Think of as the weight of air molecules stacked vertically above the place at which you measure it -- like between your ears. It *weighs* 14.7 lbs. per square inch at sealevel. Actually it "weighs" sideways too, since the *weight* gets produced by molecules in Brownian motion colliding with each other. But I prefer to think of myself walking around with a 400,000 foot wobbly stack of air on my head.

Almacen [alma-SANE] a warehouse or wholesaler's

Arawak Antillean Indians; of the 3 groups, Caribe, Ciboney and Arawak. The Arawak, post stone-age agricultural people with a large production of ceramics, fathered the Tainos (see **Taino**).

Backing Wind counter-clockwise shifting of the wind

Banks land under shallow water. The sun heats the water and the bottom. Heat will radiate from the shallow banks almost as efficiently as from land itself.

Baja Filter A California invention for use in cruising the Baja. A funnel which has nested, removable filters of successively finer mesh through which fuel gets poured into the tank. The best will have a Teflon coated filter to separate water as well.

BASRA Bahamas Air Sea Rescue Association. Volunteers, many retired foreigners, that man a chain of VHF stations up and down the Bahamas and access means of rescue.

Beaufort Wind Scale Admiral Beaufort's Scale of Wind Speed, made to enable ships of the line to classify conditions from observations. It measures wind speed 10 meters above sea level and the corresponding sea effects for open sea far from land. Refer to the section entitled *Think Beaufort* to read the Beaufort Wind Scale.

Blue Northers Colloquial expression for the arctic winds which scourge the plains states in the United States, not the scraggly tail ends of fronts in the Caribbean.

Bola [BOWL-ah] Dominican slang for a ride; *Pon* [PONE] in Puerto Rico.

Buccaneer Mean guys who jumped ship and collected on the north coast of Haiti. They survived by hunting wild cows, and selling smoked beef, called *boucain* in French, to ships. Thus they got called *boucainiers*, or, as most pirates got called, buccaneers. Praised as recruits these made the most bloodthirsty pirates.

Burgoo A pressure cooker full of everything and anything to make a nourishing meal in a passage (ref. Tristan Jones, "Ice") try a large container of yogurt, fruits and cereals thoroughly mixed, or plain old lasagna cold or hot, even potato salad.

Caribbean Sea The sea bounded by all the Antilles, Greater as well as Lesser, and South and Central America. Definitely not north of the Dominican Republic.

Christmas Winds The signal that winter trades have come, more east northeast than east southeast, and about 5 knots stronger on average. This occurs when the Bermuda-Azores winter high pressure seasonally asserts itself, usually around Christmas, but sometimes as late as late January, sometimes as early as early December.

Coastal Front Cumulus and cumulonimbus clouds created by the circulation of **seabreeze** (see below) and marking a zone of change at the margin of sea and land. In the islands these usually get pushed over the heated land by the stable sea airstream. Depending on the colors and textures of the land below, these clouds can show mariners an outline of the coast before they see the coast. Particularly true in the Bahamas where an island's colors and textures have uniformity. The island and the water behind a coastal front often get reflected in the lower surface of these clouds. On the larger islands, look for strong gusts and showers coming from **Storm Cells** (see below) spawned by the coastal fronts in the late afternoons. Don't make the mistake of forecasting sea conditions based on conditions in harbor beneath a Coastal Front, especially over an irregular coastline (e.g., Puerto Rico' south coast, Exumas to the Raggeds).

Coastal Report NOAA weather reports available in US waters on VHF WX continuous stations. In the past, coastal stations such as light houses and life boat stations sent these reports by horse or by wire. They report sea conditions in wave height and swell height. The preamble, "...up to 20 nautical miles offshore..." does not hold true for the Caribbean. In Puerto Rico and the Virgin Islands, these reports run consistently 5 knots of wind low for inshore waters of the south coasts.

Cold Front The zone of division between Tropical and Polar Maritime air masses which generally moves eastward with clear, colder air at the rear of a depression. Squalls may preceed the frontal line.

Coriolis Force Force discovered in the 19th century by French scientist Coriolis (of course) which causes anything moving above the earth's surface to curve right in the northern hemisphere (left in the southern hemisphere).

Corsaires French seamen sailing under letters of marque from the king. The letters gave them shares in any booty they could wrest from Spanish vessels. When France and England reached accommodation with Spain the letters were withdrawn. Most crews persisted, however, making them pirates. The worst of them all? Neither Bluebeard nor Morgan, but a mean little dandy named L'Olenois.

Culture Shock Reaction to sustained mismatch between cultural stimulus/response pairs.

Deathtrap Any area which appears safe in most conditions but can be surprisingly unsurvivable when attacked by wind or wave from its not always obvious weak points. Examples: Calabash Bay, Long Island, Bahamas; Attwood Harbor, Acklins Islands, Bahamas; almost all Virgin Islands anchorages; and the anchorage at Phillipsburg, St.Martins. Also, Exuma Sound in a strong easterly blow: you must claw to windward because you have nowhere to run but through life threatening passes.

DMA Defense Mapping Agency, an agency of the US Government which performs the functions of the old Hydrographic Office (**HO**) cartographic department.

DR Dead Reckoning: a method of establishing position of a vessel by projecting miles run from the simple product of average speed in knots and hours run along a stable heading. See also Estimated Postion (**EP**) below. Also Dominican Republic.

Dangerous Semicircle The half of a developed depression with cyclonic winds which contains the quadrant of highest winds, i.e., those which lie along the direction of travel of the depression.

Diurnal Variation Daily changes. For wind, the strength and direction of **surface wind**s near land during, and as a result of, the passage of the sun from horizon to horizon. **Seabreeze** (see below) becomes stronger as the sun gets higher, and weaker as the sun gets lower. Wind will usually shift somewhat to the right during the sun's transit. In **offshore waters** the **gradient wind** has small diurnal variation and none at all when the greadient wind exceeds 30 knots.

EP See **Estimated Position**

Equatorial Current (in the North Atlantic) or **North Equatorial Current** The west going part of the clockwise circulation around the Sargasso Sea. **South Equatorial Current**: the current from the equator which runs counter to the earth's rotation along the coast of South America and into the Caribbean Sea. North of the Antilles the northern current blends elements of the southern current but the southern current off South America remains nonetheless much stronger.

Estimated Postion A method of establishing postion of a vessel which biases the Dead Reckoning position with estimated *leeway*, expressed in degrees from heading, and the two vectors of *tide* and *current* whose values you show in degrees of set with magnitudes of knots.

Far Out Islands Islands to the east and south of the Exumas. "Out Islands" refers generally to all the islands out from New Providence where the capital is. Thus a weekend sailor from Miami can truthfully say he cruises the Out Islands when he goes to Bimini.

Force Beaufort See **Beaufort Windscale** above

Front The line of separation between cold and warm air masses.

GPS Global Positioning System, capable of providing 3-dimensional position data every few seconds with great accuracy (20 meters when not dithered by the military with a feature they call Selective Availability). A nearly indispensable device for confirming a navigators' dead reckoning which they should maintain hourly in the usual old way.

Gradient Wind also **Synoptic Wind** The wind forecast in the **NWS Offshore Reports**. The wind close to the surface (see **Surface Wind**) in the open sea. It will flow between pressure zones from high to low pressure, turning always to the right due to the **Coriolis Force** (see above). Weather maps feature lines called **isobars** (see below) which correlate directly to the lines of equal altitude on terrain maps. Isobars close together give the appearance of a steep incline. Far apart, they show a gradual rise. Thus the term *gradient.*

Hidalgo [ee-DAHL-go] Corruption of 'Hijos de Alguién', literally 'Sons of Somebody', implying children of rich and influential families. In the New World this usually meant the non-inheriting sons of Spanish nobility who came to seek their fortunes, often spoiled and cruel to the point of sadism, they got corrupted by the opportunities for unlimited personal power in the New World. Only the more serious stayed and took root (e.g., the Cibao Valley ranchers of the Dominican Republic).

High Pressure Center A dome of high pressure (see **Air Pressure**) seen on weather maps as rings of closed **isobars** (see below). Really air stacked higher than average. When it slides off the peak of the dome it curves right due to the **Coriolis Force**, thus setting up a clockwise rotation of wind around the center.

High Pressure Ridge A linear region of atmospheric pressure (see **Air Pressure**) bounded by lower pressures on both sides, which on weather maps gives the appearance of a ridge of terrain.

HO Hydrographic Office. Old name of the cartographer's department of government.

Hurricane From the Indian god who wreaked destruction by wind, *Oricán* [or-ee-KHAN]. Name given to the tropical cyclonic storms east of the Americas (Typhoon west). It also applies to Force 12 on the **Beaufort Windscale** regardless of cause.

Hurricane Games My name for the very serious business of posing all the "what if" questions when selecting an anchorage in the hurricane season. Draw a hurricane spiral to scale on a piece of transparent plastic and move it around on the chart.

Hurricane Hole An anchorage protected from the seas, if not the winds, of a hurricane.

Hurricane Warning A hurricane may approach within 24 hours.

Hurricane Watch A hurricane may approach within 36 hours.

Inshore Wind The wind inshore (i.e., up to two miles offshore). The winds here mostly get steered by encounter with land features such as beach, river mouths, mountains and draws, where the seabreeze begins. It extends out to sea and over land. Nocturnal winds blow strongest in this zone, and wise coastwise passagemakers angle coastward to take advantage of them on a coast clear of dangers.

Island Low Afternoon convection activity in the central regions of an island caused by daytime heating augmented by the moist tradewinds. Counter clockwise circulation about these lows can cause winds to blow along the coasts well into evening.

Isobars Lines drawn on weather maps which connect points of equal atomspheric pressure (see **Air Pressure**). As on terrain maps, these lines demonstrate the mountains and valleys, hills, cliffs and inclines of the sea of air stacked above us. Thus terms such as **ridge**, **trough** and **high** and **low centers** describe the surface of that sea at some arbitrary altitude.

Joy The only detergent I know which works as well in sea water as it does in fresh.

Katabatic A wind that flows down slope, usually at night, due to the cooling of the upper level air which then becomes heavier and flows down hill. Along with **land breeze**, the katabatic wind creates the **nocturnal wind** (see below).

Land Breeze The opposite of seabreeze, and it occurs at night with a much milder circulation than that of a **seabreeze** (see below).

Lee-bowing Using current to advance on the rhumb line. With contrary current, take the long tacks with the lee bow into the current to mitigate its effects.

Leeward Islands The Lesser Antilles which stretch from St.Martin through Dominica.

Leisure Sailor The reader of this guide. The Leisure Sailor has an old fashioned leisure class lifestyle: thus the name *The Gentleman's Guide to Passages South*. He or she needn't have wealth, only the mindset and the minimum wherewithal to leisurely enjoy cruising without the deadlines and hustle of the working classes. The Leisure Sailor may work upon occassion, usually doing maintenance chores on her or his yacht. They work for a wage only if it goes toward recouping the cruising kitty. Perhaps an athlete, but never a jock. Man or woman, power or sail, always a *seaman*.

Line Squall So named for having sunk a *ship of the line* off the Needles, beyond the Isle of Wight. A sudden squall with violent blasts of cold air occuring at the point of a V-shaped depression, or derivatives of **tropical systems** (see below). Usually preceeded by a flat black bar of cloud low to the sea. It can easily pack winds above 50 knots.

Loran A spare dinghy anchor in the Caribbean.

Low Pressure Center A depression in atmospheric pressure (see **Air Pressure**) shown as tight rings of closed **isobars** (see above) on a weather map, similar to a bowl shaped valley on terrain maps. Air falling into the center tries to fill it, but will rotate around it counter clockwise due to **Coriolis Force** (see above).

Krakatau (also Krakatoa) An Indonesian volcano whose erruption in 1893 sounded up to 2,200 miles away, and whose air pressure shook recorders around the world. It threw 5 cubic miles of rock up with a 50 mile high ash cloud, and triggered tsunamis which reached South America.

Low Pressure Trough A linear region of low pressure with or without closed **isobars** which gives the appearance on weather maps of a long valley of terrain. Called *trough,* as in the inverse of a *wave.* If the isobars close, the length of the trough renders circulation questionable. Nonetheless, winds ahead may veer slightly, and winds behind may back a bit. If the trough shrinks in length, or breaks into segments, it can become a rotating low center and eventually a Tropical Depression (see below).

Magnetic Degrees the 360° which start from 0° pointing to the northern magnetic pole

Motoconcho [moh-toh-CONE-cho] A motorbike, with or without a rickshaw-like conveyance in tow driven by an independent operator who offers rides to anywhere for half a beer (see *Beeronomy*).

Murphy's Law Even looking at it optimistically, whatever can go wrong shall, in fact, go wrong (e.g., the toast always falls buttered side down).

NAVTEX U.S. Coast Guard transmissions on 516.9 (adjusted) USB in SITOR FEC mode which include **NWS Offshore Reports** and the Puerto Rico **Coastal Reports** and notices to mariners. See *Radio Times and Frequencies.*

Night Lee A lee from wind and sea at the margin of sea and land. Created by thermal effects caused by the land cooling faster than the sea. Significantly abetted by orographic effects on mountainous coasts. See *Island Effects: Playing the Island Lees.*

Niño [KNEE-nyo] Boy child. Also the name of a world wide weather disturbance brought about periodically by a reversal in the Humboldt Current (See National Geographic Vol 165 No 2, February 1984, and again in Vol. 195 No. 3, March 1999).

NOAA National Oceanic and Atmospheric Administration, a branch of the US Government whose weather reports get regularly lost by Coast Guard Communications.

Nocturnal Wind The night wind, a combination of **land breeze** which feeds the up-drafts over the warmer water, and the **katabatic** wind (see above). The nocturnal wind begins after sundown and dies before dawn, reaching its strongest between midnight and 2 a.m. See also **sea breeze**.

Norther Colloquial expression for fierce and durable winter winds from the north. Used in New England, Holland, Iceland, Alaska, Lower Slobovia, but NOT between the Tropic of Cancer and the Tropic of Capricorn!

NWS National Weather Service

Offshore Reports The **NWS** forecasts to use for all of *Passages South.*

Offshore -Waters, -Wind, -Conditions, Passaging, whatever. Generally 8 to 12 miles offshore. Actually, as far from or as near to shore that **gradient wind** touches down and conditions go unaffected by land, the NWS Offshore Report's "more than 50 miles from shore" notwithstanding.

Parador An older house (estate or palace) renovated for use as an inn or hotel.

Passage Making The actual doing of a voyage, as opposed to a sail. Passage Making implies prudent navigation, sea-readiness and competent seamanship.

Pilot Charts Charts for each of the twelve months which give the statistics compiled of the weather, wind, current and storm tracks over a period of nearly 150 years (thanks to Lt.Matthew Fontaine Maury, USN). The British know these as Routing Charts.

Prevailing Conditions (for southern Bahamas to Grenada) east northeast to east southeast 15-20 knots. Rare extremes of northeast by east, southeast by east, and 10 or 25 knots briefly occur. Look for perturbating weather features when observations go outside these limits. For a more detailed discussion of how these prevailing conditions vary seasonally, see the chapters *Think Beaufort* and *Weather Windows*. The sailing directions in this book mean to outfox **prevailing conditions** while sailing *against* them.

Privateers The English equivalent of the French Corsaires, Henry Morgan being the most famous. See **Corsaires**.

Público [POO-blee-koh] Cars which travel fixed routes, like buses.

Rage The condition of the seas, especially the cuts in Exuma Sound, when the wind has blown hard onshore for some time.

Range Two features, marks or lights coming into line, the rearmost positioned vertically above the foremost. One can make one's own range out of any objects in foreground and background in order to stay a course (see also **Transit**).

Res [race] normal parlance for beef of any old kind in the Dominican Republic; normally chuck of old milch cow. Delicious if stewed well.

Ridge see **High pressure ridge.**

Rule of Twelfths A rough rule for estimating the variable rise or fall of the tide, and therefore the tidal current if you know peak flow. The rule states that the first, second and third hour of tide rise or fall accounts for one twelfth, 2 twelfths and 3 twelfths, respectively, of the tidal range, whereas the fourth, fifth and sixth hours account for 3-, 2-, and 1- twelfth(s), respectively. Thus, if the range is 3 feet, as in the Bahamas, 3 inches will fall (or rise) in the first hour, 6 in the second, 9 in the third and fourth hours, and finally, 6 and 3 inches in the fifth and sixth hours, for a total of 36 inches, or 3 feet. Similarly, the current, as a ratio of peak flow, runs an average of one sixth, one half, 5 sixths, 5 sixths, one half and one sixth knots, for hours one through 6, respectively. For example, if the peak flow on flood runs 1.2 knots, as on Caicos Banks, then hours one through 6 of tide rise shall average rates of 0.2, 0.6, 1.0, 1.0, 0.6, and 0.2 knots.

Seabreeze The sun heats the land during the day. The land heats the air above it which rises to be displaced by more air from the sea. A circulation begins which can create wind of up to 20 knots with effects distinguishable as far inland as 10 miles and as far at sea as 20 miles. In the tropics, seabreezes run year around, but they blow strongest in the spring and summer.

SG&T Sundowner Gin and Tonic. A mneumonic for any inflexible custom which makes the Leisure Sailor perform all passage planning so that late afternoons get spent *at leisure* in a safe anchorage with the yacht completely put away and ready for sea. This gives captain and crew a full evening of rest and relaxation with which to face the next day, or with which to face an anchor drill called invariably at 2 a.m. in the winter time Bahamas. Any other custom at sundown doesn't classify as **Leisure Sailing**, but a mark of the anxiety driven working class.

SSCA Seven Seas Cruising Association. A Ft. Lauderdale based organization for sharing information among cruisers.

Storm Cells Cells of rising or sinking air currents scattered, or occurring in lines (frontal thunderstorms). Thunderstorms from late summer afternoon **Coastal Front**s (see above) can grow vicious, especially on large or the high islands. Since winds can rotate around cells either way, you can tactically use these while crossing the Caribbean.

Storm Surge The piling up of water, like an extra tide, for hundreds of square miles to the front and right of a moving storm.

Sundowner G&T See SG&T.

Surface Wind In the open sea, the **gradient wind** (see above), or the wind forecast by the **NWS Offshore Report**, slows at the sea surface due to the force of friction. Lighter gradient winds, 5 to 15 knots, can curve 10° to 15° toward lower pressure as they brush the surface. Stronger gradient winds will bend less.

Taino Descendents of the **Arawaks** found by **Columbus** on Hispaniola, Cuba and Puerto Rico, characterized by advanced political (tribal chiefs, chiefs of chiefs, etc.) and social (specialized labor) structures. Especially noted for extreme pacifism: they preferred suicide to fighting to such an extent it became an industry after the Spaniards invaded them with the Inquisition. See the *Museo del Hombre* in Santo Domingo, and the museum at *Altos de Chavón*, near La Romana, Dominican Republic.

Thornless Path a way of **passage making** (see definition above) to windward which creates a delightful, relaxed experience.

Thorny Path a way of **passage making** (see definition above) to windward which tries the soul as well as the boat.

TPC Tropical Prediction Center (see below).

Trade Wind Winds which blow from the high pressure areas of the **tropics** to the relatively low pressure of the equatorial regions. In the Caribbean, the Northeast Trades of the Atlantic get bent with the **Equatorial Currents**, becoming easterly by the time they pour over the Lesser Antilles into the Caribbean. These winds continuously switch like a cat's tail between northeast and east southeast in the winter, and between east northeast and southeast in the summer.

Trades Short for the **trade winds**. One should always read this to include seas as well.

Transit Two features or marks, identifiable on a chart, coming into line (also **Range**).

Tropical Depression A bad weather system characterized by closed isobars of barometric pressure, precipitation and mainly ascending air in which the **gradient winds** can get quite strong and will flow counter clockwise and toward the central low.

Tropical Disturbance any large area of disturbed weather in the tropics not yet, nor perhaps ever, classified a **Tropical Depression** (see above).

Tropical Outlook The **NWS** hurricane season report of **tropical system**s as they develop.

Tropical Prediction Center The Tropical Analysis and Forecast Branch of the U.S. **National Weather Service** located in Miami, Florida. They produce excellent weather charts and reports, including the **Offshore Reports**, the broadcast that the U.S. Coast Guard Communications Division seriously bungles. Call the CG on it, and they shall predictably blame it on you and your radio.

Tropical Storm a **Tropical Depression** which has developed into a full cyclonic storm on the **Beaufort Windscale** (see *Think Beaufort*) with winds from 48 to 63 knots.

Tropical System Any of the summer weather systems in the tropics: see **tropical wave, tropical disturbance, tropical depression, tropical storm, hurricane**.

Tropical Wave Atmospheric pressure waves forming off Africa in the tropics in the Summer. These can stretch up to a thousand miles long and move between 10 and 20 knots toward the west. They usually have associated precipitation and spawn **storm cells** (see above), but like fronts, some regions of the wave can pass relatively clear.

Tropical Weather Discussion The **NWS** hurricane season report of all weather features in the northern tropics, their positions, characteristics and potential development.

Trough See **low pressure trough.**

True Degrees the 360° which start from 0° pointing to the geographic North Pole

Veering Wind Clockwise shifting of the wind (e.g., north to east)

Wait for Weather Read the section on *Wait for Weather*. This, and the **SG&T**, quite seriously form the nucleus of the *thornless path* concept. If you can afford to wait for the appropriate **weather window,** and you always lay to anchor in a snug harbor with a ready boat and getting lots of rest by late afternoon, you rate absolutely as a **Leisure Sailor** of the first order.

Weather Window The period during which wind and wave conduct themselves favorably for completing a leg of a passage in safety and comfort.

Windward Islands The islands from Martinique through Grenada.

Wx abbreviation for weather

Xenophobia Suspicion, fear or hatred of foreigners or things strange. Usually an infirmity of the French but can reach virulent degrees in homo Americanus when found aboard between the tropics.

Index

Advertisers Directory